Rural Policies for the 1990s

Rural Studies Series

Rural Policies for the 1990s

EDITED BY

Cornelia B. Flora
*Virginia Polytechnic Institute
and State University*

AND

James A. Christenson
University of Arizona

1991

Westview Press
BOULDER · SAN FRANCISCO · OXFORD

Rural Studies Series, Sponsored by the Rural Sociological Society

Published in 1991 in the United States of America by Westview Press, Inc., 5500 Central Avenue, Boulder, Colorado 80301, and in the United Kingdom by Westview Press, 36 Lonsdale Road, Summertown, Oxford OX2 7EW

Library of Congress Cataloging-in-Publication Data
Rural policies for the 1990s / edited by Cornelia B. Flora and James
    A. Christenson.
        p.   cm. — (Rural studies series of the Rural Sociological
    Society)
    Includes bibliographical references and index.
    ISBN 0-8133-7815-X — ISBN 0-8133-7816-8 (pbk.)
        1. Rural development—Government policy—United States.   2. United
States—Rural conditions.   3. United States—Social
conditions—1980–   .   I. Flora, Cornelia Butler, 1943–   .
II. Christenson, James A., 1944–   .   III. Series.
HN90.C6R815   1991
307.72′0973—dc20   90-22323
                                                                                              CIP

Printed and bound in the United States of America

⬭ The paper used in this publication meets the requirements
of the American National Standard for Permanence of Paper
for Printed Library Materials Z39.48-1984.

10   9   8   7   6   5   4   3   2   1

Contents

Foreword

The way in which scientists look at problems is reconstructed in *Rural Policies for the 1990s*. Philosophers of science once conceptualized such developments as logic-in-use, which is the flow of thinking and experiences scientists have from day to day, and reconstructed logic, periodic syntheses that reconstruct scientific and scholarly perspectives.

Like the comprehensive *Rural Society in the U.S.: Issues for the 1980s*, edited by Don Dillman and Daryl Hobbs (Westview, 1982), *Rural Policies for the 1990s* sets the tone for a decade. Whereas the first book reconstructed rural sociology in terms of research issues, *Rural Policies for the 1990s* reconstructs rural sociology in terms of policy issues that include past, present, and future research and theory. In each chapter, rural policy needs are identified by examining the flow of events and rural sociology of the 1980s.

The effectiveness of this book's mission to address rural policies may be measured by the extent to which it influences the logic-in-use that shapes such policies. Effectiveness may also be measured by how much disadvantages in rural America are prevented. And *Rural Policies for the 1990s* will, we hope, result in improved conditions for rural people and places. Not only is this desired, it is intended.

> Ronald C. Wimberley
> Chair, Editorial Board
> Rural Studies Series
> The Rural Sociological Society

1

Critical Times for Rural America: The Challenge for Rural Policy in the 1990s

Cornelia B. Flora and James A. Christenson

Whereas the 1970s was the decade of rural renaissance and turnaround, the 1980s was the decade of rural decline and turnback. Poverty in rural areas increased, as did unemployment rates and environmental problems. The 1990s will be a decade of decision for U.S. leaders regarding rural America: Either we will have two Americas, geographically and economically distinct, with the rural one considerably disadvantaged compared to the urban one, or efforts will be made to promote equity and opportunities for rural people in rural areas.

The rural disadvantage is not inevitable. Public choices are made at the local, state, and federal levels that can reverse current trends. While fiscal and monetary policy and general economic restructuring are major causes of the current problems, specific policies targeted to counteract them can make a difference.

Rural areas are crucial for the nation as a whole. The existence of rural communities provides all citizens a choice of places to live. Rural areas and people are also key for the economy of the entire nation. Not only are rural areas the primary sites for the extraction of raw materials, but they provide a major source of labor, capital, and international exchange for the rest of the economy as well.

Rural peoples serve as the guardians of our natural resources. The quality and quantity of the water we use is in part determined by how well watersheds are managed in rural areas. Rural areas receive the garbage and polluted air from the cities, and either provide a system to purify and recycle urban waste, or reinsert it into the environment in dangerous ways. We spend millions of dollars to plant trees in urban areas, but stimulate the cutting of rural forests at home and abroad. Rural areas exist as the spaces between urban areas. The quality of the transportation infrastructure determines the ability of major urban areas to move goods and people from place to place.

Rural peoples have a relative advantage in problem solution compared with urban people. Many of the same problems, such as poverty and pollution, exist in both places. But the scale of the problems and the cultural traditions of participation make the potential for successful problem solving greater in rural areas, given adequate resources and favorable policies. Rural people can be the innovators for problem solutions that can then be transferred to urban areas.

To date, there has been little attempt to address problems of rural areas beyond implementing agricultural policy. But for rural areas to provide the key functions that they do for society as a whole, active maintenance is necessary. Implementing policies that seem to be location neutral put rural peoples in unnecessarily risky situations which are not conducive to national health. We as a nation need to reexamine our commitment to rural—and urban—people and reconsider the basis of decisions.

The Global Setting

The 1970s was a decade of expanding world purchasing power, as the oil boom triggered price increases for all basic commodities. Monetary and fiscal policy in the United States further set conditions favorable for the differential growth of rural economics. A U.S. trade deficit in the early 1970s inspired President Richard Nixon to de-peg the dollar. Internationally, the costs of our exports decreased (due to a cheaper dollar), while the demand for them increased (due to increased purchasing power in many developing countries). Basic commodities such as timber, coal, and wheat, major products of rural areas, rose dramatically in price. Boom towns emerged in energy-producing areas. The low value of the U.S. dollar made imports extremely expensive, so light industries turned to rural areas of the United States in search of cheap land, low-cost infrastructure and labor force, and freedom from environmental restrictions often imposed in urban areas. But this economic growth was accompanied by high inflation, and, by the end of the decade, growth in employment had ground to a halt.

A series of macroeconomic policies was instituted in the late 1970s and early 1980s to remedy that situation. These policies included a tight monetary policy, a fiscal policy that reduced taxes and certain government expenditures but increased others, and deregulation. All of those policies had implicit urban biases. For example, deregulation and relaxation of antitrust laws have favored urban areas over rural areas. And the tax laws favoring capital-intensive urban and suburban development in the unregulated climate of the 1980s drained resources from rural areas to urban areas.

The strong U.S. dollar, coupled by the decline in commodity prices that accompanied the worldwide recession of the early 1980s, was particularly disadvantageous for rural areas. The price of basic commodities decreased as the purchasing power of developing countries declined due to the debt crisis; those same countries began to export more and more—at whatever price—to gain foreign exchange to repay their now-onerous foreign debts. Boom towns went bust. Furthermore, the factories that had moved to rural areas in the 1970s found it even easier to move overseas in the 1980s. Factory flight was furthered by the cheapening of competing imports.

Federal spending mirrored the flight of private capital from rural areas. Military spending, the growth sector of the 1980s, was substantially higher in urban than in rural areas. And while discretionary nonmilitary spending, after farm programs are excluded, has declined modestly (10 percent) in urban areas, it has declined precipitously (44 percent) in rural areas in the 1980s.

The steady recovery from the 1981–1982 recession has been an urban phenomenon in the United States. The results of the macroeconomic trends and implicit antirural policies are seen in the increasing differences in indicators of economic well-being between rural and urban areas: (1) higher unemployment in rural areas; (2) lower growth of jobs in rural areas; (3) a widening gap between median family income, as rural family income actually decreased in real terms; (4) increasing out-migration from rural areas; and (5) a higher increase in poverty in rural areas, resulting in a rural poverty rate nearly 50 percent higher than the urban poverty rate. The poor in rural areas tend to be the working poor. Rural families experience considerably more stress than do urban families. Furthermore, rural areas are behind urban areas in educational attainment, access to health care, and quality of housing; and these discrepancies are increasing.

Policies Disadvantaging Rural Areas

Public policy on the federal level, including monetary and fiscal policy, had direct consequences for rural areas, putting them at a disadvantage to urban areas. The equation of "rural" with "farm" allowed expensive agricultural programs to mask inattention to rural people and their heterogeneous economic base. No policy addresses their common problems and a dispersed population makes service delivery difficult and economies of scale in production problematic.

As a result of the inattention to rural differences, another series of federal policies was implemented in the 1980s that had implicit antirural biases. Major federal policies that negatively affected the availability of jobs and capital in rural areas included tax laws favoring capital-intensive urban and suburban development and relaxation of antitrust laws. As a result, locally owned, profitable rural firms were bought out, with the acquisition often funded by junk bonds. The resulting indebtedness of a parent company was motivation to pare back or close down a firm in order to repay the debt engendered to purchase it in the first place.

A number of federal policies had negative impacts on the poor and the delivery of services to rural areas. Inappropriate assessment of the costs of providing services in rural areas resulted in lower reimbursement for Medicare and other services. A stagnant minimum wage as well as tax policies that shifted the tax burden from the rich to lower income workers particularly hurt the working rural poor. The change from formula funding to competitive grants channeled money to urban areas and the most advantaged rural areas.

The environment and rural infrastructure were also negatively affected by federal policy changes of the 1980s. Deregulation resulted in the deterioration of both private and semipublic services in rural areas, including transportation and communication. Attempts to deal with the increasing federal budget deficit by not spending certain earmarked funds, such as those for environmental cleanup and highways, hit rural areas particularly hard. Rural areas tend to produce high-volume, low-value products that require either rail or truck transportation. As manufacturers shift from a production strategy of stockpiling inputs to "just-in-time delivery" of those materials, the decline in the quality of interstates and rural roads makes quick delivery from dispersed rural sites more problematic. Environmental problems, including the disposal of solid wastes and the problems of water pollution, have been put on a back burner at the federal level. When cleanup procedures are undertaken, they tend to be in more visible and politically vocal urban areas.

The Need for Targeted Rural Policies

While rural areas share some key characteristics that merit special policy consideration, there is also great diversity within them. There are differences in the economic activities performed, the age structure of the population, the ethnic diversity, and the natural resource base, as well as historical circumstances that lead to special problems requiring targeted solutions. The thrust of most of the policy considerations presented in this volume is to develop targeted policies based on the context of the problem a policy is designed to address. One size does not fit all Americans—or all rural Americans.

Solutions to the economically derived problems of rural areas are not simple. The nature of job creation in rural areas has made them more vulnerable, as the firms that locate there tend to create low-wage jobs, purchase few inputs locally, hire cyclically, and change sites often. Local creation of new businesses is an option, but many of the regulations, often passed at the urging of multinational corporations, mean that a new firm cannot meet the capital investment required to meet certification standards set for large plants. The availability of capital in rural areas and the way it is organized are results of both private decisions and public policies that determine, through regulation and tax laws, which forms of investment are profitable for whom.

Minorities, the elderly, the poor, and households that depend on just one adult are particularly vulnerable in rural areas. Federal funds transferred there tend to go to those who already are relatively advantaged: landowners through farm programs and land speculators through the savings and loan bailout. The unique needs of rural education and health services must be addressed through targeted programs that are not simply urban programs in miniature. Further, policies must be explicit about being inclusive. Policies that are not explicit in including women, the poor, and minorities as participants and beneficiaries will not be effective in increasing the quality of rural life.

Rural areas are uniquely dependent on their natural resource base. Natural resources may be viewed as an easily expendable source of capital or as a mechanism for investing in a sustainable source of income for an area. Decisions about natural resource quantity and quality are ones that not only affect the immediate rural area, but national and international interests as well. Often those that profit from their exploitation are not the same ones that bear the costs of their depletion. Sustaining natural resources in a way that also sustains the rural population in economic dignity will be one of the major areas of policy debate in the 1990s. A further question involves who will have access to the natural resource base, including farmland. Current policies tend toward more and more concentrated access to land and natural resources. Yet potential policies that lead to alternative private sector responses are possible.

The focus of this book is on U.S. policy that affects rural people. It is crucial to remember that U.S. policy actions have implications for rural people far beyond our borders. Thus, we include considerations of international development and population policies that stem from U.S. initiatives. The global nature of the economy requires attention to the well-being of rural residents around the world.

The Future of Rural America

Certain macro changes at the beginning of the decade suggest that the 1990s could again reverse the relative decline of rural America. The dollar is more competitively valued on the world market than it was in the first part of the 1980s. The dramatic changes in Eastern Europe, the Middle East, and elsewhere in the world have created constant dialogue on the allocation of funds for defense debt reduction or social needs. Dramatic upheavals in different parts of the world, however, often distract us from attention to our own rural people.

Technology development, if accompanied by social organization that facilitates widespread access, could overcome some of the rural disadvantage. The development of major technologies in production of goods and distribution of services, especially in computers and telecommunications, could increase the possibility of location-neutral enterprises springing from rural areas. Biotechnology could overcome a variety of natural production constraints that could help diversify and stabilize production in rural areas.

The formalization of a united Europe in 1992 and the Uruguay round of negotiations in the General Agreement on Tariffs and Trade (GATT) could all result in policy changes that increase the flexibility and respon-siveness of rural sectors of the United States and make them more than simply providers of cheap inputs for production. The possibility also exists for rural areas to offer more than wide open spaces and cheap labor—or to become further ghettoized as economic backwaters. Both public and private choices will be necessary for the possibility of diversification and prosperity to be realized.

Focus of the Book

The chapters are grouped into three areas: jobs and the economy, people and services, and the environment. In the first area, the authors address major problems of capital and economic organization that have particular impacts for rural peoples.

In the second group of selections, the services needed by rural people and special populations in rural areas, such as the aged, the poor, and minorities, are discussed. Options as to how to best meet their needs of education, health care, employment, transportation, and other services are discussed in light of the unique problems of population dispersion and a history of neglect. Because of the global nature of the linkages between rural and urban areas and between rural areas here and abroad, consideration is given to international as well as domestic policy areas.

The third set of chapters discusses the environment, focusing on land and water in its national and international context. Major policies that affect the availability and quality of natural resources are addressed, as well as the process of policy formation at the local, state, and national level. Each section overlaps somewhat, as each section deals with people issues.

This volume is designed to address the choices American people can collectively make throughout the democratic process at a variety of levels. The authors lay out the thrust of current policies and the policy options available for the future. All argue that the best policies, both domestic and international, involve mechanisms for local participation. Not all policies—and certainly not the most effective policies—are at the federal level. Clearly macroeconomic policies will have major impacts on the choices available to rural areas. We caution policymakers to be aware of these impacts. But within the parameters provided by these major structural constraints, there are many public choices that must be made. The rural social scientists in this volume outline alternative choices and their implications for the well-being of rural people in this country and abroad.

Rural policies should not be residuals of urban policies. Policies designed for urban areas overlook the unique characteristics of rural areas. Thus, we continue to be surprised by the negative results of urban based policies on rural people. With the growing urban control of the U.S. House and Senate, it is harder for the voice of rural America to be heard. Special attention has to be given to rural people's problems in order to not only solve them, but to contribute to the solution of urban problems as well.

We are extremely grateful to all the authors for their efforts in writing and rewriting their chapters. We would like to thank the editors of the Rural Sociology Society. Most of all, we would like to thank Nancy Strang, who provided extensive coordination in editing this book and maintained the high professional level of the project while the editors moved about the country.

2
Rural America and the Industrial Policy Debate

William W. Falk and Thomas A. Lyson

Rural America is in trouble. It is losing jobs; it is losing people; it is losing its identity. After eight years of "Reaganomics," record drought, and a deluge of foreign imports, rural America finds itself in a crisis. The key to resolving this crisis is to develop and nurture a more diversified industrial and economic structure.

In this chapter, we bring rural America into the industrial policy debate, a debate which has been decidedly urban in tone (see Bowles, Gordon, and Weiskopf, 1983). We focus on three distinct dimensions along which a federally directed rural development effort must turn: human resources versus available jobs, a national industrial policy versus state and local initiatives, and national planning ("steered economy" approach) versus free market principles ("laissez faire" approach) (see also Falk and Lyson, 1988; Lyson, 1989).

What We Know

Policies are only meaningful when grounded in a particular social and economic context (see Brown and Deavers, 1988). Key demographic and industrial trends in rural America provide a context for this discussion and make what we propose, in philosophy of science parlance, "necessary but not sufficient" conditions for a rural America less likely to be in crisis.

Human Resources Versus Available Jobs

During the 1970s, demographer Calvin Beale (1976) documented what was called the "rural turnaround." Based on careful analysis of 1970 census data, Beale discovered that for the first time in several decades, rural America had not suffered a net loss of people from one decade to the next. Instead, during the 1960s, rural out-migration eased in many regions of the country and at the same time new people from urban areas moved into rural areas, resulting in a net gain in the rural population.

Alas, the turnaround was short lived. Analyses in the 1980s showed that a decade of in-migration was quickly followed by a return to out-migration (Beale and Fuguitt, 1986). If anything, we suspect that the rate of out-migration may have increased in recent years. Why? Primarily because the farm crisis of the 1980s resulted in large numbers of farmers leaving the land and the countryside in search of stable jobs in towns and cities.

While farm prices have rebounded somewhat since the height of the farm crisis, farming in general continues to decline as a percentage of all adult employment. Nationally and in many regions, the rural economic structure is in transition—moving from a dependence on agriculture and manufacturing activities to service endeavors (see Singelmann, 1978; Falk and Lyson, 1988). This means that both the industrial base and the available jobs in rural America are changing.

Some scholars have labeled this movement from manufacturing to service employment deindustrialization:

> By *deindustrialization* is meant a widespread, systematic disinvestment in the nation's basic productive capacity. . . . [Investment] has been diverted . . . into unproductive speculation, mergers and acquisitions, and foreign investment. . . . Corporate managers are refusing to invest in the basic industries of the country. . . . [Deindustrialization] is the outcome of a worldwide crisis in the economic system. (Bluestone and Harrison, 1982:6)

In a similar way, Reich (1983) refers to this change in corporate investment as "paper entrepreneurialism." Simply, this means that companies pursue profit as a first-and-foremost goal. Where and in what their money is invested is a secondary concern. Little attention or worry is given to job creation (or, conversely, job loss) or to long-run investment strategies. Instead, capital seeks locales where short-run profit will be maximized. When the short-run profit picture turns down, capital seeks other markets, including those overseas. The net effect of this strategy is to deindustrialize particular localities.

Deindustrialization focuses attention on the shift away from traditional manufacturing industries, which produce goods, to service industries. What occurs, then, is a reformulation of the industrial base. A key casualty in the process is the type of work available. Consequently, a mismatch (Southern Growth Policies Board, 1986) may occur: Workers with a particular set of skills (from farming or manufacturing) must now attempt to transfer their skills to fit a different set of occupational opportunities. For some economists—and for many nonacademics who are unaware of the term's origin—worker skills have come to be called *human capital*.

The human capital thesis (Schultz, 1961) states that an individual "invests" in himself or herself, usually in the form of education, occupational training, or work experience. The resulting human capital is then parlayed into jobs of one kind or another and, ultimately, into income.

The human capital equation is not as simple as neoclassical economists make it out to be. Labor markets are not free from the discriminating effects of race, gender, region, and the like. Added to this, there may be a mismatch between the supply and demand for talent in a particular locality. So, we have a problem: Human resources on the one hand, available jobs on the other.

National Industrial Policy and Planning
Versus Free Market Principles

Industrial policy seems to be a relatively new term for practices that have occurred ever since government began to play a role in any geographic area's economy. What is industrial policy? No one definition satisfies everyone (Brinkman, 1987). To us, industrial policy is a multidimensional concept. To illustrate some of the different threads that make up the industrial policy mosaic, we selectively quote from several scholars on this topic; we then integrate key points from their comments into our own working definition.

> *Industrial policy* [italics added] . . . can be viewed broadly or narrowly. In the broadest sense, it would include all government programs and practices that significantly affect industrial performance. . . . Federal taxing, spending, and regulating activities constitute an industrial policy, albeit unintended for the most part. . . . [A] more narrow and operational definition of an industrial policy would be limited to those government programs and practices whose explicit purpose is to promote domestic and/or international competitiveness of individual firms or industries. (Bell and Lande, 1982:2–4)

> [There are] two basic approaches. . . . [One is] the targeted approach by which government offers incentives and subsidies to certain chosen industries and locations . . . either sunset . . . or sunrise [with sunset industries getting a disproportionate share of the funds available]. . . . The other approach to industrial policy is the nontargeted approach . . . [which fosters] measures that encourage savings, investment, innovation, exports, and productivity increases in our whole industrial and service structure, with market forces determining the winners and losers. . . . [This concept is] generally known as "supply-side economics." (Jones, 1981:14–15)

The key to any definition of industrial policy is the role assigned to government. Clearly, when initiated at the federal level we can expect to talk about a national policy, while state and local efforts can only result in geographically restricted policies. Yet the industrial policy debate has both national and state/local components, which raises an important point: State or local policies may conflict with national objectives. As Friedman (1982) sees it, the goal of a national policy is efficiency—to allocate resources more efficiently to industries and firms in the private sector. The goal of a regional policy, on the other hand, is equity. Garn and Ledebur (1982:48) make the same point.

> The major impetus for regional policy has been to respond to distributional issues in lagging regions. The criteria that have been taken to indicate a need for regional concern have been low income, high unemployment, and high

levels of out-migration of the potential labor force. Designing programs to ameliorate the problems of lagging regions has always led to tension between those who had either equity or efficiency concerns as of primary importance.

The twin goals of efficiency and equity are actually preceded by a larger set of goals that apply to the general issue of industrial policy: To wit, to what end might the government intervene in the marketplace? Bell and Lande (1982:4) see three goals: defensive, to protect a particular industry and its employees; stabilizing, to provide "for an orderly adjustment to excess industrial capacity"; and positive, a more proactive response to growing and declining industries, helping some to fade out and others to prosper.

Gemper (1987:16) contends that an industrial policy should improve "overall economic conditions. It [should] facilitate future-oriented, far-sighted economic policies, which strengthen and enhance the potential of the economy." Industrial policy can do this in the following ways: (1) It can help to foster and promote entrepreneurial activity by providing "starting-up assistance"; (2) for industries and firms with histories of success but confronting short-term adjustment difficulties, it can provide "adjustment assistance"; (3) for industries and firms with more regional markets and capacities, it can provide "reenforcement assistance"; and, (4) for firms that are no longer competitive, it can expedite their exit from the marketplace by providing "breaking-up assistance." Again, note that in every case, the government plays a role.

Our own position is really an amalgam of these and others. Like Reich (1983:232), we believe that "the enduring myth of the unmanaged market illustrates the power of myth over reality." As Gemper (1987:30) puts it, "The issue is not over whether or not planning exists, but rather who plans and for which purpose. While the phenomenon of economic planning in the private sector has yet to penetrate basic textbook treatment, it has taken over the economy."

For us, industrial policy is any coherent set of government- designed and initiated programs that seeks to stimulate or guide industrial (including firm-level) ventures into markets for new goods or services. Some programs may encourage totally new product or service lines; others may ease the transition or adaptation from one orientation to another. Some markets may be national and international (or have these possibilities), others may be more local and regional. And while efficiency must be a concern, our greatest concern is equity—especially between different locales in the United States, particularly between rural and urban areas.

What do we know about national industrial policies versus state and local initiatives? The results are mixed. Conservative and neoconservative (viz., orthodox) economists tend to dislike the very idea of a national industrial policy (see Wachter and Wachter, 1981). It smacks too much of government interference as opposed to government assistance. The adage here is well known: That government governs best which governs least. Ideally, then, supply-side economics should be allowed to work free of government constraints. Industrial policy, as it exists within this perspective, tends to emerge dependent, almost totally, on actions that occur in the marketplace. Industrial policy, then, becomes situated in the prevailing actions of businesses and industries (including organized labor) at any point in time. For proponents of this position, the findings on industrial policy— whether in the United States or abroad (see Eads, 1981), whether national or more local—are mostly negative.

For proponents of the counter-position—that the federal government does have a role to play in shaping alternative directions for economic activity— the findings from data analyses are interpreted with quite different results. Instead of seeing mostly negative outcomes, this group is more inclined to emphasize where industrial policies have worked (see Gemper, 1987). Indeed, from a more liberal political perspective, scholars who support this position see an increasingly important economic role for government to play. For them, it is a role not only with economic aims but social ones as well (see Brinkman, 1987; Brown and Deavers, 1989).

And as implied above, this group too is driven by a certain political/ ideological agenda. Among American economists (most of whom are classified as conservative, referring primarily to their economic perspective, although their politics may also bear that label), those working outside the fold are referred to as "liberal" or, in a very few cases, "radical." Liberal economists such as Thurow (1987) and Reich (1983) argue that the government must play a larger role in running the economy but that free market principles must also remain. Radical economists (such as Harrison and Bluestone, 1988; Bowles, Gordon, and Weiskopf, 1983) argue that the entire economy needs to be rethought and restructured. Operating out of a Marxian-oriented theoretical perspective, they see the economy as segmented—into big businesses that capture large shares of markets and small businesses that struggle in a laissez-faire, highly competitive marketplace. Again, whether liberal or radical, the interpretation given to analyses about industrial policy is that they are necessary and can be made to work.

We suspect that the findings of Chandler and Trebilcock (1986) most accurately reflect what we know about industrial policy. In a very lengthy essay, they review findings on industrial policies in Australia, Britain, France, Japan, Sweden, the United States, and West Germany. They conclude that different countries develop policies suited to their own sets of industrial dynamics. Some work better than others, but in all cases a role for government participation can be made. As we noted earlier when citing Gemper (1987:18), "The issue is not whether or not planning exists, but rather who plans and for what purpose."

National Versus State and Local Economic Initiatives

The results of various economic policy initiatives in the United States are quite mixed. This is particularly true of industrial recruitment. To recruit new industries, communities have available incentives, some of which are legislated at the state level. These include tax abatements, industrial bond programs, enterprise zones, right-to-work laws, and subsidized vocational training. Additionally, many local communities (especially in the South) also try to entice new industries by offering easy access to natural resources, cheap land, and cheap (unorganized) labor. Some areas prosper, others don't.

There is no coherent industrial policy in the United States or in any of its regions. Rather, what one finds is a potpourri of approaches. Some states have been so starved for new industry that for years virtually any industry was welcome (see Cobb, 1982). What arose from this (not just in the South but across the United States) was a set of de facto industrial policies. There was never any serious attempt to coordinate these initiatives among states. Rather, each locality was free to assemble "incentive" packages as it saw fit.

We analyzed industrial and occupational change in the South from 1970 into the 1980s (Falk and Lyson, 1988). We found that state and local de facto policies established to entice industry resulted in urban areas which prospered, attracting high-growth, high-tech industries and the jobs which came with them. Rural areas, on the other hand—and especially the Black Belt—languished. Communities must be prepared to take risks to attract an industrial winner; but taking risks means there is always the chance of losing (for example, developing an industrial park and having no tenants). Too, even in attracting a new industry, unanticipated costs may be borne. Summers et al. (1976) documented this and noted particularly that new industries often require better services, which must be subsidized by higher taxes, and that many local residents do not get the high-paying jobs they anticipate, since the best jobs are usually filled by outsiders, not locals.

More recently, Perry (1987) and John, Batie, and Norris (1988) have found that no single strategy for attracting new industries works equally well with all communities. Some communities that seem comparable in many ways (in levels of education, income, quality of schools) have radically different trajectories when it comes to success in industrial recruitment. But both Perry and John, Batie, and Norris catalog cases of communities that have succeeded. Indeed, John, Batie, and Norris focus exclusively on such communities. Their analysis concludes with six principles:

1. States should organize policies so that change can be anticipated and communities can adapt to it.
2. States should catalyze change in both public and private sectors.
3. States must be willing to provide strong support to community-based initiatives.
4. States should work at creating more public and private partnerships.
5. State and federal agencies must build new alliances, such that each does those things for which it is best suited.
6. State economic policy must support entrepreneurship at all levels, whether a firm is large or small.

The problem with any initiatives scheme is that it may become like a high-stakes poker game. Local communities are forced to compete with one another by offering more and more perks in hope of attracting a winner, a company that will move into their area. To do this, they may have to continually up the ante and, in the process, take a very large risk. The goal at this stage of the game is purely to attract a new business. The incentives used will be amortized over a long period (e.g., the life of a bond program). Thus, communities rationalize high costs at the outset on the grounds that the rewards to be reaped (jobs, income, etc.) will merit great expense at the beginning.

Firms that migrate into an area are usually attracted by the incentives offered and the cheapness of the place: cheap taxes, cheap land, cheap labor. But production costs may be even cheaper in Third World countries (which, ironically enough, leads to what are commonly called "cheap imports"). And, of course, it is low cost of production which appeals to companies trying to maximize profits. Thus, in recent years several large textile companies have shifted some of their production facilities to the Caribbean and the Far East. And rather than move to a developing country, Volkswagen of America closed its assembly plant in Pennsylvania and expanded production in West Germany.

Our message here is quite simple: There are no ironclad, tried-and-true approaches to industrial recruitment. Three possibilities exist. First, communities may spend scarce resources in the hope of attracting new industry without succeeding. Nothing more vividly demonstrates this than driving through rural areas with industrial parks which have no industries in them (see *Shadows in the Sunbelt*, 1986). Second, although communities may succeed in attracting a new business, that firm's commitment to the community is never equal to the community's commitment to the firm. The community's commitment is driven by hope for long-term employment opportunity and financial gain via increased income. The firm's commitment is driven by profit maximization. When it is no longer sufficiently advantageous to stay in one locale, the firm may negotiate for additional tax breaks and lower wages or it may move elsewhere. This type of plant shutdown/worker dislocation is not all that unusual (again, see the case of Volkswagen of America). Third, communities may be fortunate enough to attract a firm which prospers and fulfills the community's hopes; but always there is the proviso, caveat emptor, and market forces which favor one decision today may favor something else tomorrow.

Policy Options: An Agenda for Change

In recent years, "revitalization" has become a buzz word for rural America and other economic backwaters that have not shared equally in a decade of economic growth. The need to take steps to change the economic structure has been recognized (see *Shadows in the Sunbelt*, 1986; Falk and Lyson, 1988; John, Batie, and Norris, 1988). Instead of summarizing the recommended actions which could occur, we will discuss a few measures that could lead to meaningful change. In all cases, we base our discussion on the previously stated definition of industrial policy: Any set of federally coordinated programs that seeks to stimulate or guide industrial (to include firm-level) ventures into markets for new goods or services.

Human Resource Development

Human capital is dear to the hearts of policymakers and politicians who put the burden for economic success squarely on the back of the worker. For sociologists, such an attitude is akin to "blaming the victim," which emphasizes the individual over structural factors, a perspective especially popular among political conservatives (see Gilder, 1981; Murray, 1983).

While we are very critical of putting too much emphasis on the individual, we nonetheless recognize the need for individuals to fit themselves into the marketplace to find jobs for which they are well suited. Oddly, human resource development programs were curtailed drastically during the Reagan years. The Comprehensive Employment Training Act (CETA) was replaced by the Job Training Partnership Act (JTPA) in 1982. The overall effectiveness of CETA is unclear, but it did increase employment in the short run (through public works projects) when the economy was sluggish, and it succeeded in providing better employment opportunities for disadvantaged groups. JTPA, on the other hand, is characterized by decentralized administration, an emphasis on the private sector, and a focus limited to job training for poor youth and permanently displaced workers. It is a public service employment that is, quite simply, inadequate for rural America.

We believe that federal attention must be directed toward the technical and vocational skills needed for the new economic censures that will replace the branch manufacturing plants and low-skill agricultural jobs that are leaving rural America. Stuart Rosenfeld of the Southern Growth Policies Board calls for a type of "generic" vocational training that provides the individual with a set of basic industrial skills and behaviors related to independence and responsibility (Rosenfeld, Bergmar, and Rubin, 1985). Ideally, these skills would be combined with on-the-job training or apprenticeship programs where more technical and industry-specific skills would be acquired.

Infrastructure Development

A second component to an effective and socially just industrial policy concerns infrastructure development. *Public infrastructure* is defined as the physical capital investments supported by the public sector to enhance standard of living and quality of life. Infrastructure also refers to the public facilities and equipment required to support private sector economic activity. Historically, rural areas of the United States have lacked many of the infrastructure amenities found in the more urban locales of the nation. For instance, rural areas have fewer libraries, community recreation facilities, and advanced telecommunication equipment (e.g., cable TV) than do the more urban places. Likewise, rural America lacks intra- and intercommunity transit as well as the levels of police and fire protection that are available to urban residents.

Evidence indicates that infrastructure investments are precursors to economic development. The money spent for new roads, installation or expansion of water and sewer systems, school improvements and the like is a necessary step in stimulating economic development. Clearly, most firms, and especially manufacturing plants, must have access to roads, rail lines, water and sewer systems, and other necessities. Without an adequate infrastructure, localities have little hope of developing their economies.

In recent years, researchers and policymakers have begun to pay close attention to the condition of the nation's infrastructure. Perhaps the best-known study in this area is the book *America in Ruins: The Decaying Infrastructure* (Choate and Walter, 1984). With respect to rural infrastructure needs, the authors note that virtually nothing is known about the provision of basic services and the adequacy of existing facilities in nonmetropolitan America.

The federal government has historically supported infrastructure development through direct expenditures, grants, loans, and loan guarantees. However, during the 1980s the New Federalism proposals of the Reagan administration scaled back federal support for infrastructure development. State and local governments, in turn, have assumed responsibility for the financing and delivery of many infrastructure functions. Without federal funds to subsidize infrastructure development, it is difficult to see how any environment conducive to establishing and sustaining a strong economic base can be created.

What can be done? For one thing, the federal government could establish a national public works investment policy and a supporting capital budget. Such a policy would specify and meet basic levels of public works services and facilities for specific populations and geographic areas and would specify the extent to which the public sector should finance the infrastructure to support economic development (see Choate and Walter, 1984).

For rural households and communities, a national capital budget could ensure at least a minimal level of infrastructure necessary to stimulate development. Many rural localities lack the economic base to finance the development of an infrastructure that can meet both the personal needs of the local citizenry (e.g., schools and health care facilities) and at the same time establish and maintain services and facilities to attract new industry. A federally coordinated capital budget in concert with policies and programs to develop and enhance human resources would go a long way toward enhancing the economic development potential of rural America.

Equity and Justice Programs

There is a growing awareness that human resource development policies and infrastructure programs may be necessary to stimulate economic development. But these two sets of programs alone do not ensure that those rural people and communities resting on the bottom rungs of the nation's socioeconomic ladder will be brought into the mainstream of American society. To be truly effective, human resource and infrastructure programs must operate in a social and political climate that guarantees everyone an adequate and decent standard of living and access to the means, resources, and opportunities (e.g., schools, jobs, welfare programs) to achieve this standard of living. A policy agenda to address these concerns would include, but not be limited to, full employment programs and minimum wage legislation.

Full employment and minimum wage legislation are important cornerstones to an industrial policy agenda that could improve the lot of rural workers. With respect to a full employment policy, several proposals call on the federal government to assure every willing and able-bodied worker a job. One of the more radical proposals put forth by Bowles, Gordon, and Weiskopf (1983) proposes that the federal government establish a goal of no more than 2 percent unemployment. When unemployment exceeds 2 percent in a local area, they call on the federal government to make funds available to local governments to finance public employment. Other less dramatic proposals should be considered. Clearly, attention is needed in this area.

Creating employment opportunities is only one part of the solution to the problems plaguing the rural South. The jobs that are being created must pay a livable wage. In the mid-1980s, the minimum wage of $3.35 an hour translated into an annual income of less than $7,000 a year, which is less than the poverty threshold for a family of three. (While the minimum wage has recently changed, its net effect on those living in poverty has not.) Not surprisingly, industries and occupations that pay the minimum wage represent a disproportionately large share of the jobs found in rural America.

During the 1980s, the minimum wage was raised only once—in 1981. At that time, the minimum wage stood at 46.2 percent of the average hourly wage in the United States and 41.9 percent of the average manufacturing wage. By 1987, the minimum wage had slipped to 37.3 percent of the average hourly wage and 33.8 percent of the average manufacturing wage. The new minimum wage legislation passed by Congress and signed by President Bush in 1989 raised the minimum wage to $3.80 in 1990 and $4.20 in 1991. If the minimum wage had been adjusted for inflation since 1981, today it would be $4.79 per hour.

In the 1980s, several proposals were made to peg the minimum wage to the average national hourly wage. These proposals would benefit rural workers in at least two ways. First, they would establish a wage floor for rural workers that would rise when wages in the nation as a whole increased. Second, the rural hinterlands would no longer be as attractive to footloose firms whose only motivation for setting-up shop in rural America is to exploit the low-wage work force. Whether these proposals will receive serious consideration in the 1990s remains to be seen.

Conclusion

At the outset of this chapter we stated three policy issues: human resources versus available jobs, national industrial policy versus state and local initiatives, and national planning versus free market principles.

From our perspective, to emphasize human resource development with little thought to availability of jobs is the worst type of myopia. A skilled, educated work force is of little value unless there are opportunities for the application of this human capital. Social science has given too much attention to human resources and too little attention to the structural factors that restrict opportunities.

National industrial policy is a boon for some, a boondoggle for others. The federal government has an important role to play in initiating and guiding industrial development. In the absence of the federal government's playing such a role, we are likely to see a continuation of present activity, namely, states and local communities vying with one another to put together ever more generous packages of business incentives. The only real issue in competing for new business then becomes what community wants to take the greatest risk and give away the most in hopes of attracting an industrial winner. To have states and local communities engaging in this activity (even with comparable incentives at their disposal) is like sending the fox to guard the hen house. The federal government must be more aggressive in starting new programs and then monitoring them.

To call for some form of national industrial policy planning is akin to blasphemy for free market proponents. "That government which governs best governs least" is the position adopted by supply-side, free marketeers. Unfortunately, pure laissez-faire economic principles have not been the reality in the United States for decades. Instead, big business has been propped up by various forms of what could safely be called "corporate welfare." Tax breaks, loan programs, investment and reinvestment schemes— all have been made to work to the benefit of corporations. Thus, the "free" market has for years been tainted by government intervention, primarily with corporate culpability and cooperation.

The debate between national industrial policy advocates and free marketeers is driven by concerns over equity versus efficiency. To emphasize equity, which is our position, is to say that the benefits of economic development should be distributed equitably over all segments of society. To emphasize efficiency, the supply-side position, is to say that the greatest benefit must be garnered by the least investment, a ratio which favors return rather than allocation.

For us to move toward a society which emphasizes humanistic concern over profit and recognizes that skills without opportunity are of little value in the marketplace, we must take seriously the mandate of President Bush for a "kinder, gentler America." More just and equitable policies and programs that attempt to balance the benefits of national economic expansion across all groups of workers and all types of communities must be implemented (see de Janvry, Runsten, and Sadoulet, 1988). Without an overt concern for equity and justice issues, existing inequalities are destined to grow larger. A litmus test for future economic development programs should be how they affect those communities that are least able to help themselves.

To do this, we must embark on an affirmative action program for rural America. We must develop strategies and programs to remove the kinds of historical barriers that have resulted in discrimination and in a reluctance to locate facilities and new industrial projects in rural areas. To us, there are clear parallels between what we have proposed and the types of antidiscrimination suits over school desegregation and job discrimination. In these cases, individuals (or classes of them) were precluded, de jure or de facto, from any chance of equal competition. How different is it to make this same argument with respect to local communities?

Finally, a coherent set of policies must be formulated to help shape the future U.S. (including rural America) industrial structure. Gone are the days when America could dominate the world economy. The rise of the Far East, the precariousness of oil production, *glasnost* in the Soviet Union (and the subsequent revolutions in Eastern European countries), the impending economic power of the European Community (on the role of rural labor markets in this, see Newby, 1988), and the sleeping giant of South America dictate that U.S. economic policy (and policymakers) must be much more farsighted than has previously been the case. No longer can we afford to let the dynamics of the marketplace be determined purely on the basis of efficiency and profit.

Instead, we must help to develop the vast potential in all parts of America, both prosperous and poor, rural and urban. As every major industrialized country but the United States can attest, such a policy does not mean the death of capitalism or that profits will disappear. It does mean that a higher standard of living may be obtained for the general population (such as has occurred in Europe).

If the United States cannot define a national industrial policy, if free market principles are to reign supreme with little regard for the issues we have raised here, America runs the risk of having a dated economic structure, one that will be out of tune with the world economy. Just as the U.S. steel, shoe, and automobile industries found themselves antiquated without reinvestment and retooling, so too will this happen to other sectors of the U.S. economy—unless steps are taken to prevent it.

References

Beale, Calvin L. 1976. "A further look at nonmetropolitan growth since 1970." *American Journal of Agricultural Economics* 58:953–958.

Beale, Calvin L., and Glenn V. Fuguitt. 1986. "Metropolitan and nonmetropolitan population growth in the United States since 1980." Pp. 46–62 in Joint Economic Committee, ed., *New Dimensions in Rural Policy: Building upon Our Heritage.* Washington, D.C.: U.S. Government Printing Office.

Bell, Michael E., and Paul S. Lande, eds. 1982. *Regional Dimensions of Industrial Policy.* Lexington, Mass.: Lexington Books.

Bluestone, Barry, and Bennett Harrison. 1982. *The Deindustrialization of America.* New York: Basic Books.

Bowles, Samuel, David M. Gordon, and Thomas E. Weiskopf. 1983. *Beyond the Wasteland.* New York: Anchor/Doubleday.

Brinkman, Richard L. 1987. "Democratic planning in a market economy and social values." Pp. 21–36 in Bodo B. Gemper, ed., *Structural Dynamics of Industrial Policy.* New Brunswick, N.J.: Transaction Books.

Brown, David L., and Kenneth L. Deavers., eds. 1988. *Rural Economic Development in the 1980's.* Washington, D.C.: USDA, Economic Research Service.

Brown, David L., and Kenneth L. Deavers. 1989. "The changing context of rural economic policy in the United States." Pp. 255–275 in William W. Falk and Thomas A. Lyson, eds., *Rural Sociology and Development: Rural Labor Markets.* Greenwich, Conn.: JAI Press.

Chandler, Marsha, and Michael Trebilcock. 1986. "Comparative survey of industrial policies in selected OECD countries." Pp. 85–224 in D. G. McFetridge, ed., *Economics of Industrial Policy.* Toronto: University of Toronto Press.

Choate, Pat, and Susan Walter. 1984. *America in Ruins: The Decaying Infrastructure.* Washington, D.C.: TRW, Inc.

Cobb, James. 1982. *The Selling of the South: The Southern Crusade for Industrial Development, 1936–1980.* Baton Rouge, La.: Louisiana State University Press.

de Janvry, Alain, David Runsten, and Elisabeth Sadoulet. 1988. "Toward a rural development program for the United States: A proposal." Pp. 55–93 in Gene F. Summers, John Bryden, Kenneth Deavers, Howard Newby, and Susan Sechler, eds., *Agriculture and Beyond: Rural Economic Development.* Madison, Wis.: University of Wisconsin.

Eads, George C. 1981. "The political experience in allocating investment: Lessons from the United States and elsewhere." Pp. 453–482 in Michael L. Wachter and Susan Wachter, eds., *Toward a New Industrial Policy?* Philadelphia: University of Pennsylvania Press.

Falk, William W., and Thomas A. Lyson. 1988. *High Tech, Low Tech, No Tech: Recent Industrial and Occupational Change in the South.* Albany, N.Y.: State University of New York Press.

Friedman, Miles. 1982. "The political question: Can we have a national industrial policy or a national regional policy?" Pp. 21–46 in Michael E. Bell and Paul S. Lande, eds., *Regional Dimensions of Industrial Policy.* Lexington, Mass.: Lexington Books.

Garn, Harvey A., and Larry C. Ledebur. 1982. Pp. 47–80 in Michael E. Bell and Paul S. Lande, eds., *Regional Dimensions of Industrial Policy.* Lexington, Mass.: Lexington Books.

Gemper, Bodo B., ed. 1987. *Structural Dynamics of Industrial Policy.* New Brunswick, N.J.: Transaction Books.

Gilder, George. 1981. *Wealth and Poverty.* New York: Basic Books.

Harrison, Bennett, and Barry Bluestone. 1988. *The Great U-Turn.* New York: Basic Books.

John, Dewitt, Sandra S. Batie, and Kim Norris. 1988. *A Brighter Future for Rural America? Strategies for Communities and States.* Washington, D.C.: National Governors' Association.

Jones, Reginald H. 1981. "Toward a new industrial policy." Pp. 9–16 in Michael L. Wachter and Susan Wachter, eds., *Toward a New Industrial Policy?* Philadelphia: University of Pennsylvania Press.

Lyson, Thomas A. 1989. *Two Sides to the Sunbelt: The Growing Divergence Between the Rural and Urban South.* New York: Praeger.

Murray, Charles. 1983. *Losing Ground.* New York: Basic Books.

Newby, Howard. 1988. "Economic restructuring and rural labor markets in Europe: Current policy options." Pp. 41–54 in Gene Summers, ed., *Agriculture and Beyond: Rural Economic Development.* Madison, Wis.: University of Wisconsin, College of Agriculture and Life Sciences.

Perry, Stewart E. 1987. *Communities on the Way: Rebuilding Local Communities in the United States and Canada.* Albany, N.Y.: State University of New York Press.

Reich, Robert. 1983. *The Next American Frontier.* New York: Times Books.

Rosenfeld, Stuart A., Edward M. Bergmar, and Sarah Rubin. 1985. *After the Factories.* Research Triangle Park, N.C.: Southern Growth Policies Board.

Schultz, Theodore W. 1961. "Investment in human capital." *American Economic Review* 51:1–17.

Shadows in the Sunbelt. 1986. Chapel Hill, N.C.: MDC.

Singelmann, Joachim. 1978. *From Agriculture to Services: The Transformation of Industrial Employment.* Beverly Hills, Calif.: Sage.

Southern Growth Policies Board. 1986. *Halfway Home and a Long Way to Go.* Research Triangle Park, N.C.: SGPB.

Summers, Gene, Sharon D. Evans, Frank Clemente, E. M. Beck, and Jon Minkoff. 1976. *Industrial Invasion of Nonmetropolitan America.* New York: Praeger.

Thurow, Lester C. 1987. "A surge in inequality." *Scientific American* 236:30–37.

Wachter, Michael L., and Susan Wachter, eds. 1981. *Toward a New Industrial Policy?* Philadelphia: University of Pennsylvania Press.

3

Financing Rural Businesses

Mark Drabenstott and Charles Morris

The rural economy has just completed a difficult decade. Following what many labeled a rural renaissance in the mid- and late-1970s, rural America entered the 1980s with high expectations. Instead, it quickly found itself the victim of significant national and international economic forces well beyond its control. Economic adjustments in the 1980s cut across nearly all segments of the rural economy. The exceptions were rural counties that depend on retirees and government, where growth continued. Now that the decade of painful economic adjustment has passed, most rural counties look for tools to stimulate economic growth in the decade ahead.

Capital is a critical ingredient in any program to spur rural economic development. But rural financial markets underwent a significant transition of their own in the 1980s. Since the financial market deregulation, rural community banks now find themselves in a highly competitive market. Funds are scarce for traditional government direct-loan programs. And agriculture, traditionally the impetus for much public intervention in rural financial markets, is losing its uniqueness in policymakers' eyes.

Where will rural businesses find financing in the 1990s, and what public policy options, if any, should be considered to encourage rural capital formation? This chapter examines these questions and concludes that commercial banks will remain the dominant source of financing, although their role may wane somewhat. The integration of rural banks into national financial markets means that rural capital flows will be quite efficient. Most rural businesses will have ready access to debt financing, but they must be prepared to pay market interest rates. Venture capital, the key to start-up businesses, appears to merit some public policy emphasis. Overall, the role of public policy to improve rural capital formation remains uncertain without a clear rural development policy statement.

The Rural Capital Setting of the 1990s

The rural financial markets of the 1990s will be decidedly different than those of the past. Historically, rural community banks lived in an insulated world of cheap deposits and below-market interest rates. Deregulation, improved telecommunications, and a decade of economic decline have permanently changed that.

What factors define the new rural capital setting of the 1990s, and how do these factors change our assumptions about rural economic development? An uneven rural economy, financial market deregulation, emerging secondary markets, the spread of interstate banking, and fewer government lending programs sum up the likely character of rural financial markets.

Uneven Rural Economic Performance

The rural economy's performance is quite uneven as it enters the 1990s. Historically, rural America has been thought of as relatively homogeneous and dominated by agriculture, but that is no longer true. As the rural economy has been more fully integrated into the national and international marketplaces, a much more diverse and complex set of economic forces has begun to tug and pull on local rural economies. The result is a quiltlike pattern of economic strength and weakness (Henry, Drabenstott, and Gibson, 1988).

Rural economic strength is currently concentrated in relatively few counties. Retirement- and government-based counties have enjoyed steady income and employment gains. Together, these 460-odd counties represent about a quarter of the rural population. Reflecting their relatively strong prospects, retirement counties have accounted for 85 percent of the increase in rural population since 1983 (Deavers, 1989).

In the 1980s, most rural counties endured sharp economic declines from which they are just now recovering. Farm-dependent counties have had four years (1987–1990) of strong recovery, but significant structural change in the industry continues, leaving many farm communities in flux. Manufacturing counties, which account for more than a third of the rural population, remain generally depressed, with only a modest recovery in the past three years. Most rural plant shutdowns that occurred in the early and mid-1980s have not been replaced with new economic activity. And energy-dependent rural communities are quite depressed due to lower and more volatile energy prices.

Uneven rural economic performance—and the likelihood that it will continue in the decade ahead—holds far-reaching implications for rural financial markets. Geographic location and the economic base that an area represents may be a more important determinant of financing than ever before. Rural lenders are likely to attach different risks to local lending, depending on the strength of their local economy. Because the strength of the rural economy will vary widely, so will the willingness of banks to lend. Commercial banks in rural areas that were depressed through much of the 1980s may be especially cautious in lending to new rural businesses. If public policymakers choose to take steps to make financing more available to some rural borrowers, programs will have to be tailored to specific rural places. Given the diverse character of the rural economy, general rural credit programs are doomed from the start.

Loan data from nonmetropolitan commercial banks underscore the conclusion that an uneven rural economy has a dramatic effect on rural financing. The data in Figure 3.1 compare loan-asset ratios for commercial banks in all nonmetropolitan counties, retirement-dependent nonmetropolitan counties, and farm-dependent nonmetropolitan counties. Loan-asset ratios followed a similar pattern in all three types of counties from 1970 to 1982. Since then, however, loan-asset ratios have diverged sharply. Commercial banks have lent aggressively in retirement counties, where economic growth has been solid and steady. Banks in farm-dependent rural counties, meanwhile, have been much more cautious in lending due to a depressed farm economy throughout much of the 1980s. In short, rural businesses have been able to obtain credit in retirement areas more easily than in farming areas.

Deregulation of Financial Markets

As in the rural economy, rural financial markets have been integrated into national and international markets. Deregulation of financial markets in the early 1980s broke down some of the traditional barriers between rural and urban financial institutions. At the same time, improved communications introduced rural savers to more distant opportunities.

Deregulation brought three important outcomes to rural financial markets. First, rural institutions gained the tools needed to retain deposits, so deposits no longer fled rural areas in periods of high interest rates—that is, disintermediation ceased to be a problem. Second, rural savers improved their incomes. Third, as a consequence of the second outcome, rural borrowers had to pay market-based interest rates.

The integrated rural financial market of the 1990s presents both new opportunities and challenges to rural businesses. Unlike periods in the past, rural banks have a steady, ample supply of funds to lend. But those funds will be lent at money market–based interest rates. In the past, rural banks were able to offer below-market rates due to their low cost of funds. These low rates served as an indigenous stimulant to rural business activity. Rural businesses now must compete directly with urban businesses for capital.

Emerging Secondary Markets

Deregulation has integrated rural financial markets into national markets. Rural America is now open to many financial market innovations. Among the most promising rural innovations for the 1990s are secondary markets. Although secondary markets are well established in urban markets, especially for residential mortgages, rural areas have participated much less. That situation will change in the coming decade. The Agricultural Credit Act of 1987 established for the first time a secondary market for farm mortgages (Farmer Mac). By 1990, that agency should be operational, providing rural

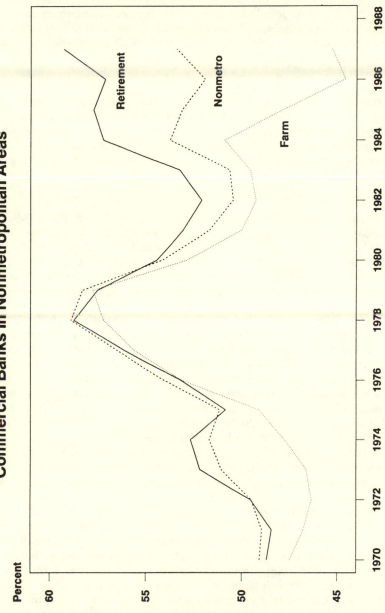

Figure 3-1
Loans as a Share of Assets
Commercial Banks in Nonmetropolitan Areas

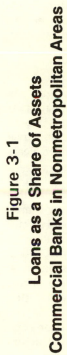

banks the opportunity to make long-term farm mortgage loans and to securitize and sell the loans to investors.

Rural secondary markets for other types of loans almost certainly will follow. The 1987 legislation allowed for the securitization of farm operating loans and rural housing loans sometime in the future. As rural lenders and financial markets grow more comfortable with securitized farm loans, opportunities should arise to extend securitization to other types of rural business loans.

Securitization offers many benefits to rural lenders and borrowers. It allows lenders to offer more complete lending services while simultaneously giving lenders the means to manage their credit and interest rate risk. Borrowers benefit from a wider offering of financial services, including fixed-rate, long-term financing. Borrowers also benefit from greater competition among lenders.

Interstate Banking

The ground rules of banking changed rapidly in the 1980s, with yet unknown consequences for rural financial markets. In the past, rural areas resisted interstate banking, believing that local independent banks would best serve the financial needs of rural communities. But economic upheaval and technological innovation in financial services during the last ten years have broken down many legislative barriers to interstate banking.

The speed with which states adopted interstate banking legislation of one form or another in the 1980s is quite remarkable. In 1982, interstate banking was prohibited by 47 states and the District of Columbia. By March 1989, only five states (Kansas, North Dakota, Montana, Iowa, and Hawaii) prohibited it ("Kansas panel votes against interstate banking," 1989). Although many states introduced interstate banking in limited form in the 1980s, allowing only banks from contiguous states, for example, to enter, most states will allow full-scale interstate banking at some future date. Thus, while the 1980s brought legislative change, the 1990s are likely to bring widespread change in bank structure itself.

What does the advent of far-reaching interstate banking mean for rural financial markets? The answer is far from clear. Most studies of bank structure agree that national and regional banking markets will become more concentrated. But the effects on rural areas are much more ambiguous.

Several factors support the conclusion that small community banks will continue to be important players in rural financial markets. First, small banks are not at a significant cost disadvantage.[1] In fact, small community banks have a history of strong profits when compared with larger, urban banks. Second, large-money-center or regional-money-center banks have demonstrated little interest in acquiring the business of small community banks. In California, for example, small independent banks prosper alongside some of the biggest banks in the nation. And third, small community banks have well-established, personalized business relationships with the local market, often a desirable trait in rural markets. Large banks simply cannot serve a local market in the same way. Thus, many studies have concluded that rural communities will continue to be served by small banks (Billington; 1988; Rhoades and Savage, 1985; U.S. Treasury Department, 1981).

Although commercial banks will remain important to rural financial flows, their predominant role may wane slightly. In a competitive market, rural borrowers will have more credit choices than in the past. Most borrowers will probably continue to choose the individualized service of a community bank. But others, especially rural borrowers with large credit lines, may find lower interest rates and a more complete array of financial services with major financial institutions in metropolitan areas.

The banking structure in rural America may be more affected in the future by the unevenness in the rural economy than by a new wave of interstate banking. As economic activity in rural America becomes concentrated in larger trade centers, financial services are also likely to be concentrated in those centers. Similarly, as some rural communities continue to lose viability, the number of banks will decline. Although rural banks will be fewer in number and somewhat larger than previously, they will still remain small when compared with regional- or national-money-center banks.

Less Government Involvement in Rural Financial Markets

In the 1990s, government will play a lesser role in rural financial markets than it has in the past. Deregulation has made rural financial markets more efficient. And while that efficiency comes at the price of money-market-based interest rates to rural borrowers, public policymakers will find fewer rural financial market failures to overcome through public programs.

Agriculture's Loss of Uniqueness. Further diminishing the justification for public policy intervention is the fact that agriculture—the principal motivator of rural credit programs in the past—is losing its uniqueness. Ten years ago, the fading of agriculture's cultural uniqueness was evident (Paarlberg, 1980); today, the loss of agricultural business and economic uniqueness has also become apparent.

Structural change in agriculture has made farm businesses more like other small businesses. Food and fiber production has shifted toward fewer and larger farms; the largest 300,000 U.S. farms now produce nearly three-fourths of the nation's food and fiber. These firms have average assets of $1.2 million and average gross incomes of $355,000. Commercial-sized farms use the same management tools and financial resources as similarly sized small businesses in other industries. Farm lenders expect the same level of financial records and management controls as they would from other small businesses. In short, farmers have lost their uniqueness in our economy.

The farm businesses of today stand in sharp contrast to the farms that have been the target of past public lending programs. Historically, federal and state governments have seen farms as businesses lacking ready access to capital. That fear gave rise to major public lending programs. The Farm Credit System, the Farmers Home Administration (FmHA), and a number of state fa.m loan programs were created out of the belief that farmers must have access to adequate capital at reasonable terms. In addition, many policymakers believed that these farm credit programs also served a rural development objective—a claim that was more justified when the rural economy depended more heavily on agriculture than it does today.

Now policymakers generally consider agriculture less deserving of public credit programs. Farm businesses already have far more access to public lending programs than do their nonfarm business counterparts. Thus, the era of free-flowing federal credit to agriculture may be past. If public credit programs are needed to stimulate rural economic activity, they will rise or fall on their own merits, apart from agriculture.

Limited Funds for Government Programs. Rural credit programs not only have less justification, they are much more limited by government finances than previously. The federal government is avoiding any new direct lending programs due to the large federal budget deficit. Loan guarantee programs are preferred over direct-loan programs due to their lower cost.[2]

States also face fiscal limits. States employed a number of linked-deposit programs in the 1980s to make idle state funds available to farmers and rural borrowers. But states generally lack the fiscal resources to implement major rural credit programs, especially in many predominantly rural states still recovering from painful economic adjustments in the 1980s.

In sum, rural credit markets will be more efficient in the 1990s, resulting in less government in rural credit programs. Deregulation and interstate banking point to ample funds for rural businesses, but at market rates of interest. The potential for securitizing rural loans will open up new opportunities for rural borrowers. Agriculture's loss of uniqueness will diminish support for new public credit programs in rural areas; the programs that do arise are more likely to be loan guarantee rather than direct loan programs.

The Need for Rural Credit Programs in the 1990s

Recent years have witnessed a public revival in rural development policy. And while the rhetoric has exceeded the action, policymakers and researchers continue to have a high level of interest in exploring public programs that will stimulate rural economic activity. Many such initiatives center on increasing rural capital formation. What role should rural credit programs have, and which programs offer the greatest promise of achieving public policy objectives?

Historically, rural credit programs have been justified on two grounds: rural credit markets are inefficient, and agriculture is a special industry facing special risks. Today both reasons are less important—some observers would say much less important. If market inefficiency no longer justifies public credit programs in rural areas, are there additional factors that do?

Rural credit programs will be justified only within the context of a coherent rural policy. The United States currently has no rural policy to guide and coordinate its public programs in rural areas (Drabenstott, Henry, and Gibson, 1987). The nation must decide what value it places on economic activity in rural places. Is the nation content to let market forces continue, with greater concentration of population and resources in metropolitan areas? Or are the social values tied to rural America important enough to merit public intervention that aims to encourage economic activity in the very rural places that market trends have left behind? Or, should public policy aim to facilitate the transition of people and resources in response to existing market forces?

Implementing rural credit programs before these questions are answered is putting the cart before the horse. The rural credit market of the 1990s will be more efficient than during any decade of the past. Thus, if the public wants to further encourage rural capital formation as part of an effort to stimulate rural economic activity, a clear rural policy with that objective should be crafted.

If the public supports programs to stimulate rural economies, an important question remains: What types of rural finance programs, if any, are needed? Recent studies of rural business starts may provide some guide to public initiatives that can overcome market gaps. Popovich and Buss (1987) and Buss and Popovich (1988) found that new businesses in Iowa and North Dakota generally found sufficient start-up funds from commercial banks and other private lenders. The exceptions were businesses in industries that were new to the area and that bankers considered more risky ventures. In short, there was a lack of venture capital for a small set of nontraditional businesses. A similar survey of businesses in Wisconsin also revealed that a sizable majority of rural businesses found ready amounts of debt capital from private lenders, even though many new businesses found equity capital difficult to obtain (Combs, Pulver, and Shaffer, 1983). These studies appear to support the earlier conclusion that rural financial markets are relatively efficient in providing debt capital.

Policy Options to Encourage Rural Capital Formation

A number of rural credit programs will be considered in the 1990s. Many state and local governments have already put some of the options into use, either as pilot programs or as full-fledged efforts. The programs can be divided into four groups: commercial bank, technical assistance, public lending, and venture capital programs.

Commercial Bank Programs

Commercial banks are the principal lenders to rural businesses; thus, it is not surprising that many rural credit programs are aimed at banks. While the role of banks in rural financial markets may decline some in the 1990s, banks will remain the most important source of credit to most small rural businesses. Increased use of secondary markets and new community reinvestment regulations are two programs aimed at encouraging commercial banks to make more loans to rural businesses. In the past, rural community banks have been reluctant to lend to firms in businesses with which the bank has little prior lending experience. Such nontypical loans are especially important to rural communities attempting to diversify their economies.

Expanding secondary markets to rural business loans may be an attractive way of increasing rural capital formation; such markets would allow commercial banks to reduce the credit and interest rate risk incurred by expanding their lending into new business lines. The bank could initiate and service loans, while the credit risk would be borne by investors who purchased packaged securities.

How such rural loan secondary markets could be formed is unclear. Farmer Mac will provide a good experiment on the overall success of secondary markets in rural America. It seems unlikely that rural business loans could be securitized if Farmer Mac fails to attract sufficient business. Governors in rural states might take the lead in promoting a new secondary market for rural loans. State banking associations also are in a position to offer leadership. Such markets will do more to help rural lending than will many state direct-loan programs, and at a fraction of the cost. To be successful, a rural business loan secondary market would need wide geographic diversification and common underwriting standards.

Some states are considering the use of community reinvestment regulations to encourage rural lending. Twenty-four states have some type of community reinvestment provision; in most cases, the law attempts to prevent banks entering the state from decreasing loan activity in the state (Peters, Stumberg, and Ward, 1988). Most state laws are patterned after federal regulation, the Community Reinvestment Act of 1977.

While the regulations provide a framework with which to assess a bank's commitment to its community, most of the regulations lack enforcement provisions. The federal law, for example, has been used almost entirely with urban banks, and even then the law comes into play only when a bank makes application to acquire another financial institution. Some researchers have suggested that states might allow rural banks to develop small, high-risk portfolios of rural business start-up loans that would be examined separately from the rest of their loan portfolios (Vaughn, Pollard, and Dyer, 1984). Such loans appear inconsistent with an overall bank regulatory goal of safety and soundness. In short, community reinvestment regulations do little to overcome the risk of lending to new businesses.

Technical Assistance Programs

Technical assistance programs serve a simple purpose: to supply the missing technical or management skills new businesses need to succeed. Often these missing links center on financing or on filling out a business plan sufficiently to qualify for financing. For that reason, many technical assistance programs incorporate lenders as key participants in bringing businesses and information together.

As rural communities attempt to diversify into new industries, two potential problems arise. First, the local bank may have little experience with the particular financial and management demands of a new business. Second, the owner of the firm may have a sound business plan but may lack technical expertise in one aspect of the business. Because of the leadership role of the community bank in financing new businesses, technical assistance programs that work through bankers may defuse both problems at once.

Several technical assistance programs are emerging. The federal government provides small business assistance through Small Business Development Centers (SBDCs), administered by the Small Business Association (SBA) in each state. SBDC programs operate directly with businesses, although banks may get involved due to participation in SBA loan guarantee programs. State bankers' associations are beginning to view technical assistance as an important, if not necessary, tool banks can use to encourage local development. The Minnesota Bankers Association, for example, has established the Enterprise Network, a clearinghouse of information on economic development issues and problems. Other states are exploring similar programs. The extension service is reevaluating its role in assisting rural businesses and will likely initiate more business development programs. One key element of the new programs will be leadership development, and community banks will be important participants in these programs.

With so many possible providers of technical assistance, state governments may play a useful role in coordinating the programs. In short, successful rural development will require the cooperation of business owners, financiers, and the specialists who can fill in technical gaps. Because the technical assistance comes from so many different sources, a public-private sector partnership to coordinate the assistance could be especially effective. Minnesota, for example, has chartered the Greater Minnesota Corporation, whose mission is to encourage applied research and technology transfer for rural areas as well as to coordinate start-up and operating financing for new rural businesses.[3] Other states will likely consider similar ways to boost rural business activity.

Technical assistance programs, in essence, attempt to be the catalysts of new rural businesses. While new products and financing are the major elements of business ventures, technical assistance programs aim to supply the missing links. Because lenders already provide community leadership, they are logical participants in programs that provide the extra expertise needed to make successful businesses. Although researchers have not verified it, technical assistance programs probably pay big dividends. The cost of the programs is relatively low, and in many cases the programs are the difference between success and failure for rural businesses.

Public Lending Programs

Public lending programs targeted at rural development will emerge in the 1990s, but the programs almost certainly will be limited in scope. Traditionally operated by the federal government, rural public lending programs are likely to shift more to state sponsorship. As discussed earlier, the justification for direct federal loan programs is waning, as rural financial markets become more efficient and as agriculture loses it uniqueness. As a result, states will likely play a somewhat larger role in loan programs. However, most rural states will have only limited funds to commit to such programs. Two low-cost types of programs will receive the most attention: loan guarantee and linked-deposit programs.

Loan guarantee programs are attractive because they share the risks of new rural business loans between the public and the private sectors. States could choose to guarantee a fixed percentage of particular rural business loans up to a given dollar amount. As a result, banks would be more willing to make new business loans that have more risk attached. However, because the bank still shares in a portion of any potential losses, the program will retain safeguards that should limit the public's cost.

With many states lacking funds for direct rural loan programs, loan guarantees are likely to gain in popularity. Currently, 14 states have small business loan guarantee programs of one type or another.[4] The programs generally are targeted at manufacturing firms and are statewide, open to both rural and urban businesses. Many rural states may create loan guarantee programs specifically for rural businesses, whether start-up or expansion of existing firms, as part of their state's rural development policy. To be most effective, such funds should be available to all types of businesses; it is unlikely that manufacturing will be the dominant engine of rural revitalization. Loan guarantee programs will stimulate more business activity than direct loan programs; sharing the loan risk with banks allows the dollars to go further.

Linked-deposit programs may also be considered in the 1990s. Under these programs, idle state funds are deposited at participating commercial banks at favorable interest rates if banks agree to lend the funds to target groups at reduced rates. In short, the programs amount to an interest subsidy to the target group. In the 1980s, 11 states began such programs, usually to assist farmers or rural businesses.[5] The programs generally do not distinguish well between borrowers that need the interest subsidy and those that do not. Even more fundamental, the programs affect the cost of loanable funds, not their availability. That is, they do not reduce the credit risk of new rural business loans. In that sense, the programs are much less effective in stimulating rural capital formation than are loan guarantees.

Venture Capital Programs

Many observers consider venture capital programs a key element in the future of rural development policy. While debt markets are generally efficient in rural America, equity markets, and especially venture capital markets, are much less developed. Commercial banks will not be viable sources of venture capital for most rural businesses. The private sector may provide more venture capital to rural America in the future, but public initiatives, possibly in partnership with the private sector, may be critical to the initial development of a well-functioning rural venture capital market. As with public lending programs, much of the impetus for that development probably will rest with state governments.

Several states already have venture capital programs of one type or another, although none is aimed specifically at rural businesses.[6] The Greater Minnesota Corporation, however, does have a strong rural orientation. The Kansas program, Kansas Venture Capital Inc., represents a strong partnership between the public and private sectors. The corporation was chartered with matching $10 million funds from the state and from Kansas banks, including many rural banks. Permanent operating funds are expected to be generated by the corporation's ongoing profits.

The success of these state programs is difficult to assess. Most of the programs were started only recently, and results are limited. But the relatively long-running program in Massachusetts (Massachusetts Community Development Finance Corporation, begun in 1975) has been quite successful in spurring business activity in depressed parts of the state. A key to that program has been a strong partnership with local community development corporations, which are generally absent in rural areas.[7] In short, state efforts to increase venture capital have had some success, but little of the improvement has occurred in rural areas.

States have two choices if they want to increase rural venture capital. They can devise new state-funded programs aimed specifically at rural businesses. Their teaming with private investors or banks, as in the Kansas case, would reduce the initial capitalization and the ongoing risk. Alternatively, states can offer tax concessions to encourage private rural venture capital funds. Indiana has followed this approach with its general venture capital corporation. In either case, the programs should be available to businesses in all industries, since diversification will be an important ingredient in overall rural development.

Conclusion

The rural financial market of the 1990s will be a critical tool in stimulating rural economic activity. After a decade of financial market deregulation, rural financial markets are quite efficient. Most rural borrowers will have ready access to loanable funds, but they must be able to pay market interest rates. In an uneven rural economy, however, borrowers in lagging regions may encounter more reluctant lenders. More borrowers will be able to take advantage of secondary markets in the decade ahead, promising a more complete set of borrowing options. Because the rural financial market is generally efficient, traditional public lending programs for rural areas probably will wane, especially at the federal level.

Public policies to encourage rural capital formation probably will be limited in scope. The need for such policies remains unclear without a clear rural development policy. Nevertheless, many rural states will undertake finance programs to stimulate rural economic activity.

Four programs offer the greatest promise. First, a secondary market for rural business loans would encourage more lending to rural small businesses. Rural states, and banks within those states, would probably have to supply leadership for such a market to develop. Second, technical assistance programs will overcome the financing and managerial gaps that naturally arise for new rural businesses. Technical assistance programs are a natural public complement to a relatively efficient rural financial market. Third, loan guarantee programs allow states to share the credit risks of new rural business activity with commercial banks, a partnership that is likely to increase rural lending. Finally, establishing rural venture capital programs may pay the greatest dividends in terms of rural development. Venture capital is generally lacking in rural areas, and public initiatives may be essential to increase its availability.

Notes

Mark Drabenstott is an assistant vice president and economist and Charles Morris is a senior economist at the Federal Reserve Bank of Kansas City. The views and opinions expressed in this chapter are strictly those of the authors and do not necessarily represent those of the Federal Reserve Bank of Kansas City or the Federal Reserve System.

1. Economies of scale studies indicate that there are some weak economies of scale for banks having less than $100 million in assets. The scale economies are not likely to be big enough to spur wholesale consolidation. For a review of the economies of scale literature, see Clark (1988).

2. Congress declared a clear preference for loan guarantees over direct-loan programs in the 1985 Food Security Act, by which FmHA funds were shifted from direct loans to loan guarantee programs over the five-year life of the bill.

3. The Greater Minnesota Corporation was created in 1987. A publicly chartered corporation, it was founded with $106 million of state funds. Over time, the founders hope that more of the operating funds will derive from fees and profits derived from new business ventures in the state.

4. The 14 states are California, Connecticut, Indiana, Louisiana, Maine, Maryland, Michigan, Minnesota, Mississippi, Missouri, Montana, New Jersey, Vermont, and Virginia (National Association of State Development Agencies, 1986).

5. By the end of 1988, 11 states had linked deposit programs in place (National Center for Policy Alternatives, 1988). In general, these programs allow a target group (typically farmers) to borrow state funds held at local banks at a subsidized interest rate. For a discussion of the costs and benefits of these programs, see Markley (1988:16–19).

6. At least ten states have venture capital programs that were started with state appropriations or were made possible through special tax concessions. The ten states are Connecticut, Indiana, Kansas, Maine, Massachusetts, Michigan, Minnesota, Montana, New York, and Wisconsin (National Association of State Development Agencies, 1986).

7. Community development corporations (CDCs) are nonprofit entities that promote economic development by providing assistance, including some forms of financing, to start-up firms or existing businesses that are expanding. Banks are allowed to

establish CDCs or participate in them under a 1963 Comptroller of the Currency regulation.

References

Billington, Wilbur T. 1988. *Community Banks, Surviving with Change.* Kansas City, Mo.: Federal Reserve Bank.

Buss, Terry F., and Mark G. Popovich. 1988. *Growth From Within: New Businesses and Rural Economic Development in North Dakota.* Washington, D.C.: Council of State Policy and Planning Agencies.

Clark, Jeffrey A. 1988. "Economies of scale and scope at depository institutions: A review of the literature." *Economic Review.* Kansas City, Mo.: Federal Reserve Bank. September/October.

Combs, Robert P., Glen C. Pulver, and Ron E. Shaffer. 1983. *Financing New Small Business Enterprise in Wisconsin.* Research Bulletin R3198. Madison, Wis.: University of Wisconsin–Madison, College of Agricultural and Life Sciences.

Deavers, Kenneth. 1989. "Rural policy: Facing the 1990s." *Positioning Agriculture for the 1990s: A New Decade of Change.* Symposium proceedings. National Planning Association.

Drabenstott, Mark, Mark Henry, and Lynn Gibson. 1987. "The rural economic policy choice." *Economic Review.* Kansas City, Mo.: Federal Reserve Bank. January.

Henry, Mark, Mark Drabenstott, and Lynn Gibson. 1988. "A changing rural economy." Chapter 2 in *Rural America in Transition.* Kansas City, Mo.: Federal Reserve Bank.

"Kansas panel votes against interstate banking." 1989. *American Banker* 154(47):15.

Markley, Deborah. 1988. *Availability of Capital in Rural America: Problems and Options.* Washington, D.C.: National Governors' Association.

National Association of State Development Agencies. 1986. *Directory of Incentives for Business Investment and Development in the United States. A State by State Guide,* 2nd ed. Washington, D.C.: National Association of State Development Agencies.

National Center for Policy Alternatives. 1988. *Legislative Sourcebook on Financial Deregulation.* Washington, D.C.: National Center for Policy Alternatives.

Paarlberg, Don. 1980. "Agriculture loses its uniqueness." Chapter 2 in *Farm and Food Policy: Issues of the 1980s.* Lincoln, Neb.: University of Nebraska Press.

Peters, Farley, Robert Stumberg, and Roxanne Ward. 1988. *Legislative Sourcebook on Financial Deregulation.* Washington, D.C.: National Center for Policy Alternatives.

Popovich, Mark G., and Terry F. Buss. 1987. *Rural Enterprise Development: An Iowa Case Study.* Washington, D.C.: Council of State Policy and Planning Agencies.

Rhoades, Stephen A., and Donald T. Savage. 1985. "The viability of the small bank." *The Bankers Magazine* 168(4):66–72.

Scheld, Karl A., and Herbert Baer. 1986. "Interstate banking and intrastate branching: Summing up." In *Toward Nationwide Banking: A Guide to the Issues.* Chicago: Federal Reserve Bank.

U.S. Treasury Department. 1981. *Geographic Restrictions on Commercial Banking in the United States. The Report of the President.* Washington, D.C.: Government Printing Office.

Vaughn, Roger, Robert Pollard, and Barbara Dyer. 1984. *The Wealth of States: Policies for a Dynamic Economy.* Washington, D.C.: Council of State Policy and Planning Agencies.

4
Rural Banking

Gary P. Green

Over the past decade banking deregulation has structurally transformed the commercial banking industry.[1] The central policy issue in the debates over banking deregulation is the extent to which the costs of credit and services, the geographic location, and the variety of services offered by banks should be regulated. The merits of banking deregulation have been widely debated. Proponents contend that deregulation will make the banking industry more efficient and competitive and place banks on a level playing field with nonfinancial institutions. Deregulation provides a competitive environment that allegedly encourages banks to provide a wider variety of services and to charge less for services and credit. Critics of deregulation charge that banking regulations have provided security and restricted monopolistic power in the banking industry. Banking deregulation will increase concentration in local banking markets, insert additional risk into the financial system, and contribute to higher costs for credit and banking services.

This chapter reviews the social science evidence on the consequences of banking deregulation for rural communities and evaluates responses to these changes at the national, state, and local levels. The basic choice in rural banking policy is between further deregulation or reregulation. Deregulation would remove all restrictions on the permissible activities and geographic location of commercial banks. Reregulation would eliminate many of these same restrictions, but it would require financial institutions to demonstrate they are meeting the credit needs of communities.

Since 1980, Congress has eliminated many of the regulations surrounding the commercial banking industry. Prior to 1980, Regulation Q placed a ceiling on the interest rates commercial banks could pay on deposits. In effect, this regulation limited price competition for deposits, and thus it subsidized borrowers. Regulation Q was removed because of increased competition for funds from newly developed alternative investment instruments (e.g., money-market funds and certificates of deposit) offering higher interest rates to borrowers. During the 1970s, capital flowed rapidly into these alternative investments and shifted overseas where there were fewer banking restrictions on interest rates. With the elimination of Regulation

Q, commercial banks are allowed to compete for deposits. As a result, bank depositors earn a higher interest rate on their deposits and borrowers pay higher interest for loans. Interest rate deregulation, however, may have contributed to the problems of many rural banks and savings and loan institutions that were forced to pay their depositors more interest than they had paid in the past.

The United States is one of the few industrialized countries that have geographic limitations on where banks can do business. Prior to the mid-1980s, banks were not permitted to cross state lines. The spark to merger mania in the banking industry was the Supreme Court's decision in June 1985 that interstate banking was constitutional. By the end of 1986, 35 states had enacted legislation providing for regional or national interstate banking. Regional banking pacts with reciprocal relationships now exist in several regions. Alaska, Arizona, Maine, Texas, and Wyoming permit interstate banking from any state without reciprocity requirements.

The third prong of banking deregulation concerns the types of services offered by financial institutions. In the 1970s, nonfinancial institutions (i.e., those not restricted by banking regulations, such as Sears and Merrill Lynch) invaded commercial banking markets by offering products and services (e.g., money-market funds) traditionally provided only by financial institutions. These nonfinancial institutions were immune from banking regulations because they were not considered "banks" by regulators. *Commercial banks are defined as institutions that take deposits and make loans; if a firm only does one of these tasks, it is not considered by regulators to be a commercial bank.* Commercial banks were at a competitive disadvantage with these nonfinancial institutions and called for a level playing field. Financial institutions asked regulators for permission to become involved in activities not related to finance, such as real estate, insurance, and securities. The central question facing legislators and regulators today is: How far should banks be allowed to enter into activities not directly related to banking?

Policy Context

A number of social science studies have been conducted on the lending policies and practices of commercial banks in rural areas. Research on rural banking has identified three general sets of variables influencing commercial bank performance: local economic growth, local credit market structure, and organizational and managerial influences.[2] Banking policy is directed primarily at influencing the latter two factors. From the bankers' standpoint, however, the poor quality of local loan opportunities and the undiversified economies of many rural communities severely limit the capacity of banks to increase lending.

Much of the social science literature on rural banking has examined the consequences of banking structure (bank size, market concentration, and absentee ownership vs. independent bank) on bank performance (e.g., costs of services and credit, availability of services, differential access to credit, and capital flows within and between communities). Although there are many inconsistent findings in this literature, there is a consensus that structural variables are related to lending practices and to the performance of rural banks.

Critics of deregulation have been concerned that the elimination of many banking regulations would lead to a centralized and concentrated industry. According to these critics, a shift from independent banks to holding company affiliates and branch banks would have deleterious consequences for the availability of credit in rural communities. Research findings on this issue are mixed. Rural bank mergers increase the availability of financial services (Markley, 1984) and the proportion of a bank's assets available for loans (Barkley and Potts, 1985). Several studies have found that bank mergers, however, lead to a smaller ratio of agricultural loans to total loans (Markley, 1984). Ownership structure is not related to the cost of credit, but it does influence access to credit; holding company affiliates and branch banks are less likely than independent banks to lend to small farmers (Green, 1984).

The literature on the relationship between market concentration and rural bank performance suggests that competition and performance are weakly linked (Heggestad and Shepherd, 1986; Milkove and Weisblat, 1982). Contrary to the expectations that banking deregulation would lead to market concentration, Kaufman and Kormendi (1986) show that concentration ratios (the percentage of assets in the local market held by the four largest banks) for commercial banks in metropolitan statistical areas (MSAs) and counties have generally decreased over the past 15 years. The shift from independent banking to holding company affiliates and branch banks decreases concentration in local credit markets because new branch offices are opened in the community. At the national level, however, the evidence clearly suggests that concentration in the banking industry has increased over the past decade.

Strong evidence indicates that bank size is significantly related to bank performance. Bank size is positively related to the number of services offered, the percentage of assets (loans) committed to consumer and industrial loans, the size of loan limits, and formalization of lending policies (Milkove, 1985). In addition, Milkove found that bank size is also positively related to the aggressiveness in attracting large deposits and the risk orientation of banks.

Less evidence is available on the effects of managerial influences on the performance of rural banks (Markley, 1988a). A recent study of rural banking in West Virginia (Boggs, Sorenson, and Isserman, 1988) found that banks using collateral as the major criterion for evaluating loan applications made fewer loans and were much less aggressive than were banks using the capacity to repay the loan as the major criterion. This study also reported that active involvement by the board of directors in evaluating loan applications negatively influenced rural bank performance. This finding is consistent with other studies that have found that loan limits on loan officers and formalization of lending policies restrict access to credit (Green, 1984).

The available evidence on banking deregulation does not suggest that the growth of multibank holding companies and proliferation of branch banks will drain capital from communities (Dunham, 1986). Research does suggest that banking structure influences access to credit in rural communities. Smaller businesses, the poor, and minorities have more problems gaining access to capital and pay more for banking services in holding company affiliates and branch banks. Also, bank size has been found to have a strong positive correlation with the performance of rural banks. Overall, however, other elements of banking deregulation, such as the cost of credit and services, may have more serious consequences for rural areas than does the structure of local credit markets. There is considerably less research on how these other elements of banking deregulation have influenced local economic development.

Assumptions Guiding Policies

The central assumption behind banking regulation since the 1930s has been that commercial banks were major contributors to the Depression. To avoid another financial collapse, policymakers have promoted policies for safety and security in the financial sector. One of the most important pieces of legislation was the Glass-Steagall Act of 1933, which forced commercial banks out of the investment banking business. The basic activity for investment bankers is to provide credit to stock investors.

A second assumption guiding banking policy is that commercial banks are different from other economic organizations. These financial institutions play a unique role in the economy; therefore, they need to be protected from competition. Banks occupy a special niche in capitalism by linking producers and consumers as they channel a universal and essential resource— finance capital. To play this role, however, banks must maintain the public's trust. Banking policy, therefore, has focused more on maintaining the public's confidence than on the profit orientation of commercial banks.

Assumptions about commercial banks and their role in the economy have changed considerably in recent years. For example, many analysts believe it is unreasonable to assume that expanding banking powers will produce a financial collapse as large as the one in the 1930s. In fact, support for a more centralized banking system with expanded powers was expressed recently by officials of the U.S. Treasury Department. Treasury officials favor the creation of *superbanks*, which are conglomerates consisting of large commercial banks and industrial companies. These officials believe that superbanks would be more competitive with large European and Japanese banks. Another assumption made by proponents of banking deregulation is that banks are like any other business and will become more efficient with increased competition. It is also assumed that financial institutions are primarily responsible to their stockholders and that by serving their stockholders bankers can best meet community needs.

Changes in the commercial banking industry have been met with a variety of responses by organizations, communities, and policymakers at the national, state, and local levels. The responses are examined below.

National-Level Responses

National policy organizations are concerned with three issues: lending disclosure laws, the boundary between banking and nonbanking activities, and the extension of the Community Reinvestment Act (CRA) to nonbank financial institutions.

Financial institutions are not required to publicly disclose much information about their lending practices. The Home Mortgage Disclosure Act (HMDA) of 1975 requires banks and thrifts with more than $10 million in deposits in MSAs to report: (1) the annual number and volume of residential loans, (2) the volume and amount of mortgage loans by census tract and zip code in MSAs, and (3) the aggregate number and volume of mortgage loans outside the MSA. The HMDA was recently amended by the Financial Institutions Reform, Recovery, and Enforcement Act (FIRREA) to include other financial institutions (e.g., mortgage and home finance corporations) and to expand disclosure requirements. FIRREA requires lenders to disclose the race, sex, and income of loan applicants and recipients. HMDA data are of little use to rural communities, because information on capital flows outside MSAs is not provided by lending institutions. In addition, communities need information on loans other than residential loans (e.g., commercial and industrial, agricultural) to be able to assess how well institutions are meeting community needs.

Although commercial banks have expanded their range of activities in recent years, debate continues over the extent to which they should be allowed to enter into additional nonbanking activities. Critics of expanding the powers of commercial banks are particularly concerned with the risk to the financial system associated with commercial banks' underwriting securities. The stock market crash of 1987 and the large number of thrift and bank failures in the 1980s, however, have slowed the impetus behind expanding bank powers into this area.

The CRA, along with the HMDA, was designed to prevent lenders from redlining neighborhoods on the basis of race or economic class. Financial institutions are required to provide data on lending activities in their local community. These data are used by federal regulators to evaluate applications for branch establishment, relocation of branch headquarters, or for corporate mergers and acquisitions. National organizations concerned with banking deregulation, such as the National Center for Policy Alternatives, the Center for Community Change, and the Woodstock Institute, have recognized that the CRA taps only a small segment of the financial industry and have argued that nonregulated institutions should also be monitored. These organizations contend a broader approach to monitoring and regulating financial institutions with regard to community reinvestment should be taken in a more deregulated environment.

State-Level Responses

Much of the effort to improve the social responsibility of commercial banks is taking place at the state level. Five states (Massachusetts, New

York, Ohio, West Virginia, and Indiana) have enacted reinvestment laws. These laws are based on a quid pro quo policy (see Siegel, Kwass, and Reamer, 1986). For example, in New York, banking powers are linked to CRA activity; with a better rating, banks are allowed to invest a larger proportion of their assets in real estate. In Massachusetts, CRA ratings are tied to eligibility to receive deposits of state funds. In Maine, financial institutions acquiring in-state banks are required to demonstrate that the transaction will lead to a net increase in funds to the state and will benefit the communities being affected. Although states have adopted a wide variety of community-oriented policies, none address the specific needs of rural areas.

In addition to reinvestment laws, many states have created new institutions to provide capital to underdeveloped sectors and regions and to small businesses and minority groups (Green and McNamara, 1988). State programs range from providing seed capital and venture capital to small business loans and home mortgage loans. A central concept behind many of the community-oriented financial institutions is the pooling of risk. Capital access programs and business industrial development corporations are two examples of innovative institutions being created to fill the credit gap in rural communities. Many states have organizations that provide technical assistance to community organizations in rural areas seeking ways to finance economic development.[3]

Local-Level Responses

In many low-income communities, commercial banks are closing branches and adding charges for services to customers (e.g., check cashing and checking accounts) that were provided "free" in the past. Banking deregulation also has contributed to the large number of bank mergers and to the loss of many locally owned banks. In response to these changes, community and neighborhood organizations have used the CRA to challenge the lending practices and operating policies of commercial banks attempting to acquire an existing bank or establish a new branch in a community. These challenges have produced several agreements with banks, providing additional loans for home mortgages and small businesses, and credit for low-income and minority groups. CRA challenges have produced at least $5 billion in additional loan commitments by commercial banks (Fishbein, 1988). These challenges have been primarily limited to urban areas because much less data are available and fewer community organizations are located in rural areas.

CRA challenges have proliferated, and community organizations across the country are using banking deregulation as a lever to obtain reinvestment agreements with financial institutions. Since 1978 over 100 CRA protests have been filed by community groups. The community reinvestment movement is somewhat limited, however, by its focus on commercial banks. Other financial institutions, such as insurance companies, are not covered by reinvestment laws. A broader movement to make all financial institutions socially responsible would be more effective in revitalizing rural communities.

Policy Options

Rural banking policy options are based on different assumptions about the relationship between the credit system and economic development and the effects of market concentration. The different assumptions regarding credit and its role in development focus on whether the credit system is considered to be creating or reacting to economic development. Proponents of deregulation contend that financial institutions are passive, simply responding to demand. By lending capital to the most profitable firms, industries, and regions, bankers promote efficiency and equity. The system of regulations established in the 1930s prevents the banking system from efficiently responding to the demand for credit.

On the other hand, critics of deregulation assume the banking system plays an active role in rural economic development. In its role as an intermediary between savers and borrowers, the financial system creates and defines the character of economic development (Green, 1987). This position assumes that the supply of capital will influence lending decisions more than will the demand for capital.

Proponents and critics of banking deregulation also disagree on what effects increasing market concentration will have on credit allocation. Proponents assert that consumers and businesses will benefit from the increased size and concentration of financial institutions through better access to services and credit and more competitive interest rates on deposits. Critics argue that increased size and concentration will result in monopolistic pricing practices and less access to credit for minorities, the poor, and small businesses.

Where Are We Going?

Banking deregulation has had a more profound effect on rural banks than on urban banks (Nejezchleb, 1986). Prior to deregulation, rural banks were not tightly integrated into the financial system and did not have to compete for deposits with other financial institutions. Increased integration of rural banks into the financial system has contributed to the volatility of interest rates and the higher costs of credit for rural borrowers.

Deregulation also encouraged a rapid increase in bank mergers over the past decade. This process has led to a net loss of independent banks in many rural areas and an increase in the number of communities served by a new affiliate or branch bank. In 1987, 203 banks failed, the highest number since 1938. The majority of these failures were small banks with less than $25 million in assets. It is projected that deregulation will reduce the number of banks by as much as one third, which will lead to a more concentrated financial system (Hughes et al., 1986).

We appear to be moving toward a banking system in which banks offer a wide array of financial and nonfinancial services (e.g., insurance and real estate). Commercial bankers anticipate that these activities will provide their banks with higher profits than do their lending activities. At the same time, the cost of these services will increase. In the past many services were provided by banks at little or no direct cost to customers. The emerging financial system excludes a large segment of the rural population from access to these services; the poor will not be able to afford the increased costs of many of these services. Similarly, commercial banks will close down branches that are located in areas with large numbers of poor people, because these operations are less profitable than suburban branches.

Where Should We Go?

Although a deregulated financial system has several advantages, it also carries many costs and risks. The costs are borne primarily by the poor, minority groups, and small businesses, all of which have increasing difficulty obtaining credit. An unregulated financial environment places the "real economy" in jeopardy by encouraging speculation.

An alternative to the emerging financial system would be one that provides access to credit for all qualified borrowers and ensures the soundness of the economy rather than injecting risk and insecurity. A democratic financial system would require the creation of new community-oriented financial institutions and a politically open monetary system that would include the Federal Reserve (Greider, 1988).

Reregulation is an important step in democratizing the financial system. Some form of reregulation could provide many of the advantages of financial deregulation while encouraging social responsibility among financial institutions. The key to this policy would be a quid pro quo feature allowing banks to broaden their activities if they demonstrate that they are meeting community needs. Reregulation places less emphasis on government control of market structure but focuses more on establishing the means by which social responsibility by financial institutions can be assessed and encouraged. The success of this option, however, would depend on tough enforcement of existing CRA regulations and disclosure of additional data on lending, particularly in rural areas.

Conclusion

The debate over banking policy has been portrayed as a choice between regulation or deregulation. Given the restructuring of the American economy and the current political environment, it does not appear that we can return to the form of banking regulations that existed before the 1980s. The basic choice in rural banking policy for the 1990s is thus between further deregulation and reregulation (see Table 4.1).

The most basic element of a policy that pursues deregulation would be the virtual elimination of the Glass-Steagall Act, which places constraints on the array of activities in which commercial banks may be involved. Further deregulation may also remove existing geographic limitations on

TABLE 4.1   Policy Options for Rural Banking

Deregulation

> Eliminate limits on banking activities
> Eliminate geographic limits, encourage interstate banking
> Reduce reserve requirements

Reregulation

> Better enforce existing laws on reinvestment
> Require data on lending by type of loan and geographic area
> Establish community-oriented financial institutions; it may be part of a quid pro quo policy
> Apply community reinvestment laws and standards to all financial institutions taking deposits or making loans

banking activities, which would in effect produce an interstate banking system. Finally, deregulation could include a provision for reducing further the reserve requirements for commercial banks. Proponents contend that these changes in banking regulations are necessary for financial institutions to compete effectively against nonfinancial institutions. Bankers warn that if these changes are not made the commercial banking industry will be further weakened and the entire financial system will become increasingly vulnerable.

Reregulation, on the other hand, permits greater flexibility in the form and content of banking practices and organizational structure, but it places more emphasis on the social responsibility of banks. Rather than regulating the economy, the state would introduce "structures of accountability" that would allow the economy to become accountable to the people it affects (Bruyn, 1987:7). Reregulation is based on four basic components. First, CRA laws must be enforced more rigorously. Fishbein (1988) indicates that in 1986, 99 percent of the banks evaluated received a favorable rating by regulators. Much of the evaluation problem is due to the limited resources available for these activities. Second, to assess whether commercial banks are meeting their community's needs we must have additional data on lending patterns. In particular, we should require commercial banks and other lending institutions to provide data on the geographic locations of all loans, not only residential loans. Third, states and communities should be encouraged to develop new financial institutions to address gaps in financing. Finally, community reinvestment laws and standards need to be applied to all financial institutions (e.g., insurance companies and pension funds). If nonfinancial institutions are to be granted the same privileges as financial institutions, they should also have the same responsibilities.

The financial system is changing rapidly, and it will have a significant influence on rural economic development in the 1990s. The goal of policymakers should be to design a set of policies ensuring the stability of the financial system and promoting equal opportunity in the economy.

Notes

I appreciate the comments of Arnold Fleischmann, Cornelia Flora, Davita Glasberg, Tsz-Man Kwong, Paul Lasley, Kevin McNamara, David Myhre, Mark Smith, Leann Tigges, and Deborah Tootle.

1. The most important laws regulating the banking industry are the Federal Reserve Act of 1913, McFadden Act of 1927, Glass-Steagall Act of 1933, Banking Act of 1935, Federal Deposit Insurance Act of 1935, Banking Holding Company Act of 1956, and Regulation Q. Two major pieces of legislation are responsible for most aspects of banking deregulation: the Depository Institutions Deregulation and Monetary Control Act of 1980 and the Garn–St. Germain Depository Institutions Act of 1982.

2. Markley (1988a) and other economists argue that the social science literature on rural banking has focused too much on the supply-side factors and ignored the demand-side factors influencing bank lending practices. Research on the demand for credit will make an important contribution to the literature on rural banking. However, several studies have demonstrated that supply factors have a stronger effect than demand for credit (Shlay, 1986). In addition, Dominguez (1976) demonstrates that in minority communities the demand for credit is inelastic; the supply of credit determines the financial condition of these communities. Due to the limited competition in many rural financial markets, one could assume an inelastic demand for credit in rural communities as well.

3. See Markley (1988b) for an excellent review of public and private rural capital options.

References

Barkley, David L., and Glenn T. Potts. 1985. "Will branch banking increase credit and competition in rural communities?" *Rural Development Perspectives* 1(June):26–30.

Boggs, Bruce S., David J. Sorenson, and Andrew M. Isserman. 1988. *Commercial Lending Patterns and Economic Development in West Virginia.* Berea, Ky.: Mountain Association for Community Economic Development.

Bruyn, Severyn. 1987. "Beyond the market and the state." Pp. 3–27 in Severyn T. Bruyn and James Meehan, eds., *Beyond the Market and the State.* Philadelphia: Temple University Press.

Dominguez, John. 1976. *Capital Flows in Minority Areas.* Lexington, Mass.: Lexington Books.

Dunham, Constance R. 1986. "Interstate banking and the outflow of local funds." *New England Economic Review* March/April:7–19.

Fishbein, Allen. 1988. "The implementation and enforcement of the Community Reinvestment Act of 1977." Testimony before the Committee on Banking, Housing and Urban Affairs, United States Senate, March. Washington, D.C.

Green, Gary P. 1984. "Credit and agriculture: Some consequences of the centralization of the banking system." *Rural Sociology* 49(4):568–579.

———. 1987. *Finance Capital and Uneven Development.* Boulder, Colo.: Westview Press.

Green, Gary P., and Kevin McNamara. 1988. "Traditional and nontraditional alternatives and opportunities for local economic development." Pp. 288–303 in L. Beaulieu, ed., *The Rural South in Crisis.* Boulder, Colo.: Westview Press.

Greider, William. 1988. *Secrets of the Temple: How the Federal Reserve Runs the Country.* New York: Simon & Schuster.

Heggestad, Arnold A., and William G. Shepherd. 1986. "The banking industry." Pp. 290–324 in Walter Adams, ed., *The Structure of American Industry.* New York: Macmillan.

Hughes, Dean W., Stephen C. Gabriel, Peter J. Barry, and Michael D. Boehlje. 1986. *Financing the Agricultural Sector: Future Challenges and Policy Alternatives.* Boulder, Colo.: Westview Press.

Kaufman, George G., and Roger C. Kormendi. 1986. *Deregulating Financial Services: Public Policy in Flux.* Cambridge, Mass.: Ballinger.

Markley, Deborah Morentz. 1984. "The impact of institutional change in the financial services industry on capital markets in rural Virginia." *American Journal of Agricultural Economics* 66(December):686–693.

———. 1988a. "Changing financial markets and the impact on rural communities: An alternative research approach." Pp. 158–169 in *The Rural South in Crisis.* Boulder, Colo.: Westview Press.

———. 1988b. "Availability of capital in rural America: Problems and options." Background paper submitted to the Task Force on Rural Development, National Governor's Association. Washington, D.C.

Milkove, Daniel. 1985. *Do Bank Size and Metro-Nonmetro Location Affect Bank Behavior?* Rural Development Research Report No. 47. Washington, D.C.: UDSA, Economic Research Service.

Milkove, Daniel, and David B. Weisblat. 1982. *The Effects of Competitive Structure of Financial Institutions on Rural Bank Performance and Economic Growth.* ERS Staff Report No. AGES820226. Washington, D.C.: UDSA, Economic Research Service.

Nejezchleb, Lynn A. 1986. "Rural financial institutions: Trends and prospects." Pp. 422–430 in R. C. Wimberley, D. Jahr, and J. W. Johnson, eds., *New Dimensions in Rural Policy: Building Upon Our Heritage.* Washington, D.C.: Congress of the United States, Joint Economic Committee.

Shlay, Anne B. 1986. *A Tale of Three Cities: The Distribution of Housing Credit from Financial Institutions in the Chicago SMSA from 1980–1983.* Chicago: The Woodstock Institute.

Siegel, Beth, Peter Kwass, and Andrew Reamer. 1986. *Financial Deregulation: New Opportunities for Rural Economic Development.* Washington, D.C.: National Center for Policy Alternatives.

5

Small Businesses

Jan L. Flora and Thomas G. Johnson

The Small Business Administration (SBA) defines a *small business* as one that is independently owned and operated (not a branch firm or franchise), is not dominant in its field, can be operated and managed by one person, and employs fewer than 150 people (cited in Combs, Pulver, and Shaffer, 1983). We will use the SBA definition with one modification: Since we are dealing with nonmetropolitan America and placing emphasis on smaller rural communities, we will set the upper limit at 20 or fewer employees, including those with no employees.[1] We have chosen to relate our discussion principally to private firms that are in the retail, manufacturing, or service sectors. We do not discuss farms and other primary sector firms, financial institutions, wholesale firms, and transportation firms, since most of these are dealt with elsewhere in this book. The three types of firms we have chosen are typically thought of in terms of creating or attracting small business to rural communities.

Important Policy Issues

The following issues are central to defining appropriate contributions of small businesses to the vitality of rural communities:

1. Should states have a small business policy, a rural development policy, simply an economic development policy, or some combination of these?
2. What role should small business retention, growth, and recruitment play in local policy in rural areas?
3. What small business and economic development policies at federal, state, and local levels are detrimental to the well-being of rural people and communities? Should they be changed? If so, how?

Policy Context

What Do We Know About the Issues?

The development of a global economy in which manufactured goods and capital move more easily across national borders has resulted in the growth of new forms of productive organizations. These include the expansion of small and medium-sized firms and growing informalization of national economies throughout the world, including the United States. In the United States, between 1980 and 1986, Fortune 500 companies reduced their labor force by 2.8 million workers, while 10 million jobs were added to the economy as a whole. A substantial majority of the fastest-growing firms began the period with fewer than 20 employees (Birch, 1987). Over the past decade, the number of women entrepreneurs (unincorporated firms) grew more than three times as fast as did their male counterparts (Lichtenstein, 1990).

Independent firms (a very rough proxy for small businesses) in rural areas account for a much higher proportion of new jobs than they do in urban areas. Between 1980 and 1984, nonmetro independent firms grew in employment by 1.2 percent, accounting for all net new nonmetro job growth (branch plants experienced a 1.4 percent decrease). In comparison, in metropolitan areas independent firms grew at half the rate of branch plants (5.2 percent and 11.9 percent, respectively) (Reid, 1988).[2]

In this information age, knowledge-generation operations can be geographically separated from the labor-intensive operations in the same industry. Research and development and management activities may well be carried out in urban areas, whereas production, involving low-paid labor, may occur in rural areas. Further, these activities do not have to be carried out by the same firm.

A Kansas study shows that in nonmetro, nontrade-center counties, during the 1980s job growth in the service sector—the only private sector to experience growth—was in low-paying or part-time jobs (relative to jobs in that sector at the beginning of the period) (Flora et al., 1989). Most of those jobs were in small businesses as we have defined them. Other studies have shown that manufacturing sector jobs in nonmetro areas continue to be traditional production jobs, while more complex industrial activities (including managerial positions) are increasingly located in metropolitan areas (Reid, 1989). Are such patterns a necessary consequence for rural areas, and what government policies related to small business would contribute to maintenance of population, infrastructure, and services in rural areas and would ensure that some degree of equity exists between rural and urban incomes and quality of life?

Geographic and economic centralization is occurring—from nonmetro to metro and within nonmetro areas—as service centers devour the economic activities in their hinterlands. While firm size is declining in many sectors, control of capital is becoming more centralized. Farm people know of this phenomenon through contract broiler and laying operations. Fast-food and 24-hour convenience store franchises are more recent entrants on the rural scene, often replacing mom-and-pop operations. Similar centralizing patterns in the banking industry have a negative impact on small businesses in small rural communities. For instance, North Carolina banks in many small communities have virtually stopped making business loans. Small-business people from those communities must go to the branches in larger cities to seek financing.

The low local utilization of capital available to rural areas is illustrated by the low loan-to-deposit ratio of agricultural banks, which was only about 50 percent for all agricultural banks in the Midwest in 1987 (Barkema, Drabenstott, and Froerer, 1988). Rather than risking capital by investing in small businesses or other ventures in their communities, rural bankers prefer to invest it in government securities.[3] Capital flows out of rural savers' home communities into regional trade centers and metropolitan areas. The challenge is to devise mechanisms to put that capital to work locally through the expansion or creation of small businesses (see Chapters 3 and 4).

A related centralizing trend affecting rural small businesses is the merchandising revolution. Retail goods merchandising is geographically becoming centralized, and some firms in this sector are growing in size, while the number of firms is declining. Kansas data show that during the 1970s, total personal income grew in all major economic sectors of nonmetro, nontrade-center counties except two, farming and retail trade (Flora et al., 1989). In retail trade during the expansive years of the 1970s, nonmetropolitan America provided a high return on capital investment, attracting regional and national firms. A retail merchandising revolution was initiated, much as occurred in metropolitan areas in the 1950s and 1960s. Retail activities became concentrated in trade center counties, resulting in a sharp decline in goods-based retail activities in small rural communities. That trend has continued in the 1980s, encouraged by the farm crisis (J. Flora and C. Flora, 1988).

This "Wal-Marting" of rural America has threatened many locally owned small rural firms. In an effort to survive, these so-called mom-and-pop stores reduce wages and employees. One overall result is increased income inequality between metro and rural areas and within rural areas.

Rural areas are experiencing a decline in manufacturing income and employment as manufacturing branch plants seek cheaper labor overseas. In the recovery period of the late 1980s, some manufacturing activity has returned to certain nonmetropolitan areas. The growth that has taken place has not been in branch plants but in locally owned manufacturing, including the purchase of branch plants by local investors and recruitment of entrepreneurs who move into and become part of the community; occasionally a local person will start up a business (John, Batie, and Norris, 1988).

The service sector is the only sector that is growing in much of rural America. This is predominantly a small business sector. As already suggested, the more rural the firm the greater the likelihood that it will offer low-paying and part-time work.

Assumptions That Have Guided Past Policies

In the past, two truisms have operated with respect to economic development. One, which comes from the national level, state capitals, and main street, says that industrial recruitment and economic development are synonymous. The other comes from the agricultural establishment, land-grant universities, and county governments in rural areas. It says that agricultural and economic development cannot be separated; the best way to ensure a healthy rural economy is to have a healthy agriculture.

Industrial recruitment is synonymous with economic development. Statistically, this perspective is no longer viable. The ratio between communities seeking industry and the number of industrial enterprises willing to move in any particular year is quite unfavorable to the communities. Everyone has heard of community X, which sold its soul to attract a firm that, when the building was amortized, left for greener pastures—probably overseas. Still, in practice, smokestack chasing lingers. City managers and administrators, economic development department heads, and chambers of commerce are still often seduced by the idea of attracting outside industries to solve employment problems in one fell swoop. Often an empty building in an industrial park creates the "need" to recruit outside industry. Working to attract an outside firm creates solidarity among community leaders and enables them to avoid the difficult decisions regarding which local entrepreneurs to aid. Thus, one often finds the curious situation in which a group of small business persons works to bring in large businesses and employs local resources that could be used to strengthen the community's own economic activities.

In farming-dependent areas, agricultural development is synonymous with rural development. This assertion is much less true than it was before World War II. Even in many farming-dependent counties, farming's contribution to the entire economy is no greater than is income from transfer payments or from the service sector. At least in the Midwest and in much of the West, as a smaller number of farmers come to represent a higher proportion of agricultural production, those large-scale farmers tend to bypass the local community in purchasing inputs, marketing agricultural products, and making their consumer purchases as well. Hence, the economic impact of agriculture on the local community has diminished (C. Flora and J. Flora, 1988).

Current Small Business Policy Trends
at the National, State, and Local Levels

Rural small business policy is closely related to rural development policy. An effective rural development policy must support small businesses, because in rural areas a high proportion of persons in the labor force are self-employed—even when farmers are excluded.

During the 1980s, federal funding for 63 rural and related domestic programs fell 63 percent (from $35 billion in fiscal year 1980 to $14.6 billion in fiscal year 1989). On the other hand, state spending on economic development in rural and metro areas together more than quadrupled in that period. States have expanded programs in the following areas: more aid to small and new firms, investment in science and technology, promotion of exports, encouragement of international education, improvement in education, and training for adult workers (John and Norris, 1989). However, state programs are designed for the state as a whole, with little attention paid to the peculiar needs of its rural areas (see Johnson, 1987).

In the 1980s, rural communities and sometimes entire counties were very active in economic development efforts. Those efforts were often oriented toward creating or expanding small businesses, because macro trends are unfavorable to traditional industrial recruitment. There has been a trend toward hiring city economic development directors or, for small towns, city administrators who have economic development experience. In other cases, rural communities appear willing to tax themselves so they can hire an economic development manager in a public-private capacity (e.g., shared by city government and the chamber of commerce). There has also been a trend toward using public monies to support or assist private development corporations or committees. While industrial parks, tax abatements, and smokestack chasing are still around, there is a growing tendency to diversify approaches, support local entrepreneurs, hire outside expertise while maintaining local ownership, and use local monies to leverage outside capital. There is greater public support of locally owned small business firms than in the past.

Policy Options

Federal Policies

Small business policy is related to economic development policy. Federal spending has an important impact on the viability of rural communities in terms of income that is available to be spent locally and is turned over chiefly through the small-business-dominated retail trade sector. Per-resident federal spending in nonmetropolitan areas is 18 percent below that for metropolitan areas (Dubin and Reid, 1988).

Table 5.1 shows federal development programs which might benefit small businesses and, where available, the share which goes to *rural counties*, defined here as counties with an urban population of less than 20,000. Such counties represent 16 percent of the total U.S. population (U.S. GAO, 1989). For programs not specifically targeted to small businesses, it is clear that the average size of loans and grants is much larger than that needed by the typical small business in rural areas. In surveys conducted in Iowa and Minnesota, most jobs generated by new businesses in rural areas were in firms with three employees or less. Half the new Iowa businesses required $20,000 or less to start (Popovich, 1988). Yet in the case of business and industrial loans through the Farmers Home Administration, the average loan was $1.5 million; urban development action grants which went to small cities (those of less than 50,000, both suburban metro and nonmetro cities) averaged $350,000; and single-purpose, small-cities community development block grants (CDBGs) averaged $350,000.

TABLE 5.1 Federal Loans and Grants Which Potentially Could Go to Rural Small Businesses, 1985, 1987

Program	Amount, FY 1987 (Millions of Dollars)	Percent Rural, 1985	Average Loan or Grant, 1987 (Thousands of Dollars)
Department of Housing and Urban Development			
CDBGs[a]/State's program	$844	n.a.[b]	(determined by formula)
Urban development action grants	306	7	959[c]
CDBGs/Small cities	38	29	350[d]
CDBGs/Technical assistance	12	4	n.a.
Department of Agriculture			
Business and industrial loans	96	35	1,500
Small Business Administration			
Small business loans (guaranteed)	2,232	18	150
Bond guarantees for surety companies (guaranteed)	957	16	100
Certified development company loans			
Section 504 (guaranteed)	355	n.a.	230
Section 503 (direct and guaranteed)	2	11	210
Loans for small businesses			
Guaranteed	24	13	118
Direct	19	8	56
State and local development co. loans (guaranteed)	36	7	187
Management and technical assistance (grants) for socially and economically disadvantaged businesses	9	8	variable

[a]CDBGs = community development block grants.
[b]n.a. = data not available.
[c]Small-city average; large-city average was $2 million.
[d]Single-purpose loans. For comprehensive loans, $550,000.

Source: U.S. General Accounting Office (1989:35, 37, 42).

Even those loans administered by the Small Business Administration tend to exceed the initial capital needs of small businesses in rural areas by at least a factor of five. Only the direct loans for small businesses, which are for businesses owned by low-income persons or located in high-unemployment areas, average less than $100,000 (U.S. GAO, 1989).

State and Local Policies

Tax exemptions on corporate incomes, capital investments, equipment and machinery, and manufacturers' and retailers' inventories, as well as accelerated depreciation for industrial equipment spread to a growing number of states during the 1960s and 1970s (Miller, 1983); if anything, their use has increased in the 1980s. Such policies have an antirural bias for two related reasons: Small businesses are de facto excluded from or are disproportionately under-represented in such programs, and small businesses are disproportionately located in rural areas.

Perhaps the most notorious of these mechanisms are industrial revenue bonds (IRBs), which are used extensively by state and local governments to finance machinery, equipment, and new buildings for businesses. In the late 1970s, IRBs surpassed federal economic development loans in value. IRBs are popular among state and local governments because the interest income from these bonds is exempt from federal taxes. Thus, they attract jobs and income to the state or locality issuing them, but they do not generate new jobs for the nation as a whole (Miller, 1983). The federal government forgoes taxes which would otherwise have been collected. Small businesses rarely receive IRBs because these companies are perceived as a high risk and the cost of preparing the paperwork for an IRB is the same regardless of its value.

Some state and local programs have direct potential for aiding small business development. These programs include small business incubators, revolving loan funds, and retention and expansion programs. These are discussed in more detail in Johnson (1987).

Small Business Incubators. A business incubator is a flexible, locality based means of assisting start-up firms. The incubator usually includes a physical structure to house the new firm at a reduced rental rate; it may also provide space, equipment, management and technical assistance or training, accounting services, and office support such as computers and photocopiers (Johnson, 1987). Central to the incubation concept is a limited "incubation period," usually about two years. After this time the firm must leave this protected environment and compete independently with other firms.

Only 14 percent of incubators are in nonmetropolitan counties, and most of those are in trade centers. Many small rural communities have unused buildings on main street or in their industrial parks. In some instances, owners have been willing to provide these buildings rent free to new businesses for a limited time, with the hope that the new businesses would pay rent on the building later. Other services provided by incubators are beyond the financial capacity of small rural communities, but a local-state partnership could be developed in which incubators would receive technical assistance from state or regional institutions such as community colleges.

Revolving Loan Funds. The concept of revolving loan funds is an important one for rural communities. Even SBA loans, which leverage funds from local banks for fixed asset financing, are too large to benefit the size firm that is predominant in small nonmetro communities. However, if the administrative cost can be borne by local government in conjunction with community volunteers, then a larger loan can be given to the community which can then administer a revolving loan fund for small businesses; this has worked well in some instances with federal community development block grants. A state-local matching, revolving-loan program could increase investment of local private funds in the community.

Retention and Expansion Programs. A retention and expansion program for existing small businesses would work well in conjunction with a revolving loan program. "The primary tool of retention and expansion programs is the industry visitation. . . . Volunteers are trained to survey local businesses and to detect problems and opportunities. When surveyors discover an opportunity to aid an existing industry, economic development specialists are brought in to help out" (Johnson, 1987:69).

Interviews with individual business persons are to be kept confidential. Confidentiality poses a problem in small towns, where often everyone knows (or seeks to know) everyone else's business, and secrets are not readily kept. A retention and expansion program works best in trade centers or in small towns where mutual trust is high. It is most effective if it involves collaboration between local leaders and a statewide or regional organization, such as the Cooperative Extension Service, the state economic development department, or a regional planning agency.

What is central to most of these approaches is cooperation between the state and localities and a clearly defined state strategy, not simply for economic development but for strengthening small businesses and for rural development. Such a strategy will encourage and provide direction to local efforts.

Where Are We Headed and What Should Be Done?

Federal Level. It is clear that the federal government will continue to play a reduced direct role in encouraging small business development and growth so long as the federal budget deficit remains a major problem. The greatest impact of the federal government on rural small business is through macro policies, including tax and spending policies. The reintroduction into the tax code of accelerated depreciation, investment tax credits, and lower capital gains rates, while of some short-term help to small businesses, would favor large businesses, partly because of their more capital-intensive nature.

If rural small businesses are to prosper, rural communities must have access to the sophisticated telecommunications infrastructure to transfer facsimile documents, use modems, and gain access to value-added data networks. They must also have access to touch-tone and custom-calling features and, in the future, video devices (see Chapter 6 of Parker et al., 1989). With federal leadership, this will require cooperative efforts among the federal and state governments and the private telecommunications firms.

Local Level. Localities need to recognize the trend away from the location of branch plants in rural areas and to engage in self-development activities— locally initiated, locally controlled, and at least partially locally financed efforts at generating jobs and income. A study of rural self-development activities throughout the United States indicates that although such grassroots efforts do not generate as many jobs as do successful industrial recruitment efforts, they have a number of advantages: They do not create the public service problems that result from large-scale industrial development, they rely less heavily on government incentives, they tend to create skilled and managerial jobs, and they overwhelmingly recruit local personnel (Green et al., 1990).

Localities need to encourage innovative institutions for financing local development, such as revolving loan funds and innovative investment schemes, to keep local wealth in the community and to leverage outside funds; promote expansion and retention of existing businesses; establish incubators and small business assistance centers, for which the investment per job created is quite low; develop value-added firms (see Kraybill and Johnson, 1989); and create community-controlled or worker-owned firms and other alternative legal entities, if adequate technical and managerial assistance are available at the state or regional level. Tourism and recreational and cultural projects were found to be the most prevalent form of self-development. While there are many pitfalls to tourism development, communities that have a comparative advantage in terms of physical location or cultural or historical heritage can generate income and employment through collective effort. If appropriately designed, such activities can contribute to small business vitality. Most self-development efforts, however, do not effectively reduce poverty, and they enjoy the greatest success in midwestern communities with high educational levels and out-migration rates.

State Level. In most states, economic development policy does not differentiate between rural and urban areas. Hence, it is tailored principally to the needs of metropolitan areas. Rural constituencies need to be mobilized to ensure that programs are developed which are appropriate to rural areas and, especially, to small businesses. A small business focus is especially important if small localities are to be included in a state development program.

State policy should involve the coordination of capital provision for small businesses in rural areas with a realistic human capital policy—not only for rural areas, but for the entire state. Human capital problems must be solved at the same time that decent jobs are created. States with different problems will have to devise different approaches. In states with substantial high school dropout rates, economic transformation must occur at the same time that the quality of public education is raised. The local public school system can contribute to long-term training of its citizens through school-based firms, cultural journalism programs, conversion of school buildings into community learning resource centers, and other involvement of the school in the community (Wigginton, 1985; Hobbs, 1988). The state can set the tone for involvement of local schools in such programs.

In much of the Midwest, where population decline, not low educational levels, is the problem, a more targeted, postsecondary approach is more appropriate. Such a program would involve special training and management courses, perhaps through the community college or vocational technical system. Directly involving the educational institution in economic development activities would facilitate such an approach. Thomas (1989) has highlighted instances of successful community college involvement in economic development.

A third element of state policy is state officials' willingness to work in partnership with localities for rural, community, and small business development. Important state contributions to such partnerships include providing information and expertise in targeted programs; developing cost-sharing and matching programs with localities in locally initiated programs which foster small businesses; tailoring certain small business and related programs to the unique needs of rural areas; encouraging cooperation, including financial, among adjacent communities, where labor markets and service catchment areas are larger than in a single rural community; and finally, crafting programs which favor creation and expansion of small, locally owned businesses over attracting branch plants of large firms. The state should discourage local recruiting efforts which are a zero-sum game by placing restraints on tax abatements and narrowly delimiting state programs such as enterprise zones, which allow localities to compete with one another for firms by using state resources.

Conclusion

Small firms are the fastest-growing firms in most economic sectors of metro and nonmetro areas. Small businesses account for a large majority of economic activity in nonmetro and, particularly, small rural communities. The question is not whether there should be a small business policy, but rather how to devise policies which explicitly include rural areas and which enhance the quality of life through population retention in regions where population decline is a serious problem, through upgrading human capital in areas where high school dropout rates are high and through developing quality jobs in all rural regions.

The policy issues stated at the outset were (1) whether states should have a small business policy per se or whether an economic development or rural development policy is adequate; (2) what the role of small business retention, growth, and recruitment should be in rural areas; and (3) what policies at federal, state, and local levels are most detrimental to rural small business vitality, and how they might be changed. Below are summary responses to the three policy questions.

The focal points of economic development efforts during this era of tight federal budgets will be states and localities. States can set the tone by continuing to emphasize economic and rural development and by making the growth of small businesses the centerpiece of their development efforts. Economic development, as currently practiced by most states, represents the indiscriminate pursuit of economic expansion without concern for geographic balance, workplace quality, or commitment of recruited firms to the community to which they move. Rural development has the political disadvantage of appearing to cater to a special interest group—rural people. (Economic development, since it is not called urban or suburban development, does not suffer from that liability.) However, because most small businesses are linked to other businesses in a chain of product development and marketing or service provision, a state small business program would demand an explicit examination of how businesses relate to each other and to governments. Such a program should take into account the quality of jobs that are created and where the high- and low-quality jobs in the product or service chain would be located.

Local governments and their private and public partners in economic development should balance creation, retention, and recruitment of small businesses. Retention maintains the economic and social base, creation brings in new leadership, and recruitment adds quickly to the economic base. Public officials should not limit themselves to encouraging traditional for-profit firms but should consider community-owned, worker-owned community development corporations, cooperatives, and various nonprofit forms. The legal entity chosen should match the need.

State and federal policy should not foster—indeed should actively discourage—competition among localities for existing economic activity. Federal and state policy should be carefully examined to eliminate overt or hidden ways in which such competition is subsidized. Eliminating federal tax exemptions on interest from IRBs would be a useful first step.

Achieving such objectives cannot be left to chance; it requires explicit rural-oriented, small business policies at all three levels of government.

Notes

1. According to figures from the SBA Office of Advocacy, there are over 14 million self-employed entrepreneurs in the United States, including moonlighters and entrepreneurs without employees. That compares with 8.6 million by the Bureau of the Census definition. Over 3.3 million firms employ between 1 and 19 workers (87 percent of all firms with employees). There are over 11 million businesses with annual receipts up to $100,000, which represents one sort of outer limit on the number of "microenterprises" (although it does not include those informal sector activities for which income is not reported to the IRS). It is these microenterprises which have increased numerically faster than any other size firm in the 1980s. (See Lichtenstein, 1990, for details on these calculations.)

2. Headquarters establishment employment declined by more than 5 percent in both metro and nonmetro areas.

3. Drabenstott and Morris (1989) argue that the reduced level of rural commercial lending is a demand, and not a supply, phenomenon. Johnson (1989) argues that if other business ingredients were in place, particularly venture capital and technical assistance, the demand for bank loans would rise.

References

Barkema, Alan, Mark Drabenstott, and Landell Froerer. 1988. "A new era in farm lending: Who will prosper?" *Economic Review: Federal Reserve Bank of Kansas City* 73(6):22–38.

Birch, David L. 1987. "The booming hidden market." *Inc.* (October):15–16.

Combs, Robert P., Glen C. Pulver, and Ron E. Shaffer. 1983. *Financing New Small Business Enterprise in Wisconsin*. Agricultural Research Bulletin R3198. Madison, Wis.: University of Wisconsin, College of Agriculture and Life Sciences.

Drabenstott, Mark, and Charles Morris. 1989. "New sources of financing for rural development." *American Journal of Agricultural Economics* 71(5):1315–1323.

Dubin, Elliott, and Norman Reid. 1988. "Do federal funds help spur rural development?" *Rural Development Perspectives* 5(1):2–7.

Flora, Cornelia B., and Jan L. Flora. 1988. "Public policy, farm size, and community well-being in wheat and livestock farming systems." Pp. 76–129 in Louis E. Swanson, ed., *Agriculture and Community Change in the U.S.: The Congressional Research Reports*. Boulder, Colo.: Westview Press.

Flora, Jan L., and Cornelia B. Flora. 1988. "The effects of different production systems, technology, mixes, and farming practices on farm size and communities: Implications for the conservation reserve program." Pp. 75–83 in John E. Mitchell, ed., *Impact of the Conservation Reserve Program in the Great Plains*. General Technical Report RM-158. Fort Collins, Colo.: USDA, Forest Service. April.

Flora, Jan L., Dwight Dickson, Yu-ching Cheng, Mohummed Amin Ul-Karim, and Qian Yun-Ji. 1989. "The changing structure of farming dependent communities in the 1980s." Paper presented at "Sustainable Rural Communities in Canada," rural policy seminar sponsored by the Canadian Agriculture and Rural Restructuring Group, Saskatoon, Saskatchewan. October.

Green, Gary, Jan L. Flora, Cornelia Flora, and Fred Schmidt. 1990. "Local self-development strategies: National survey results." Paper presented at the annual meeting of the Southern Regional Science Association, Washington, D.C. March.

Hobbs, Daryl. 1988. "Educational reform and rural economic health: Policy implications." In *Risky Futures: Should State Policy Reflect Rural Diversity?* Louisville, Ky.: Appalachian Educational Laboratory Conference.

John, Dewitt, and Kim Norris. 1989. "State governments can help." *Choices* 4(2):12–15.

John, DeWitt, Sandra S. Batie, and Kim Norris. 1988. *A Brighter Future for Rural America? Strategies for Communities and States*. Washington, D.C.: National Governors' Association.

Johnson, Thomas G. 1987. "Success stories in rural development." Pp. 65–72 in David Mulkey and Rodney L. Clouser, eds., *Agriculture and Rural Development Issues in the South*. Southern Natural Resource Economics Committee, Publication No. 25. November.

———. 1989. "Entrepreneurship and development finance: Keys to rural revitalization." *American Journal of Agricultural Economics* 71(5):1324–1326.

Kraybill, David S., and Thomas G. Johnson. 1989. "Value-added activities as a rural development strategy." *Southern Journal of Agricultural Economics* 21(1):27–36.

Lichtenstein, Jules. 1990. "Helping the unemployed start businesses: Strategies and results." Paper presented at the annual meeting of the Southern Regional Science Association, Washington, D.C. March.

Miller, James P. 1983. "Interstate competition for business: Changing roles of federal and state initiatives." Staff Report No. AGES 831012. Washington, D.C.: USDA, Economic Research Service. December.

Parker, Edwin B., Heather E. Hudson, Don A. Dillman, and Andrew D. Roscoe. 1989. *Rural America in the Information Age: Telecommunications Policy for Rural Development.* Lanham, Md.: Aspen Institute and University Press of America.

Popovich, Mark. 1988. "New businesses, entrepreneurship, and rural development: Building a state strategy." *New Alliances for Rural America.* Background paper submitted to the Task Force on Rural Development. Washington, D.C.: National Governors' Association.

Reid, J. Norman. 1989. "Rural America: Economic performance, 1989." Agricultural and Rural Economic Division. Economic Research Service. Washington, D.C.: USDA, Economic Research Service.

_____. 1988. "Entrepreneurship as a community development strategy for the rural south." Pp. 325–343 in Lionel J. Beaulieu, ed., *The Rural South in Crisis: Challenges for the Future.* Boulder, Colo.: Westview Press.

Thomas, Margaret. 1989. *A Portfolio of Community College Initiatives in Rural Economic Development.* Kansas City, Mo: Midwest Research Institute.

U.S. General Accounting Office (USGAO). 1989. *Rural Development: Federal Programs That Focus on Rural America and Its Economic Development.* GAO/RCED-89-56BR. Washington, D.C.: U.S. Government Printing Office. January.

Wigginton, Eliot. 1985. *Sometimes a Shining Moment.* New York: Anchor.

6

Issues Facing Agricultural Policy

Louis E. Swanson and Jerry R. Skees

Policy Issues

Agricultural policies, including the Food, Agriculture, Conservation, and Trade Act of 1990, have remained remarkably constant since the temporary provisions of the Agricultural Adjustment Act were enacted in 1933. Now there is mounting evidence that most dimensions of agricultural policy are facing qualitative changes, requiring a reformulation of the basic assumptions on which U.S. policy rests. A sampling of assumptions increasingly under review includes: Who should be entitled to federal funds? How safe should production be for the environment and for consumers? and What should be the public mission of the U.S. Department of Agriculture (USDA) and the land-grant universities (LGUs)? Consideration of new directions for agricultural policy necessarily must incorporate issues related to the dual structure of U.S. farming, the contribution of off-farm work to farm income, and the balance of nonfarmers' environmental concerns with farm profitability. The 1990s will confront all of us with the difficulties and opportunities of reworking agricultural policy for the first time in over 50 years.

Central to the process of reworking agricultural policy are issues of public legitimacy. From the 1930s to the early 1970s, the farm problem was one of farm income. Consequently, policy legitimacy was grounded in helping financially strapped family farmers. But the transformation of U.S. farming, global market restructuring, and the uncertainty and risks of both monetary markets and nonfarm financial policy place farmers in a vastly different business environment than that of the 1930s, when current policies were developed. Today farmers are not a disadvantaged group, as they have been portrayed. Their average wealth (i.e., their net assets) is much above average. This does not mean there are no financially stressed farmers but, on the whole, farmers are doing as well as, if not better than, the average citizen. Farm income is no longer the central problem confronting policy formulation. Instead, a primary problem is the risk and volatility of income and wealth. Assessing the farm policy problem in this way requires a rethinking of past assumptions.

Among the most significant challenges to current agricultural policy are (1) record federal Commodity Credit Corporation (CCC) outlays during a period of large deficits, (2) a fractured and polarized class farm structure, (3) recognition of the enormous off-farm environmental costs of production, (4) increased consumer concern regarding pesticides in the food supply, (5) international trade negotiations at the General Agreement on Tariffs and Trade (GATT), and (6) renewed discussions on who should be the beneficiaries for future federal entitlements. Other issues that have gained prominent positions on the policy agenda and that may grow even more important include the nutritional quality of food, the rapid consolidation of market share by multinational agribusinesses, the alarming expansion of hunger among low-income citizens, and new rural development initiatives. Collectively, these issues have triggered widespread and sometimes heated discussions on restructuring agricultural policy.

The New Agenda

Don Paarlberg (1980) has attributed the present political environment to the advent of a "New Agenda" during the last two decades. This New Agenda reflects the increase in nonfarm interests in agriculture policy—most notably environmental concerns—and the political division and decline of the once monolithic influence of the farm lobby in Congress. To no one's surprise, the influence of the New Agenda is less visible at USDA, since its current organizational structure reflects commercial farm interests of the past. Moreover, congressional power now resides with representatives of urban constituencies, and it is with these representatives that consumer and environmental groups have the most influence. The next reapportionment of the Congress following the 1990 Census of Population will only enhance the power of these nonfarm interest groups.

Despite the impressive array of fundamental issues confronting U.S. agriculture, *food security*, defined as the ability to produce enough food, is not an issue at this time. Even given adverse environmental conditions, including the worst drought in 50 years (1988), the farm sector still demonstrated an overcapacity for producing food. Rather, practical and political concern is directed toward the ways in which food and fiber are produced and distributed.

As these issues have emerged, so too have questions regarding the performance of the USDA and its LGUs. Traditionally, both the USDA and the LGUs have focused their mission on serving commercial farms. Rural nonfarm needs seem to be, at best, an afterthought, even though USDA has a congressional mandate to coordinate rural development. At this time there are burgeoning calls for a redetermination of that mission to emphasize public research and extension agendas (Buttel, 1985). Where private sector research and extension provide the necessary services or similar information, it is recommended that the LGUs pull away. The array of issues listed above suggests that in the 1990s both the USDA and the LGUs will be expected to expand their efforts on environmental quality; profitable, sustainable agricultural systems; and rural development. However, this redirection of mission will likely be imposed by nonfarm congressional and state legislative interests, rather than by agricultural administrators. Learning to deal with new and not always sympathetic constituencies likely will be a major challenge and opportunity for the USDA and LGUs during the next decade.

The Policy Context

Current Dilemmas

Agricultural policy is actually a multitude of separate policy initiatives built around specific commodities. Each commodity policy has a different set of constituencies and a different social and economic history. This makes most generalizations about the nature of agricultural policy, and therefore about policy reforms, at best problematic. At a minimum, farm policies are the public's investment in the agricultural sector. They embody economic, social, and philosophical dimensions that are often at odds with one another. Consequently, each reflects the political economy in which it is embedded. According to Allen (1989:4), the present agricultural support systems were "conceived and born of economic necessity, grew and prospered by drawing on social and philosophical arguments that trace their lineages back to Thomas Jefferson, and continue largely because of astute political bargaining and coalition building on the part of all groups interested in agricultural policy."

However, even astute coalition building now seems to be at risk. Difficulties associated with coalition building are due less to astuteness than to fundamental disarticulations over policy goals within the agricultural policy arena. While farm and commodity organizations have continued to foster a cultural identity with small-scale family farming and the entrepreneurial values associated with it, their clients have ceased to reflect this ideal. They have become more industrial in their scale, workplace structure, and business rationality (Mooney, 1988). This discontinuity between what the programs propose to do and the actual policy consequences is now the object of public debate. At the heart of this debate are the questions of who should be entitled to federal support and what limits should be placed on farm production to protect the environment and enhance food quality.

Policy Goals and Farm Structural Change

The public goals of farm policy over the last half century are familiar, even if they have not always been consistent with the policymakers' actual intent or successful in their consequences. Four goals have formed the centerpiece of stated agricultural policy: a plentiful and cheap supply of safe food; stabilization and enhancement of farm income, which includes maintenance of family farms and assistance to rural communities; technological development to improve productivity; and soil and water conservation. Together these goals provide a strong bond between actual agricultural policies and popular American culture. Therefore, past farm programs have depended on a social contract between the public and those formulating farm policy that public policy would simultaneously preserve the family farm and ensure a plentiful food supply. Since most people are unfamiliar with the myriad agricultural policies, they have placed their trust in what they have been told. But what they have been told is not accurate. In fact, because of a combination of historical economic forces and government policies, the first goal has not been achieved. The evaluation of farm programs, then, requires some definition of a family farm.

This is neither an easy nor an academic exercise. It is a central political issue as long as the family farm is a cornerstone of farm policy legitimacy. Strange (1988:32) remarks that "what makes any social system functional is shared values and goals, collectively and individually expressed in the behavior of its members. The glue that holds the system together is a consensus about how things ought to be, not necessarily how they are."

It is especially important for those who do not fit even the popular image but have greatly benefited from it. If one simply defines a family farm as one owned by a family, as do many operators of industrial farms, then all but the most vertically integrated corporate operations[1] are family operations. Such a broad definition is useless, since it only distinguishes between two types of private property: family and corporate.

Applying such a broad definition to the past half century would lead to the conclusion that while there have been significant quantitative changes in the trend toward fewer but larger farms, there have been no qualitative changes. That is, there are considerably fewer farms, but the great majority of agricultural wealth is produced by family farms. In fact, there have been many qualitative changes. Today the United States has a dual farm structure, essentially divided into commercial and noncommercial farms. It is estimated that only 15 percent of all farms produce more than 85 percent of the agricultural wealth. Or, conversely, 85 percent of the farms yield no more than 15 percent of the wealth.

Within this dual structure, the midsized farms (about $40,000–$500,000 in gross farm sales[2]) are disappearing most rapidly. Are farms with sales of less than $40,000 and with most of the family income earned in the nonfarm sector family farms? For our purposes, these part-time operations are noncommercial family farms. Yet they account for the great majority of all farms. On the other hand, farms with sales of $500,000 or more tend to depend on the employment of much more hired labor than the family provides. Among the largest farms, we find industrial relations of production, where a family or corporation owns the capital but employs hired managers and hired laborers.

We propose that Rodefeld's (Goss, Rodefeld, and Buttel, 1980) definition will suffice. For Rodefeld, a *family farm* is one on which a family owns half the land, makes the management decisions, and provides at least half of the labor. He also identifies two other types of farms on which a family or an individual provides most of the management but does not own most of the land or machinery. Farms where a family owns most of the capital resources and makes the management decisions but has more hired labor year round than family labor are identified as *larger-than-family operations*. Farms where a family rents most of the land and other capital resources but provides most of the labor are referred to as *modern tenant operations*. These latter two types are not what we think of as traditional family farms but as ascendent commercial farm types. All three of these farm types tend to be midsized. These midsized farms represent the smaller end of the commercial farm-scale continuum.

USDA farm management studies and LGU studies have identified midsized farms as the most efficient farms (Strange, 1988; Ahearn, 1986; Madden, 1967). Contrary to popular belief, in commercial farming the largest farms are *not* the most efficient. Moreover, most midsized farms are characterized by a great deal of family labor, even though the family may not own most of the capital (as in modern tenant farms) or provide most of the labor (as in the larger-than-family farms). As we approach the twenty-first century, the midsized farm best fits the popular image of the traditional family farm. This farm scale also tends to be the most adept at successfully adjusting to market and government policy nuances.

Assuming that maintenance of the family farm will continue to be central to farm policy legitimacy in the 1990s, the myths surrounding it must be recognized for meaningful policy reform to occur. Family farms are no more likely to preserve the environment than are other types of farms (Lovejoy and Napier, 1986). Nor do family farmers see farming only as a way of life (Coughenour and Swanson, 1989). Indeed, most of these farms are not as financially stressed as the media has portrayed (Collins et al., 1990; Bentley et al., 1989). However, family farms and other types of midsized farms, in their efficiency and their adaptability to markets and policy change, represent the best of the farm types for achieving farm policy goals. Therefore, we suggest that the focus should be on midsized farms when farm policy is formulated (see also Strange, 1988; Swanson and Skees, 1987).

Beneficiaries of Farm Programs

Public entitlements are meant to reflect society's values of what is fair and who should be helped. While most of the public probably believes that family farmers are the primary beneficiaries of government farm programs, in fact, a wide variety of citizens, including some of the nation's wealthiest residents and corporations, also directly benefit. Current program entitlements tend overwhelmingly to benefit landowners, even though many of these do not work the land. Examples would include the owners of large sugar and cotton farms (many of whom trace their ownership to pre–Civil War times), or owners of large farms that benefit from federally subsidized water in the West. Shaffer (1989) succinctly refers to the inequities of current entitlement benefits as a transfer of scarce public resources from the less well-off to the more well-off, since most recipients are property owners with personal assets much greater than those of the average American.

Over the last half century, many farm policies have contributed to the steady loss of family farms. Among the lost farms were many efficient family operations that were discontinued because the succeeding generation chose not to stay in farming. In fact, most farms have gone out of production because the children did not stay in farming, often choosing a nonfarm sector profession with a more stable income. An unanticipated consequence of this social phenomenon is that almost half the land under production is not owned by the operator. Explanations for this phenomenon, as well as for farm concentration in general, fall into at least two general categories: market structure and public policy.

Market Factors Contributing to Farm Concentration

Three related market factors are often cited as being responsible for the concentration of commercial farming: a dual economy in the sphere of agricultural production, the tendency of competitive markets toward concentration, and a technological treadmill.

Agricultural production should include those firms providing the factors of production (labor- and land-saving technologies, financial institutions, etc.) as well as those purchasing, processing, and marketing farm commodities. A dual economy now exists between these firms and the farm sector due to unequal terms of trade. Most farmers operate in highly competitive sectors while they buy from and sell to only a few agribusinesses, especially at the local level. This dual economy has led to such colloquialisms as "farmers are price takers, not price makers" and "farmers buy retail and sell wholesale." Tweeten (1979) proposes that these unequal terms of trade have contributed to a cost-price squeeze.

Farm concentration also has occurred because competitive markets tend to reward concentration. The deregulation of the airline industry and the rapid concentration of the personal computer industry during the 1980s provide other examples of this market phenomenon outside of agriculture. Historically, farmers have found it necessary to increase their scale of operations to retain their share of the market. However, because most farm markets are characterized by inelastic demand, what is a rational decision by a farmer to expand contributes to overproduction at the aggregate level and lower prices for each unit produced. This contradiction has likewise aggravated the cost-price squeeze.

The process of increasing farm scale was facilitated by rapid technological change. Cochrane (1979) refers to the necessity for farmers to purchase new technologies in order to remain viable competitors on the technological treadmill. However, he is careful not to propose a technologically deterministic relationship between farm concentration and technological change. Rather, he emphasizes that the various commodity markets and federal farm policies have offered incentives for such technological change. After all, as Dickson (1975) notes, it is not the development of technologies that drives farmers to maximize their profits; rather, it is the need to maximize their profits that induces farmers to adopt technologies to remain competitive. Both the agribusinesses and the LGUs have been at the forefront of this continuous technological revolution. Collectively, these market factors have encouraged both the quantitative change of fewer and larger farms and the qualitative change toward a dual farm structure and the decline of the family farm.

Policy Factors Contributing to Farm Concentration

Agricultural economists have demonstrated that most farm policies have probably increased the rate of concentration. Or, put differently, rather than preserving and enhancing family farming, most farm policies likely have facilitated the eclipse of family farms as the dominant farm type. Some policies, especially those characterized by price supports but no supply control, have contributed to the technological treadmill by encouraging a maximization of production unrelated to market demand.

Another important way that farm policies have influenced farm structure is in risk management, by manipulating market and farmer decision making. Government actions that are capitalized into land prices provide an element of risk within the farm economy that affects both farm prices and asset values. Indeed, risk associated with government policy may be more important than other forms of market and financial risk. Historically there has been an interdependency between federal price-support policy and the price of land. To the degree that federal price and income supports increase, there often is a significant increase in the capitalization of farmland. The contradictory policy conclusion of this interdependency is to assume that price supports need to be increased as land prices increase in order to cover higher costs of production. Such policies eventually hamper U.S. exports, since the nation's competitive position is reduced by higher commoditiy prices.

This capitalization of farm program benefits into land prices has still another contradictory effect because it presents formidable capital barriers to entry into farming. Because such policies overvalue agricultural land, it is less possible to service debt associated with either entry into or success in farming. This contradiction is further accentuated by the unreliable and widely variable cash flows associated with farming.

If farm policies have not preserved the family farm, then what have they done? Agricultural economists suggest that their primary policy goal has been to "maximize efficiencies in the market," that is, to promote the accumulation of societal wealth. This is hardly an undesirable goal. However, whereas farm programs were legitimized by identification with family farming, the consequence has been, in part, to maximize the economic fortunes of the largest commercial producers at the expense of their smaller commercial competitors, even though the larger producers were no more efficient.

Farm Policy and the Environment

Agricultural commodity programs often have been at cross-purposes with conservation efforts. Conservation programs have gone to great lengths to promote voluntary soil conservation techniques, while commodity programs often have unintentionally promoted environmental degradation. In 1933, concern for the environment was confined to the on-farm loss of productivity from soil erosion. Moreover, a primary cause of soil erosion was considered to be the farm financial crisis. To counter this threat to the economic recovery of the farm sector and the farm environment, the Soil Conservation Service (SCS) was established. From the beginning, its programs were voluntary and broad based.

By the 1950s, agricultural economists were expressing concern that the primary cause of soil erosion was not low farm income but was rooted in the nature of short-term farm management practices. Heady and Allen (1951) demonstrated that most farmers were unlikely to practice conservation because most practices were so costly in capital or labor that economic gains could only be realized in the long term. They even argued that farmers adopting conservation techniques were probably not economically rational. They pointed out that most conservation efforts were unprofitable in the short term and possibly not profitable even in the long term. Rather, it was cheaper to externalize the costs of soil erosion. That is, it was cheaper to accept marginal losses in soil productivity (which could be cheaply regained by greater application of fertilizers) and let someone else pay for off-site cleanup.

More recently, the assumption that the costs of soil erosion, and also of chemical applications, are confined to lost productivity have been dispelled (Crosson, 1982). Environmental studies show that the off-farm costs of erosion and chemical applications might be many times the on-site costs— probably billions of dollars annually (Phipps and Crosson, 1986). During the 1970s, a period of high farm prices and incomes, soil erosion actually increased as marginal land was brought into production and conservation structures were removed from the land. Also during this period, the total volume of chemicals used in farming continued to increase. The possible health costs of contaminated drinking water are only now being assessed, with most observers fearing the worst.

Not surprisingly, nonfarm political concern for environmental degradation caused by agricultural production has brought environmental groups and their considerable metropolitan-based political influence into the farm policy arena. The quasi-regulatory provisions of swampbuster, sodbuster, and conservation compliance, as well as the targeting of benefits of the Conservation Reserve Program, represent qualitative departures from the earlier voluntary programs of the SCS (Napier, 1990).

Reichelderfer (1989:2), in a broad review of the literature, points out that "agricultural commodity markets inherently fail to incorporate the environmental costs of agricultural production" and that farm programs have aggravated this phenomenon. Indeed, farm policies may have actually encouraged greater natural resource degradation by encouraging farmers to apply more toxic chemicals than even the existing markets might have warranted.

Other Federal Policies and Farm Structural Change

While farm policies have been blamed for the most recent farm financial crisis, other federal policies also have had a decided influence. The most notable example was the Federal Reserve's decision in 1979 to greatly reduce inflation while simultaneously increasing real interest rates. The effect was a massive decapitalization of assets in the farm sector and the inducement of a debt crisis for farmers and farm lenders.

Other federal policies affecting taxes, worker safety, the environment, registration of pesticides and drugs, and even the rate of corporate mergers are having increased influences on farm structure. For example, consideration of the renewal of the Clean Water Act in 1992, which will not occur in any of the congressional agricultural committees, is likely to directly influence farm use of toxic chemicals.

Policy Options

Summary of Issues

The list of complaints against U.S. farm policy include program expense relative to the small and generally prosperous population served, tendency to benefit the largest producers and thereby contribute to the demise of family farming, inefficiencies in design, degradation of the environment, and inability to cure the economic and social problems of rural communities. Another complaint that so far has not been discussed is the loss of foreign markets, such that the United States may become a supplier of last resort. Together, these complaints strongly suggest that the programs of the last 50 years are at risk of losing public legitimacy. At root is a general inability for the programs to effectively adapt to the changing realities of farm structure and agricultural trade.

The foundations are being laid for qualitative change in farm policy. However, whether these foundations will eventually support new programs will depend on the political and economic environment of the 1990s. Bonnen and Browne (1989), citing most of the issues listed above, argue that while farm programs are in need of change, there are potentially expensive transition costs for any qualitative policy adjustments. At an even more fundamental level, Shaffer (1989) reminds the policy community that issues of entitlements—who should justly benefit from the federal treasury?—are at the base of all federal policies. Furthermore, macroeconomic, social welfare, and environmental policies outside the general domain of the congressional agricultural committees also influence agricultural policy. Therefore, although the direction of agricultural policy in the 1990s is impossible to predict, there are multiple options ranging from more of the same to a reformulation of entitlements.

Difficulties of Staying the Course

The Food, Agriculture, Conservation, and Trade Act of 1990 provides further marginal changes with little departure from the Food Security Act of 1985. Maintenance of farm incomes through expanded trade remains central to the 1990 legislation. One of the most significant changes is the provision for a flexible base, which allows farmers to produce nonprogram crops on 15 percent of their traditional base acreage. This change, although important, probably would not have occurred if Congress was not embroiled in a federal fiscal crisis that forced the congressional agriculture committees to reduce program costs. In short, the 1990 legislation demonstrates how difficult it is to change agricultural policy. Staying the course means a continued lack of response to many of the pressing issues noted above.

Difficulties of Changing Agricultural Policies

Qualitative changes likely will occur only under certain conditions, none of which is sufficient. First, the legitimacy of the present programs will have to be eroded to the point of public disillusionment. Earlier we noted that aiding family farms and maintaining a plentiful food supply were two key cultural values legitimizing current programs. It is possible for the public to accept that current policies are legitimate without inclusion of rhetoric for preserving the family farm, so long as the food supply is plentiful. However, the public will probably frown on entitlements to the wealthier segments of the population if family farming is eliminated as a policy objective. But, as Bonnen and Browne (1989) have stated, continued use of family farming by the various farm groups to legitimize most current farm programs is little more than a cynical manipulation of culture.

Second, if reduction of the federal budget deficit continues to be a political issue, then among nonmilitary entitlements, agricultural expenditures are the most likely candidates for significant cuts. Justifications for these budget cuts will likely trigger what we believe is an impending legitimacy crisis. However, the emergence of increased real concern over the federal budget deficit probably will result in a national economic crisis. After all, it was the economic crisis of the late 1920s and early 1930s that set the stage for the last period of qualitative change in farm policy.

Third, it is possible that environmental concerns will force significant adjustments in farm policy. Already the issue of entitlements is part of the environmental agenda. The most salient issue is the debate between the rights of private property and the rights of the public (i.e., the state).

A fourth condition might be macroeconomic policy changes due to multinational trade agreements at the General Agreement on Tariffs and Trade. Should a reduction of protectionist policies be agreed on, with bipartisan support in Congress, the terms of such agreements may externally impose changes in U.S. farm policies.

Certainly there are other factors. But any qualitative change will require difficult public policy choices in defining and setting goals for the new programs. Central to such a debate will be the issue of entitlements. Shaffer (1989:1) argues that "current policy analysis and debate are often biased or incomplete because of selective perceptions about the rights and the consequences of rights that should be taken into account. . . . Ultimately the fight [is] over jurisdictional boundaries and power: whose perceptions would determine the rules of property?"

Central questions that any policy reform must confront are Who should benefit from government farm programs? and What, if any, contingencies must be met? The historic changes in farm structure and in the ownership of farmland discussed earlier call into question the social fairness and economic benefits of current entitlements. For policy reform to occur, the entitlement assumptions that determine the beneficiaries of scarce government resources will have to be addressed directly.

Policy Options

While current programs are most likely to continue in the early 1990s, the critical issues confronting agricultural policy are not going to dissipate. What, then, are some equitable options? We propose that any new programs should at least include the following assumptions. First, new policies must take into account the dual farm structure of American agriculture. Second, public entitlements must be reformulated so that social objectives are treated as separate from economic objectives. Third, commodity policies must be coordinated with environmental policies. Fourth, rural development policy must be separated from farm policy. Fifth, a redetermination of the research and research agendas of USDA and the LGUs is needed. We will briefly examine each and then offer a framework for a new policy for commercial farms.

Building new farm programs around the structural realities of U.S. agriculture should be self-evident. As already noted, midsized farms are worthy targets of any federal benefits. These farms have several characteristics that justify establishment of policies to protect them, including a proven record of market and policy flexibility and the highest efficiency ratings as measured by USDA. But it is farmers in this scale of operation who are leaving farming at the fastest rate, causing the "disappearing middle" phenomenon.

Another structural reality is the importance of hired farm labor. This group of U.S. workers is the most disenfranchised. It is neither socially moral nor economically wise to base food security on a highly exploited labor force. The LGUs must help to demonstrate to U.S. farmers that hired labor is an important human resource for American agriculture. They must document that improving the material well-being and work skills of hired labor is profitable for both farmers and rural communities.

These policy recommendations will, of course, require a change in priorities of who should receive entitlements. For instance, if the preservation of the remaining family farms continues to be a public objective, then policymakers should consider a social policy that will support family income rather than the current policy that enhances farm income. A negative income tax has been proposed as one mechanism for a family income support—although this proposal would not be limited to family farms. Agricultural entitlements should go to the producers of food and fiber, and then only to midsized farms and hired laborers. The super-farms have demonstrated they have sufficient economies of scales, market share, and financial clout to remain profitable without direct federal assistance.

The protection of the environment must also be of paramount importance. The low-input sustainable agriculture (LISA) effort by USDA is a good first step in this direction. Soil conservation programs should emphasize micro-targeting, since only about 10 percent of all U.S. cropland is considered highly erodible (see Lovejoy, Lee, and Beasley, 1986). Moreover, no commodity program should be at cross-purposes with the conservation programs, including programs to reduce the harmful application of toxic chemicals.

There is already movement toward separating rural development from agricultural policy. Recent socioeconomic research suggests that, except where farming is still the primary source of income, farm programs will not directly benefit most rural people. USDA has estimated that less than 7 percent of the U.S. rural population lives in agriculturally dependent counties. In 1986, more than two-thirds of the rural labor force was employed in manufacturing, service industries, or government. In fact, in many areas it is the well-being of the nonfarm economy that influences not only rural community well-being but also the stability of family farming through viable off-farm employment.

Finally, the USDA and the LGUs need to redetermine their mission toward public research and extension. This does not mean agricultural production research should be abandoned. It does mean that such research should focus on lower input, sustainable farming systems, since agribusinesses are unlikely to do so. USDA and LGU research should be targeted to midsized commercial farms. These research programs should be expanded to include extension efforts in the areas of environmental quality and rural development. In doing so, they will create a new general mission that will legitimize their existence well into the twenty-first century by cultivating both urban and rural nonfarm constituencies.

Policy Recommendations for Commercial Farms

If one accepts that the farm problem is not the level of income, but rather the variability of income, then commercial farm policy should be altered. We have established that government actions designed to support incomes are generally bid into land prices. Therefore, it follows that changes in such government actions can adversely affect land prices. This element of risk threatens farm viability to the extent that a change in any of several government farm and financial policies can directly affect the balance sheet.

Given the problems with current programs, we propose that federal farm policies move toward a decoupling of the farm sector from price and income support programs. We also recognize that without a clear set of policy goals, a move toward decoupling will cause hardships. Moreover, there are other aspects of risk that also must be addressed. Among these, the new international markets provide a significant element of risk and uncertainty. Consequently, any effort to decouple farming from current programs will be difficult, even if approached incrementally. What is needed are new institutions and ideas that will help farmers cope with risk by sharing the costs without artificially inflating land values or degrading the environment. Any program transition, of course, will be shaped less by what might seem to economists to be optimal policy than by the political and institutional environment. The following general proposal attempts to work within what we feel are the considerable constraints of what is politically possible.

Congress has demonstrated that it recognizes the types of institutions needed to meet the future requirements for risk management. The policy trick is to effectively manipulate markets to simultaneously commit the farmer in more effective risk management strategies, while not causing the value of land to be bid upward. Commercial farmers need government and market signals that will help them reduce the risk associated with farming but will not create hardships for international markets.

During the 1980s, Congress appears to have worked on two fronts to accomplish these policy goals. Legislators have made significant changes in federal multiple-peril crop insurance and have reopened options trading in the futures market. Further, it is significant that Congress continued to support crop insurance during the 1990 debate despite attempts from Secretary of Agriculture Yeutter to abolish the program. Both crop insurance and futures options are market mechanisms that require farmers to pay for risk protection. In the case of crop insurance, farmers must pay a premium in order to collect when yields drop below a specified level. In the case of option markets, farmers pay to have an option that gives them the right to sell at a specified price should the market price drop below that level. In principle, both programs work the same way. With each, farmers must pay to protect against either a yield or a price decline. Since farmers pay for the risk protection, the benefits of these programs are not bid into land prices. In addition, to the extent that farmers pay according to the relative risk of their farming operation and environment, these programs should produce a more efficient allocation of resources, assuming farmers will not produce using high-risk management practices. These market mechanisms should make participation in international trade less uncertain.

A policy that would accomplish a number of objectives and ease the process of decoupling is the "targeting of revenue." This policy option would establish a revenue target, by acre, for program crops. Since prices and yields tend to move in opposite directions, in years when yields are high and prices are low the target revenue would compensate for low prices. In years when yields are low and prices are high, the target revenue would compensate for low yields. The current commodity programs could be redesigned to this end. Such a plan should provide stability. Moreover, this policy option could lay the groundwork for providing a revenue insurance program for farmers. In such a program, farmers would pay to protect their per acre revenue at specified levels. This type of program has clear advantages. Farmers pay the costs of such protection, yet it does not bid up land prices. Convincing farmers to work through futures markets will require more strict oversight by the federal government to ensure that insider trading does not occur. Given recent allegations involving the Chicago Board of Trade, insider trading could be a serious problem. Strict regulation is justified given past instances of market fraud and because the federal government is expected to ensure that markets are fair and competitive.

These program options should also address some of the concerns about environmental degradation. First, by eliminating the current programs, farmers will no longer have a government incentive to overproduce. Second, there will be less incentive to cultivate marginal land. Third, it will complement current federal efforts to lower farm inputs. However, these proposals will also reduce the penalties of current conservation cross-compliance programs. In order to counter this consequence of decoupling, as we propose above, the SCS should be given the resources for a comprehensive microtargeting program. This program would include the option of purchasing the production rights of highly erodible land.

Obviously, such program changes would require institutional reform of the federal crop insurance program and a major restructuring of the support system for current programs, including the LGU mission. The benefit is that farmers would pay their fair share for protection with only a modest amount of support from the public. This farm policy would represent a type of decoupling. The savings from this decoupling should be passed along to rural development initiatives (Swanson and Skees, 1987). Enhanced rural development programs should help subcommercial farm operations by improving off-farm employment opportunities.

Any transition to this type of program must take into account potential social costs, especially the loss of family farms. While the negative income tax would be one part of a transition policy that would support family income, some calculation of possible decapitalization of farm assets caused by program changes should be made. In this way, the transition from one entitlement system to another could be made more politically palatable.

Conclusion

U.S. agricultural policy faces the potential for fundamental challenges in the 1990s. While many may feel threatened, the opportunity for meaningful policy reform is greater now than at any time since the beginning of the New Deal. Agricultural issues are no longer the domain of farmers. Representatives of the New Agenda and of hired farm labor have brought concerns for the environment, worker and food safety, food distribution, and rural development into the fray. We believe U.S. agriculture has already benefited and will continue to benefit from their involvement. We also believe that U.S. agriculture can support midsized commercial farms while at the same time producing an abundance of safe and nutritious food without drawing large sums of money from the federal treasury. However, whether or not these opportunities for change are seized remains uncertain.

Notes

1. There is an important difference between a *corporate* farm and farms that are *incorporated* for tax and business purposes. The former is a type of industrial farm structure in which there is not only a separation of ownership, management, and labor but also a direct vertical integration with an agribusiness. When the Census of Agriculture records a corporate farm it is referring to a legal structure and not a workplace structure.

2. Strange (1988) makes a good argument that in some areas of the country there are successful commercial farms with $20,000 to $40,000 in gross sales. We accept this argument. However, most farms below $40,000 in gross sales get more than half their income from nonfarm sources.

References

Ahearn, Mary. 1986. *Financial Well-Being of Farm Operators and Their Households.* Agricultural Economic Report No. 563. Washington, D.C.: USDA, National Economics Division, Economic Research Service.

Allen, Kris. 1989. "Reflections on the past, challenges for the future: An examination of U.S. agricultural policy goals." Pp. 3–26 in Kristen Allen, ed., *Agricultural Policies in a New Decade.* Washington, D.C.: Resources for the Future.

Bently, Susan E., Peggy F. Bartlett, F. Larry Leistritz, Steve H. Murdock, William E. Saupe, Don E. Albrecht, Brenda L. Ekstrom, Rita R. Hamm, Arlen G. Leholm, Richard W. Rathge, and Janet K. Wanzek. 1989. *Involuntary Exits from Farming: Evidence from Four Studies.* Agricultural Economic Report No. 625. Washington, D.C.: USDA, Economic Research Service.

Bonnen, James T., and William P. Browne. 1989. "Why is agricultural policy so difficult to reform?" Pp. 7–33 in Carol S. Kramer, ed., *The Political Economy of U.S. Agriculture: Challenges for the 1990s.* Washington, D.C.: Resources for the Future.

Buttel, Frederick H. 1985. "The land-grant system: A sociological perspective on value conflicts and ethical issues." *Agriculture and Human Values* 2(Spring):87–95.

Cochrane, Willard W. 1979. *The Development of American Agriculture.* Minneapolis, Minn.: University of Minnesota Press.

Collins, Timothy, Kurt Stephenson, Catheryn Alexander, Louis E. Swanson, and Jerry R. Skees. 1990. "A matter of life and debt: Some new measures of farm financial stress." Agricultural Economics Staff Paper No. 276. Lexington, Ky.: University of Kentucky.

Collins, Timothy, Kurt Stephenson, Jerry R. Skees, and Louis E. Swanson. 1990. "Kentucky agricultural survey highlights." *Review and Perspectives* Vol. 15. No. 1.

Coughenour, C. Milton, and Louis E. Swanson. 1989. "Rewards, values, and satisfaction with farm work." *Rural Sociology* 53(4):442–459.

Crosson, P. R. 1982. *Conservation Tillage and Conservation Tillage: A Comparative Assessment.* Ankey, Ia.: Soil and Water Conservation Society of America. University Books.

Dickson, David. 1975. *The Politics of Alternative Technology.* New York: University Books.

Goss, Kevin F., Richard D. Rodefeld, Frederick H. Buttel. 1980. "The political economy of class structure in U.S. agriculture: A theoretical outline." Pp. 83–132 in Frederick

H. Buttel and Howard Newby, eds., *The Rural Sociology of the Advanced Societies.* Montclair, N.J.: Allanheld, Osmun.

Heady, Earl, and Carl Allen. 1951. *Returns from Capital Required for Solid Conservation Farming Systems.* Research Bulletin No. 381. Ames, Ia.: Agricultural Experiment Station, College of Agriculture, Iowa State University.

Lovejoy, Stephen, John Lee, and David Beasley. 1986. "Integration of social and physical analysis: The potential for micro-targeting." Pp. 108–120 in Stephen Lovejoy and Ted Napier, eds., *Conserving Soil.* Ankey, Ia.: Soil and Water Conservation Society of America.

Lovejoy, Stephen, and Ted Napier. 1986. *Conserving Soil: Insights from Socioeconomic Research.* Ankeny, Ia.: Soil Conservation Society of America.

Madden, J. Patrick. 1967. *Economies of Size in Farming.* Agriculture Economic Report No. 107. Washington, D.C.: USDA, Economic Research Service.

Mooney, Patrick. 1988. *My Own Boss.* Boulder, Colo.: Westview Press.

Napier, Ted L. 1990. *Implementing the Conservation Title of the Food Security Act of 1985.* Ankey, Ia.: Soil and Water Conservation Society of America.

Paarlberg, Don. 1980. *Farm and Food Policies: Issues of the 1980's.* Lincoln, Nebr.: University of Nebraska Press.

Phipps, Tim P., and Pierre R. Crosson. 1986. "Agriculture and the environment." Pp. 3–34 in T. T. Phipps, P. R. Crosson, and K. A. Price, eds., *Agriculture and the Environment.* Washington, D.C.: Resources for the Future.

Reichelderfer, Katherine. 1989. "Policy issues arising from implementation of the 1985 Farm Bill conservation provisions." Pp. 144–159 in Farm Foundation, ed., *Increasing Understanding of Public Problems and Policies—1988.* Oak Brook, Ill.: Farm Foundation.

Shaffer, James D. 1989. "Selective perceptions and the politics of agricultural policy." Pp. 61–77 in Carol S. Kramer, ed., *The Political Economy of U.S. Agriculture: Challenges for the 1990s.* Washington, D.C.: Resources for the Future.

Strange, Marty. 1988. *Family Farming.* Lincoln, Nebr.: University of Nebraska Press.

Swanson, Louis E., and Jerry R. Skees. 1987. "Funding new ideas for old objectives." *Choices* (Fourth Quarter) 8–12.

Tweeten, Luther. 1979. *Foundations of Farm Policy.* Lincoln, Nebr.: University of Nebraska Press.

7

Agricultural Labor

William H. Friedland

Agricultural labor in the 1990s will be affected by policy in six major areas. The policies that have been continued or put into place have very different impacts for agricultural workers and their agricultural employers. Since labor is recruited internationally as well as nationally, the federal government has vested interests as well. The major policy areas are:

1. worker remuneration, including policies affecting conditions of work and benefits;
2. who will determine or control remuneration, including policies affecting workers' ability to organize collectively in unions;
3. worker health and safety, particularly pesticide use and who determines what is safe;
4. conditions for employment—that is, who is eligible to work (particularly citizenship and age requirements) and who bears the penalty if eligibility is not met;
5. the quality of the labor force, who pays to upgrade it, and what skills are transmitted; and
6. the maintenance of control over international migration and national borders, which are state and federal concerns.

The policy context for agricultural labor, more than for any other policies in rural America, is determined by class position, with workers and employers generally in favor of distinct policies. In the past, agricultural workers have been exempt from the labor laws that protected most workers in the United States. Because of their ethnic and class status, farm workers generally have lost the struggles to determine policy in their favor.

From the viewpoint of governments, policy matters will probably continue to focus on two major issues and a third emergent one. First, there is the contradiction between the need to maintain the labor supply, on the one hand, and for the nation-state to maintain control over its national borders on the other. Thus, there will be continued attempts by the federal government—and at times state government—to put into place policies that ensure availability of labor at crucial points in the agricultural cycle. Migration policies, including the ability of non-U.S. citizens to work legally under specific conditions, will be critical. A related issue is the special vulnerability of agriculture to the shortfall of seasonal labor. This could either be a key tool for labor organization or it could legitimize the repression of organized labor and labor-organizing efforts. Emergent issues relating to the nonagricultural impact of agricultural practices include the use, overuse, and abuse of agricultural chemicals and the treatment of animals. Labor and management have distinct stances on these issues.

The Context for Agricultural Labor Policies

Four important structural conditions provide the context for understanding the development of agricultural labor policies. First, there is the structure of agriculture with the increased importance of economic concentration and the significance of a relatively small percentage of very large units of production, which now employ the bulk of agricultural labor.

Second, there are the factors of geographical/regional and commodity variation. There are such substantially different regional patterns that agricultural labor in a region like the Midwest is significantly different from that of the Sun Belt states. The labor processes of the many agricultural commodities produced in the United States also manifest striking differences, and thus the character of the labor force in the various commodities varies. Agricultural labor, like production, is highly dispersed spatially. Labor is also increasingly stratified by organizational levels (i.e., managerial, supervisorial, technical, white and/or pink collar, permanently employed workers, and seasonal workers) and by ethnicity.

Third, the distinctive price characteristics of agricultural production make labor one of the few production expenditures over which agricultural producers have some margin of discretion. Finally, the state of knowledge about the numbers, characteristics, remuneration, spatial distribution, and occupational standards of agricultural labor is abysmal (Friedland, 1984). Although national and state governments maintain apparatuses to collect and distribute data on agricultural labor, the results are noteworthy for their lack of reliability. Because accuracy of counts determines funding, improved data collection is a crucial issue.

These structural features have had continuing effects on the development of agricultural labor policies. Thus, unlike the experiences with other categories of workers brought under protective legislative coverage during the New Deal period, agricultural labor has remained anomalous as far as government intervention has been concerned. Where other workers were covered by national minimum wage, social security, and labor relations legislation during the 1930s, agricultural workers were extended such coverage in a piecemeal fashion only several decades later. To this day, these workers nationally remain outside the legal system for establishing formal recognition of organization, that is, the National Labor Relations Board procedures.

Despite the relatively small number of persons represented by grower organizations, they have considerable resources in effecting political blocs. This advantage has meant that the agricultural workers, whom they employ, constitute the last group of workers to be considered in providing coverage and the first to be ignored in the enforcement of standards.

An assessment of the overall situation of agricultural labor since World War II must recognize several basic continuities that have existed during the four decades since then.

First, there is the changing structure of agriculture in which the largest units of agricultural production have continued to produce ever-larger shares of total U.S. agricultural production. Thus, "the share of sales accounted for by the largest 5 percent of farms has gradually increased from 39 percent in 1949 to 42 percent in 1960, 47 percent in 1970, and 50 percent in 1982" (Marion, 1986:7). These agri-industrial firms are large not simply in acreage; their significance rests in the degree to which, as an aggregate group, they dominate the totality of agricultural sales. These firms have emerged as the significant, albeit unstudied, organizational form in U.S. agriculture.[1] Although primarily found in Sun Belt states, these firms are now spread throughout the United States. These large agricultural firms have begun to manifest organizational characteristics similar to those of medium-sized corporations, although many—if not most—are still in family ownership. In their internal structures, owners have become distinct from employed managers and technical workers such as agronomists. There are also middle-level, lower-level, and field supervisors; and of course, there are workers who engage in manual labor in a variety of occupations, some employed year round and others who are seasonal, that is, employed only during the harvest or other peak labor demand times.

Second, because of a "perturbation" in the labor situation from the mid-1960s through the 1970s, a perturbation that witnessed the first successful and relatively continuous organization of farm workers, agricultural employers have begun to develop some degree of sophistication in labor relations. Dragged kicking and screaming at the end of the 1960s into a legal situation similar to the labor-industry relations of the 1930s by the formation and success of the United Farm Workers (UFW) union, agricultural employers began to develop some of the sophistication of their industrial brethren. Although considerable work remains, the establishment of agricultural personnel relations capability in the United States and in such institutions as the University of California has created the conditions for much greater sophistication in the management of agricultural workers.[2]

The perturbation created by the UFW has now been largely dissolved. On the one hand, political tactics by organizations such as the Farm Bureau have effectively blocked attempts at legislation favoring farm workers. Other more sophisticated approaches have also been used to create employer-oriented farm labor legislation in several western states. On the other hand, the techniques of class warfare of agricultural employers have been sustained by the political ineptness of the unions in general and the self-destructive leadership of the UFW in particular. Now only a hollow husk of its former robust self, the UFW can still mobilize highly visible urban liberals, especially when Cesar Chavez engages in media-oriented hunger strikes. Chavez's inability to make room for a secondary leadership has led, however, to the destruction of the original organizing cadre of the union. Chavez turned the union away from organizing workers in the fields or in their neighborhoods (where the union won its original constituency) to organizing liberal urban populations through the use of sophisticated computer mailings intended to raise funds and sustain boycotts.

At the national level, the inability of agricultural workers to develop their own organizations and to effect blocs with other workers or interests has meant there have been only modest efforts by agricultural employers to create parallel organization. Although the National Council of Agricultural Employers (NCAE) has been in existence since 1964, the organization has not emerged as a powerful force, particularly since the regional interests of agricultural employers remain highly variant. The NCAE remains available, however, should a powerful farm workers' union ever emerge.

What this has meant is that there is relatively little incentive for national intervention on the subject of union representation among agricultural workers. It is only when organizations and issues peripheral to agriculture become central that government involvement in agricultural labor occurs. Thus, regarding the major issue in the 1980s of the supply of immigrant agricultural workers, the subject arose not because of concerns about agricultural workers but because of the incredible volume of workers turning up in urban employment and the symbolic importance of enforcing the legal myth about the integrity of national borders. The larger issue of undocumented immigration—which included farm workers—became the basis for involvement of agricultural employers and the consequent provision of special interest legislation to guarantee the continuous flow of labor to Sun Belt states. This key element of national agricultural labor policy, therefore, has been largely a nonpolicy issue in the sense that segments of the agricultural community did not drive the debate.

At the level of state government, policy issues have emerged almost entirely in the West. In California, the initial success of the UFW in organizing farm workers led to the adoption of the Agricultural Labor Relations Act (ALRA) in June 1975. In turn, agricultural employers developed two countering strategies. In California employers set out to capture the state apparatus created to regulate labor relations. In this case it was the Agricultural Labor Relations Board (ALRB), whose membership initially was composed of people sympathetic to the UFW. After employers harassed the ALRB budgetarily for several years, ALRB was brought under their control with the election of Republican Governor George Deukmejian. The second strategy developed in a number of other western states where agricultural employers introduced bills in state legislatures on representational legislation that established employer control over the governmental apparatus.

At the local level, it is difficult to generalize about policies. Several points, however, can be made. First, there is what might be referred to as the "irrelevance" of locality on agricultural labor policy matters; these are issues that are fought out and determined on national and state levels, to the extent that policy issues are determined. Second, local policies most frequently develop when dramatic actions such as strikes take place; in these cases, the classical class position usually emerges with local sheriffs playing their traditional role of keeping workers "in their place," especially when they are of ethnic or racial origin.

Policy Options for the 1990s

There is little indication that policies for the 1990s will produce significant changes in agricultural labor. Agricultural employers can be expected to continue to worry about quantity and quality of the labor force. In the East, Midwest, South, and West, small and medium agricultural producers who hire little or no labor will remain relatively unconcerned about this issue. For organizations such as the Farm Bureau, even in states where agricultural employees are inconsequential, the maintenance of the labor supply and resistance to any forms of organization will continue to be preoccupations. The significant units of agricultural production, the large farms producing over $200,000 of sales, can be expected to remain very much concerned.

That concern can be expected to take several different forms. First, the matter of maintaining a continuous labor supply adequate for peak harvest periods will continue to worry employers. Historically, employers have dealt with this problem by hiring an oversupply of labor. Employer concerns now focus less on public discourse than on the maintenance of informal arrangements so that government agencies will not enforce immigration legislation during periods of peak labor demand. Despite formal denials by government agencies, this is an old and well-institutionalized practice, and there is little reason to believe that well-established behavior patterns will change.

Second, an increasing number of employers are becoming interested in training programs for their agricultural employees. These programs cover such topics as improving management skills, operating and repairing tractors, and having safe industrial practices. It is already possible to see growing interest in short training courses as well as in extension activities geared at developing the skills of managerial, supervisorial, and manual permanent employees.

Third, it is reasonable to expect an increase in the organizational density of agricultural employers. At this time there is only one weak organization of these employers nationally, the National Council of Agricultural Employers, and relatively few organizations that operate systematically at the local level. Many associations, however, emerged out of the organizational drive of the UFW, organizations intended to provide substitute services for those being developed by the UFW. These organizations provide benefits such as health care, insurance, and vacation. Organized by clusters of employers in a specific location, these organizations monitor developments among lower ranking workers and can provide quick response when organizational activity begins.

Unionism alone, however, does not increase employer organization. As agriculture becomes more capital intensive, employers need more highly trained workers who are capable of operating very expensive equipment. During the peak season, for example, an agricultural employer cannot risk having an insufficiently trained or irresponsible operator combine grain or harvest winegrapes. The costs of these production problems can be expensive to machinery, equipment, plantings, and personnel. Thus, some employers are finding it necessary to maintain, in addition to managers and supervisors, a cadre of reasonably paid, permanently settled workers. Other large agricultural operators have begun to contract out capital-intensive work. In the Midwest, grain harvesting is frequently contracted to a specialist who brings in a crew of workers specifically for the summer harvest. In California, winegrape harvesting is also being contracted out. In these operations, the contractor has the specialized skills for maintaining equipment or hires a few highly qualified personnel to repair and keep the machinery operating.

As agricultural labor becomes more specialized, there is an increased need for publicly funded training programs, which are based on the classical arguments about the economic value to society of training workers. This demand will conflict with the fiscal crisis, that is, the inability to expand public services because of limits on taxation. The 1990s may become the decade in which the consequences of the tax revolt of the late 1970s and 1980s are brought home to the American public; even now legislators and business leaders are frustrated with society's inability to produce key services. The decrepit state of American education, which has been producing an increasingly segmented labor force, a large portion of which reflects the debilitated condition of the system, has reached a point where some business leaders are beginning to confront the consequences of the tax revolt.

On the organized labor front, there is little indication that significant new developments will unfold. The UFW union, having abandoned organizing farm workers in the fields or in their homes, shows no signs of making a turnaround. UFW leader Cesar Chavez continues to exercise total control over what is left of the union, maintaining an appalling hegemony that precludes significant new initiatives. There have been independent organizations such as the Farm Labor Organizing Committee in the Michigan-Ohio area and UFW spin-offs such as the Arizona Farm Workers and the Texas Farm Workers unions. These organizations have proven to be relatively weak and unable to expand from a localized farm worker base. Thus, the prospect that farm-worker action will produce any new policy initiatives is somewhat less than optimistic.

With employers preoccupied with the quantity and quality of labor supply and the prospects for unionization very weak, what policy options can be expected from the third actor, governments (i.e., the state)? Few new policy developments can be anticipated from the government itself. The state does not simply represent "the executive committee of the bourgeoisie," as Marx and Engels held; rather, the bourgeois-liberal state (which characterizes all major capitalist societies) rarely looks for trouble and intervenes only when there is a clamor for intervention. The state, for example, must respond if the social order is threatened. Thus, when California was torn by years of turmoil during the organization of the UFW and the resistance of employers, Governor Jerry Brown intervened to create the ALRA. Once the law was created, agricultural employers begrudgingly accepted the new state of affairs and actively and aggressively captured the ALRB in their own interests.

Certainly the abstract concept of distributive justice cannot be expected to inform state policy; the decades of defining farm workers as exceptional excluded them from the standard protective legislation that covered all other workers. On what grounds can the state now be expected to become concerned with distributive justice? There are two potential areas, however, within which some possibilities for change and new policy developments may be feasible—the use of agricultural chemicals and the treatment of agricultural animals. Both topics have been largely ignored by the organized manifestation of farm workers, the UFW. Whereas Chavez's hunger strike in 1988 called attention to the effects of agricultural chemicals on farm workers, the UFW's handling of the pesticides issue has been inconsistent and narrowly focused. UFW concern about agricultural chemicals has been sporadic, waxing when the union is in difficulty or engaged in a struggle with employers, waning when contracts are signed. Moreover, the UFW has concentrated its concerns almost exclusively on the effects of chemicals on farm workers. Both the environmental and the long-term effects on consumers have essentially been ignored by the union.

The issue of chemicals, however, will not go away. Despite arguments by some scientists dismissing the dangers of agricultural chemicals, the increasing skepticism about food safety has begun to undermine scientific hegemony. There are simply too many cancer clusters; in addition, the disclosures about the dangers of asbestos, PCBs, DBCP, and other pesticides and chemicals in the environment have led to increasing worries despite reassurances from segments of the agricultural scientific community. At some stage a catastrophic event or combination of events involving chemicals will trigger a backlash of unparalleled magnitude that will bury the reassurances of the epidemiologists and toxicologists. In such a context, the situation of the farm workers, who are on the front line in exposure to a multiplicity of chemicals and are thus the human equivalent of canaries in the mine, may again come to the fore.

Somewhat less likely might be a coalition between farm workers and animal rights constituents. While more responsible elements in this protest movement have been concerned with weak controls and poor care of animals in experiments, too much of the protest has focused on issues (e.g., the use of animals to test ways to improve human health) which can hardly be expected to engage the majority of the population.

Another segment of the animal rights movement has focused on the miserable conditions of chickens, pigs, cattle, and other animals that are raised for food. The emergence of chicken and pig factories has created a spirited opposition in Scandinavia which has become so strong that some elite segments of the agricultural community are now taking the protests seriously. Farm-worker leaders have manifested little sympathy for this movement. They are appalled, with some justice, about the "white liberals" who worry more about the health and happiness of chickens and pigs than of human beings, that is, farm workers. Thus, until now, there have been no possibilities of alliances between animal-rights and farm-worker activists. Should such an alliance become possible and should it encompass the broad-scale concerns about chemicals in the environment and the particular role of agricultural chemicals, the creation of a new coalition to which the state must pay attention may become feasible.

Conclusion

Agricultural labor is unlikely to become an arena for major policy initiatives in the 1990s. Although employers will continue to be concerned about the volume and the quality of the labor supply, it is unlikely that they will be threatened by agricultural unionism, a force calculated to develop conscious class interests and organization. It is equally unlikely that employers will seek major national initiatives on any front, preferring to work informally to ensure that state intervention is minimized in their employment of undocumented workers. Employers will also work locally to resolve problems of quality of labor; that is, they will develop their employees' technical skills through local school and training systems.

With no anticipated actions being manifested by workers, there is little likelihood that the formal instrumentalities of government can be expected to worry a great deal about labor. There will undoubtedly be individuals and organizations who will be concerned, but it is highly unlikely that such matters will produce policy options at the national, state, or local levels.

The resurgence of an environmental/animal rights movement, if brought into conjunction with farm worker interests, has considerable potential for change. Whether such a movement will develop during the 1990s is uncertain. While it is evident that the basis for such a movement is increasing, it is not yet clear whether a sufficient number of urban Americans feel threatened enough by environmental poisoning that they are willing to turn their attention away from their preoccupation with material pursuits.

Notes

1. Most of the literature on large-scale agricultural firms can be found only in journalistic accounts. A somewhat scholarly work can be found in Drache (1976). Serious scholarly treatments of large-scale agricultural enterprises remain to be initiated.

2. See, for example, Agricultural Employment Work Group (1982) for a statement on the importance of developing agricultural personnel management skills. The University of California's Division of Agricultural Sciences has published a series of

leaflets on various aspects of labor and personnel relations. These are on such topics as farm labor contracting (#21071), pesticide regulation (#21077), child labor (#21081), workers' compensation (#21082), wages and agriculture (#21083), collective bargaining and seasonal farm workers (#21147), California's Agricultural Labor Relations Act (#21159), and various other topics. In addition, newsletters such as "People in Ag Personnel Management and Safety" are now being issued by agricultural extension specialists in labor relations in California.

References

Agricultural Employment Work Group of the U.S. Department of Labor. 1982. *Agricultural Labor in the 1980's: A Survey With Recommendations.* Berkeley, Calif.: University of California, Division of Agricultural Sciences.

Drache, Hiram M. 1976. *Beyond the Furrow: Some Keys to Successful Farming in the Twentieth Century.* Danville, Ill.: Interstate Printers and Publishers.

Friedland, William H. 1984. "The labor force in U.S. agriculture." Pp. 143–181 in Lawrence Busch and William B. Lacy, eds., *Food Security in the United States.* Boulder, Colo.: Westview Press.

Marion, Bruce W., and NC 117 Committee. 1986. *The Organization and Performance of the U.S. Food System.* Lexington, Mass.: Lexington Books, D.C. Heath.

8
The Rural Poor:
The Past As Prologue

Kenneth L. Deavers and Robert A. Hoppe

Welfare reform legislation was a major accomplishment of the 100th Congress. The Family Support Act (FSA) became law when it was signed by President Reagan in October 1988. The act, as summarized by Rovner (1988:2825):

> requires states to establish an education, training and employment program to move welfare recipients from the dole into permanent jobs that pay enough to support their families. States must enroll 20 percent of their cases in this JOBS (Job Opportunities and Basics Skills) program by 1995 and must guarantee child care, transportation and other services needed to allow welfare recipients to participate. To minimize the need for mothers of young children to go on welfare to begin with, the legislation mandates stricter enforcement of child-support orders, including automatic wage-withholding of court-ordered support payments.

The FSA focuses largely on the population that is currently served by Aid to Families with Dependent Children (AFDC). AFDC has primarily benefited families with a female head and no spouse present. However, only 31 percent of the rural or nonmetro[1] poor live in these families. Strictly speaking, FSA affects welfare that is provided to only a segment of the rural poor population. Further changes in the welfare system could help other segments.

In this chapter we examine characteristics of the rural poor and program changes likely to benefit different groups. We do this in the context of some of the basic beliefs about the poor that have conditioned past policy and that will continue to have a strong influence on future policy. These beliefs are important because any proposals for policy reform that ignore them are unlikely to be accepted by lawmakers or the public.

Beliefs and English Poor Laws

The evolution of our present welfare system, including the reform measures in the FSA, has been strongly influenced by beliefs about the poor that are older than our nation. Poverty was a serious problem in the colonies. Almost half of the early settlers arrived as indentured servants with few resources, and others fell into poverty on the frontier (Salamon, 1978:66). Colonial leaders, as British subjects, drew heavily from the English Poor Laws for ideas about how to deal with the poor. The three central elements of the English Poor Laws are:[2]

1. The poor should be categorized into the deserving and undeserving poor. Some poor, particularly the able-bodied, do not deserve aid. (Poverty among those able to work is a result of personal failings, particularly laziness and vice.)
2. Aid to the poor must not interfere with the private labor market.
3. Aid to the poor is a local responsibility.

Time has modified these beliefs (Salamon, 1978). Economic catastrophes, especially the Great Depression of the 1930s, showed that a weakened economy, as well as personal failings, can cause poverty. Limited financial resources have reduced the role that local governments can realistically play in aiding the poor. And most Americans no longer object on general principle to federal aid to the poor (Heclo, 1986).

Nevertheless, the first two beliefs of English Poor Laws continue to exert a strong influence. Personal failings, particularly refusal of the able-bodied to work and behavior resulting in illegitimate children, are still commonly seen as major causes of poverty where the public responsibility to assist is minimal. When the current welfare system was established, aid was largely targeted at various groups of deserving poor (Ellwood, 1988:26–33); this categorization is still reflected in the programs. Also, effects on private employers are still discussed whenever aid to the working poor is debated.

In addition, the strong work ethic of the Poor Laws still prevails among some groups of people, as anyone who grew up in a rural area can attest. According to Williams (1970:459):

> This "metaphysical drive to work" permeated the older agrarian culture of this country and exists today in practically the original quasi-religious form in some rural areas and among other subgroupings that have not yet fully assimilated the more recent cult of success and conspicuous consumption. The emphasis on work is strong in some professional and executive circles. Even in leisure and expressive behavior, the purposive and obligatory emphases often persist.

This strong belief in the value of work that is common in many rural areas hinders local acceptance of antipoverty programs that do not involve work for the undeserving poor.

Of course, the central beliefs of the English Poor Laws are not the sole determinant of our nation's treatment of the poor in either rural or urban areas. Sociopolitical changes and general economic conditions continually interact to affect attitudes about the poor and to influence policy decisions. A genuine desire to help the poor, as expressed by Ellwood (1988:15), also exists: "I think America's support for the poor comes not from our most selfish instincts or greatest fears, but from our highest virtues. Helping is motivated by a sense of compassion and a desire for fairness. People are troubled when they see or even think of hungry or homeless people."

Compassion for the poor does not necessarily conflict with the Poor Laws. Ideally, aid to the poor should go to those who need it, should not discourage work, and should not interfere with the private labor market. Conflicts, however, can and do arise in assessing how well programs meet these ends.

The Current Welfare System

Here we limit our discussion to major "income maintenance programs" targeted specifically at the poor, rather than including social insurance programs such as unemployment insurance and Social Security. Although such programs play an important role in alleviating poverty (Bentley, 1986:19–21), they are based on a person's past participation in the labor market and are not targeted at the poor per se. The major welfare programs are summarized below.

Aid to Families with Dependent Children (AFDC). This program was established in 1935 to help poor children deprived of support because of the death, incapacity, or absence of a parent. The program is targeted largely at female-headed families. Starting in 1961, legislation gave states the option of providing AFDC to two-parent families if the breadwinner is unemployed (U.S. Congress, 1989:535). The FSA will extend this provision to all states, although the states may limit participation of such families to six months in a twelve-month period (Rovner, 1988:2825, 2830). Benefits are set by the states and vary widely. Federal and state governments currently share the costs of the program, but states administer the program.

Work requirements were not added to AFDC until 1967. AFDC was originally intended to allow poor widows to stay home and raise their children (Solomon, 1988:3), because poor widows with young children were among the deserving poor (Salamon, 1978:66–68). As more and more mothers joined the labor force and as AFDC became a program for separated, divorced, and unwed mothers and their children (Solomon, 1988:3), the consensus that AFDC mothers need not work weakened.

Supplemental Security Income (SSI). The federal SSI program pays nationally uniform benefits to the aged, blind, or disabled poor (Hoppe and Saupe, 1982:33). Starting in 1974, SSI replaced state-administered programs serving the same groups. Because states may supplement the program, total benefits for similar recipients differ from state to state. All of the groups served by SSI are traditionally classified among the deserving poor.

Food Stamps. The Food Stamp Program was enacted to alleviate malnutrition and to increase sales of agricultural products (Hoppe and Saupe, 1982:34). The program is funded solely by the federal government, and its benefits are uniform across the nation, except in Alaska and Hawaii. Although households made up entirely of AFDC or SSI recipients are automatically eligible for food stamps, other poor can participate if they meet the income and asset requirements (U.S. Congress, 1989:1106–1115).

Medicaid. Medicaid, the medical program for the poor, is targeted largely at AFDC and SSI recipients (U.S. Congress, 1989:1127–1129). Medicaid must also cover children less than seven years old who live in a family with income less than the AFDC standard, even if the child's family does not qualify for AFDC. Pregnant women with income and assets below the AFDC standard are also eligible, even if they are not receiving AFDC. The federal and state governments share in the cost of the Medicaid program.

General Assistance.[3] This program evolved from the concept of local responsibility for the poor (U.S. Congress, 1974:349) mentioned above. The statutory basis for general assistance dates back to early state, colonial, and territorial laws regarding the care of paupers and the indigent. State or local governments provide general assistance to families or individuals who do not qualify for other programs. No federal funding is used in this program.

The support system for the poor is a complex set of overlapping programs supported by federal, state, and local governments. Serious problems exist in coordinating eligibility for the several programs and adjusting the size of benefits as earnings change (Levitan, 1985:88–90). Schiller (1984:188) aptly summarizes the current welfare system:

> There is no coherent *system* of income maintenance in the United States. Instead, we rely on a variety of diverse income transfer programs, designed and implemented independently of each other. Despite these patchwork origins, however, current public assistance and Social Security programs do provide much aid for the poor.

Rural Poverty

The American public generally perceives poverty as an urban problem. This perception likely stems from the greater visibility of the metro poor, particularly in central cities. However, the incidence of poverty is actually higher in nonmetro areas. In 1987, the nonmetro poverty rate was 16.9 percent, 4.4 percentage points above the metro rate. Examining the nature of poverty in rural areas may suggest relevant policy changes to help the rural poor.

Rural Delivery Problems

Delivering help to the rural poor is often more expensive and difficult because, by definition, the rural poor are more dispersed than the metro poor (Institute for Research on Poverty, 1980:6). Organizations and agencies that serve the poor in rural areas are also smaller and fewer than in urban areas (Watkins and Watkins, 1984:49). Thus, relatively fewer social work services and fewer resources address the problems of the rural poor.

Regional concentration presents another problem for the rural poor in that a large share live in relatively poor states (particularly in the South) which are unable to support welfare programs or other services at the same level or to the same extent as more prosperous states (Deavers, Hoppe, and Ross, 1986:295–297; Institute for Research on Poverty, 1980:5–6).

Who Are the Rural Poor?

The rural poor numbered 9.1 million in 1987 (Table 8.1), or about 17 percent of all rural people. They can be sorted into three major categories— families with a female householder, no husband present; other families; and unrelated individuals.

The first category, "female-headed household," has been the principal target of the AFDC program since its inception. In 1987, these female-headed families contained about one-third of all poor rural people. The female heads themselves made up about 30 percent of this category, while children under age 18 made up nearly 60 percent. "Other families" consist of married-couple families and families with a male householder, no wife present. Nearly half of the rural poor lived in these families in 1987, of which 92 percent were married-couple families. The "unrelated individuals" category consists of people who are at least 15 years old, do not live with relatives, and are not inmates of institutions. About one-fifth of the nonmetro poor in 1987 were unrelated individuals (Table 8.1), and about one-third of the nonmetro poor in this category were elderly women (U.S. Census Bureau, 1988b.)

During the past two decades, the share of the nonmetro poor living in female-headed families increased, while the share living in other families decreased. By 1987, the number of poor female-headed families reached 860,000, while the number of poor other families was more than 1.2 million. More than 1.7 million unrelated individuals lived in poverty in the same year.

Contrary to popular belief, many poor persons work (Table 8.2). Among the nonmetro poor, householders of other families are much more likely to work than either female householders or unrelated individuals. About 60 percent of other family householders worked, including 25 percent who worked full time, year round.

Policy Options

The family status (Table 8.1) and recent work history (Table 8.2) of the rural poor suggest four principal groups that might be the target of policies to reduce rural poverty.[4] These groups are (1) families (primarily female-headed) eligible for AFDC, both before and after FSA; (2) the aged and disabled poor; (3) the working poor; and (4) the unemployed poor.

TABLE 8.1   Nonmetro Poor Persons, by Family Status and Selected Personal
Characteristics, 1987

	Number (Thousands)	Distribution (%)
Family status		
People in families with a female householder, no husband present	2,799	30.7
Householder[a]	862	9.4
Children under 18 years old[b]	1,618	17.7
Other family members	319	3.5
People in other families[c]	4,389	48.1
Householder[a]	1,225	13.4
Spouse	1,125	12.3
Children under 18 years old[b]	1,751	19.2
Other family members	288	3.2
People in unrelated subfamilies[d]	175	1.9
Children under 18 years old	98	1.1
Other	77	0.8
Unrelated individuals	1,760	19.3
Total	9,123	100.0
Selected personal characteristics[e]		
White	6,508	71.3
Black	2,285	25.0
Hispanic[f]	514	5.6
Aged	1,154	12.6

Note: Population count as of March 1988. Poverty status is based on 1987 income.
   [a]Person in whose name the home is rented or owned.
   [b]Related to the householder by blood, marriage, or adoption.
   [c]Married-couple families and families with a male householder, no wife present.
   [d]See U.S. Census Bureau (1988a:156).
   [e]Detail adds to more than the total because a person may be in more than one group.
   [f]Hispanics may be of any race.

Source: U.S. Census Bureau (1988b).

An effective attack on the poverty of these four groups would be a major step in eliminating rural poverty. About 613,000 family heads and unrelated individuals were retired,[5] 811,000 were ill or disabled, 695,000 had trouble finding work, and 488,000 worked full time for a full year (Table 8.2). These groups together made up 67.8 percent of all poor householders and unrelated individuals. In addition, 380,000 families reported that they received public assistance,[6] which includes AFDC (U.S. Census Bureau, 1988b). To avoid double counting, however, we excluded these families from our count above,

TABLE 8.2 Work Experience and Selected Personal Characteristics of Poor Householders and Unrelated Individuals in Nonmetro Areas, 1987

	All Householders and Unrelated Individuals		Female Householder, No Husband Present		Other Family Householder		Unrelated Individuals	
	Number (Thousands)	Distribution (%)	Number (Thousands)	Distribution (%)	Number (Thousands)	Distribution (%)	Number (Thousands)	Distribution (%)
Work experience								
Worked last year	1,760	45.7	397	46.1	740	60.4	623	35.4
Full year (50–52 wk)	690	17.9	124	14.4	362	29.6	204	11.6
Full time[a]	488	12.7	80	9.3	310	25.3	98	5.6
Part time[b]	200	5.2	43	5.0	52	4.2	105	6.0
Part year (1–49 wk)	1,071	27.8	273	31.7	378	30.9	420	23.9
Full time[a]	614	16.0	156	18.1	250	20.4	208	11.8
Part time[b]	455	11.8	116	13.5	128	10.4	211	12.0
Did not work last year	2,077	54.0	465	53.9	475	38.8	1,137	64.6
In armed forces	10	0.3	0	0.0	10	0.8	0	0.0
Total	3,847	100.0	862	100.0	1,225	100.0	1,760	100.0
Main reason for not working at all or for working part of year								
Ill or disabled	811	25.8	129	17.5	239	28.0	443	28.5
Keeping house[c]	640	20.3	361	48.9	46	5.4	233	15.0
Unable to find work	695	22.1	160	21.7	305	35.8	230	14.8
Retired	613	19.5	12	1.6	165	19.3	436	28.0
Other	389	12.4	77	10.4	98	11.5	214	13.7
Total	3,148	100.0	738	100.0	853	100.0	1,557	100.0
Personal characteristics								
White	2,908	75.6	505	58.6	1,002	81.8	1,401	79.6
Black	805	20.9	323	37.5	174	14.2	308	17.5
Graduated from high school[d]	1,532	45.9	409	58.0	541	47.6	582	38.9
At least 65 years old	970	25.2	51	5.9	199	16.2	720	40.9

Note: Count of householders and unrelated individuals as of March 1988. Poverty status is based on 1987 income.
[a]Worked at least 35 hours per week in a majority of the weeks worked.
[b]Worked less than 35 hours per week in a majority of the weeks worked.
[c]People keeping house usually are women. They may also take care of young children or sick or aged adults, which limits their ability to leave home and work.
[d]Excludes householders and unrelated individuals less than 25 years old.

Source: U.S. Census Bureau (1988b:24).

because some public assistance recipients are already included in the other policy groups.

Families Eligible for AFDC

As we noted earlier, female-headed families receiving AFDC will be the main beneficiaries of the welfare reforms contained in the FSA. Of the 380,000 poor rural families receiving public assistance, 267,000 were female-headed. However, the FSA will extend AFDC coverage to two-parent families in all states, if the main earner is unemployed and meets other program eligibility criteria. Until this provision of the FSA is implemented on October 1, 1990, coverage of such families is a state option. These families have been excluded from coverage in about half of the states, and many of these states contain large rural poor populations.

About 70 percent of the 862,000 female-headed poor families in nonmetro areas do not receive public assistance. Nevertheless, these families may also benefit from FSA. For a fee, they can participate in FSA's efforts to increase child-support collections (Solomon, 1988:73).

Additional changes in AFDC that were not incorporated in the FSA could also benefit the rural poor. Nonmetro AFDC recipients are more likely to live in states where low benefit levels have been established (Deavers, Hoppe, and Ross, 1986:301.). If the test of equity in national programs is that poor families in similar situations are treated the same, then the wide variation in AFDC payments suggests that the program has failed. For example, the maximum monthly AFDC payment for a family of three is $629 in Vermont but only $118 in Alabama (U.S. Congress, 1989:546–547). Clearly, this is not just a reflection of cost-of-living variations alone. Establishing national minimum benefit levels and providing federal funds to assist low-income states meet these minimums would especially help the rural poor.

As the national standard of living improved, public policy has increased the support provided to many transfer payment recipients. Most notable were the 20 percent increase in Social Security benefit levels in 1972 and the automatic indexing of Social Security benefits to compensate for inflation after 1975 (U.S. Congress, 1989:23). AFDC benefits, however, are not indexed. As a result, AFDC recipients have fallen behind in all but three states as inflation has eroded the real value of benefits (U.S. Congress, 1989:545). The median decline in real benefits for a family of three was 37 percent between 1970 and 1989.[7] Adjusting benefit levels for inflation would benefit the rural and urban poor alike.

It is unlikely that more uniform benefits or indexing will soon be added to the AFDC program. Because the FSA has just become law, Congress is probably not willing to consider additional welfare reform proposals soon. And, these changes would be expensive. For example, provisions to encourage states to raise benefit levels were dropped from the FSA during negotiations between the House of Representatives and the Senate. This action saved an estimated $1.1 billion over five years (Rich, 1988:A3).

Furthermore, some policymakers may fear that a minimum benefit level will create work disincentives in states where benefits are increased. Reforms instituted by the FSA to move AFDC recipients off the welfare rolls and into jobs, however, may ultimately establish stronger work efforts among recipients and blunt this argument against a national minimum benefit level.

Fears that more uniform benefits will reduce work effort may actually be unfounded because the statistical relationship between AFDC benefit levels and work effort appears weak. Only 18 percent of the variation among the states in the share of AFDC families with earnings is explained by state-to-state variation in benefit levels.[8]

Aged and Disabled Poor

Establishing a federal minimum SSI payment at least equal to the poverty level could significantly reduce poverty among the aged poor. The 1.2 million aged rural poor (Table 8.1) would benefit disproportionately from such a policy, since about 60 percent of them live in the South (U.S. Census Bureau, 1988b) where state supplementation of the program tends to be low (Deavers, Hoppe, and Ross, 1986:299). Because more than half of the poor elderly households receive Social Security but not SSI (U.S. Congress, 1989:930), increasing Social Security benefits to low-income elderly would also reduce poverty.

A strategy combining Social Security and SSI could virtually eliminate poverty among the rural aged. Such a strategy would, however, cost billions of dollars. The 1987 poverty gap, or the difference between the poverty level and income received, was estimated as $3.9 billion for the nation's elderly households (U.S. Congress, 1989:970).

Pressure for higher Social Security benefits for all elderly, poor and nonpoor alike, may come from the growing surplus in the Social Security trust fund, which makes large benefit increases appear to be free. Clearly they are not, because the surplus will be required to help pay benefits to the large number of "baby boomers" retiring after the turn of the century. Saving the surplus and investing it productively is crucial to both the nation's future economic growth and future retirees (Rauch, 1988).[9] Any efforts to help the elderly poor through Social Security must be carefully targeted to control costs.

Progress against poverty among the rural disabled likewise depends largely on provisions in Social Security and SSI. Benefit levels could be increased, higher supplementation of SSI could be mandated, or eligibility criteria for disability payments could be relaxed. Any combination of these policies would help the 811,000 householders and unrelated individuals reporting illness or disability (Table 8.2).

The Working Poor

Almost half a million rural householders and unrelated individuals worked full time for a full year and still were poor (Table 8.2). Because the working poor have earned income, nearly all pay payroll taxes and many also pay income taxes. Thus, they can be aided by changes in the tax codes. For example, 1986 tax legislation increased the working poor's earned income tax credit (EITC), and Congress is considering raising it again (Rovner, 1989:326–328). The EITC, in effect, is a subsidy to workers with low earnings that is paid through the federal tax system. The EITC is available to married couples, surviving spouses, and unmarried heads of households if they have children (U.S. Congress, 1989:790–792). This credit, enacted in 1975, was designed to improve work incentives, to provide relief from the Social Security tax, and to aid poor workers with children.

Increasing the minimum wage is another way to help the working poor. Late in 1989, President Bush signed a bill raising the minimum wage from $3.35 per hour to $4.25 by April 1, 1991 (Ciccone, 1989). A lower training wage was also established for teenagers.

Perhaps the strongest argument for the latest increase in the minimum wage is its symbolic importance. The minimum wage is a statement of national policy about the minimum purchasing power that we find acceptable for American workers. Inflation has seriously eroded the value of the $3.35 minimum wage established in 1981. In real terms, the purchasing power of the minimum wage is lower than at any time since the mid-1950s (Smith and Vavrichek, 1987:25). Even at the $4.25 level, however, the minimum wage will have limited ability to move people out of poverty. A full-time, year-round worker paid $4.25 per hour would earn 96.6 percent of the 1987 poverty level for a one-parent family with two children.[10]

Increasing the minimum wage is controversial. There is some concern that minimum wage increases may decrease the number of jobs for the poor, if such increases make it unprofitable for businesses to hire new or retain old workers (Levitan, 1985:124–125). An additional factor acts against a minimum wage increase: it would interfere with private labor markets by forcing some employers to pay higher wages than they would otherwise.

Raising the minimum wage may also be a relatively inefficient way to reach the working poor, because relatively few poor workers are covered by minimum wage legislation. A recent study found that about 38 percent of poor workers who worked year round (primarily full time) were self-employed or unpaid workers (Smith and Vavrichek, 1987:29). These workers are exempt from minimum wage legislation, and would be unaffected by a minimum wage increase. The self-employed are especially common in rural areas. In 1986, self-employment provided 23.4 percent of all jobs in nonmetro areas, compared with only 13.2 percent in metro areas (U.S. Department of Commerce, 1988).

In addition, some wage earners are not covered by the federal minimum wage. The new federal minimum-wage law does not cover most businesses grossing under $500,000 per year (Ciccone, 1989). Lowering the cut-off from the $500,000 level could extend minimum wage coverage to more workers in nonmetro areas. On the other hand, lowering the cut-off might drive small, marginal firms out of business, costing low-income workers their jobs. The effect on small businesses may not be as great as it would appear, because some small businesses exempt from federal law are covered under state minimum wage laws.[11]

Extending coverage of Medicaid to all needy children would also help the working poor. Currently, only children under seven years of age are potentially covered by Medicaid in low-income families not receiving AFDC, and many of the working poor lack medical insurance. For example, about 40 percent of working, two-parent poor families across the nation have no medical coverage at all (Ellwood, 1988:103).

In the long run, educational programs or job training would be desirable to help the working poor upgrade their skills and earn income above the poverty level. Unfortunately, the poor who already work are unlikely to be helped by the Job Training Partnership Act (JTPA) or similar programs. According to Levitan (1985:123),

> The plight of these adult working poor receives little attention in training and employment programs. . . . These programs tend to be preoccupied with the unemployed, youths, and those outside the labor force. The goal of most training programs is full-time employment; that this may be no real solution to poverty is often ignored, as are the needs of those who are already laboring at full-time, low-paying jobs.

What policy changes to help the working poor are likely? Another increase in the minimum wage is unlikely in the near future, mainly because it was just raised by the 1989 legislation. However, regular increases to keep up with inflation should be considered.

Perhaps a more generous EITC is more likely. In recent congressional debates, a higher EITC was proposed to help low-wage workers without the negative effects on employment that might result from an increase in the minimum wage (Ciccone, 1988). In addition, the EITC applies to the self-employed and to wage earners not covered by the minimum wage. On the other hand, the working poor benefited from several tax changes in 1986 legislation, including a higher EITC (U.S. Congress, 1989:872–874). This recent legislation might make it more difficult to achieve further tax benefits.

The Unemployed Poor

The unemployed poor are a fairly large group in rural areas. Nearly 700,000 poor householders and unrelated individuals reported having trouble finding work (Table 8.2). The unemployed poor with recent wage and salary employment may be eligible for unemployment insurance. We cannot tell from the available data how long these people have been unemployed or whether they have exceeded the maximum period during which they can receive benefits. We also lack information on the benefit levels for which they may be eligible.

We do know, however, that unemployment payments are related to previous wages and that the states determine the percentage of wages replaced by the program, up to a state-determined maximum benefit (U.S. Congress,

1989:450–451). As a result, benefit levels vary substantially from place to place. Given the relatively low wage levels of many rural workers and the frequency of less than full-time work, unemployment benefits may provide only modest help for the unemployed rural poor. In addition, unemployment insurance intentionally provides only a short-term solution.

Programs that improve employment opportunities for the rural unemployed clearly are important. Macroeconomic policies that assure the highest levels of national growth consistent with reasonable price stability are essential, because no other policies can work without adequate overall economic growth. High economic growth for the nation as a whole, however, may not help all areas. As the economic recovery since 1982 has demonstrated, even a relatively robust national economy is no assurance of job availability in all rural areas. Rural development programs for slowly growing or depressed rural areas are another component of rural poverty policy. (See Chapter 2 for more detailed ideas to help depressed rural areas.)

Even where there is strong local employment growth, the poor may find themselves at a serious disadvantage when competing for the newly created jobs. Programs such as JTPA that provide training, education, and job placement for the poor may be more useful in the long run.

Summary of Policy Options

Table 8.3 provides a summary of the policy options discussed above. Although we discussed each option as if it helped only one group, this table indicates additional groups that might benefit from a given policy change. For example, some female householders of AFDC families work, full time or part time (U.S. Congress, 1989:563), and they obviously could benefit from measures, such as an increase in the minimum wage, that help the working poor. Similarly, unemployed AFDC mothers could be helped by policies dealing with the unemployed.

The Future of Rural Poverty Policy

It seems unlikely that major new policies or program changes will be enacted in the near future specifically to benefit the rural poor. One reason is that most of the options would be expensive. Given both the need to reduce the budget deficit and the low priority currently given to rural poverty, no broad political consensus will mandate significant new spending on the problem. Therefore, we did not present a single, unified (and expensive) welfare system that would simultaneously aid all the rural poor. We suggested instead a series of policy changes that could be enacted independently of each other to help the four categories of the rural poor as budgetary conditions and interest in rural poverty allow.

Enacting policy changes to aid the rural poor will also be difficult because poverty continues to be perceived as an urban problem, especially a central-city problem. One indication of this perception is the recent emphasis in the poverty literature on the urban underclass (see Wilson, 1987). This view

TABLE 8.3 Summary of Policy Options to Help the Nonmetro Poor

| | Groups Affected | | | |
Policy Option	Families Eligible for AFDC	Aged and Disabled Poor	Working Poor	Unemployed Poor
Make AFDC benefits more uniform	X			
Index AFDC benefits for inflation	X			
Legislate higher Social Security or SSI benefits		X		
Make criteria for Social Security or SSI disability payments less stringent		X		
Increase the minimum wage	X		X	
Extend coverage of minimum wage	X		X	
Make changes in the EITC, income tax, or payroll taxes	X		X	
Extend Medicaid to all needy children			X	X
Target educational and training programs at poor who already work	X		X	
Institute macroeconomic policies that favor growth	X		X	X
Provide traditional education programs that are targeted at the unemployed, youths, and people outside the labor market	X			X
Legislate rural economic development programs	X		X	X

of poverty leads policymakers to design policies, such as the recently enacted FSA, for the poor in female-headed families. For poverty areas[12] of central cities, where 54 percent of all the poor and 71 percent of poor children live in female-headed families, this is a reasonable focus. But in rural areas, this family type contains only 31 percent of all the poor and 47 percent of poor children.

Simple questions of fairness should motivate some changes. Where a national commitment exists to provide transfers to certain categories of the poor, large variations in benefit levels from state to state clearly are unfair. AFDC and SSI are targets for change on these grounds. As an example, the maximum SSI benefit levels in 1987 for people with no income were sufficient to lift aged couples out of poverty in 11 states and aged individuals in 4 states.[13] Are the aged poor in the remaining states really less deserving of assistance?

We also question the fairness of allowing widespread poverty among full-time, year-round workers. The traditional reluctance to provide help to the poor who can work arose from fear that such aid would reduce their work effort (Salamon, 1978:68–69). Experimental evidence on this topic suggests, however, that assistance causes only moderate reductions in work by the poor.[14] In addition, any attempts to lift the nonworking poor out of poverty through transfers, while ignoring the working poor, may actually create disincentives for low-income workers (Levitan, 1985:140).

One does not need to be an advocate of rural causes to argue for more uniform benefits or aid to the working poor. As Schiller, author of *The Economics of Poverty and Discrimination* (1984:188), says:

> Public assistance programs are particularly inequitable in their disregard of the needs of poor families with working fathers. These working poor are excluded from assistance due to a misplaced concern for work motivation and a general desire to contain public expenditures. Also maltreated are those who are eligible for categorical assistance programs but reside in impoverished or unsympathetic states. Even after receiving assistance, they remain pitifully below acceptable standards of living.

For those able to work, solving the problems of rural poverty requires adequate employment opportunities and higher wages. For those not expected to work—the elderly and the disabled—changes in poverty status are tied to eligibility for transfer payments and to the level of benefits. Labor market strategies may also have only an indirect effect on rural poor children.

Finally, the severe recessions of the early 1980s demonstrated that the overall performance of the national economy has large and direct effects on the level of poverty in the United States (Hoppe and Bellamy, 1989). Efforts to reduce poverty while the national economy falters will fail. Likewise, the current recovery, which has been slower in rural areas, suggests that economic growth for the nation as a whole may not necessarily narrow the differences in the poverty rate between rural and urban places. Rural areas, and many of the rural poor, are disadvantaged in competing for new jobs and higher incomes even in a growing economy. Public programs, when they are carefully targeted, can assist the development of rural areas and upgrade the human capital of the rural poor who can work.

Notes

1. "Rural" and "nonmetro" are used interchangeably in this chapter. Areas outside of metropolitan statistical areas (MSAs) are nonmetropolitan (nonmetro). Generally speaking, an MSA is a county or group of counties with a city or an urban population concentration of at least 50,000 (U.S. Census Bureau, 1988a:151).

2. Summarized from Salamon (1978:66–70).

3. General Assistance is a relatively minor program, particularly in nonmetro areas. General Assistance recipients are concentrated in large cities (Levitan, 1985:41–42), and the program provides few benefits in nonmetro areas, except in the Northeast (Bentley, 1986:23–24). We discuss General Assistance anyway, however, because it is a good example of how the English Poor Laws continue to influence our welfare system.

4. Discussion of policy options reflects existing legislation as of late January 1990, when this chapter was last revised.

5. Strictly speaking, "retired" is not the same as "elderly." People may retire before they are 65, some elderly may give another reason for not working, and some elderly continue to work. In addition, elderly women keeping house may not consider themselves retired.

6. As used here, public assistance includes AFDC and general assistance, but excludes SSI and in-kind programs such as food stamps.

7. Food stamps, which are indexed for food inflation, help alleviate part of the decline in real AFDC benefits.

8. Simple regression was used to examine the relationship between: the maximum AFDC benefit in January 1987 for a family of three and the percent of AFDC units in fiscal year 1987 that reported earned income. The observations were the 50 states plus the District of Columbia, and the data were from U.S. Congress, 1989 (pp. 546–547 and 576–578). The R^2 for the regression was .1757.

9. While letting the surplus accumulate on paper, Congress currently borrows against it to help cover the deficit in the rest of the federal budget. In January 1990, Senator Daniel Moynihan of New York proposed a Social Security payroll tax cut to stop the growth of the program's surplus (Dentzer, 1990:16–18). His proposal would prevent the use of regressive Social Security payroll tax to offset deficit spending.

10. A full-time, year-round job, as defined here, provides 40 hours of work per week for 52 weeks per year.

11. For example, nine states automatically set their minimum wage rates to equal or exceed the federal minimum and do not exempt small businesses (U.S. Department of Labor, 1989).

12. Metro poverty areas are census tracts where at least 20 percent of the population was poor based on the 1980 Census (U.S. Census Bureau, 1988a:152).

13. Based on data in U.S. Congress (1989:681–684, 689).

14. The negative income tax experiments found that a guaranteed income reduced work effort by an average of 17 percent among women but only 7 percent among men (Munnell, 1987:33–34). These reductions were larger than advocates had hoped for, but less than predictions from earlier, nonexperimental research.

References

Bentley, Susan E. 1986. "Income security and the nonmetro poor." *Southern Rural Sociology* 4:17–30.

Ciccone, Charles V. 1988. *Minimum Wage Earnings and the EITC: Making the Connection.* Washington, D.C.: Library of Congress, Congressional Research Service, 88-736E. November 30.

———. 1989. *Provisions of H.R. 2710, 101st Congress, The Fair Labor Standards Amendments of 1988.* Washington, D.C.: Library of Congress, Congressional Research Service. Memorandum. December 7.

Deavers, Kenneth L., Robert A. Hoppe, and Peggy J. Ross. 1986. "Public policy and rural poverty: A view from the 1980s." *Policy Studies Journal* 15(2):291–309.

Dentzer, Susan. 1990. "Paycheck politics: A plan to cut Social Security taxes makes Washington flip out." *U.S. News & World Report* 108:(4):16–18.

Ellwood, David T. 1988. *Poor Support: Poverty in the American Family.* New York: Basic Books.

Heclo, Hugh. 1986. "The political foundations of antipoverty policy." Pp. 312–340 in Sheldon H. Danziger and Daniel H. Weinberg, eds., *Fighting Poverty: What Works and What Doesn't.* Cambridge, Mass.: Harvard University Press.

Hoppe, Robert A., and Donald L. Bellamy. 1989. "Rural poverty: A continuing problem." Paper presented to the Washington Statistical Society.

Hoppe, Robert A., and William E. Saupe. 1982. *Transfer Payments in Nonmetropolitan Areas.* ERS Staff Report No. AGES820827. Washington, D.C.: U.S. Department of Agriculture, Economic Research Service.

Institute for Research on Poverty (University of Wisconsin–Madison). 1980. "On not reaching the rural poor: Urban bias in poverty policy." *Focus* 4(2):5–8.

Levitan, Sar A. 1985. *Programs in Aid of the Poor.* Baltimore: The Johns Hopkins University Press.

Munnell, Alicia H. 1987. "Lessons from the income maintenance experiments: An overview." *New England Economic Review* May/June:32–45.

Rauch, Jonathan. 1988. "Cracking the nest egg." *National Journal* September 24:2395–2398.

Rich, Spencer. 1988. "House offers to cut back welfare bill." *Washington Post* July 29:A3.

Rovner, Julie. 1988. "Congress approves overhaul of welfare system," *Congressional Quarterly Weekly Report* 46(41):2825–2831.

———. 1989. "Congress shifts its attention to the working poor." *Congressional Quarterly Weekly Report* 47(7):326–328.

Salamon, Lester M. 1978. *Welfare: The Elusive Consensus.* New York: Praeger.

Schiller, Bradley R. 1984. *The Economics of Poverty and Discrimination.* Englewood Cliffs, N.J.: Prentice Hall.

Smith, Ralph E., and Bruce Vavrichek. 1987. "The minimum wage: Its relation to incomes and poverty." *Monthly Labor Review* 110(6):24–30.

Solomon, Carmen D. 1988. *The Family Support Act of 1988: How It Changes the Aid to Families with Dependent Children (AFDC) and Child Support Enforcement Programs.* 88–79 EPW. Washington D.C.: Library of Congress, Congressional Research Service. November 7.

U.S. Census Bureau. 1988a. *Poverty in the United States: 1986.* Series P-60, 160. Washington, D.C.: U.S. Government Printing Office.

———. 1988b. Unpublished tables from the March 1988 *Current Population Survey.*

U.S. Congress. 1974. *Studies in Public Welfare, Handbook of Public Income Transfer Programs: 1975*. A staff study prepared for the use of the Subcommittee on Fiscal Policy of the Joint Economic Committee. Washington, D.C.: 93rd Congress, Second Session.

———. 1989. *Background Material and Data on Programs Within the Jurisdiction of the Committee on Ways and Means*. Prepared for the use of the Committee on Ways and Means, U.S. House of Representatives, by its staff. Washington, D.C.: 101st Congress, First Session.

U.S. Department of Commerce, Bureau of Economic Analysis. 1988. Unpublished tables of total, metro, and nonmetro employment by industry, 1969–1986.

U.S. Department of Labor, Division of State Employment Standards Programs. 1989. Minimum Wage and Overtime Premium Pay Standards Applicable to Nonsupervisory NONFARM Private Sector Employment Under State and Federal Laws, August 14, 1989. Photocopied table.

Watkins, Julia M. and Dennis A. Watkins. 1984. *Social Policy and the Rural Setting*. New York: Springer.

Williams, Robin M., Jr. 1970. *American Society: A Sociological Interpretation*. New York: Alfred A. Knopf.

Wilson, William Julius. 1987. *The Truly Disadvantaged: The Inner City, the Underclass, and Public Policy*. Chicago: The University of Chicago Press.

9

Work and Poverty in Rural America

Ann R. Tickamyer and Cynthia M. Duncan

Working poverty is a serious problem in rural areas. Jobs are scarce relative to the number of job seekers and steady, good-paying work is hard to obtain. Consequently, many rural workers and families are poor even though they work as much as they can. In 1987, 10 percent of the 11.3 million working householders in rural America were poor. Two-thirds of the working poor were unable to find full-time work, while one-third worked full time but for such low wages that they could not escape poverty.

The plight of the working poor is linked to the structure of opportunity in rural America and to the development of the skills of its labor force. Policy directed toward the working poor must address both human resource and economic development issues to consider ways to raise the income of a population for whom work effort is not at issue. Options available include encouraging migration from economically depressed areas, improving the skills and education of rural workers, raising wages and benefits for existing jobs, and developing depressed rural economies to bring more and better jobs. Each of these has played a role in past policies and will continue to be part of the policy debate for designing future programs.

This chapter considers possible policy directions for the rural working poor in the 1990s, based on the premise that continued lack of such a policy will perpetuate the high incidence of poverty among working householders in those areas with constricted work opportunities. Such policies and programs are necessary to the continued economic health of the entire country, because at the same time that rural areas languish from lack of employment, high-growth centers and industries face an impending shortage of skilled labor. We review policy to deal with rural poverty among able-bodied adults over the last several decades, including both economic development programs and human resource policies. We argue that policy issues for the future will include a combination of national efforts to make work pay, youth service programs designed to draw young people into the labor force, and specific rural programs to target public sector jobs for areas where no other opportunities exist. The goal is to improve options for individuals and communities whose current choices are limited. These policies are most likely to come from national policy initiatives, but they could be augmented effectively by state and local initiatives. The quality of state and local program implementation would be critical to their success.

Policy Context

Poverty, Work, and Workers

The central theme in the current poverty policy debate focuses on the work effort of poor people and the degree to which welfare programs provide incentives or disincentives to work. The welfare reform bill that Congress passed in late 1988 responded to these concerns by requiring greater work participation from those receiving public assistance. Much of this discussion concerns stereotypes based on popular misconceptions about the poor, rather than on solid analyses of their circumstances and behavior (Duncan and Tickamyer, 1988). Empirical analyses of work and poverty show that many of the able-bodied poor already work, especially in rural areas, but they cannot find employment that is either steady enough or pays enough to lift them out of poverty. Indeed, as Deavers and Hoppe point out in Chapter 8, compared to urban areas, the working poor make up a larger proportion of poor persons in rural areas; rural areas have higher rates of poverty among workers; poor workers in rural areas work more hours and jobs than their urban counterparts; and, finally, more children in rural areas grow up in poor households with at least one worker. In addition to the large numbers of actual workers at any particular time, there are also large numbers of unemployed and discouraged workers who augment the rolls of the working poor (O'Hare, 1988; Levitan and Shapiro, 1987; Tickamyer, 1988).

These statistics indicate that the problem is not lack of individual work effort or desire to work. Rather, rural poverty is explained by a complex combination of the lack of good jobs in rural areas, a regional imbalance in the supply and demand for labor, and deficits in the human capital of rural workers and communities. Economic development practitioners throughout the rural United States can document time after time when local plants have advertised only a handful of job openings and yet received hundreds of applicants. In rural areas it appears that people are glad for any work they can find, and one study showed that even "make work" jobs that accompany workfare experiments are welcomed by householders receiving public assistance (MDRC, 1986). Furthermore, analysis of job vacancies for welfare recipients shows that there are clearly not enough jobs for the unemployed, let alone for "work-qualified" AFDC recipients (Bloomquist, Jensen, and Teixeira, 1988). Ironically, while rural areas and workers become increasingly marginalized by diminished opportunities, analysts predict a skilled labor shortage looming ahead for urban areas (*Business Week*, 1987).

However, lack of skills and low educational attainment mean that rural workers will be unable to help fill this demand, just as lack of facilities and infrastructure development make it unlikely that well-paid jobs will be located in rural areas. The options for individuals and communities are severely limited.

When poverty debate focuses on individual motivation, the structural problems associated with lack of employment are ignored. These debates have neglected penetrating social and economic analysis of why the working poor are such a significant segment of the poverty population and why this is especially the case in rural areas. To answer these questions we must examine the economic structure of rural America, recent changes in the national economy, and how the opportunity structure intersects with persons living in these places.

The Rural Economy and Opportunity Structure

Although rural economies have been among the hardest hit during the recession and economic restructuring of the 1980s, the roots of the rural economic crisis have been apparent for decades. Research on rural labor markets demonstrates that rural poverty has persisted for decades because of the volatility and instability of rural labor markets and significant inequality in the distribution of income, jobs, and resources (cf. Tickamyer and Duncan, 1990).

Economic Instability. Many industries in rural areas are inherently unstable because they are vulnerable to cyclical trends. For example, resource-based markets change according to unpredictable production factors, including weather conditions, labor relations, and the affect of international relations on commodity prices and international trade. Rural workers in resource industries expect booms and busts in their local economies, and most families working in the agriculture, mining, or timber industry can recount ups and downs experienced by each generation. They have always pieced together a variety of income-generating activities, combining timber work with dairy farming, odd jobs with coal mining, and so forth. However, most analysts agree that the "bust" in resource industries during the recession of the early 1980s appears to represent a structural and not merely a cyclical downturn.

Rural manufacturing also appears to have turned a corner. Since the 1960s, rural economies have become increasingly dependent on manufacturing employment as companies that had routinized production moved to rural areas where wages were lower and where job scarcity made people grateful for any opportunity for work. By 1980 manufacturing made up the largest sector of rural employment. While these jobs mostly paid low wages to low-skilled workers, they nonetheless brought an element of stability and diversity to rural economies accustomed to volatile resource-based industries. In the 1980s growth slowed, and the recessions of the early 1980s led to reduced manufacturing employment in rural as well as urban areas. Since that time the manufacturing sector has stabilized with little expectation of significant renewed growth. Economists predict that most growth will be in the service-producing industries, which are increasingly likely to locate within the embrace of expanding metropolitan areas (Noyelle, 1986; Rosenfeld, Bergman, and Rubin, 1988).

Labor Market Inequality. Changes in labor market opportunities have affected some rural areas and workers more than others. Minorities and women are especially vulnerable to tight labor markets and limited opportunities, and higher levels of poverty and working poverty are particularly prevalent among these groups in those rural labor markets dominated by industries with seasonal or volatile demand for labor, such as agriculture and resource extraction (Tickamyer and Tickamyer, 1988; Tickamyer, 1988). In mining areas particularly, both income and work are ill-distributed, and poverty rates are high even during periods of growth. When good jobs are scarce, public sector jobs are much sought after, and control over them leads to a corrupt patronage system that exacerbates inequality (Duncan, 1988).

Recent studies suggest that the scarcity of work and the inadequacy of wages are becoming even more serious problems for young people in rural areas. Poverty for young adults aged 18 to 44 increased 55 percent between 1979 and 1986, compared to 29 percent overall and 22 percent for older workers (O'Hare, 1988). In some remote areas like the Appalachian coal fields, more than one-third of the young people were idle in 1980, neither working, looking for work, nor in school. Out-migration reminiscent of the 1950s and 1960s has resumed, and those remaining scramble to do odd jobs, trade goods and services in the informal sector, and piece together livelihoods with work and income from a variety of sources.

In sum, the rural economy of the 1980s is characterized by high unemployment and underemployment rates for rural residents, high rates of discouraged workers, high rates of out-migration, and a large number of the working poor. While these trends mark a reversal from the temporary turnaround of the 1970s, they nonetheless reflect long-term problems associated with the marginality, volatility, instability, and inequality of rural labor markets. Furthermore, there appears to be little prospect for immediate improvement. Although the recession, farm crisis, and energy glut have somewhat abated, the level of the working poverty remains high. All economic forecasts continue to point to shifts in U.S. industries away from goods-producing to service sector jobs, and clearly this shift hurts rural areas particularly hard. The overall supply of jobs in rural areas is unlikely to grow, and demand for unskilled labor throughout the United States is likely to decrease further. Without policy intervention, the plight of the rural working poor will only grow worse.

Human Resource Issues. While the shape of the economy defines the demand side of the opportunity structure, human resource and labor supply also play important parts in structuring opportunity. At the same time that there is little prospect for revitalization of rural economies, the characteristics of rural workers neither encourage new economic growth within rural areas nor increase their chances for employment in the larger economy.

Low educational attainment is foremost among the factors which limit both the supply and demand sides of the rural economy. Educational facilities in rural areas are often inadequate, poorly funded, and the object of political manipulation. This is partly the result of fewer resources and partly the reflection of the realities of rural labor markets. There are few opportunities to find jobs requiring high skill or education levels. In fact, historically in some rural regions the highest paying jobs have discouraged continued education. For example, the mining industry of Appalachia and the unionized paper mills of northern New England offer only high-wage jobs that do not require much education. Many men discontinue education for jobs in these relatively highly paid but volatile industries. Economic hardship for these workers resulting from cyclical trends is compounded by structural shifts as employment in these industries contracts with the development of more capital-intensive production processes. Without education these workers have few options, even if other jobs are available.

At the same time, inferior educational systems and educational attainment limit the likelihood of economic growth in depressed areas. Growth industries are concerned with the quality of the labor force as well as the cost. While rural areas may supply cheap labor, they lack skilled labor, and thus discourage prospects for new industrial development. Finally, the lack of opportunity means that those who do get a good education are unlikely to remain where jobs are scarce. This out-migration depletes the supply of skilled labor in rural areas. It also creates ambivalence about education among those left behind which may perpetuate the failure to support improved educational facilities and standards. Education simultaneously becomes the means of mobility for educated workers and the force which accelerates the separation of families and the demise of communities.

Policy Options

Past Policies

Past policies addressing the lack of stable jobs have included both economic development policies, to stimulate new jobs and economic diversity in depressed areas, and human resource policies, to build the human capital of potential workers. We review the impact of these past efforts and then suggest some new directions.

Economic Development Programs and Strategies. With the exception of New Deal policies designed to relieve temporary economic distress in the 1930s, U.S. economic policy before the 1960s largely followed the neoclassical economists' model of growth promotion in the private sector and a laissez-faire stance toward the social and spatial distribution of growth (North, 1961; Kolko, 1963; Chinitz, 1974). It was assumed that workers would move to find jobs and that capital would move to find workers. Any public intervention to affect this flow of labor and capital was deemed an unnecessary and unwelcome intervention into the private sector's domain (Nugent and Yotopoulos, 1979).

After World War II, regional development scholars argued that market-driven economies stimulated polarized growth, with rich areas gaining at the expense of depressed areas that became trapped in a cycle of under-development (Hirschman, 1958; Myrdal, 1973). They advocated a variety of public investment strategies to stimulate new growth in lagging economies and thereby achieve more balanced regional growth (Hansen, 1980; Newman, 1980). However, these arguments were not taken seriously by policymakers until the 1960s.

By the early 1960s, unemployment was higher than it had been in 25 years, and the impact of the recession plagued the industrial Northeast as well as rural areas dependent on resource extraction. Congress passed the Area Redevelopment Act (ARA) in 1961, and other public development programs were subsequently developed to directly address regional inequal-ities and concentrated, chronic employment problems. Development scholars consider the ARA a significant departure from the federal government's previous laissez-faire policy that made out-migration the de facto solution to unemployment and underemployment in rural areas (Miernyk, 1980; Newman, 1980). The clearly understood rationale for the act was to assist areas with combined problems of low income and high unemployment or underemployment. Loans and grants were made either to develop infra-structure or to invest directly in private enterprises that would locate in depressed areas.

Despite Congress's apparent commitment to support development inter-ventions, neither this program nor the more public works–oriented Economic Development Administration (EDA) programs which soon superseded it had sufficient resources to make the substantial investment necessary to stimulate lagging economies. To gain political support in Congress, eligibility for participation was extended to include areas that were not severely depressed, thus diluting potential impact because limited funds for investment had to be spread over much greater areas. Furthermore, local and state political forces had tremendous influence on the allocation and shape of investments, further undermining the potential for significant developmental impact in some of the most depressed areas (Briggs, 1986).

The combination of political pressures to spread resources broadly and local pressure to ensure that publicly supported development did not compete with private enterprises complicated program delivery at every juncture. In this politically sensitive environment, program administrators and local politicians generally regarded public works as safer and less controversial investments (Miernyk, 1982). In fact, in many poorer rural states, development funds were used to subsidize provision of basic public services for residents rather than invested in development efforts to stimulate new enterprises and jobs. Two-thirds of the EDA budget went to public works, and of the remaining development funds only 13 percent were used for business loans (Miernyk, 1980).

Similarly, the Appalachian Regional Commission (ARC), established in 1965 to address underdevelopment problems in the notoriously poor Ap-palachian region, represented in principle a commitment to public policy initiative to address employment problems in a depressed region. Like ARA and EDA, ARC was designed to include a large area to secure political backing; it therefore had inadequate funds and political leeway to concentrate investment in ways that might address development problems. Again, the ARC adopted a politically safer tack of investment in basic public infrastructure. Almost 60 percent of the funds went to highway development, and the balance has, in many ways, bolstered the deficient resources of the local public governments by financing sewer and water systems, clinics, and vocational education. While these public goods have improved the quality of life in many Appalachian communities, they do not contribute to diversifying their economies.

Debate continues over the effectiveness of these development programs. Some argue that the resources were spread too thin (Hansen, 1980), others argue that political pressures made it impossible to accomplish development goals (Pressman and Wildavsky, 1973). Many regional development scholars in the United States would argue that resources for regional economic development have never been adequate, and thus evaluations tell little about the strategies' potential. In addition, political constraints invariably confound even the best development practitioners' goals, and macroeconomic trends can subvert even the most diligent planning and investment strategies of development policymakers.

Development practitioners and scholars who have worked in the field generally agree that the fundamentally political character of economic development makes it extremely difficult to achieve progress (Hirschman, 1958; Myrdal, 1973; Pressman and Wildavsky, 1973; Miernyk, 1980; Hansen, 1980; Newman, 1980). Development inherently entails change, and change challenges the status quo of the existing political and social structure. Struggles over who gains and who loses with the introduction of new resources and new actors in the economy are always present, and they frequently undermine a project's success or alter its impact. The political nature of development at the local level, combined with ideological debate over the role of the public sector in the economy and with debates over the allocation of whatever public resources are made available, make economic development very difficult to implement and to evaluate. Human resource programs seem quite simple in comparison.

Human Resource Policies. Human resource policies emerged at the same time as these federal development initiatives. Just as growing economic problems in the early 1960s had given rise to the first national development programs, the accompanying growth in unemployment stimulated congressional concern that led first to the Manpower Development and Training Act and later to the Job Corps, the Comprehensive Employment and Training Act (CETA), and its more private sector–oriented heir, the Job Partnership Training Act (JTPA). Although these programs have never generated great controversy since their inception (Sundquist, 1968; Levitan and Gallo, 1988), their form and level of support have been shaped by the prevailing political climate.

When the Manpower Development Training Act was first passed by Congress, the guiding assumptions were that problems of unemployment were due to the inadequate skills and training of potential workers. However, it soon became clear that employment was reviving in many growing economies while those in the inner cities and remote rural areas were bypassed (Levitan and Gallo, 1988). Subsequently, training programs were frequently incorporated into development programs as part of a package of incentives to attract private enterprises to depressed areas.

Although federal commitment to these programs has fluctuated over the last 20 years (from a low of $4.9 million in 1967 to a high of $18.1 billion in 1978, with a 1986 level of $5.3 billion), the fluctuation largely reflects political trends rather than changes based on evaluations of program efficacy (Levitan and Gallo, 1988; Ross and Rosenfeld, 1987). The Job Corps, while expensive, is praised by both liberal and conservative policymakers for its success in helping severely disadvantaged youth gain training crucial for their participation in the labor force. Similarly, basic skills training has had remarkable success rates in helping the poor and unskilled gain their first foothold in the work world (Sum, Taggart, and Berlin, 1987). Even the less comprehensive, more private sector–oriented JTPA is widely praised by politicians (Levitan and Gallo, 1988).

Future Policies

These past policy experiences suggest that broad-based area development programs are riddled with obstacles and that people-oriented policies that can benefit both urban and rural workers are more likely to gain political backing. Within these political parameters, two general areas deserve attention. First, the rural working poor would benefit significantly from national policies that "make work pay," as policy analysts call it, wherever they live and work. Second, policymakers should consider much greater investment in human resource programs, including greatly expanded youth employment programs and public service employment for rural areas.

National Policies to Make Work Pay. During the early 1990s, policymakers will face continued problems arising from the restructuring of the national economy and the way the shift from goods-producing to service-producing industries is changing the occupational structure and labor force needs. While the debate about growing inequality persists (Harrison and Bluestone, 1988), there is nonetheless growing concern among policymakers that too many Americans are poor even though they work.

Policy analysts argue that those who are working and still poor need policy that makes work pay (Berlin and Sum, 1988; Ellwood, 1988; Reischauer, 1988; and Greenstein, 1987). In *Poor Support*, Ellwood distinguishes poverty among single heads of households, whose poverty reflects a complex web of social problems, and poverty among two-parent families, the working poor, whose poverty is the result of low wages or unemployment. Ellwood and others make a convincing case for raising the minimum wage so that full-time, full-year household heads can raise their families out of poverty by working. Analysts also propose expanding the earned-income tax credit and Medicaid coverage. Provisions in the Family Support Act that extend coverage of Aid to Families with Dependent Children to two-parent families provide rural families an important new buffer during bad times. (See Chapter 8 for more details of problems and advantages of these measures.)

But for many of the working poor in rural areas, poverty is caused not only by low-income and low-wage levels but also by the lack of stable, year-round work opportunities. Diversifying rural economies would certainly help these problems, but past policy experience suggests that the level of public investment required is impractical under current fiscal conditions and in the current policy climate. Two policy directions, however, deserve consideration.

Specific Rural Initiatives. Expanded efforts to provide public service employment would be an important policy initiative to help the problems of volatile and scarce work in rural areas. Some public employment occurs already—prisons are often located in rural areas, and in the past, military bases frequently saved remote areas from complete decline when natural resource industries underwent transitions. But conscious efforts not only to achieve regional balance in those public programs that exist but also to increase programs that support conservation of natural resources and recreation areas could have a profound effect on some of the most depressed rural areas with the highest numbers of part-year or part-time workers.

Past experience suggests that public sector employment programs and human resource investment must be coordinated to succeed. Evaluation of CETA programs suggests that public service employment has been an important component of human resource policies, particularly in rural areas (Briggs, 1986; Briggs, Rungeling, and Smith, 1984; Levitan and Shapiro, 1987; Nathan and Cook, 1981). Public sector employment is steadier and better paying than most rural jobs, and therefore government work is highly sought. Since public resources are more limited in rural areas where the economy is less diverse and weaker, these jobs can provide much-needed public services without substituting for work that would otherwise be provided by local governments. Similarly, public sector employment is less likely to compete with private employers in rural areas because jobs, rather than workers, are in great demand. Numerous analysts familiar with human resource development programs argue that their effectiveness has been demonstrated time and time again (Briggs, Rungeling, and Smith, 1984; Levitan and Gallo, 1988; Levitan, Mangum, and Marshall, 1982; Berlin and Sum, 1988). But as with the development programs themselves, their effectiveness has been limited by funding levels and by political pressures to disperse benefits widely.

Today, however, the shift in the national economy toward service-producing goods and the expectation that growth industries will be those that are more flexible and employ skilled workers have made it clear to most rural policy analysts that human resource development is a sound economic policy, critical to the nation's future prosperity. Rural youth today, like inner-city youth, are isolated from the mainstream economy and see few avenues for successful participation in the labor force. Expanded training programs for young people, including some variations of current proposals to establish a national youth service program, could simultaneously expand these young people's horizons, provide basic skills training which they are clearly not obtaining from local public schools, and, in the long run, contribute crucial human capital to the nation's future labor force.

Conclusion

In the long run, new economic development initiatives that include national and regional planning will be necessary to revitalize rural economies and reverse the trend toward rural decline (see Chapter 2). While expanded policies to diversify rural economies in remote areas—the traditional economic development programs such as EDA and ARC—are unlikely to gain political support in the current fiscal climate, human resource policies are less controversial and assist people wherever they work. Given predictions of an impending labor shortage in the United States, investing in young rural workers would be in the national interest and would give workers the opportunity to find better jobs with more options for where they choose to work. Combining these programs with a renewed commitment to public service would directly benefit rural areas and their 54 million rural residents as well as provide more fertile ground for future development policies.

References

Berlin, Gordon, and Andrew Sum. 1988. "Toward a more perfect union: Basic skills, poor families and our economic future." Project on Social Welfare and the American Future, Occasional Paper No. 3. New York: Ford Foundation.

Bloomquist, Leonard, Leif Jensen, and Ruy Teixeira. 1988. "Workfare and nonmetro America: An assessment of the employment opportunities for nonmetro welfare clients." Paper presented at the 9th annual research conference of the Association for Public Policy Analysis and Management (APPAM), Bethesda, Md., October.

Briggs, Vernon. 1986. "Rural labor markets: The role of government." Pp. 160–183 in M. Killian, L. Bloomquist, S. Pendleton, and D. McGranahan, eds., *Symposium on Rural Labor Markets Research Issues.* Washington, D.C.: USDA, Economic Research Service.

Briggs, Vernon, Brian Rungeling, and Lewis Smith. 1984. *Public Service Employment in the Rural South.* Austin, Tex.: University of Texas, Bureau of Business Research.

Business Week. 1987. "The coming labor shortage." August 10:48–53.

Chinitz, Benjamin. 1974. "Regional development." Pp. 247–273 in James W. McKie, ed., *Social Responsibility and the Business Predicament.* Washington, D.C.: Brookings Institute.

Duncan, Cynthia. 1988. "Poverty, work, and social change in the Appalachian coal fields." Paper presented at the annual meetings of the American Sociological Association, Atlanta, August.

Duncan, Cynthia, and Ann Tickamyer. 1988. "Poverty research and policy for rural America." *American Sociologist* 19(3):243–259.

Ellwood, David. 1988. *Poor Support.* New York: Basic Books.

Greenstein, Robert. 1987. "The rural poor—Working and non-working." Presentation at the Rural Economic Development in the 1980s seminar, National Rural Electric Cooperative Association and the Aspen Institute, November.

Hansen, Nils. 1980. "Policies for nonmetropolitan areas." *Growth and Change* 11(2):7–13.

Harrison, Bennett, and Barry Bluestone. 1988. *The Great U-Turn.* New York: Basic Books.

Hirschman, Albert. 1958. *The Strategy of Economic Development.* New Haven: Yale University Press.

Kolko, Gabriel. 1963. *The Triumph of Conservatism: A Reinterpretation of American History, 1900–1916.* New York: Free Press.

Levitan, Sar, and Frank Gallo. 1988. *A Second Chance: Training for Jobs.* Kalamazoo, Mich.: W. E. UpJohn Institute for Employment Research.

Levitan, Sar, and Isaac Shapiro. 1987. *Working but Poor: Americas Contradiction.* Baltimore: Johns Hopkins University Press.

Levitan, Sar, Garth Mangum, and Ray Marshall. 1982. *Human Resources and Labor Markets.* New York: Harper and Row.

MDRC (Manpower Demonstration Research Corporation, West Virginia). 1986. "Final report on the community work experience demonstrations." Executive summary. New York: MDRC. September.

Miernyk, William. 1980. "An evaluation: The tools of regional development policy." *Growth and Change* 11(2):2–6.

Miernyk, William. 1982. *Regional Analysis and Regional Policy.* Cambridge, Mass.: Oelgeshlager, Gunn, and Hain.

Myrdal, Gunnar. 1973. "Growth and social justice." *World Development* 1(3,4):119–120.

Nathan, Richard, and Robert Cook. 1981. *Public Service Employment: A Field Evaluation.* Washington, D.C.: Brookings Institute.

Newman, Monroe. 1980. "The future of multistate regional commissions." *Growth and Change* 11(2):14–18.

North, Douglas. 1961. *Economic Growth of the United States, 1790–1860.* Englewood Cliffs, N.J.: Prentice-Hall.

Noyelle, Thierry. 1986. "Economic transformation." *Annals of the American Academy of Political and Social Science* 488(Nov.):9–17.

Nugent, Jeffrey, and Pan Yotopoulos. 1979. "What has orthodox development economics learned from recent experience?" *World Development* 7:541–554.

O'Hare, William. 1988. *The Rise of Poverty in Rural America.* Washington, D.C.: Population Reference Bureau. July.

Pressman, Jeffrey, and Aaron Wildavsky. 1973. *Implementation.* Berkeley: University of California Press.

Reischauer, Robert. 1988. "Welfare reform and the working poor." *Reducing Poverty and Dependency.* Washington, D.C.: National Academy Press, Center for National Policy.

Rosenfeld, Stuart, Edward Bergman, and Sara Rubin. 1988. *Charting Growth in the Rural South: A Re-View of After the Factories.* Research Triangle, N.C.: Southern Growth Policies Board.

Ross, Peggy, and Stuart Rosenfeld. 1987. "Human resource policies and economic development." Chapter 15 in D. L. Brown, J. N. Reid, H. Bluestone, D. McGranahan, and S. M. Mazie, eds., *Rural Economic Development in the 1980's.* Washington, D.C.: USDA, Economic Research Service.

Sum, Andrew, and Robert Taggart with Gordon Berlin. 1987. "Cutting through." Ford Foundation project on Social Welfare and the American Future, Occasional Paper. New York: Ford Foundation.

Sundquist, James. 1968. *Politics and Policy: The Eisenhower, Kennedy, and Johnson Years.* Washington, D.C.: Brookings Institute.

Tickamyer, Ann. 1988. "The working poor in rural labor markets in the southeastern United States." Paper presented at the annual meetings of the American Sociological Association, Atlanta, August.

Tickamyer, Ann, and Cynthia Duncan. 1990. "Poverty and opportunity structure in rural America." *Annual Review of Sociology* 16:67–86.

Tickamyer, Ann, and Cecil Tickamyer. 1988. "Gender and poverty in central Appalachia." *Social Science Quarterly* 69(4):874–891.

10

Meeting Rural Family Needs

Janet L. Bokemeier and Lorraine E. Garkovich

One out of four American families who live in rural areas experiences chronic stresses that are rooted in the social risks associated with rural residence. A critical purpose of public policies for the 1990s should be to reduce the impact of these stresses so that rural families can more effectively utilize their personal and community resources to improve their well-being. To achieve this purpose, policymakers must recognize that (1) rural and urban families and communities differ to such a degree that social policies and programs designed to address urban family needs are both inappropriate and ineffective for rural families, (2) rural family needs cannot be addressed in isolation from the condition of the communities in which these families are located, and (3) rural social and economic conditions are very diverse, which necessitates developing local initiatives that address the unique nature of the social and economic problems confronting their rural families.

Family Stress and the Rural Environment

In general, stress refers to threats to the steady state of the family which may arise from a variety of conditions either internal to the family (e.g., alcoholism) or from the external environment (e.g., high unemployment). Some stresses are unexpected and arise from a unique situation (e.g., a sudden illness, a flood). But other stresses are chronic. "A chronic stressor is a situation that runs a long course, is difficult to amend, and has a debilitating effect on the family" (Boss, 1987:699). The debilitating effect of a chronic stressor is primarily due to the uncertainty concerning its cause, development, and eventual outcome. In some situations, chronic stressors may "pile up" or accumulate. If chronic stressors begin to accumulate, they may exceed the family's resources to meet these growing pressures and create a situation of family strain.

We will argue that the characteristics of the rural social environment, to a greater degree than the urban, generate chronic stresses that pile up and produce strains. While all families experience stresses, on the average rural families more continuously face a greater variety of stresses, and with fewer coping resources or supporting services than do urban families. As a result, rural families are more likely to experience family strain and an attendant restructuring of the family system that may lead to a breakdown of the family.

What chronic stressors are associated with the rural environment? Across most indicators of well-being, compared to urban families, rural American families have significantly more disadvantages, including higher rates of poverty, unemployment, underemployment, and mortality. Rural families also have less education, fewer vocational training opportunities, and more limited access to health-care services, social services, and public water systems. The consistency and range of the comparative disadvantages between rural and urban families is systematic, indicating that residence constitutes a critical factor conditioning life opportunities (Zvonkovic, Guss, and Ladd, 1988). This chapter examines the effects of three chronic stressors from the external environment that seriously threaten the well-being of rural families: financial instability; inadequate housing; and inadequate, inaccessible, and inappropriate social services.

Financial Instability

Rural residents are more likely than urban residents to experience financial instability throughout their lives. Financial instability is a chronic stressor because it is enduring and intractable, its source or cause is difficult to identify, its course is uncertain, and its consequences are far-reaching (see Chapters 8 and 9). The pervasive financial instability in the rural environment is an encompassing stressor for rural families because it exacerbates the stress associated with many other conditions in the rural environment.

Most rural families are at risk of financial instability. Rural families with gainful employment and an income over the poverty level experience financial instability as do the rural poor. In the abstract, *financial instability* refers to the limitation of economic security created by the intersection of the range of opportunities available through local economic institutions, the individual's and family's relationship to these economic institutions, and the family's economic expectations. Financial instability affects those families with incomes below official poverty guidelines and those families whose incomes, while above the poverty line, do not provide a dependable cash flow adequate to sustain a quality of life or standard of living comparable to that of urban families. Financially unstable families must cope with higher day-to-day risks due to the inadequacy or uncertainty of their economic resources and their greater likelihood of job turnover, underemployment, and unemployment. These families have no buffer against unexpected events and their economic consequences (e.g., a furnace breaking down, a sudden illness) and they are vulnerable to changes in their environment that threaten their cash flow (e.g., changes in levels of assistance, no overtime this month) or the adequacy of their cash flow in sustaining the family economy (e.g., increases in heating oil prices). Financial instability is associated with residence in communities with limited economic diversity and poorly developed human resources.

Inadequate Housing

The size and the nature of the rural housing market represents another chronic stressor for rural families. Although they make up only 14 percent of the nation's households, rural Americans occupy 22 percent of the nation's housing units that have severe physical deficiencies. The rural housing crisis is especially serious in the South where rural households are three times more likely than their counterparts in the rest of the nation to occupy substandard housing. The housing stock in many rural communities is insufficient to meet demand, especially given the chronic financial instability that affects many families. Without a stable source of income, many families are unable to meet the minimum financing requirements established by lenders and therefore have limited access to the housing market. For example, in 1985, four out of ten rural poor families paid at least half of their income on housing and utilities and one out of four actually paid 70 percent or more of their income for housing. Since *affordable housing* is defined as costs at 30 percent or less of income, the rural housing market clearly offers limited alternatives for the rural poor. Moreover, the rural housing market is less diverse in terms of types of structures (e.g., single-family versus multifamily units) and the range of costs (e.g., subsidized, low- or moderately priced units). Finally, the quality of rural housing is substantially below that of urban areas, with many substandard or deteriorating housing units.

The interaction of financial instability with the size and the quality of the rural housing market contributes to a pileup of stressors. Financially unstable rural families must allocate a greater proportion of their income to housing than their urban counterparts or they must live in inadequate housing. Rural families have a higher density per room, signaling the crowding that results from sharing housing with extended family members and the limited housing choices available. The fact that rural homes are less likely to have access to public water systems reflects the absence of such systems or the prohibitive costs of hooking up to them. Rural homes are less likely to have central heating sources, indicating the age and condition of the homes and the high cost of centralized energy. Separately and together these housing conditions add to the stresses already affecting rural families. For example, the ability of the rural family to respond to the needs of kin or adult children for temporary housing in times of crisis is often hampered by inadequate housing conditions. In sum, limited opportunities for privacy combined with the problems of maintaining a supply of potable water or keeping the house warm, and simply generating the income to stay in the home can disrupt the family. Thus, inadequate and crowded housing places a constant stress on families that is added to the potential threat of losing one's home due to financial instability.

Inadequate, Inaccessible, and Inappropriate Support Services

Rural families face the same problems as urban families—drugs, crime, delinquency, marital stress, chronic physical and psychological conditions, and the need to provide for dependent family members. Yet, rural communities do not offer the range of specialized social and family services found in urban areas. For example, urban families facing a housing crisis have several options within their communities. On the other hand, in over 30 rural eastern Kentucky counties there was only one homeless shelter, and it closed in the fall of 1989. Rural health services are seriously deficient with respect to advances in medical and therapeutic treatment (see Chapter 12). Many rural communities engage in desperate searches to replace retiring physicians, and rural hospitals are closing at an alarming rate because of insurance problems or a lack of qualified personnel. Treatment programs for families with alcohol or abuse problems or for juveniles in trouble are simply nonexistent in most rural communities.

The limited range of social and family services available to rural families is apparent in many other areas. Despite the growing proportion of elderly in rural communities, few long-term-care facilities are available, and even the supporting services such as Meals on Wheels and in-home health care that enable older persons to remain independent are often absent (see Chapter 11). Although many local economies rely on occupations with high accident rates—farming, mining, lumbering—rehabilitative services are not available in most rural communities. Rural youth find few recreational activities outside of traditional sports (e.g., baseball, football, basketball). Moreover, rural youth have limited vocational or pre-employment training opportunities and minimal career counseling. Thus, regardless of the type of supporting service needed, rural families often have to travel to distant urban communities or simply have to deal with chronic stressors without organized or professional assistance. This is a situation made more difficult by families' chronic financial instability.

The lack of adequate and accessible services and programs for rural families can be attributed to several factors. By definition, the rural environment is characterized by low population density, which typically translates into geographic and social isolation. The wide geographic area combined with small populations in rural communities creates structural barriers to the development of an infrastructure capable of delivering services at a level comparable to that available to urban families. Family financial instability and a local economy offering few employment opportunities with benefits limit the amount of private monies available to pay for services. Finally, rural communities themselves are financially unstable, relying on a limited tax base to generate the resources to support an ever-growing number of fiscal responsibilities. Limited funds must be spent to support, often at minimal levels, essential government services (e.g., police and fire protection, roads), while human services go unsupported.

Consequences of Chronic Stressors

Chronic stressors have multiple effects on family life. Some are the direct effects of a particular stressor and others represent the impact of the pileup of stressors that strain the family's ability to cope with accumulating pressures, making it ever more difficult for the family to deal with even the most simple demands. The following describes some of the direct and cumulative consequences of chronic stressors.

Chronic financial instability reduces the family's economic resources needed to meet both daily needs and unexpected demands. The lack of consumer opportunities in rural communities and the higher costs of social and other services deepen the financial stress on families and increase the sense that family resources are incapable of meeting even basic needs. Another consequence is that, when people perceive blocked opportunities or experience changing work hours or conditions or fluctuating incomes, they have psychological and physical responses in terms of stress, depression, unstable family life, and illness (Walker and Walker, 1987). Marotz-Baden (1988) found that rural couples report higher levels of financial and business strains than do urban couples, and are more likely to report major changes in their financial status. The physical responses to financial instability can be exacerbated by poor housing conditions (Fitchen, 1985). Inadequate housing means drafty homes, limited access to water or unsafe water, crowded conditions and the consequent psychological stress that they cause, all of which contribute to heightened rates of illness.

Limited and erratic income diminishes opportunities for rural families to acquire a standard of living comparable to that of other families with similar educational levels and occupations. For some rural families, status inconsistency, or high educational achievement but low job status due to underemployment, typifies their economic lives. For these couples, their investments in education and training do not pay off in terms of the well-paying or even full-time jobs that they would find in urban areas. For many rural couples, the inability to reap comparable benefits from personal investments in education and training is an indirect but stressful effect of financial instability.

Financial instability diminishes parents' opportunities to provide for their children's educational and occupational attainment. Children of financially unstable parents may lose their incentive for personal improvement. In other words, there may be negative reinforcement between the educational attainment of rural residents and the condition of the rural economy. Furthermore, limited opportunities and inadequate services mean that even when parents can maintain a strong interest in their children's education and instill in them a strong work ethic, the lack of career counseling and vocational/work training programs may limit the development of human resources in rural families (see Chapter 13).

In an attempt to cope with financial instability, many rural family members hold more than one job. Multiple jobholding is associated with stress from trying to juggle incompatible or competing role demands, difficulties in finding child care, and the lack of available time and thus may further strain families. Multiple jobholding may also contribute to the accumulation or pileup of stressors. Families may then become more aware of existing tensions that to this point they have ignored, thus overloading a family's coping abilities (McCubbin, Cauble, and Patterson, 1982).

For other rural families, stress is increased by employment strategies that produce role reversals (e.g., wife employed, husband unemployed or underemployed). Role reversals strain the marital relationship as individuals are forced into roles that they are unaccustomed to, have no training for, or do not define as acceptable (Scanzoni and Arnett, 1987; Rosenblatt and Anderson, 1981). Keating, Munro, and Doherty (1988) note that farm men who work off the farm see their off-farm work as taking away from their primary role as farmers. Farm women, on the other hand, feel they lack the knowledge or skills to perform farm tasks for husbands now working off the farm or feel unable to meet traditional role expectations as wife, mother, and worker. Because rural people hold more traditional sex role orientations, stress arises from the sense of not meeting the expectations of themselves or others, or the "incongruence between how roles 'should' be defined according to their expectations and the definitions prescribed by their extended families and the community, and how the roles were operationally defined on a day-to-day basis" (Norem and Blundall, 1988:25). The high unemployment in the smokestack industries during the recession of the early 1980s highlighted the crippling psychological effects of job losses, layoffs, and underemployment for men socialized to assume that they would be the breadwinner in a family. For many rural couples, this is a permanent, not a temporary condition.

Lack of supporting services can further strain chronically stressed rural families. For some families, an event added to the cumulative effect of multiple chronic stressors may produce a crisis. If supporting services are not available or financially accessible, the crisis may immobilize or break down the entire family or particular members (Boss, 1987). The event precipitating the crisis may not be, on the face of it, that serious (e.g., a car breaking down), but on top of a myriad of other stressors—an unexpected doctor's bill, no overtime that month, a high heating oil bill—the family's financial and emotional resources are overwhelmed and there is no outside support.

Even when supporting services are available, rural families are less likely than urban families to take advantage of government support programs (e.g., cash assistance, food stamps, Medicaid). Why? Rural families in poverty are more likely to be intact husband-wife couples who own their home or have other assets and are therefore ineligible for assistance under most state assistance programs. In addition, strong cultural traditions prevent many rural families from using public assistance and the intimate nature of social interaction in rural communities makes others aware of individual or family decisions to access public assistance. As a result, rural people are less likely to express a need for social services or to utilize them if they are available. These tendencies are confirmed by Marotz-Baden and Colvin (1986), who find that use of public services ranks fifth as a preferred coping strategy of rural families. In other words, "where the need for public assistance is greatest, the constraints against using welfare programs appear to be strongest" (Rank and Hirschl, 1988:204).

A last example of the consequences of chronic stresses on rural families is their effects on the functioning of kinship networks. Traditionally, in rural communities, extended family networks have served as safety nets providing financial and other types of assistance to kin in need. In this sense, kin social networks have buffered particular families from the effects of chronic stress. For example, relatives are often relied on to bring sick children to distant health-care facilities when parents cannot afford to take time from work. Chronic stress hampers or limits the ability of rural families to fulfill these kinship obligations. Families in financial or personal stress have few economic or psychological resources with which to assist kin. Alternatively, when financial instability forces families to leave in search of better opportunities, they leave behind kin, such as elderly parents, who no longer have access to their support. Indeed, Lee (1988) found that rural nonfarm elderly are less likely to have kin nearby or to have weekly contacts with those kin who are in the community than urban elderly. The persistence of financial instability in rural communities and the accumulation of other stressors limit families' resources and may induce migration, thus reducing the mediating effect of kinship networks on family stress.

Nature of Past and Current Policies

What has been the national response to the financial instability of rural families and communities? Federal attention to the spatially based social risks associated with rural residence has been fleeting due to three stereotypes of rural families and communities. The assumptions are that (1) families thrive in rural communities which offer the ideal environment for raising children; (2) all communities, regardless of ecological position or size, have equal opportunities to generate economic growth; and (3) national economic growth eventually benefits all families regardless of residence. These assumptions have shaped the policies of both federal and state governments so that they fail to adequately address the needs of rural families in crisis. Some examples will illustrate the ways in which society has failed rural families.

Implicit in many national economic development efforts is the assumption that economic growth is beneficial for all families because economic benefits trickle through all segments of the community. Yet, depending on their labor requirements, new firms may not hire the unemployed in a community. Rather, they may attract better educated or more skilled migrants from other places, or local people may be hired but at the lower end of the wage scale. Economic development policies that may have the desired effects in urban communities because of the size of the labor markets and the diversity of the labor pool may be inappropriate for rural communities.

Underlying specific flaws in past and current economic development policies is the absence of policies explicitly directed toward improving family welfare. The United States is the only industrialized nation that does not have a national family policy and that does not acknowledge there is a vested public interest in and responsibility for family welfare. A long cultural tradition of privatizing family issues has left individual families to their own resources. Individual families are viewed as being responsible for their own economic situation and its consequences. As a result, there is no perceived need to develop programs and policies designed to enhance family economic stability or the quality of family life.

For example, given the increasing proportion of dual career families in rural communities as well as the significant number of elderly rural persons, there is a great need for support services such as child care, Meals On Wheels, in-home health care, and transportation for dependents (Hughes, 1987). Family and community financial instability limits the ability to purchase or provide such services. This is especially true for older rural Americans who have accumulated fewer financial resources than their urban counterparts due to the lifelong effects of limited economic opportunities.

The assumption that the rural environment is somehow conducive to an idealized family life overlooks some negative aspects of this environment. For example, the geographic isolation of rural families makes delivery of services less cost-effective than in urban areas, making access to family support services more difficult. Yet national efforts to provide social services do not account for incapacitating effects of geography. Funds are typically allocated on a per capita basis without regard to the higher costs of delivering services to more dispersed populations.

When there is an effort to establish policies or programs directed at family welfare, they are designed to fit the political images of the ideal family—working father, housewife mother, and dependent children. Demographically, however, this ideal family represents an increasingly smaller proportion of American families. Social trends including increases in the divorce rate, the level of cohabitation, the number of single women with children, women's labor force participation, and multigenerational households have produced diverse family structures. Policies shaped to address the needs of the ideal family by providing alternatives that fit its structure benefit only a few families. Other family types are excluded from participation because eligibility requirements do not acknowledge the heterogeneity in the American family.

Finally, national policies and programs rarely are evaluated for their effects on family well-being. It is as if policymakers assume that families function in a social vacuum, isolated from the effects of the forces of social change. For example, consider workfare proposals that make no adequate provisions for child care, especially for isolated rural families. Parents are thus forced to choose between providing economically for their children or providing appropriate care.

Existing programs and policies are seriously flawed because they fail to directly address the needs of rural families or to take into account their effects on family well-being. Families have been left to their own devices under the misguided belief that general economic growth benefits individual families and that negative consequences reflect individual family pathologies rather than structural conditions such as rural residence. As a result, current and past programs have done little if anything to alleviate the financial instability of rural families or the accumulation of other stresses in the rural environment. The consequences of this situation affect all generations and their communities.

Assumptions Underlying New Policy Initiatives

New policy initiatives to address family financial instability must be based on the following set of new assumptions. First, society has a vested interest in assuring that all families, regardless of residence, have opportunities to acquire the minimal level of financial stability necessary to ensure their survival. Failure to do so extracts a high penalty, since the total society pays the costs of rural residents who must function without educational, health, or economic skills comparable to those of urban residents. Urban areas cannot continue to operate as islands of wealth, opportunities, economic growth, and high standards of living in a rural sea of poverty, limited opportunities, stagnant growth, and low standards of living.

Second, society has a vested interest in assisting families to increase their internal resources—psychological, physical, and emotional—so that they can meet their basic needs. Given the opportunity to strengthen their personal resources, families can develop their own strategies for adapting to changing conditions. The resiliency of families in the face of the most debilitating conditions demonstrates their adaptive strengths. But these strengths have been undermined by the pileup of chronic stressors and the lack of supporting services in their communities. Without access to a wide range of supporting services, families in crisis have no means of buffering the effects of chronic stress. Local programs are needed that can help families in crisis when their own resources are stressed to the breaking point.

Finally, policies for rural families in the 1990s must be based on the recognition of the great diversity among rural communities and rural families and the essential differences between the rural and urban environments. Diversity and flexibility in program requirements are essential. Emphasis must be placed on rural families and communities using their strengths, their knowledge of local conditions, and their particular competencies to develop their own approaches to diversifying and strengthening local institutions and families. The standardization and centralization of past programs have contributed heavily to their failure to address the particular needs and concerns of rural families.

These assumptions are the basis of a new way of viewing the relationship between the national government and the family. Policy and program initiatives based on these assumptions would acknowledge that the national government has a vested interest in reducing family and community financial instability in rural areas. It would also acknowledge that the rural environment is characterized by chronic stresses that have placed rural families at greater social risk than urban families.

New Policy Initiatives

There are four areas in which new policy initiatives can address the needs of rural families. New policies should seek to:

1. reduce rural family financial instability by increasing the number, diversity, and quality of employment opportunities;
2. reduce the social isolation of rural families by increasing access to a greater number of more diverse supporting services;
3. reduce the effects of chronic stresses on rural families by increasing family resources and providing alternative uses of these resources; and
4. develop programs that take into account the diversity of conditions between rural and urban families and among rural communities.

Reducing Family Financial Instability

This policy initiative will be accomplished only with a national commitment to rural economic development that strengthens and diversifies local economies. There are several necessary conditions underlying such an effort. One critical factor in reducing family financial instability is ensuring that family members have opportunities to find employment that is not susceptible to periodic business cycles, enables them to work the necessary number of hours, fits their education and work experiences, and provides a living wage. In other words, what is needed is a development policy directed at reducing both rural unemployment and rural underemployment. More jobs and a better match between job requirements and workers' skills are necessary preconditions for rural financial stability. Since self-employment is quite common in rural communities (e.g., farm operators, small business owners), an unemployment insurance pool that would provide assistance during business crises (i.e., drought, collapse of markets, input shortages) could alleviate family financial instability. Similarly, programs that assist self-employed business operators to diversify their economic activities and consequently lessen the effects of business crises would also be desirable.

Reducing the Social Isolation of Rural Families

Policies are needed that take into account the scale of community life. Policies that are suitable to large concentrations of population, manufacturing, service and retail firms, the large agglomerations of wealth, and the well-developed infrastructure of urban areas may be inappropriate for rural communities with small, geographically dispersed populations; few economic enterprises; limited community wealth; and a limited and deteriorating infrastructure. While centralized social service programs in cities with mass transit may meet the needs of urban families, centralized services may not be accessible to rural families.

Alternative service delivery programs need to be developed for rural families. Rural social services must be responsive to the geographic isolation of rural families and the socioeconomic and demographic characteristics of clients. For example, income-support programs that presume single-parent families may be appropriate in urban areas but automatically exclude the great majority of rural families seeking assistance. Income-support programs with eligibility requirements that exclude families with property also exclude a substantial proportion of rural families seeking assistance, although most urban families seeking assistance would qualify. In this sense, we must develop programs and policies suitable for rural families and communities and not simply apply urban biases and presumptions to rural people.

Similarly, few services and programs are targeted to rural youth. In a time when four out of ten youth will experience a parental divorce, over half live in poverty, nearly a fifth are unemployed, and increasing numbers are affected by substance or physical abuse, rural youth find few programs of assistance. Otto (1988) identifies three general areas of youth service needs: health and fitness, prevention and treatment of drug or alcohol abuse, and pre-employment training. Pre-employment training is especially critical given the high youth unemployment rates and the incidence of high school dropouts, two situations that are especially problematic in rural communities. Rural communities offer youth little beyond recreational programs such as baseball or football, and financially strapped rural school systems have few resources to develop programs that address broader issues such as life goals or personal counseling. Access to a variety of youth services is an investment in the future of rural communities, yet it is an investment that most families and communities cannot afford to make.

Reducing the Effects of Chronic Stresses

Developing employment policies that enable families to mesh work with family role demands is the most critical policy initiative. Given the spatial distribution of employment opportunities and residence in rural communities and the fact that a growing number of farm families depend on off-farm jobs, employers should be encouraged with tax incentives or new employment regulations to adopt innovative approaches to work scheduling. Options such as flextime, compressed work schedules, shift work, and job sharing, or an increased reliance on home-based or contract work would broaden family members' opportunities to work given the constraints of rural residence. The importance of entrepreneurs as small business owners suggests a need for programs that provide financial and technical assistance for new business start-ups or that provide incentives to banks to make higher risk loans. Such innovations would contribute to family financial stability by diversifying employment options.

Access to affordable, quality child care is an essential factor in the employment decisions of family members. Child care is especially problematic for rural families because of the lack of licensed facilities, the cost of limited child care spaces, and the time involved in moving children to and from distant care centers. As the proportion of rural families with both spouses employed or seeking employment increases, access to adequate child care will become more critical. All levels of government must work toward new approaches to assure access to affordable child care for all families, regardless of residence or work schedule. This would further expand rural employment opportunities and reduce a chronic family stress.

Employment alternatives can be in the form of employee benefits such as health and life insurance, retirement plans, unemployment coverage or temporary leaves of absence without losing seniority, which represent significant noneconomic contributions to a family's financial condition. As noted earlier, employment alone does not guarantee family financial stability. If a job does not provide benefits, offer a salary adequate to purchase these benefits, or cover employees with state unemployment insurance programs, workers are susceptible to financial instability due to health problems or job losses.

Simply mandating that employers offer such benefits is not a solution. Small employers dominate the rural labor market and, on their own, many of these businesses cannot afford to offer benefits and remain competitive. Yet, within the rural labor market, workers have few alternatives to low-wage, minimum-benefit employment. This is the dilemma of the rural labor market: How to enhance worker benefits to provide employees with financial stability without jeopardizing the viability of small rural businesses. One way to accomplish this is to provide financial or other forms of assistance to small employers so that such benefits do not constitute an unfair economic burden. For example, national or state-sponsored health insurance pools for small employers or self-employed persons would enable such businesses to offer competitive benefits and thereby provide more financial security for their employees.

Programs and services are needed that enhance other family resources and coping strategies. Programs that enable established kin social networks to function more effectively would be most appropriate for rural communities. Family counseling or alternative treatment programs that strengthen kinship ties by involving relatives outside the immediate family or rely on kin to assist in delivering services (e.g., family day care for the elderly) illustrate this approach. In effect, local communities must multiply the effectiveness of organized services by enlisting and organizing kin networks' support for efforts designed to improve the quality of family life.

Finally, the range of social services provided by rural service agencies needs to be diversified. Given the low population density in rural communities, prevalence rates tend to be inadequate to sustain specialized services. Providers of public and private services must be offered both incentives and assistance to broaden their program offerings and expand their target populations. Rural families will have greater access to a wider variety of supporting services only when programs can overcome the physical barriers of geography.

Designing Programs for Residential Diversity

Development efforts must be oriented toward reducing the rural communities' dependence on larger places for services; the dependence of local businesses and institutions on larger centralized institutions limits their ability to focus on local concerns (Hughes, 1987). An example of such a program is one developed and administered by MACED (Mountain Association for Community Economic Development) to a consortium of banks in eastern Kentucky. The program provides technical assistance on using FmHA and other federal programs to provide low-interest housing loans. An evaluation of the program, which included a multimillion dollar bond issue, found a substantial increase in the use of these programs by local banks due to a greater understanding of the technical requirements for participation and the opportunity provided by the consortium to pool high-risk loans. Bank officals admitted that prior to this intervention they did not use these federal loan programs because either they did not understand the paperwork required or, on an individual basis, they did not generate sufficient usage to justify program participation. In this case, federal loan programs suited to the nature and needs of urban housing markets were inappropriate for rural banks and so unsuited to addressing the housing needs of many rural families.

Conclusion

Rural families and rural communities have suffered from neglect due to a narrow focus on urban America and the assumption that the benefits of economic growth eventually trickle through society. This neglect has led to the high level of financial instability among rural families and the piling-up of other chronic stresses, a situation that reflects conditions imposed by their residence rather than any characteristic particularly unique to the structure and functioning of rural families. If rural families are ever to achieve equity with their urban counterparts in living standards and quality of life, national policies must be consciously designed to reduce the social risks associated with rural residence.

References

Boss, Pauline. 1987. "Family Stress." Pp. 695–723 in M. B. Sussman and S. K. Steinmetz, eds., *Handbook of Marriage and the Family*. New York: Plenum.

Fitchen, Janet. 1985. *Rural Poverty*. Boulder, Colo.: Westview Press.

Hughes, Robert, Jr. 1987. "Empowering rural families and communities." *Family Relations* 36(4):396–401.

Keating, Norah, Brenda Munro, and Maryanne Doherty. 1988. "Psychosomatic stress among farm men and women." Pp. 64–73 in Ramona Marotz-Baden, Charles B.

Hennon, Timothy H. Brubaker, eds., *Families in Rural America: Stress, Adaptation and Revitalization*. St. Paul, Minn: National Council on Family Relations.

Lee, Gary. 1988. "Kinship ties among older people." Pp. 176–182 in Ramona Marotz-Baden, Charles B. Hennon, and Timothy H. Brubaker, eds., *Families in Rural America: Stress, Adaptation, and Revitalization*. St. Paul, Minn: National Council on Family Relations.

Marotz-Baden, Ramona. 1988. "Stressors: A rural-urban comparison." Pp. 74–83 in Ramona Marotz-Baden, Charles B. Hennon, Timothy H. Brubaker, eds., *Families in Rural America: Stress, Adaptation and Revitalization*. St. Paul, Minn: National Council on Family Relations.

Marotz-Baden, Ramona, and P. L. Colvin. 1986. "Coping strategies: A rural-urban comparison." *Family Relations* 35(2):281–288.

McCubbin, H. I., A. E. Cauble, and J. M. Patterson, eds. 1982. *Family Stress, Coping and Social Support*. Springfield, Ill.: Charles Thomas.

Norem, Rosalie H., and Joan Blundall. 1988. "Farm families and marital disruption during a time of crisis." Pp.21–31 in Ramona Marotz-Baden, Charles B. Hennon, Timothy H. Brubaker, eds., *Families in Rural America: Stress, Adaptation and Revitalization*. St. Paul, Minn: National Council on Family Relations.

Otto, Luther. 1988. "America's youth: A changing profile." *Family Relations* 37(4):385–391.

Rank, Mark, and Thomas Hirschl. 1988. "A rural-urban comparison of welfare exits: The importance of population density." *Rural Sociology* 53(2):190–206.

Rosenblatt, P. C., and R. M. Anderson. 1981. "Interaction in farm families: Tension and stress." Pp. 147–166 in R. T. Coward and W. M. Smith, Jr., eds., *The Family in Rural Society*. Boulder, Colo.: Westview Press.

Scanzoni, John, and Cynthia Arnett. 1987. "Policy implications derived from a study of rural and urban marriages." *Family Relations* 36(4):430–436.

Walker, Lilly Schuber, and James L. Walker. 1987. "Stressors and symptoms predictive of distress in farmers." *Family Relations* 36(4):374–378.

Zvonkovic, Anisa M., Tom Guss, and Linda Ladd. 1988. "Making the most of job loss: Individual and marital features of underemployment." *Family Relations* 37(1):56–61.

11

The Aged in Rural America

Marvin A. Kaiser

The greying of the population is the demographic revolution of the twentieth century. In 1900, the United States had three million persons 65 years of age and older, 4 percent of the population. By 1986, the number of aged had increased tenfold and represented 12 percent of the population. It is estimated that by 2025 the aged will comprise 19.5 percent of the population.

This population transition is having a significant impact on rural places. In general, as the population of a place declines, its proportion of the elderly increases. Thus, rural areas tend to have disproportionately more older citizens. This phenomenon represents an unprecedented yet urgent policy and program challenge to ensure that quality of life for the rural aged matches their longevity. Rural America is experiencing increasing numbers and percentages of older persons, shrinking family support systems, and limited formal support services. Moreover, these events are occurring in the context of changing rural social and economic structures, changes that challenge the very vitality of rural life.

Three broad policy arenas emerge from the aging of rural populations. First, the availability of and accessibility to health and social services that respond to the unique characteristics of the rural aged and the rural environment are inadequate. Second, the elderly's resources must be developed through the expansion of opportunities for the rural aged to remain productive members of their communities. Third, policy and program initiatives involving the rural aged must support and enhance the viability of rural communities. Each of these policy arenas encompasses policy initiatives to be addressed during the 1990s. The first two arenas focus directly on the humanitarian needs and development potential of the rural aged. The third arena recognizes that policy and program initiatives are intimately intertwined with the maintenance and development of strong and vital rural communities.

Policy Context

Who are the rural aged? While chronological markers inadequately represent the various dimensions of aging, a wide range of such markers is used for public policy purposes. For example, in the United States age discrimination legislation covers those 40 and over, and full Social Security benefits are shifting from age 65 to 67. Moreover, we now recognize that there is significant variability between the young-old and the old-old. We might more accurately talk about a "third and fourth quarter of life," with the former referring to the years from 50 to 75. Nevertheless, unless otherwise noted, *the aged* here refers to persons 65 years of age and older.

According to the U.S. Census Bureau, 10.9 percent of the rural population was 65 years of age and older in 1980. More important, those 59 million aged who live in the small towns, rural communities, and farms of the United States comprise 26 percent of the aged population of this country, or every fourth elder (Coward and Lee, 1985). Atchley (1975) notes that 21 states have at least 40 percent of their older population in rural areas. Additionally, in more rural states such as Kansas, two thirds of the aged, nearly 68 percent, live in small towns and rural areas.

The more rural states in the Midwest and most of the Northeast have high proportions of elderly. This geographic concentration of the elderly population is principally due to "aging in place." While immigration of the aged may have a significant impact on the proportion of elderly in places such as Florida, the major migratory impact related to rural aging is more accurately reflected by the out-migration of the young in search of economic opportunities.

Approximately 17 percent of the 13 million minority aged lived in rural places in 1980. While little is known about rural minority elderly, as a minority within a minority, they are likely to be even more disadvantaged than their majority rural counterparts. As Soldo and Agree (1988:14–15) note, "Minority elderly, in particular, are more likely to have a greater per capita need for services such as income maintenance, housing, meals, transportation, and health care." Minority elderly are likely to receive services targeted to their needs only in large metropolitan areas.

In 1985, the ratio of females to males aged 65 and older was 147 to 100. In rural areas, however, the proportion of elderly men is higher than that of women. In the United States in 1980, 68.6 percent of all men 65 and older lived in rural areas, whereas only 23.4 percent of females did so. This difference tends to reflect differing migration patterns for men and women based on marital and family status. Most older men, 80 percent aged 65 to 74 and 66 percent of those 75 and older, are married and living with a spouse. By contrast, 51 percent of women 65 to 74 and 22 percent of those 75 and older are married and living with a spouse. In rural areas, the major impact of widowhood is the move to town, while widowers tend to remain in place. Thus, small towns in rural America tend to become "grey ghettoes," principally for widowed women.

In 1986, 12.4 percent of the elderly, 3.5 million, had incomes below the poverty level. These figures, however, mask significant variations. For example, poverty rates increase with age (18 percent for those 85 and over), for women (15 percent versus 8 percent for men), and for blacks (31 percent). The impact of residence is also significant: a greater proportion of the elderly poor live in rural areas. In 1980, 21 percent of the rural elderly were poor, nearly double the urban rate at that time. Goudy and Dobson (1985) report that older nonfarm families and individuals in rural areas are the most economically disadvantaged. They state that "the poverty rate for those 65 and over was 7.5 percent in farm areas and 15.4 percent in nonfarm areas (in 1980). Thus, the problem of insufficient income for the elderly was greatest in rural nonfarm localities" (p. 67). The vast majority of these rural nonfarm poor are women.

The rural elderly tend to report their incomes as adequate, regardless of their actual income. According to Goudy and Dobson (1985:70), "Although rural residence is associated with substantially lower incomes for the elderly, there do not appear to be large or consistent rural-urban differences in older individuals' evaluations of their financial situations."

For rural residents, illness and disability rates vary. Male farm residents in the 65 to 74 age group report the greatest number of restricted activity days compared with those in other residential categories. Beyond 75, farm men and women have more restricted days and more bed days than nonfarm residents. The rural elderly may suffer from the "poverty-illness syndrome" (McCoy and Brown, 1978). Poverty combined with geographic isolation increases health risk factors, including lifestyle characteristics that lead to chronic illness, with limited treatment opportunities.

Family and kin relationships of the rural elderly have been subject to stereotypes of closeness and provision of care. On the other hand, as noted earlier, "aging in place" suggests that the rural young are moving from rural places in search of employment, leaving the aged behind. Lee and Cassidy (1985) report that when the farm elderly's children move, they tend to go beyond the immediate neighborhood, restricting interaction opportunities. Additionally, the rural nonfarm elderly "are the least likely to have proximate children of any residential category" (p. 163). They conclude:

> If the rural elderly really were uniquely advantaged by embeddedness in strong, supportive kin networks, in contrast to the isolated nuclear families of the urban elderly, . . . their needs for public services might indeed be less. The fact is that they are not. . . . We do contend that the available evidence should serve, at least, to demolish the myth that rural families possess any unique strengths which ameliorate the effects of other privations upon their family members. We therefore cannot assume that the needs of the rural elderly for supportive public services are any less than are those of other groups because the classical family of Western nostalgia . . . is alive and well and living in the country. It is not. (p. 165)

The rural aged are more likely to have contact with friends and neighbors and have a confidant than are their urban counterparts (Schooler, 1975).

These informal relationships, fostered by homogeneity and length of residence, are important to the rural aged due to the limited avenues available for social contact and services. Thus, such contact may serve as sources of transportation and emergency assistance.

The rural aged are also less likely to belong to and actively participate in organizations than the urban aged. It has been suggested that this is due to lower incomes, poor health status, lack of adequate transportation, low population density, and fewer formal organizations. When the rural aged do participate, much of the focus is on church-related activities, special-interest farm organizations, agricultural cooperatives, and national political parties. Karcher and Karcher (1980:410) found that "the single most important and trusted institution, outside the family, in the lives of the rural elderly, is the church." For the rural elderly, a high level of church membership translates into high levels of activity and participation, particularly for older rural women.

This analysis suggests that the needs of the rural elderly, whether for health care, social services, financial support, or transportation, are at least equal to those of the urban elderly and in many cases greater. Moreover, the availability of family, friends, and neighbors to provide assistance in meeting these needs is more limited in rural than in urban areas.

The development and expansion of formal services is a response to the inability of the informal sector to meet the need. There is evidence that while the services are being expanded in rural areas, they still lag significantly behind urban settings. As Coward and Lee (1985:8) explain:

> Services for many rural residents are less accessible, more costly to deliver, narrower in range and scope, and fewer in number. . . . This does not mean that health and human services are completely absent from rural environments; rather, relative to their more urban counterparts, many rural residents suffer a disadvantage in their ability to utilize the formal helping structure during periods of crisis.

Krout (1988) notes that often fewer services for the aged in rural areas are directly tied to limited financial resources. Whether in the area of private or public funding, rural areas appear disadvantaged. Addressing the limited private foundation support for rural areas, Greene (1988:12) states:

> The crux of the problem may be that grant seekers in rural America are at an inconvenient distance—physically, culturally, and psychologically—from grant makers perusing applications in their urban offices. . . . Crossing that gap requires spending more time, money, and energy than many people on either side seem equipped or inclined to spend.

In the public funding of services for the rural elderly there are numerous examples to support the "urban bias" argument. In addition to the urban/ rural disparity in Medicare reimbursements for hospitals and physicians, there remain significant variations in funding Older Americans Act services and transportation. The National Center on Rural Aging (1989:8) notes that the "mean budgets of most rural agencies on aging (funded largely through Older Americans Act funds) are one quarter the size of the most urban ones." The National Association for Transportation Alternatives (1988) reports that while 41 percent of the transportation disadvantaged (elderly, poor, and disabled) live in rural areas, in fiscal year 1987 these areas received only 3.5 percent of the UMTA (Urban Mass Transportation Act) Transit Assistance funding.

The limited availability of health and human service professionals contributes to fewer services in rural areas. The availability of physicians in small rural communities is improving, but it is still one-half that of physicians in urban areas. These shortages continue for most provider groups, including nurses, social workers, psychologists, and allied health professionals.

Even where services may be available, accessibility is conditioned by the attitude toward services and distance. While negative attitudes toward formal services may be breaking down, distance remains a barrier. Schooler (1975) reports that 82 percent of the rural aged, as opposed to 10 percent of the urban aged, live far from a core set of services. Delivering services to widely dispersed rural elderly is expensive and time consuming. For the elderly, the limited availability of funds for public transportation exacerbates the problem.

There are major variations in the availability of services among rural communities. Community-level variables, particularly supportive leadership and community cohesion, can significantly contribute to the availability of services for the rural aged. Given a policy environment that appears to be systematically biased against rural services, it is important to acknowledge the significant role that individual rural community dynamics can play in providing services for the elderly.

Policy and program initiatives for older persons in the United States have focused principally on "humanitarian" services that meet the special needs of the aged in such areas as health and nutrition, social welfare, housing, and financial support. The major federal initiatives supporting policies and programs to meet the special long-term-care needs of the aged have been the Older Americans Act, with its 1971 and 1978 amendments, Medicare, Medicaid, the Social Services Block Grant, and the Medicare Catastrophic Coverage Act of 1988. The Older Americans Act mandated an additional 5 percent of allocations for rural areas and required support for the implementation of rural model projects. The Medicare Catastrophic Coverage Act expanded the availability of home and community-based services in those states where it was supported. This enabled some rural areas to gain increased access to case management, homemaker, and other support services.

The Urban Mass Transportation Act of 1964, although very limited in its assistance to rural areas, has provided financial support and training to states to help meet the needs of the rural elderly. The White House Rural Elderly Housing Initiative of 1977 supported the expansion of rural elderly congregate housing. In that same year the Farmers Home Administration increased the level of 504 low-income housing repair loans and grants to help meet the needs of the rural elderly. In 1978, support for the expansion of primary health care facilities for rural areas and for the training of health care professionals was initiated.

In the 1980s, rural aging issues were "left off the list" of the federal agenda. A rural aging agenda is now beginning to reappear under the auspices of health legislation. Examples of this rekindling of interest in rural aging include the congressional language in the 1988 National Institute on Aging budget to update the White House Conference on Aging report as it related to the health and socioeconomic status of the rural elderly. The 1989 budget appropriation requested the institute undertake a feasibility study on establishing a center for studies of aging and health in rural areas. The Administration on Aging recently established the National Resource Center for Rural Elderly. Additionally, the Department of Health and Human Services recently established an Office of Rural Health Policy to help monitor and support the development of health policy for rural Americans.

State support for rural aging issues is mixed. Twenty-one states now have Offices of Rural Health. While their focus is not exclusively on the rural aged, they obviously are concerned about health issues for this group. The extant literature tends to focus on statewide programming for long-term care, with little distinction between rural and urban settings. It is clear, however, that for rural states most federal and state expenditures for long-term care go to Medicaid-supported institutional care. In reviewing state financing for long-term care services for the elderly, Lipson and Donohoe (1988:22) conclude, "Virtually every state allocate(s) their own funds above and beyond federal matching requirements. . . . Among the states, there are tremendous differences in the magnitude of those state general revenues and the role that they play in each state's long-term care financing and delivery systems."

Several states with large rural elderly populations, including Alaska, Minnesota, and Missouri, rank among the top ten states in per-capita state expenditures for long-term care services. Conversely, such states as Kansas, Nebraska, and South Dakota, which also have large rural elderly populations, rank in the bottom 10 percent. Thus, there appears to be no clear policy or agenda among the states to address the needs of the rural elderly.

The "development" dimension of population aging, that is, the contributions and impact of population aging on the socioeconomic life of the community, has received little attention. Where development activities have occurred, they have mainly focused on promoting employment and volunteer opportunities for older persons. The major federal initiatives supporting employment include Title III of the Older Americans Act, the Senior Community Service Employment Program (Title V of the Older Americans Act), and the Job Training Partnership Act with its 3 percent set-aside for disadvantaged older workers. Additionally, the U.S. Employment Service supports Job Service offices that may serve the older workers. A number of state and community-funded programs also assist older workers in job identification and training. While it is clear that many of these programs, such as the Arkansas Abilities Based on Long Experience and the Kansas Older Kansans Employment Program, serve the rural elderly, the proportion of elderly served remains quite small.

Volunteer opportunities have received their principal federal support through the ACTION programs, including the Senior Retired Volunteer Program and Senior Companion and Foster Grandparent programs. As in the employment programs, the number of rural elderly involved is far smaller than those eligible. Recognition of and support for volunteer activities on the part of the elderly is particularly significant in rural areas, as these places rely heavily on volunteers for a wide range of services and community activities.

One consequence of this nearly exclusive focus on the humanitarian dimension of population aging is that the elderly have come to be viewed as dependent beneficiaries of society's development, rather than active contributors to it. Only recently has attention been given to the considerable positive economic impact of transfer payments and spending patterns of the aged on local economic development. Peter Townsend (1981) argues that the dependency of the elderly in our time, "acquiescent functionalism," is a creation of social policy.

The policy and programmatic consequences of such a construct are particularly important for rural areas given their higher incidence of poverty and growing proportion of elderly. In such a view, the elderly may be considered an obstacle to community and economic development as they drain finite resources to meet their needs. This dependency stigmatizes them as individuals in need of society's care, rather than as partners in community and economic development. They become marginalized, a social burden is created, and a major development potential for rural communities is lost. Pifer (1986:403) summarizes the policy implications of this dependency construct:

> A significant proportion of the population, about 20 percent, or some 50 million people, falls within the third quarter (fifty to seventy-five years of age) today. What is especially startling is that, by the year 2010—only twenty-five years from now—some 85 million Americans will be in the third quarter, and they will comprise close to a third of the population! How the nation is going to deal with this large group of citizens, and what opportunities it will offer them to stay in the mainstream of its life, therefore constitutes a public policy issue of immense magnitude.

Given the high proportion of the aged in rural America, the development potential of the rural aged is a major public policy opportunity. Several conclusions emerge from this discussion of rural population aging. First, the phenomenon of the "grey ghetto" resulting from aging in place is increasingly characteristic of rural places. Rural America, particularly the Midwest and the Northeast, is experiencing population aging. There is little reason to believe this trend will be altered in the near future.

Second, the needs of older rural residents are at least equal to and in many cases greater than the needs of their urban counterparts. As discussed earlier, the health, transportation, family, and economic statuses of the rural aged are generally worse than those of the urban elderly.

Third, although rural places are expanding their service availability for older persons, significant gaps in services persist. Public policy and programming, particularly at the federal and state levels, have tended to ignore the rural aged or have assumed that urban service models are sufficient to meet their needs. Compared with urban places, formal services such as home health care, homemaker, transportation, and meal services are simply less available for individuals who grow old in rural places. For those in need of long-term care, a disproportionate emphasis is placed on institutional care.

Fourth, while the family remains the principal structure for caregiving for the frail elderly, the family's ability to continue this function is seriously compromised in rural areas. The out-migration of the young combined with the aging of the remaining population, including neighbors and friends, means that the availability of informal interaction and support is reduced for the rural aged.

Fifth, the role of the local rural community as a partner is a crucial, but insufficiently developed, element in meeting the needs of its older citizens. As one considers service delivery as a public/private partnership, the institutions that undergird life in rural communities (i.e., churches, schools, and voluntary associations) can play a major role in meeting the needs of and developing opportunities for older citizens.

Finally, limited attention has been given to the community and economic development role of older rural citizens. While older persons represent a major resource in rural America, their perceived contributions to the economic life of the community tend to focus on transfer payments and jobs provided to meet their social and health needs rather than on the broad range of productive aging, including employment, volunteering, and entrepreneurship.

Options

As we look to the future in public policy development, it is important to summarize several assumptions that appear to have guided policy and program initiatives related to rural aging and the rural elderly over the past several decades. The first assumption is that the rural elderly are a self-sufficient group, embedded in family and community networks. Given this assumption, the notion of public responsibility to assist in meeting their needs can be avoided. Private resources embodied in informal networks of family, friends, and neighbors, plus private community institutions such as the church, are perceived as meeting the needs of the rural aged. As noted earlier, evidence suggests that while informal support is part of rural life, the out-migration of the young has placed serious strains on that system's ability to support the elderly.

A second major assumption underpinning rural aging policy is that transplanting programs designed for urban settings is sufficient to meet the needs of rural places. Such an assumption tends to ignore the issues of low density, distance, few formal service providers, policies which prohibit direct service provision on the part of some public agencies, limited expertise to obtain external funding, and limited financial resources, all of which tend to disadvantage the rural aged.

A related, third assumption is that service delivery is less costly in rural areas, principally due to reduced labor costs. Little consideration is given to cost implications of low density and distance in providing service. One consequence of this assumption is the reimbursement differential between rural and urban areas in the Prospective Payment System for hospitals and physicians.

A fourth assumption focuses on the dependency or nonproductivity of the elderly in both urban and rural settings. Pifer (1986:401) summarizes this assumption, "In the popular view, a person past sixty-five is still considered to be 'over the hill,' 'past it,' 'ready to be put out to pasture,' and so on—in short, already suffering from bad health, diminished physical vigor, and declining mental acuity."

A fifth assumption is that rural places with their more diffuse and less visible problems are more prosperous, stable, and self-sufficient than their urban counterparts. Given such an assumption, rural issues, whether focusing on aging or other concerns, are not a priority with funders, public or private.

To move beyond these assumptions, which have disadvantaged the rural aged, is both a challenge and an opportunity. We cannot continue to leave the rural aged "off the list," invisible and forgotten. The only viable option is to institute "an affirmative action plan" for the rural elderly (Hunter, 1989). Such a plan must include three major policy arenas if we are to ensure that the rural elderly are to live with dignity and opportunity.

First, it is evident that the changing rural family and community network will require enhanced formal support services to meet the social and health needs of the rural elderly. Following the lead of the National Center on Rural Aging, the following policy initiatives are urged:

- Establish a rural policy and program office within the Administration on Aging to monitor and develop policies and programs that support the rural elderly;
- Encourage the Administration on Aging to target the rural aged as a priority area within its discretionary grants program;
- Expand the Office of Rural Health in the Department of Health and Human Services to monitor and support the development of health services that respond to the needs of the rural elderly;
- Stimulate the development of housing and housing repair programs for the rural elderly;
- Adjust the regulations and allocations of the Older Americans Act to recognize the paucity of providers, ensure fair distribution of resources

for rural areas, and support the added costs of delivering services in low-density, high-distance areas;
- Target program funds within the Older Americans Act to address the special needs of rural minority elders;
- Adjust and expand allocations under the Urban Mass Transit Act to ensure equity in allocations and adequate transportation support for community service delivery in rural areas;
- Encourage state governments to establish offices or programs of rural aging within state level health and social service agencies; and
- Encourage private granting agencies and foundations to give priority to the needs and opportunities associated with rural population aging.

Second, as the aged increase proportionally in rural areas, they can remain a valued resource for the economic and social well-being of rural America. A major challenge for rural America is to develop and support those policies and programs that allow the rural elderly to remain productive citizens. The following policies are recommended:

- Establish or expand job programs that target the aged in both the private and public sectors;
- Establish community and economic development programs, both public and private, which focus on rural issues and integrate the aged into their activities;
- Encourage economic development agencies and state units on aging to develop model programs of employment, senior entrepreneurship, and volunteerism in rural communities;
- Establish microenterprises developed for and by the aged through banks or development funds; and
- Adjust tax policies at the federal and state levels to ensure that the rural aged can continue to receive income from employment without penalty.

Third, formal service program development for the rural aged, whether humanitarian or developmental, must be driven by policies that ensure the viability of rural communities. Public policy and programming for the rural aged must support and enhance, not displace, rural community systems. The following policy initiatives are recommended:

- Ensure rural representation on governing and advisory boards in programs established to serve the rural aged;
- Integrate programs for the rural aged into existing community-based institutions; and
- Have state economic development agencies analyze the economic impact of population aging on rural communities.

Conclusion

Three major policy issues were identified at the outset: the development of formal health and social services for the aged; the provision of opportunities for rural persons to age productively; and the need for policy initiatives that enhance the viability of rural communities—an "affirmative action plan" for the rural elderly. These policy issues provide a framework for the plan. The substance of the plan is outlined in the specific policy initiatives above.

The grey revolution is sweeping both urban and rural America, as well as all the developed and the developing world. It is a revolution that is particularly powerful in rural America, where between one fourth and one third of all older persons live. Our rural places are becoming "grey communities." This represents both a challenge and an opportunity that will involve every citizen and virtually every institution in rural America. Through our public policy responses we will have the opportunity to create a future that ensures dignity, support, and opportunity for those who have spent their lives building and supporting our rural communities.

References

Atchley, R. C. 1975. *Rural Environments and Aging*. Washington, D.C.: Gerontological Society.

Coward, R. T., and G. R. Lee. 1985. *The Elderly in Rural Society*. New York: Springer Publishing Company.

Goudy, W. J., and C. Dobson. 1985. "Work, retirement, and financial situations of the rural elderly." Pp. 57–77 in R. T. Coward and G. R. Lee, eds., *The Elderly in Rural Society*. New York: Springer Publishing Company.

Greene, S. G. 1988. "Despite dire problems, rural America is ignored by many philanthropies." *The Chronicle of Philanthropy*. Vol. 1. No. 4.

Hunter, J. B. 1989. *Decline and Promise in Rural America: New Directions for Rural Transportation, Development, and Health and Human Services*. Paper presented at The National Council on the Aging Preconference (no. 120), New Orleans, March.

Karcher, C. J., and B. C. Karcher. 1980. "Higher education and religion: Potential partners in service to the rural elderly." *Educational Gerontology* 5:409–421.

Krout, J. A. 1988. "The elderly in rural environments." *Journal of Rural Studies*. Great Britain 4(2):103–1114.

Lee, G. R., and M. L. Cassidy. 1985. "Family and kin relations of the rural elderly." Pp. 151–169 in R. T. Coward and G. R. Lee, eds., *The Elderly in Rural Society*. New York: Springer Publishing Company.

Lipson, D. J., and E. Donohoe. 1988. *State Financing of Long-Term Care Services for the Elderly*, Vol. 1: Executive Report. Washington, D.C.: The George Washington University, Intergovernmental Health Policy Project, May.

McCoy, J. L., and D. L. Brown. 1978. "Health status among low-income elderly persons: Rural-urban differences." *Social Security Bulletin* 41:14–25.

National Association for Transportation Alternatives. 1988. *Equity in Transportation*. Washington, D.C., National Center on Rural Aging Public Policy Statement. (March):33–34.

National Center on Rural Aging. 1989. *Public Policy Statement*. Washington D.C., National Council on Aging. P. 33.

Pifer, A. 1986. "The public policy response." Pp. 391–413 in A. Piper and L. Bronte, eds., *Our Aging Society: Paradox and Promise*. New York: W. W. Norton & Company.

Schooler, K. 1975. "A comparison of rural and non-rural elderly on selected variables." Pp. 262–280 in R. C. Atchley, T. O. Byerts, and M. Arts, eds., *Rural Environments and Aging*. Washington, D.C.: Gerontological Society.

Soldo, B. J., and E. M. Agree. 1988. "America's elderly." *Population Bulletin*. Vol. 43. No. 3. Washington D.C.: Population Reference Bureau.

Townsend, P. 1981. "The structured dependency of the elderly: A creation of social policy in the twentieth century." *Ageing and Society: The Journal of The Centre for Policy on Ageing and The British Society of Gerontology*. New York: Cambridge University Press, 1.

12

Health Care in Rural America

Doris P. Slesinger

During the 1990s, the United States must address three major policy issues regarding rural health care: the economics of health care, equity in access to health services, and special health problems related to rural populations. These issues generate important policy decisions that the nation must face immediately. Although these are health issues, they cannot be regarded as matters separate from the economic strength of rural communities or of the federal government. Indeed, more attention must be paid to the symbiotic relationship between the strength and vitality of the United States as a nation and the strength and vitality of the rural communities that provide the food on which this strength is based. Strong rural communities require strong economies, and the infrastructure underlying this vitality consists not only of a basic and quality educational system, but a basic and quality health system as well.

Just as our nation has solved some of the inequities of the educational system, so too must we solve the inequities of the health-care system. Historically, our rural lands were dotted with small, one-room schoolhouses. Most rural primary schools have now been consolidated into larger districts, and regional high schools that serve much larger geographic areas have been created. States, educational districts, and local school boards planned the location and use of these district and regional schools. These schools are able to provide high-quality education in a broad array of subjects because of the larger population they serve and the larger pool of resources they can tap. The successful regional system is fueled by the linkages between the local communities that support primary education and the larger educational districts that control the curriculum in the regional high schools. Thus, quality programming is provided to children living in wide geographic areas. Such progress in rural education serves as a model for improving rural health care.

In the past, these small communities not only had a one-room schoolhouse but an "old family doc" as well. While the educational needs of the rural children have been addressed by the communities themselves and linked to a planned and coordinated regional system for higher education, no such activity has taken place in the area of health care. Many small communities have tried to keep, or replace, a one-person medical practice. But the statistics indicate that the number of rural, one-person practices has declined and will continue to decline because of trends in medical practice and market forces.

In the mid-1960s, the movement that produced the Comprehensive Health Planning Act started the planning process for coordinated regional health care. However, with the national swing toward free market forces' determining the availability of health services, coordinated health planning had all but disappeared by the beginning of the 1980s. This has left small and mid-sized rural communities without the opportunity to link to any organized or consolidated system of health-care services.

Many small communities lack not only day-to-day primary health-care services, they also lack hospitals that provide obstetrical care, general surgery, and some routine acute care. The more complex hospital care as well as trauma centers and neonatal intensive care units are located in tertiary care centers in large metropolitan areas and serve a regional population. Thus, the medical equivalent of regional high schools appears to have been established, but we lack the consolidated "medical" districts.

Improving the health status of rural people must be regarded as the shared responsibility of individuals, employers, health providers, and governments at local, state, and national levels, just as the improvement of the educational level of rural people was considered the responsibility of individual citizens and educational experts, as well as local, state, and national governments.

Economics of Health Care

The mounting costs of health care for both urban and rural dwellers in the United States are well documented. One major constraint on costs has been the institution of the diagnostic-related groupings (DRGs) dollar ceilings that are reimbursed by the federal government for hospital stays. Created in 1983, these regulations have dramatically reduced the length of hospital stays. Although DRG regulations apply primarily to Medicaid and Medicare patients, many private health insurance companies have also set similar caps on the hospital costs for their insurees. And a set of maximum reimbursable charges for outpatient procedures is already beginning to fall into place.

One way of approaching medical charges is to take a fresh look at physician reimbursements. Instead of accepting the traditional scale of payment (i.e., higher charges for specialized medicine than for primary care and extremely high charges for medical care that involves high-tech procedures such as laser surgery or nuclear magnetic imaging), there is a new effort to evaluate doctors' services based on three components: work performed by the physician; practice costs, including malpractice premiums; and cost of postgraduate or specialty training. Researchers at the Harvard

School of Public Health have proposed an alternative physician-payment system, called the *resource-based relative-value scale*, which they applied to various types of physician services (Hsiao et al., 1987; Hsiao et al., 1988a). In a simulation model for family practice, internal medicine, general surgery, and thoracic and cardiovascular surgery, the authors note that a family practitioner could receive 60 percent more revenue from Medicare, whereas the average ophthalmologist could lose 40 percent of current revenues. The effects on other specialties fall between these two (Hsiao et al., 1988b).

The implications for changing the fee structure for physicians are considerable. For example, if physicians were reimbursed at a higher rate for primary care procedures, more physicians might be attracted to perform these procedures rather than to opt for specialized postgraduate training. Such a change could reduce the overabundance of specialists that the United States produces each year and permit a more balanced distribution of physicians between urban and rural locations.

A change in the reimbursement policy might improve the quality of health care in rural areas. For one, it might help redress the lack of primary care providers who can assist aging rural persons with chronic illnesses. Also, such a change might improve the availability of mental health services as well as psychiatrists and other mental health providers in rural areas. Primary care and mental health services do not require the application of high technology in hospital settings. Each involves the need for practitioners to spend sizable amounts of time with patients over a long period. If physicians were reimbursed commensurate with the time spent ministering to the ill, perhaps more physicians would turn their attention to aiding the sick in these ways.

Equity in Access to Health Services

Many scholars have expressed concern with the nation's health-care delivery system (Roemer, 1986; Starr, 1982; Rosenblatt and Moscovice, 1982; Navarro, 1976, 1987). In general, the United States has developed a "market" system rather than one based on the unmet needs of its citizens. Medical care originated from a simple exchange of service for money, not unlike one's transactions with the local shoemaker. As a result, health-care services are generally established in areas where profits can be generated.

Following the passage of the Social Security Act of 1964, health (or, more properly, "illness") insurance started to be aggressively marketed, mainly to cover the high costs of hospital charges. Also, Medicare, a health insurance program for older citizens tied to the Social Security program, was developed. This meant that most persons 65 and over were able to obtain both inpatient and outpatient medical care at very low out-of-pocket expenses. Note the word "medical," not "health," care. Public funds were targeted to supplying the elderly with medical care provided by medical personnel in their offices and in other facilities in which they worked. Such care eliminated a whole array of other professional workers who minister to the health of the population, among them occupational therapists, nurse practitioners, psychiatric social workers, and chiropractors. Since then, other types of health insurance plans have developed—some quite comprehensive, others still limited to hospital costs.

Concern with equity means that one must examine underserved populations. The majority of citizens who fall into this category are those who cannot pay for their health care, mainly the poor. Local governments and charitable organizations, since the turn of the century, have attempted to service the poor. In the 1960s, the federal government was also prodded into developing health insurance programs for the "deserving" poor. Medicaid is a program based on joint financing by the states and the federal government. In most states, persons have to be recipients of one of the means-tested programs of social aid to qualify for this medical insurance. The *deserving poor* are defined as those who have fallen into poverty through situations that were no fault of their own and includes, for example, widows, children, and victims of war.

Who remains in the underserved populations? A small group of the "undeserving" poor—those who are defined as derelicts, perhaps because of alcohol or drug abuse, or those who are "lazy" and don't want to work. However, many other groups are also the underserved and uninsured: the "near" poor, who work but do not earn enough to buy health insurance; the long-term unemployed; those who work part-time or for small companies that do not offer group health insurance; and self-employed persons who cannot afford individual health insurance policies. Many of these conditions are more prevalent in rural areas. Recent research indicates that among the poor and near poor, more people without health insurance and fewer people with Medicaid coverage live in rural areas than in urban areas (Wilensky and Berk, 1982).

A statewide survey was recently conducted in Wisconsin to ascertain the numbers and characteristics of those who did not have health insurance. Review of the characteristics of the uninsured revealed some startling facts. Of the total Wisconsin population of 4.2 million, 12 percent, or about 550,000 persons, had no health insurance; about three-fourths were adults, and one-fourth were children. However, of all the uninsured, 85 percent lived in households in which at least one person was employed. Moreover, only 18 percent of the uninsured lived in households with incomes below poverty (the poor having probably been covered by Medicaid or Medicare); 25 percent were in households between 100 to 199 percent of poverty; and 44 percent (the largest proportion) lived in households with an annual income at 200 or more percent of the poverty cutoff (Soref, 1988). The stark facts are that many of the uninsured persons are employed workers and their families who have low-paying jobs or who do not work full time at one job (but may work a number of jobs part time).

Some data are available about health insurance coverage among farmers. In a sample of Wisconsin farmers, Jensen (1983) notes that farm families that rely only on farm income are slightly less likely to have health insurance

(86 percent) than are families with nonfarm income (90 percent). However, farm families are less likely to have group plans than are other families; only 43 percent of farm families have group insurance compared with 62 percent of the total population. Moreover, of the state's total population, 26 percent of the farm population have private individual plans, compared with only 8 percent of the total population (Jensen, 1983). Farm families are likely to get group health insurance through plans sponsored by farm or religious organizations or through their off-farm work. Private individual plans are much more expensive than group plans and often provide fewer benefits.

Although national health insurance proposals have been brought before the Congress, none has ever been enacted, and today the inequities of coverage across the country are great. Persons who suffer most are neither the unemployed nor the very poor; they are the hard-working, low-paid workers and the self-employed craft and service persons, many of whom live in rural areas. They deserve to be insured just as much as the assembly-line workers in manufacturing plants. But because of employer, not worker, characteristics, they do not have access to reasonable health insurance plans. A national or universal health insurance plan which would include these hidden workers needs to be enacted.

Table 12.1 provides data from national health surveys conducted in 1976 and 1982 and compares urban and rural residents. The first column shows that in 1976 and 1982, rural farm residents are the ones most likely to be uninsured. Over the six-year period, however, the proportion of uninsured in most categories declined, while it increased for rural farm residents.

In the second column, we see that farm residents had the lowest proportion of persons stating that they had no regular source of care. This has held true for the 20 years the National Center for Health Statistics (1984) has been surveying the nation's population, mainly because the rural respondents can name the family doctor in town. However, even though they could name their health provider, the farm residents had the lowest proportion (71 percent) who saw a doctor in the previous year (column 3). This was a full 10 percentage points below the national average of 81 percent.

As an example of receipt of preventive services, women from rural farm areas had the lowest proportion who reported a Pap screening test for cervical cancer in the previous year (column 4). Although the gap between rural and urban women narrowed between 1976 and 1982, the rural rate was still considerably below the national average.

Finally, hospital use in 1976 (column 5) reflected a long-standing trend—rural residents had higher rates of hospitalization than most urban groups. Researchers speculated that this pattern was related to rural residents' having lower numbers of doctor visits; they suggested that postponing doctor visits caused rural patients to be sicker than their urban counterparts when they finally received care. However, the hospitalization data indicate that by 1982 the farm population was similar to all other residence groups. Currently, because of shorter hospital stays since the inception of the DRGs, there

TABLE 12.1 Receipt of U.S. Medical Procedures by Residence, 1976 and 1982

Residence	Percent with No Insurance (1)		Percent with No Regular Source of Care (2)		Percent Who Saw MD in (3)		Percent Who Obtained Pap Test (4)		Percent with 1+ Hospital Days (5)	
	1976	1982	1976	1982	1976	1982	1976	1982	1976	1982
Total	10	9	12	11	n.a.	81	54	60	11	10
SMSA central city	12	11	15	12		82	58	63	13	10
SMSA other urban	8	7	13	10		83	55	61	10	9
Non-SMSA urban	8	9	10	11		79	51	55	13	10
Rural nonfarm	10		10				52		12	
Rural farm	12	14	7	7		71	35	54	8	10

n.a. = not available.

Source: Aday and Andersen (1984). Reprinted by permission.

appears to be a trend toward more uniformity across areas, and the differential has almost been eliminated.

Access to hospitals in rural areas is currently being studied. Small hospitals are finding their economic viability threatened unless they branch out into new and less traditional services for their communities. Some suggested services include long-term care, health education, elderly and disabled day care, and other outpatient services. The Small or Rural Hospital section of the American Hospital Association notes that financially unstable hospitals have been closing in the United States. If the trend continues, the most vulnerable facilities are those with less than 100 beds (American Hospital Association, 1988).

Demographics and Physician Distribution

Miller (1982) predicted that rural health issues for the 1980s would concern the rapidly increasing rural population resulting from the "turnaround," that is, persons moving from the cities back to rural lands. Miller feared that such a turnaround would worsen the situation in rural areas, where physicians are already in short supply. He also predicted that rural population growth would increase the use and acceptance of midlevel practitioners in place of family doctors to alleviate the shortage.

None of these issues turn out to be of major importance today because the turnaround movement has ceased. Beale and Fuguitt note that the metropolitan areas are once again growing at a faster rate than are the nonmetropolitan. However, even in agricultural counties with population losses, the process is rather "a slow bleeding than a demographic hemorrhage" (1986:61). The nonmetropolitan areas that are gaining population are in the retirement states of California, Florida, and Arizona. Although the turnaround has ceased, the nonmetropolitan counties today still have larger populations than they would have had if the turnaround movement of the 1970s had not taken place. And a large proportion of these newcomers are of retirement age.

The distribution of physicians in rural areas has changed since the 1970s. In 1980, a report of the Graduate Medical Education National Advisory Committee suggested that class size in medical schools be increased to produce a surplus of doctors that would diffuse to areas of underservice. Medical schools responded by increasing class size and producing more physicians. Although the majority of these additional physicians still settle in urban communities, there appears to be some improvement in rural areas. Kindig, Li, and Movassaghi (1988) calculate the change in numbers of physicians practicing in nonmetropolitan counties from 1975 to 1985. They note that the absolute number of physicians in patient care increased from 36,850 to 53,365, a 44.8 percent increase, whereas the total population of these counties decreased by 3.5 percent. Thus, the physician/population ratio in nonmetropolitan counties increased from 65.3 physicians per 100,000 population in 1975 to 97.9 per 100,000 physicians in 1985, an average annual rate of growth of 4.1 percent. This rate of growth was faster than the U.S.

rate as a whole (2.9 percent) and was faster than the rate in all metropolitan counties (2.7 percent) over this ten-year period.

Two other interesting changes in nonmetropolitan counties were noted by Kindig, Li, and Movassaghi. First, the proportion of board-certified physicians increased from 40 percent in 1975 to 60 percent in 1985. Also, during the same ten-year period, the proportion of physicians who were 65 years of age and over decreased by 11 percent, whereas the proportion of those under 44 years of age increased by 93 percent.

These improvements, however, were not equally distributed across nonmetropolitan counties. The larger the county's population, the more likely the physicians were board-certified and of younger age. In addition, the physician to population ratio in nonmetropolitan areas also varied by regions of the country. The highest ratios in the nonmetropolitan counties in 1985 were found in the Northeast, followed by the West, and then the South. The lowest physician to population ratios were found in the North Central region.

Probably because of the increased number of physicians, there is less acceptance now than there was ten years ago of the roles of physician assistants and nurse practitioners in areas physically removed from physicians. Today most of these physician "extenders" work directly with physicians and have not fulfilled the original hope of providing services in communities that do not have a physician.

To summarize, the inability to pay for services is the major barrier to health care. The poor and those with no or limited health insurance are less likely to receive care. The small size of rural communities and their distance from urban centers are other barriers, with residents of smaller places having much less access to doctors and hospitals than residents of larger places. When persons live in rural areas and are poor and uninsured, they are at "triple jeopardy" (Rowland and Lyons, 1989).

Special Problems in Rural Areas

Three special health problems are common in rural areas: accidents and injuries; chemical contamination of the environment from agricultural inputs; and the severe stress to farmers, their families, and farm communities from such factors as the recent devaluation of land, foreclosures of farming enterprises, and unusual weather problems (e.g., drought and flooding).

Accidents and Injuries

It is well known that the agriculture industry has one of the highest accident and injury rates, if measured by fatalities. Many of these rural accidents happen to urban residents who are visiting or passing through rural areas. As an example, rural revitalization efforts to develop the economy of an area are often based on recreational resources. Medical emergencies are often created from auto accidents on rural roads, as well as skiing, boating, motorcycle, and snowmobile accidents.

Policies to address these problems include continued support for emergency medical care systems. Because of the high farm accident rates that result in death when rapid medical attention is not available, we must continue to support and improve rural schemes for such first responders as emergency medical technicians and med-flights that use helicopters.

Evidence indicates that we have learned how to address rural emergency problems. Large medical complexes with specialists trained in burn, trauma, and cardiac treatment are able to save lives if the patients are brought there quickly and in relatively stable condition. A regional approach based on local supporting structures appears to be the solution to this problem.

Contamination of the Environment

The health of rural residents and of the larger public is affected by the overuse of pesticides and herbicides. These chemicals seep into groundwater and contaminate drinking water. They are sometimes sprayed on workers in the fields (Wilk, 1986). Conveyed on fruits, vegetables, and feed, they enter the nation's food chain.

Contamination of the environment is difficult to trace, especially when the contaminants accumulate over a long period. Stokes and Brace (1988), however, were able to analyze cancer mortality rates in selected rural counties for five types of cancer over a 20-year period (1950–1969), correlating the cancer rates with the use of agricultural chemicals in those counties since 1964. Their findings indicate that the use of herbicides is statistically predictive for genital and lymphatic cancer mortalities and that insecticide use correlates with the incidence of respiratory cancer. The use of fertilizers, however, was not related to any of the cancer deaths. Because of the limitations of the measurements, the authors note that these results must be considered as suggestive, not definitive. However, it is likely that evidence will continue to accumulate that relates illnesses to environmental toxins.

Environmental protection laws must be strengthened and the cleanup of toxic sites and dumps must continue. Only federal policies can make an impact on the total environment. Our rural hinterland is used for nuclear waste dumps and landfills from city garbage systems; cities and industries discharge sewage into our lakes and streams. The health of our citizens depends on clean air and water and an uncontaminated food chain. A clean environment requires federal regulations, inspections, and expert cleanup teams. We cannot contaminate the environment and expect to lead fruitful, healthy lives and produce healthy offspring.

Stress

Another set of problems involves the extreme mental stress of farmers, farm laborers, rural bankers, rural storekeepers, and others due to the faltering rural economy, foreclosure of family farms, and failure of rural banks (Heffernan and Heffernan, 1986). Rural adult male suicide rates are increasing. Children of rural families in stress are exhibiting alcohol and drug-related maladies. Although rural people have never been interested in supporting mental health programs as such, the need is now greater than ever to direct mental health outreach programs specifically toward rural populations (Bachrach, 1983).

Conclusion

Three areas of concern have been noted: the costs of health care, the inequities in access to health services, and the special health needs of rural residents. In general, rural areas have characteristics that are likely to continue into the twenty-first century. These include diverse populations and lands, low population densities, and greater proportions of the elderly, poor, and lesser educated among their residents. In order to meet the health needs of these populations, we must consider a national health insurance program to provide insurance for the self-employed, the near poor, and the part-time workers.

Inequities in access to physicians still exist in rural areas because of maldistribution problems. We need to investigate new ways of reallocating our dollars by evaluating physician charges for various types of care. If primary health care and prevention services carried higher charges, it is likely that more physicians would be attracted to this type of service. One proposed plan, the resource-based relative-value scheme, is now under investigation. This plan would redirect some of the monetary rewards that have been placed on the practice of high-tech medicine, which is available to very few, to more general services needed by the majority.

Finally, we must address some of the unique health problems of rural areas: the stress of living in areas with declining economies, the high accident and injury rates, the aging population that requires long-term care, and the contamination of the environment. The federal government should strengthen its efforts to clean up toxic wastes; control the distribution and use of herbicides, insecticides, and pesticides; and prevent additional spoiling of the land by prohibiting the disposal of nuclear wastes and toxic chemicals near farmlands and streams. Accessible, necessary, and coordinated quality health care for rural America is possible by the turn of the century if attention is directed to these problems.

References

Aday, Lu Ann, and Ronald M. Andersen. 1984. "The national profile of access to medical care: Where do we stand?" *American Journal of Public Health* 74(12):1331–1339.

American Hospital Association. 1988. *Profile of Small or Rural Hospitals 1980–86.* Chicago: American Hospital Association.

American Medical Association. 1985. *Physician Characteristics and Distribution in the U.S.* 1984 ed. Chicago: American Medical Association.

Bachrach, Leona. 1983. "Psychiatric services in rural areas: A sociological overview." *Hospital and Community Psychiatry* 34(3):215–226.

Beale, Calvin L., and Glenn V. Fuguitt. 1986. "Metropolitan and nonmetropolitan population growth in the United States since 1980." Pp. 46–62 in *New Dimensions in Rural Policy: Building Upon Our Heritage.* Washington, D.C.: U.S. Congress, Joint Economic Committee.

Heffernan, William D., and Judith Bortner Heffernan. 1986. "Impact of the farm crisis on rural families and communities." *The Rural Sociologist* 6(3):160–170.

Hsiao, William C., Peter Braun, Edmund R. Becker, and Stephen R. Thomas. 1987. "The resource-based relative-value scale: Toward the development of an alternative physician payment system." *Journal of the American Medical Association* 258(6):799–802.

Hsiao, William C., Peter Braun, Douwe Yntema, and Edmund R. Becker. 1988a. "Estimating physicians' work for a resource-based relative-value scale." *New England Journal of Medicine* 319(13):835–841.

Hsiao, William C., Peter Braun, Daniel Dunn, Edmund R. Becker, Margaret DeNicola, and Thomas R. Ketcham. 1988b. "Results and policy implications of the resource-based relative-value study." *New England Journal of Medicine* 319(13):881–888.

Jensen, Helen. 1983. *Farm People's Health Insurance Coverage.* Rural Development Research. No. 39. Washington, D.C.: USDA, Economic Research Service. December.

Kindig, David A., Man Chun Li, and Hormoz Movassaghi. 1988. "Trends in physician availability and selected characteristics in the nonmetropolitan counties of the United States, 1975–1985." University of Wisconsin–Madison. Unpublished.

Miller, Michael K. 1982. "Health and medical care." Pp. 216–223 in Don A. Dillman and Daryl J. Hobbs, eds., *Rural Society in the U.S.: Issues for the 1980s.* Boulder, Colo.: Westview Press.

National Center for Health Statistics. 1984. *Health Characteristics by Geographic Region and Other Places of Residence.* Series 10. No. 146.

Navarro, Vicente. 1976. "Health and medicine in rural United States." In *Medicine Under Capitalism.* New York: Prodist.

———. 1987. "Federal health policies in the United States: An alternative explanation." *The Milbank Quarterly* 65(1):81–111.

Roemer, Milton I. 1986. *An Introduction to the U.S. Health Care System,* 2nd ed. New York: Springer.

Rosenblatt, Roger A., and Ira S. Moscovice. 1982. *Rural Health Care.* New York: Wiley and Sons.

Rowland, Diane, and Barbara Lyons. 1989. "Triple jeopardy: Rural, poor and uninsured." *Health Services Research* 23(6):975–1004.

Soref, Michael. 1988. *The Uninsured in Wisconsin.* Madison, Wis.: Wisconsin Department of Health and Social Services, Center for Health Statistics.

Starr, Paul. 1982. *The Social Transformation of American Medicine.* New York: Basic Books.

Stokes, C. Shannon, and Kathy D. Brace. 1988. "Agricultural chemical use and cancer mortality in selected rural counties in the U.S.A." *Journal of Rural Studies* 4(3):239–247.

Wilensky, G., and M. Berk. 1982. "Health care, the poor, and the role of Medicaid." *Health Affairs* 1(Fall):93–100.

Wilk, Valerie A. 1986. *The Occupational Health of Migrant and Seasonal Farmworkers in the United States,* 2nd ed. Washington, D.C.: Farmworker Justice Fund, Inc.

13

Rural Education

Daryl Hobbs

The issues pertaining to public education in rural America must be considered in the context of a perceived national public education crisis. Publication of *A Nation at Risk* in 1983 symbolized public awareness of this crisis. The study's title accentuates an enduring American connection between education and the economy. The study emphasized that the nation's future economic competitiveness was being jeopardized by declining student test scores and rising dropout rates. In response to that assertion, educators, policymakers, business leaders, and others have called for and instigated numerous educational reforms. Most reforms that were proposed and adopted have attributed poor student performance to poor school performance. From this viewpoint, instructional, organizational, and curricular changes within the schools are essential to improvement.

The education crisis follows several decades during which schools increasingly became instruments of social, economic, and industrial policy as well as agents for education. Because schools are unique in that they daily bring together the youth of all classes and races, they have been publicly mandated and offered incentives to add noninstructional services such as transportation, nutrition, health, counseling, child care, and recreation to their education role. Although schools, as much as any sector, have adopted the mass society principles of management and organizational specialization, they have in fact become less specialized. Their societal purposes have become more comprehensive in response to social, economic, and political changes outside the schools.

This enlarged role of the schools is seldom taken into account in analyses of the declining productivity of the public education sector. For example, a 1983 analysis concludes that "public school productivity, as measured by the number of employees required to process a given number of students, seems to have declined by 46 percent between 1957 and 1979" (Brimelow, 1983:62). Two features of that statement are striking. One is that students are referred to as being "processed," a notion that reflects a widely held industrial perspective regarding education. The second is that it is not clear what proportion of the "employees" are performing noninstructional services that schools, at public insistence, have added in recent decades. Such added services are not usually included in assessing the effectiveness of schools. *A Nation at Risk* and the other assessments it has inspired tend to confine attention to test scores, dropout rates, and costs per student. Indeed, we will emphasize that what is revealed as declining student (school) performance is highly associated with changes in family, community, and economic structure outside the school. As some writers contend (e.g., Carnoy and Levin, 1986), reproduction rather than change of the existing social and economic structure has become a societal expectation of the school.

It has been puzzling to some that, despite the recent spate of educational reforms, little improvement in student test scores has occurred and dropout rates in some states and regions remain unacceptably high. But other factors known to greatly influence student performance have been largely ignored. For example, while test scores have been declining (or at least not improving) and dropout rates have been increasing, the proportion of the nation's children living below the poverty line has increased to the highest levels since the mid-1970s. Rural areas have been most adversely affected. Indeed, by 1987 rural (nonmetro) poverty rates were 50 percent higher than metro rates and even higher than inner-city poverty rates (Greenstein, 1988). This statistic is highly relevant because student socioeconomic status has repeatedly proved to be the most powerful predictor of student academic performance (Walberg and Fowler, 1987; White, 1982). Our analysis of the 1989 version of the nation's report card produced a correlation of .78 between average state test scores and percent of each state's children living below the poverty line (Hobbs, 1989).

Perceptions of Rural School Problems

Public perception of a national educational and concurrent economic competitiveness crisis has contributed to some modification of policy perspectives affecting rural education. For several decades rural schools were thought to represent a problem to be solved, because most had small enrollments and therefore were economically incapable of offering all the features of the large, comprehensive school (DeYoung, 1987; Rosenfeld, 1987). Since they offered less they were, by extension, generally thought to be educationally inferior. Consequently, the most prominent rural school "improvement" policy for decades was to encourage consolidation to achieve larger size and therefore greater presumed economic efficiency and educational effectiveness. The presumption of an unambiguous linkage between school size, efficiency, and effectiveness was at the heart of what Tyack (1975), in a critique of U.S. public education, referred to as the "one-best system" perspective; that is, public education would be improved to the extent that all schools came to resemble the consensually validated model of the "good" school. But since the one-best system itself is now perceived to be in crisis, simplistic prescriptions for rural school improvement are somewhat attenuated. A number of states, however, in their apparent impatience to improve school performance, have again turned to attempts to mandate further rural school consolidation (Sher, 1986).

The perception of crisis contributes to some rethinking of standardization policies. Location-specific educational problems, such as urban desegregation, have contributed to the restructuring of some urban secondary schools into specialized magnet schools, and decentralization strategies are being employed in New York City and Chicago. A concomitant trend is open enrollment; that is, students can attend whichever secondary school they choose as long as desegregation is not adversely affected. Such an open enrollment policy is in place in Minnesota and has been adopted by Iowa. Other states are considering it. Choice is becoming a more operative concept for both rural and urban schools, although spatial considerations make choice a limited rural alternative.

The Situation: Rural Schools

Some writers contend that social and economic changes have virtually eliminated a distinctive rural society. Whether one agrees with that assertion or not, rural life and institutions have undoubtedly been transformed by mass society and its emphases on specialization, centralization, and standardization. No institutional sector manifests this transformation more than does public education.

Over the past 50 years rural schools have been transformed following criteria embodied in the national trend toward standardization. The most visible effect has been a dramatic reduction in the number of schools and school districts through consolidation. Encouraged by state policies, consolidation reduced the number of districts from 128,000 in 1930 to about 15,700 by 1985 (U.S. Department of Commerce, 1988). The average number of students per district increased from about 200 in 1930 to nearly 3,000 by 1972 (Walberg and Fowler, 1987). There are approximately 84,000 public schools—57,000 elementary, 22,000 secondary, and 1,600 elementary and secondary combined. Seventy-one percent of the elementary schools have an enrollment of less than 500. Among secondary schools, 43 percent have an enrollment of less than 500, 29 percent an enrollment from 500 to 999, and 28 percent an enrollment over 1,000 (U.S. Department of Commerce, 1988).

About three-quarters of the 15,700 districts have an enrollment of 2,500 or less. Most of these are nonmetropolitan. Rural America now includes about three-quarters of the nation's school districts, which serve about one-quarter of the nation's students. Many of today's small-enrollment rural districts are what Nachtigal (1980) refers to as "necessarily existent," since low population density makes further consolidation impractical. That factor, along with growing rural resistance, slowed the pace of consolidation after 1975. Only about 900 districts were consolidated out of existence between 1975 and 1985.

The merger and consolidation of rural schools have been accompanied and encouraged by a shift in sources of funding and control of rural schools.

The long-term trend has been toward more state funding of schools. Although states vary substantially, about 50 percent of public school revenues are currently supplied by state governments, about 6 percent by the federal government (mostly category programs), and the remainder by localities. Public schools differ from other public services in that there is a minimal federal role. Federal policy and funding have had little direct effect on public education.

The absence of a federal role has not prevented public schools, including rural schools, from becoming a national system, which has emerged as the state became an increasingly prominent part of the production system (Carnoy and Levin, 1986). Standardized tests, national publication and marketing of textbooks, growing professionalism among educators and state education officials, and state regulations, as well as the dictates of a mobile society, have produced what is, in effect, a national education system, despite funding that is dispersed among state governments and localities. Rural schools have clearly been incorporated into the system and greatly affected by it, although levels of funding and perceptions of differences in school quality vary greatly among rural localities, even within the same state.

Both schools as an organization and education as an institution tend to be more visible and prominent features of the community in rural areas than in urban. In many rural communities the school is the largest employer, the largest claim on the public treasury, and the locus of many community events. The school is thus more closely connected with community life (cf. Peshkin, 1978). Lowe and Pinhey (1980) report that, contrary to popular belief, rural people place as great a value on education as do urban people. Their analysis of national sample surveys reveals that rural residents place improving the nation's educational system higher among national concerns than do their urban counterparts. The prevalence of rural-to-urban migration of youth and the perceived importance of education to successful migration (Tweeten, 1980) also contribute to the value rural people place on education. Indeed, education itself changes some traditional rural values. Flinn and Johnson (1974) report a strong inverse association between agrarianism and educational attainment.

The Effect of Rural Diversity on Policy

Rural America has become exceptionally diverse—economically, socially, and occupationally (Bender et al., 1985). In recent years many new and different versions of rural America have emerged. An important policy implication is a need to disaggregate policy initiatives. Also, policies must provide sufficient flexibility to enable adaptation to local circumstances (National Governors' Association, 1988). A need for local adaptation has become especially important for schools because of the tremendous variation between schools and districts in funding capacity, population density, student characteristics, and ability to attract and retain essential educational services. For both rural and urban schools the effect of interaction between school and neighborhood or community is coming to be better understood as a factor associated with effective schools.

The economic diversity of rural America compounds the problem of equity in school funding. Not only is the gap between rural and metro income widening, but variation in rural localities' financial capacity to support education is increasing as well. At the same time, educational costs are rising substantially for all schools. Most state foundation formulas take into account local resource variations in allocating state funds, but variations in school revenues per student remain greater for rural than for urban schools. Resource-poor districts have less money to spend than do wealthier districts. Federal funds help supplement poor districts, but they are not sufficient to produce equity. A result is the recent emergence of court challenges in several states and an effort by some states (e.g., Colorado) to take more local factors into account in funding formulas (Nachtigal and Hobbs, 1988).

Rural Education: Analytically Separable Issues

Education has become an increasingly comprehensive public service sector. Because of changes in the family, community, and economy, schools are now expected, at public insistence, to provide a growing range of social services in addition to education. Consequently, public education represents a complex set of human resource policy issues. Accordingly, our discussion divides rural education into four analytically separable issues: schools, student performance, effect of schooling on students' future income and mobility, and control. Each issue pertains to an outcome thought to be important to rural and national quality of life, but each outcome is attributable to a different mix of factors. Public policy tends to group them together or to assume that public investments in schools have a direct and exclusive effect on student academic performance and future income. Research clearly shows that while school improvement policies can be justified on their own merits, alone they are unlikely to produce substantial changes in student performance or to produce much effect on income distribution within the society (Mulkey, 1988).

The School

Recent education reforms have generally concentrated on the school and its teachers, programs, methods, and requirements. Most rural school issues emanate from their necessary (and often locally desired) small size and associated effects on costs, funding, staffing, and curriculum. Small schools generally have small budgets and are therefore less able to offer the breadth of curriculum and other components of the comprehensive school. A leaner curriculum, less teacher specialization, and fewer inputs have been a principal basis for the frequent assertion that smaller rural schools are more costly and educationally inferior. Research supporting that assertion is mixed.

If anything, recent research has tended to downplay the effect of school (district) size on either costs or student performance. Indeed, Walberg and Fowler emphasize that "research on district size . . . is at best equivocal; and much of it suggests that bigger districts yield low achievement and poor student, parent, and staff morale" (1987:6). Similarly, from a study of New York state school districts, Butler and Monk (1985:3) conclude, "The analysis of scale economies enjoyed by larger districts can come at the expense of the efficient production of educational outcomes. . . . Empirical evidence . . . shows that lower levels of efficiency exist in large as compared to small districts."

Fox's (1980) extensive review of research on educational scale economies concludes that educational cost curves are U-shaped; for example, the lowest cost per student for an equivalent quality (quantity of inputs) of education lies between the extremes of small and large. In rural areas, the relationship is significantly affected by student population density. White and Tweeten (1973) found that districts with a student density of 0.6 per square mile achieved minimum costs with as few as 300 enrollment; whereas for districts with a student density of 3.0 or greater per square mile, an enrollment of 1,075 was required to reach a minimum cost per student. Such situational factors led Sher (1986) to conclude that the relationship between educational costs and district size should be evaluated on a case-by-case basis rather than mandated by statewide policies.

Aside from costs, some debate concerning school size focuses on the validity of using the quantity of inputs as a measure of school quality. Again the research is equivocal. In a synthesis of research regarding school inputs, Bridge, Judd, and Moock (1979) found only one input, student socioeconomic status, among 35 inputs surveyed, to be consistently associated with learning. Monk's (1987) curriculum study found a direct linear relationship between school size and curriculum offerings, but he found the association to be of little practical importance beyond a high school enrollment of 400, since only small numbers of students took advantage of the greater offerings of these larger schools.

Growing concern for student performance and dropout rates has shifted research emphases away from school size. More research is now being directed toward the effect of size on the school's social environment. Goodlad (1984) argues that size influences the ethos of the school and social relationships between students and teachers and among school, parents, and community. One such effect is the greater opportunity for student participation in small schools. Otto's (1975) longitudinal study of student performance found that student participation in extracurricular activities produces a powerful independent effect on academic performance, controlling for academic abilities and family socioeconomic status. In a classic study of behavioral effects of high school size, Barker and Gump (1964) conclude that a school should be sufficiently small that all its students feel they are needed for its enterprises.

While research on school size is voluminous, much of it lost relevance when the very smallest schools were eliminated through consolidation. As emphasized by Rosenfeld (1987), once consolidation had eliminated the smallest schools, research on the effects of consolidation failed to produce evidence of links between standard educational outcomes and size of school.

In sum, research consistently concludes that school or school district size is not a very important factor in affecting student learning outcomes (Sher, 1986; Smith and DeYoung, 1988). Indeed, what is often interpreted to be the poor educational performance of small rural schools is more likely attributable to the number of rural districts serving predominantly poor and lower income students.

Student Academic Performance

How well a student performs academically is attributable to a combination of individual abilities, the quality of instruction, the measures of academic performance used, and the social and economic environment both within and outside the school. Although both individual and structural factors affect student performance, most assessments have been limited to the individual's traits or the characteristics of the school. Apple and Weiss (1986) stress that the mainstream of educational research has been overly psychological and has neglected inquiry into the larger context in which schools exist and which may make it difficult for them to succeed by existing standards and measures.

Although research consistently shows a direct connection between students' socioeconomic status and academic performance, there is a distinction regarding that relationship which underscores its structural nature. Socioeconomic status is a strong and powerful predictor of student performance (accounting for 60 to 70 percent of the variance) when aggregated to the level of a school, a district, or a state, but the association is much weaker in accounting for individual student performance (White, 1982; Walberg and Fowler, 1987). The effect is more powerful in aggregate than it is for the individual.

The effect of social class on student performance is especially germane for rural areas, since the current nonmetro poverty rate is 50 percent above the metropolitan rate. But neither the level of student academic performance nor rural poverty rates are uniformly distributed geographically. Rural poverty rates tend to be highly concentrated (Bender et al., 1985), and student outcomes vary widely between states and regions (a 9 percent dropout rate in Minnesota compared with 41 percent in Florida at the other extreme). The performance of rural students (schools) ranges from the best in the country to the worst, depending largely on the socioeconomic environment in which the school is located. In many rural localities students suffer the double jeopardy of poverty and poor, underfunded schools.

Since rural areas include a disproportionate share of the nation's poor, evaluations of the academic performance of rural students and schools, either in comparison with each other or in comparison with urban students and schools, should consider students' economic status. Rural-urban differences in academic performance in New Mexico disappeared when the effect of family income was taken into account (Vaughn, 1984; Edington and Martellaro, 1985).

Students' social class affects educational outcomes from within the school as well. In-school factors include the frequently contested economic and cultural biases of standardized tests, as well as the focus and content of the curriculum. Apple and Weiss (1986:11) contend that "by defining certain groups' knowledge as legitimate for reproduction and/or distribution . . . schools help not only in the production of useful technical/administrative knowledge but in the reproduction of the culture and ideological forms of dominant groups." From his cross-national analysis of educational achievement, Swarzweller (1976:213) concludes:

> Social class origin appears to manifest a greater direct impact on (American) scholastic performance and therefore a somewhat more indirect influence on educational ambition than it does in the European (Norway, Germany). Evaluation procedures in American schools, it seems, and perhaps even classroom learning situations, may be more vulnerable to the intrusion of social class biasing than in the European schools.

In the case of rural schools, the standardized curriculum and procedures can contribute to student alienation by depreciating the importance and value of a student's culture and experiences. As an alternative, Wigginton (1986), the inspiration for the *Foxfire* books and educational philosophy, advocates using the locality as a focus for learning, while students simultaneously acquire an ability to learn how to learn. The contention is that such methods enhance student motivation while legitimizing multiple conceptions of knowledge. Although such a philosophy is far from widespread, more rural schools are beginning to emphasize experiential learning and are incorporating students' study of their locality into the curriculum (Nachtigal and Hobbs, 1988).

With regard to social class, the role of the school incorporates conflicting expectations. On the one hand, given the historically strong link between education and economy, schools serve as a major mechanism of meritocracy— in effect reproducing inequality. But schools are also expected to teach and stress democratic and egalitarian values. Carnoy and Levin (1986) observe that when there are contradictory purposes, one of the purposes will be dominant at different times. In the late 1960s and early 1970s the social equality purpose was somewhat more dominant. But because the current perceived education crisis is linked to concern about national economic competitiveness, most recent reforms (e.g., more courses, longer school days, more technically trained teachers) have emphasized the economic dimension over social equality. Correspondingly, improvements in student performance have occurred, but they have tended to be most impressive in more affluent communities and regions. But those gains are offset by higher dropout rates and absence of improvement in other communities and regions, resulting in little overall net improvement in student performance.

Policies intended to improve student performance will likely continue to be met with limited net effect until adverse social and economic conditions affecting student performance are concurrently addressed.

Social and Class Mobility and Rural Development

Social class position and characteristics such as gender and race not only affect student academic performance but also, for persons with the same level of education, great differences in earnings and class mobility (Falk and Lyson, 1988). Tweeten (1980) reports significant income discrepancies between rural white and black males with the same educational attainment and even greater discrepancies between white and black females. Thus, educational attainment does not uniformly produce the same reward for races, sexes, and social classes—an important consideration in interpreting the powerful effect of social class position on student performance. If rewards are different, student motivation and alienation are likely to differ as well.

On a structural level, public investment in education and training is increasingly being advocated as an essential part of rural economic development strategy (Deaton and McNamara, 1984; DeYoung, 1985; Rosenfeld, Bergmar, and Rubin, 1985). Although human capital theorists have demonstrated a direct connection between education or training and economic development, the connection is attenuated for many rural areas. Lichter and Costanzo (1987) did find that level of education of the labor force was the most important factor in accounting for regional differences in nonmetro underemployment. But they stress that upgrading rural human resources is unlikely to reduce local (regional) employment marginality without concomitant increases in the quality and quantity of employment opportunities. Neither education/training without jobs nor jobs without education/training is likely to be of much help to the local labor force.

Since higher paying, higher skill jobs are disproportionately concentrated in metro areas (Falk and Lyson, 1988), more highly trained rural residents often migrate to areas that provide a higher return on their educational investment. In effect, rural localities lose a return on their investment in the education of their youth (Deaton and McNamara, 1984). This has prompted some economists (e.g., Deaton and McNamara, 1984; Tweeten, 1980) to advocate, on equity grounds, greater public subsidy of education in rural areas.

A policy implication is that there is little evidence that education or training alone directly *causes* either individual economic or social mobility, or rural community or regional economic development. Evidence is stronger in support of investments in education/training/counseling that are combined with local and regional economic development strategies.

School/Educational Control

Although public education has evolved into a national system, there remains at least an ideological perception of local control of schools. However, the actual amount of local control has dwindled as state governments have taken on a larger funding and regulatory role. Indeed, these changes, along with economic changes, are adding to rural perceptions of external dependency.

Given education's range of public responsibilities and its prominence in state and local budgets, it is difficult to separate education issues from larger political issues. Hogan (1982) identifies four categories of political issues surrounding public education: (1) structural politics, including alignment of the school with the economy and conflicts over authority relations within schools; (2) human capital politics—efforts of parents and communities to retain a benefit from education; (3) cultural capital politics—conflicts over competing definitions of legitimate knowledge (e.g., textbooks, curriculum, methods); and (4) displacement politics, whereby educational issues become a proxy for other community conflicts.

All these political control issues are identifiable and operative in the rural school environment. In fact, because of the greater relative prominence of the school in community life, control issues are often more intense in rural localities (Peshkin, 1978). Two factors especially pertinent to rural schools, consolidation and the concomitant shift in funding from locality to state, are productive of both structural (authority) and cultural capital (content) control concerns. Resistance to further rural school consolidation (cf. DeYoung, 1987; Sher, 1986) appears to reflect Hogan's (1982) displacement politics category—that is, possible loss of the school being perceived as an added threat to rural community survival. As aptly described by Smith and DeYoung (1988:9):

> Educational control, rather than educational quality, is of most importance in the "appropriate" school size debate. Fundamental philosophical, social, and economic questions continue to lie at the heart of educational controversies. . . . Are the schools agents of the local community, agents of the state, agents of the national economy, or the playground for an urban-based profession?

They speculate that answers to these questions may have more to do with the future existence and operation of rural and small schools than empirical data concerning school size and schooling outcomes.

Because of rural schools' small size and geographic dispersion, control issues often are confined to conflicts within a school district. Despite their large numbers, "small town and rural schools have never enjoyed a powerful constituency to speak for their more subtle benefits" (Cole 1988:141). Moreover, there is a growing sense that rural interests cannot be achieved through resolution of issues only at a community level. Recognition of a need to represent the specific interests of rural and small schools appears to be the foundation for the recent emergence of rural school organizations in many states. However, with few exceptions, these organizations are most representative of teachers and administrators. Consequently, other special interest organizations (e.g., farm organizations) often represent rural school issues from their organization's perspective and interest.

Directions for Rural Education Policy

Public education policies have narrowly focused on the school. But schools and education do not exist in isolation; they affect and are affected by the larger community as well as the regional and national environment. Below are some specific policy considerations pertaining to each of the four issue areas.

The School

Setting aside social, economic, and community factors known to affect student performance, all children, regardless of location or wealth, should have access to a quality school program. The most effective rural school reforms will likely provide for some adaptation to local circumstances. Educationally effective variations should be encouraged. To facilitate such reforms, states should evaluate regulations that impose standardization but that show little evidence of being either educationally or cost effective. States should establish data bases, including relevant research, to facilitate state and local decisions about effective reforms. Localities should be encouraged to establish broad educational goals and policies for achieving these goals.

States should also continue to evaluate funding formulas to determine if they are equitable and should fully take into account local differences in ability to support quality schools. Because of out-migration of more highly educated youth, equity considerations argue for greater state and federal support for many rural districts.

Student Performance

Because of the powerful influence of socioeconomic status on educational outcomes, educational reform policies should be more effectively linked with rural development efforts. Evidence clearly shows that reducing the number of rural poor would significantly improve educational outcomes. Such efforts should be especially targeted toward persistent poverty localities and populations. Further, more effective coordination in the delivery of human services (including education) would improve access for the neediest, who are most likely to benefit from such services.

Evaluators of school performance should take into account the social and economic characteristics of the student population being served, especially in cases where measures of performance affect resource allocation. If this is not done, schools and localities which are in greatest need may be placed at even greater risk. New methods of evaluating performance are also needed. In addition, school curriculum reforms should include ways to make learning more interactive with the community outside the school to place more emphasis on linking learning with experiences.

Class Mobility and Rural Development

The traditional labor force framework for rural areas is inadequate, particularly the measures of need used, such as unemployment. Employment services tend to be fragmented and organizationally and geographically separated, thus making them less accessible to rural than to urban populations. More effective collaboration among the public agencies and organizations providing manpower training, counseling, and other human services is needed. State rural development councils should include representation from state education agencies.

Rural development efforts should be more explicitly linked with various education and training programs and initiatives at the locality level so that employment preparation is coupled with improved employment prospects. Rural development efforts should also be directed toward improvements in both quantity and quality of employment. Minimum-wage, low-skill jobs in rural localities have exacerbated rural-urban economic differences.

Control

Operating within the framework of a broad public mandate, control of education has been lodged largely within the public school system. Accordingly, control issues have been concerned with control of the school, its budgets, and its programs. Advocates of school reform and restructuring emphasize that reforms, in order to be effective, must include greater sharing of responsibility with community and families. However, new initiatives to share responsibility will evoke new conflicts about control.

Rural schools are already decentralized and generally enjoy a close connection between school and community. Nevertheless, neither rural schools nor communities have been effectively organized to represent their interests. Rural localities should establish broad representative community organizations to identify education and community goals and to determine how best to achieve them. University extension services and public agencies having rural development responsibilities should provide organization and support assistance.

State policies should also encourage schools and communities to experiment with alternative methods of education and conceptions of the school's role. The state of Washington has undertaken such a program (Schools for the Twenty-first Century) by offering competitive grant funds to schools that are willing to experiment with educational innovations and alternatives. The program stipulates broad community participation in devising the alternatives.

Conclusion

Improving rural education no longer means simply making rural schools larger and more like urban schools, although that might be appropriate in some cases. A good school—a safe and effective learning environment regardless of size—should be accessible to all rural youth. Such a goal should be a high priority. Achieving that goal will require great attention to who is going to pay for overcoming existing inequities. The uneven location of economic growth has diminished many rural localities' capacity to support more effective schools.

Improving student performance and reducing the marginality of rural employment will require more than good schools. Rural education interacts with rural development; that is, the lack of rural development and the persistence of low income contribute greatly to poor academic performance in many rural localities. The most effective rural development strategies will likely be those that combine education and training with efforts to improve rural income and its distribution.

References

Apple, Michael W., and Lois Weiss. 1986. "Seeing education relationally: The stratification of culture and people in the sociology of school knowledge." *Journal of Education* 168(1):7–31.

Barker, Roger G., and Paul Gump. 1964. *Big School, Small School: High School Size and Student Behavior.* Stanford, Calif.: Stanford University Press.

Bender, Lloyd B, Bernal L. Green, Thomas F. Hady, John A. Kuehn, Marlys K. Nelson, Leon B. Perkinson, and Peggy J. Ross. 1985. *The Diverse Social and Economic Structure of Nonmetropolitan America.* Rural Development Research Report No. 49. Washington, D.C.: USDA, Economic Research Service.

Bridge, R. G., C. M. Judd, and P. R. Moock. 1979. *The Determinants of Educational Outcomes: The Impact of Families, Peers, Teachers and Schools.* Cambridge, Mass.: Ballinger.

Brimelow, Peter. 1983. "What to do about America's schools."*Fortune* 108(September 19):62.

Butler, R. J., and D. H. Monk. 1985. "The cost of public schooling in New York State: The role of scale and efficiency in 1978–79." *The Journal of Human Resources* 20:3–38.

Carnoy, Martin, and Henry Levin. 1986. "Educational reform and class conflict." *Journal of Education* 168(1):35–45

Cole, Bob. 1988. "Teaching in a time machine: The 'make-do' mentality in small-town schools." *Phi Delta Kappan* October.

Deaton, Brady, and Kevin McNamara. 1984. *Education in a Changing Environment.* Mississippi State, Miss.: The Southern Rural Development Center. February.

DeYoung, Alan J. 1985. "Economic development and educational status in Appalachian Kentucky." *Comparative Education Review* 29(1):47–67.

———. 1987. "The status of American rural education research: An integrated review and commentary." *Review of Educational Research* 57(2):123–148.

Edington, Everett, and Helena Martellaro. 1985. *Does School Size Have Any Relationship to Academic Achievement?* Las Cruces, N. Mex.: New Mexico State University, Department of Educational Management and Development.

Falk, William W., and Thomas A. Lyson. 1988. *High Tech, Low Tech, No Tech: Recent Industrial and Occupational Change in the South.* Albany, N.Y.: State University of New York Press.

Flinn, William L., and Donald E. Johnson. 1974. "Agrarianism among Wisconsin farmers." *Rural Sociology* 39(2):187–204.

Fox, William F. 1980. *Relationships Between Size of School and School Districts and Cost of Education.* Technical Bulletin No. 1621. Washington, D.C.: USDA, Economic Research Service.

Goodlad, John. 1984. *A Place Called School: Prospects for the Future.* New York: McGraw-Hill.

Greenstein, Robert. 1988. "Barriers to rural development." Paper presented at annual National Rural Electric Cooperative Manager's Conference. Baltimore, August.

Hobbs, Daryl. 1989. "Rural education and the people still being left behind." Paper presented at The Rural Agenda of Educating All Our Children for the 1990s. University of Missouri, Kansas City, May.

Hogan, D. 1982. "Education and class formation: The peculiarity of the American." In M. W. Apple, ed., *Cultural and Economic Reproduction in Education: Essays in Class, Ideology and the State.* Boston, Mass.: Routledge and Kegan Paul.

Lichter, Daniel T., and Janice A. Costanzo. 1987. "Nonmetropolitan underemployment and labor-force composition." *Rural Sociology* 52(3):329–344.

Lowe, George D., and Thomas K. Pinhey. 1980. "Do rural people place a lower value on formal education?: New evidence from national surveys." *Rural Sociology* 45(2):325–331.

Monk, David. 1987. "Secondary school size and curriculum comprehensiveness." *Economics of Education Review* 6:137–150.

Mulkey, David. 1988. "Rural education policy: A southern perspective." Paper presented at Rural Development Policy Options Workshop. Birmingham, Alabama, October.

Nachtigal, Paul. 1980. *Improving Rural Schools.* Washington, D.C.: U.S. Department of Education, National Institute of Education.

Nachtigal, Paul, and Daryl Hobbs. 1988. *Rural Development: The Role of the Public Schools.* Washington, D.C.: National Governors' Association.

National Commission on Excellence in Education. 1983. *A Nation at Risk: The Imperative for Educational Reform. A Report for the Nation.* Washington, D.C.: U.S. Government Printing Office. April.

National Governors' Association. 1988. *New Alliances for Rural America: Report of Task Force on Rural Development.* Washington, D.C.: National Governors' Association.

Otto, Luther B. 1975. "Extracurricular activities in the educational attainment process." *Rural Sociology* 40(2):162–176.

Peshkin, Alan. 1978. *Growing Up American.* Chicago: University of Chicago Press.

Rosenfeld, Stuart. 1987. *How Big Is Too Big? High School Size and Quality of Education. SGPB Alert.* Research Triangle, N.C.: Southern Growth Policies Board.

Rosenfeld, Stuart, Edward Bergmar, and Sarah Rubin. 1985. *After the Factories: Changing Employment Patterns in the Rural South.* Research Triangle, N.C: Southern Growth Policies Board.

Sher, Jonathan. 1986. *Heavy Meddle.* Raleigh, N.C.: North Carolina School Boards Association. April.

Smith, Dan T., and Alan J. DeYoung. 1988. "Big school vs. small school: Conceptual, empirical and political perspective on the re-emerging debate." *Journal of Rural and Small Schools* 2(2):2–11.

Swarzweller, Harry K. 1976. "Scholastic performance, sex differentials and the structuring of educational ambition among rural youth in three societies." *Rural Sociology* 41(2):194–216.

Tweeten, Luther. 1980. "Education has role in rural development." *Rural Development Perspectives* October:9–13.

Tyack, D. B. 1975. *The One Best System.* Cambridge, Mass.: Harvard University Press.

U.S. Department of Commerce. Bureau of the Census. 1988. *Statistical Abstract of the United States*. Washington, D.C.: U.S. Government Printing Office. December 1987.

Vaughn, Rosco. 1984. "The relationship of school enrollment size and student achievement in reading, language and mathematics in New Mexico schools." Unpublished D.Ed. dissertation. New Mexico State University, Las Cruces, N.Mex.

Walberg, Herbert J., and William J. Fowler. 1987. "Expenditure and size efficiencies of public school districts." *Educational Researcher* October:1–22. (Reprinted as a Heartland Policy Study No. 22. Chicago, Ill: The Heartland Institute. September 1988.)

White, Fred, and Luther Tweeten. 1973. "Optimal school district size emphasizing rural areas." *American Journal of Agricultural Economics* 55:45–53.

White, Karl R. 1982. "The relation between socio-economic status and academic achievement." *Psychological Bulletin* 91(3):461–481.

Wigginton, Eliot. 1986. *Sometimes a Shining Moment: The Foxfire Experience*. Garden City, N.Y.: Anchor Books.

14
American Indian Development Policies

C. Matthew Snipp and Gene F. Summers

Since the late nineteenth century a stated goal of U.S. policy has been social and economic equality for American Indians. A variety of measures have been used over the past century to hasten American Indians' integration into the mainstream of American society. Nearly a hundred years later, how well has this goal been achieved?

Indicators of Social and Economic Well-being

Although once considered destined for extinction, the American Indian population has grown rapidly throughout the twentieth century (Thornton, 1987; Snipp, 1989). In 1890, the American Indian population was less than 250,000; today there are probably six times that number. The 1980 census count was 1.36 million.

American Indians are about evenly divided between rural and urban areas; many are newcomers to city life. In 1930, barely 10 percent of American Indians resided in urban areas, compared with 49 percent in 1980 (U.S. Bureau of the Census, 1937; Snipp, 1989). About two-thirds reside west of the Mississippi River. Also, over a third live on land held in trust as federal reservations, and all but a handful of these reservations are in the western United States.[1]

Historically, American Indians have been among the poorest of Americans. Table 14.1 illustrates the relative social and economic well-being of American Indians in 1970 and 1980 and compares them with blacks and whites in 1980.[2] Two conclusions can be drawn from the data in Table 14.1. First, between 1970 and 1980, American Indians made significant improvements in several key areas of socioeconomic well-being.[3] Second, in 1980, they reached economic parity with blacks but, like blacks, continued to lag far behind whites. For example, American Indian family incomes were only 66 percent of the family incomes of whites.

TABLE 14.1 Socioeconomic Characteristics of American Indians,[a] Blacks, and Whites

	American Indians, 1970	American Indians, 1980	Blacks, 1980	Whites, 1980
Percent with 12+ years of school[b]	22.0	55.5	51.2	68.8
Median family income[c]	$11,547	$13,724	$12,598	$20,835
Percent of families living in poverty[c]	33.0	23.7	26.5	7.0
Unemployment rate[d]	10.9	13.2	11.8	5.8
Percent not in the labor force[e]	50.7	41.4	40.6	37.8

[a]Includes Alaska natives; information not reported separately by the Census Bureau for American Indians and Alaska natives.
[b]Persons age 25 years and older.
[c]Income data reported for 1969 and 1979 in constant 1979 dollars.
[d]Percent of the civilian labor force without work.
[e]Persons age 16 years and older.

Source: U.S. Bureau of the Census (1983).

One of the significant gains made by American Indians in the 1970s was in education. In 1980, 56 percent of American Indians over age 25 had 12 years or more of school, more than double the 22 percent level of 1970. Likewise, median family income in real 1979 dollars increased from $11,547 in 1969 to $13,724 in 1979. These gains for American Indian families were reflected in lower poverty rates, which dropped from 33 percent in 1969 to 24 percent in 1979. Other indicators of economic well-being, such as labor force participation, also followed this pattern of improvement.

The 1970s saw American Indians catch up to, and in some instances surpass, the economic position of blacks. For example, by 1980 they had a slightly higher percentage of persons with 12 years or more of school than did blacks (51.2 percent). They also had slightly higher median family incomes than blacks ($12,598). Likewise, fewer American Indian families than black families (26.5 percent) had incomes below the official poverty threshold.

U.S. Policy in Historical Perspective

Understanding modern public policies directed at achieving social and economic parity for American Indians requires some knowledge of past policy. Since the founding of the United States, American Indian policy has followed four distinct approaches: isolation, assimilation, termination of Indian reservations, and self-determination.[4]

Isolation

American Indian policy has not always been directed at integrating American Indians into the mainstream of the U.S. economy. Beginning with the founding of the republic, the federal government sought to isolate American Indians from the rest of American society. President Thomas Jefferson urged that a part of the Louisiana Purchase be set aside as a special preserve for American Indians. This preserve later became the Indian Territory, in the area of what is now the state of Oklahoma.

President Andrew Jackson proposed to Congress and later implemented the legislation that most profoundly isolated American Indians. In the 1830s, Jackson's removal legislation resulted in thousands of American Indians being moved, often forcibly, from their homes in the East to points west of the Mississippi River that were distant from frontier settlements. In the balance of the nineteenth century, treaty negotiations, military action, and federal reservations were used to resettle American Indians in places distant from the newly emerging cities of the West.

Assimilation

After the Indian Wars, relocation, and massive population losses, federal policy moved toward a more benign view of how to fit surviving American Indians into American society. By the late 1800s, it was widely believed that American Indians were on the verge of extinction. Proponents of Indian rights advocated that those remaining should be encouraged to assimilate into the mainstream of white society (Utley, 1984; Prucha, 1984; Hoxie, 1984).

To the reform groups, assimilation meant that American Indians must adopt white lifestyles. The assimilation advocates were effective lobbyists, and with support in Congress, the federal government undertook a vigorous campaign to assimilate American Indians. A particularly important component of this campaign was aimed at ending the communal land tenure practices on federal reservations. The General Allotment Act of 1887 (the Dawes Act) sought to transform American Indians who had been communal agriculturists or nomadic hunters into yeoman farmers with Jeffersonian ideals (Carlson, 1981; Lewis, 1988). Male heads of Indian households were allotted simple title to 160 acres of land, provided with a few basic farm implements such as a mule and plow, and expected to adopt the agricultural lifestyles of their white neighbors (Carlson, 1981).

Assimilation policy was a dismal failure. Fewer Indians were farming and ranching after allotment than before (Carlson, 1988). Without experience or fertile cropland, some Indians were unable to become successful farmers (Carlson, 1981). Others, especially those who had been nomadic hunters, simply had no desire to become farmers (Lewis, 1988).

Allotment resulted in losses of millions of acres of Indian land (Snipp, 1986). Where reservation lands exceeded the amount needed for allotments, the Bureau of Indian Affairs (BIA) had the option of holding it in trust. Often, however, it opted to sell the "surplus" land or opened it for settlement by non-Indians. Within a short time after allotment, many Indians gave up the title to their land, often without fully appreciating the implications of this act; others lost their lands in bank foreclosures and tax auctions.

Recognizing the devastating impact of the allotment policies, the Meriam Report (Institute for Government Research, 1928) provided the impetus for the Wheeler-Howard Indian Reorganization Act of 1934, which formally repudiated Indian land allotments (Prucha, 1984; Deloria and Lytle, 1984). However, the act did not restore all the land that Indians lost through the allotment process.

Termination

With the failure of the allotment acts to hasten Indian assimilation, the Indian Reorganization Act of 1934 curtailed land allotments, returned some allotted land to trust status, and restored authority to tribal governments. This legislation provided a brief hiatus in efforts to assimilate American Indians while the federal government struggled with the Great Depression and World War II. However, shortly after the war, efforts to assimilate American Indians began anew.

The goal of federal policy after World War II was to close the outstanding accounts with Indian tribes, extinguish the relationship between the tribes and the federal government, and help individual American Indians move ahead with their lives like other Americans in urban postwar prosperity (Fixico, 1986). These goals were carried out by establishing the Indian Claims Commission (ICC), making efforts to terminate the trust status of reservation lands, and creating urban relocation programs.

The Indian Claims Commission eventually resolved many claims resulting from treaty violations and broken agreements. It restored some lands for tribal use, but it usually made remunerative awards for damages done and land illegally seized. However, the ICC proceedings were often highly complex and protracted, with some claims taking 20 years or more to settle (Fixico, 1986).

Termination became official policy in 1953 with the adoption of House Concurrent Resolution 108, which called for the dissolution of the special trust status of reservation lands and the elimination of federal responsibility for this land. In exchange, reservation residents were to receive title to tribal land and natural resources to dispose of as they wished (e.g., through timber sales). Termination was to begin with only a few reservations and then extend to all reservations. Perhaps recalling the experience of allotment, many Indian leaders actively opposed termination, and only a few reservations were ever terminated. The largest terminated reservations were the Klamath in Oregon and the Menominee in Wisconsin. In 1975, the Menominee reservation was restored to trust status by a special act of Congress; the Klamath are still actively seeking restoration of their reservation.

Of the postwar termination programs, the BIA urban relocation programs were the most active efforts to assimilate American Indians into the mainstream of society. In 1953, the BIA Direct Employment Program established relocation centers in a handful of cities such as San Francisco, Los Angeles, Chicago, and Cincinnati. American Indians participating in these programs were provided with moving expenses, job counseling and training, a temporary stipend, and help finding employment. From their inception until the early 1970s, the BIA relocated over 100,000 American Indians from reservations to ten urban locations (Sorkin, 1978), although the number staying in these locations was probably much smaller. In fact, critics accused the program of being a revolving door for reservation Indians (Fixico, 1986).

Not much is known about the success of relocation programs in assimilating American Indians. There is some evidence that program participants, especially those who were younger and better educated, did benefit from more employment and higher incomes (Clinton, Chadwick, and Bahr, 1975; Sorkin, 1978). However, these studies were limited only to persons completing the program and seeking employment in the city. The success of relocation for persons who never completed the program or who returned to the reservation is not known, nor is it known how many eventually went back to the reservation. Anecdotal information suggests that this number is large (Sorkin, 1978; Fixico, 1986). Furthermore, at least one study suggests that the benefits of rural-urban migration are highly selective and relatively small for the Indian population as a whole (Snipp and Sandefur, 1988).

Self-Determination

The protracted legal struggles in the ICC, the Indian leaders' resistance to termination, and the charges by critics that relocation programs were ineffective at best and a reservation "brain drain" at worst made federal policymakers rethink their past efforts to assimilate American Indians. Perhaps bolstered by the civil rights movement of the 1950s and 1960s, "self-determination" became a rallying cry for American Indian activists and their supporters throughout the United States.

The concept of American Indian self-determination was well received by sympathetic members of Congress and by proponents of the so-called New Federalism in the Nixon administration. On January 5, 1975, self-determination became official policy with passage of the American Indian Self-Determination and Education Act, which called for tribal governments to become increasingly responsible for reservation administration. The act has resulted in greater federal support for the development of tribal administration capabilities and for ancillary activities such as the development of tribal judicial systems.

In practice, tribes have assumed the management of programs for welfare assistance, housing, job training, education, natural resource conservation, and the maintenance of reservation infrastructures such as roads and bridges.

On some reservations tribal governments have nearly complete control of reservation management while on others, particularly smaller ones, the BIA continues to have a significant role in reservation affairs.

A much broader view of self-determination, one embraced by many tribal leaders, sees in this policy a federal recognition of the political autonomy of tribal governments. This interpretation goes well beyond the mere granting to tribal governments greater responsibility for administration. It reaffirms the concept of tribal sovereignty (Deloria and Lytle, 1984; Barsh and Henderson, 1980). While it accepts as superior the sovereignty and authority of the federal government, it rejects that of state and local governments. However, the exercise of tribal sovereignty is highly controversial, especially since it denies the authority of state and local governments to control, regulate, or otherwise intervene in affairs on reservations. Combined, the principle of tribal sovereignty and the policy of self-determination mean that tribal leaders are free to develop their community however they please, regardless of state and local restrictions, and are subject only to federal oversight. According to Prucha (1984:1188):

> Tribes can exercise the right of eminent domain, tax, and create corporations. They can set up their own form of government, determine their own members, administer justice for tribal members, and regulate domestic relations and members' use of property. They can establish hunting and fishing regulations for their own members within their reservations and can zone and regulate land use. They can do a great many things that independent political entities do, insofar as federal law has not pre-empted their authority.

In practice, this can mean imposing taxes and vehicle registration and controlling access to fish and game and recreational facilities. It also gives tribes the right to undertake development projects without regard to locally enforced regulations such as zoning or building codes. A growing number of tribes have taken this opportunity to establish gaming operations, especially bingo parlors and tax-free tobacco shops. The inability to control or regulate these operations, or gain access to the proceeds from them, often outrages local authorities.

The policy of self-determination remained intact throughout the Reagan administration, although in the face of massive cutbacks in federal assistance, some tribal leaders came to view self-determination as a hypocritically veiled attempt to return to the termination policies of the 1950s. However, two developments are notable because they anticipated future policy. Officially, the Reagan administration embraced a "government-to-government" relationship between federal and tribal governments (PCIRE, 1984). On the other hand, the administration discouraged tribal governments from undertaking business enterprises traditionally regarded as the domain of the private sector, especially controversial ones such as gaming and duty-free outlets (PCIRE, 1984).

The rejection of tribally owned businesses prompted former Interior Secretary James Watt's widely publicized remark that reservations exemplified

"failed socialism." Moreover, the Reagan administration supported the passage of 1988 legislation that restricts gaming on Indian reservations. Tribal
leaders greeted this legislation with ambivalence; some believe that it infringes
on tribal sovereignty, while others argue that, while regulation of gaming
restricts their freedom to a degree, it also implicitly recognizes the tribal
right to establish gaming without state or local government interference.

The authority increasingly exercised by tribal governments has generated
considerable resentment among non-Indians, especially among local citizen
groups. Many of these groups are pressing for access to hunting, fishing,
or other natural resources now under tribal control. So-called "equal rights"
groups are engaged in lobbying against tribal entitlements throughout the
western United States. In the state of Washington, for example, an active
campaign is being conducted against tribal entitlements to a share of the
annual salmon harvest. In Wisconsin, antitreaty rights groups are strenuously
objecting to Ojibwa off-reservation spearfishing, even though federal courts
have affirmed their right to do so under treaties of the past century.

The direction of public policy for American Indians is unlikely to change
dramatically under the Bush administration. Most likely, tribal leaders will
continue to push for greater self-determination and tribal sovereignty, while
local officials and equal rights citizen groups will campaign against them.
American Indians may find more opportunities in the next ten years than
they have in the past, but the pursuit of these opportunities may be more
threatened than it has been for many years.

Policy Options for Self-Determination

Social and economic inequality can be viewed as a reflection of the
unequal distribution of access to productive assets, either through ownership
or other legally protected means. Productive assets include all the various
income-earning factors of production such as land, labor, capital, and
institutions. Large differences in the distribution of these factors among
groups in society primarily account for the wide divergence between the
rich and the poor. Thus, achieving social and economic parity through the
self-determination policy requires legal instruments that will increase American Indians' access to income-earning factors of production—as individuals,
as tribes, or both.

Land

The land and natural resource base of American Indian reservations
varies enormously. In size, the reservations range from California rancherias
of a few acres to the Navajo reservation, which overlaps three states and
covers an area about the size of West Virginia. Some reservations are richly
endowed with such natural resources as mineral and petroleum deposits,
timber, fertile soil, and pristine wilderness areas. Others have few, if any,
of these resources.

Tribes have at least three alternatives for increasing their access to land and other natural resources. First, they may purchase or lease additional lands for their reservation. This is obviously not a viable strategy for tribes without sufficient capital or income. However, some tribes, such as the Wisconsin Oneida, have made progress in planning or establishing land acquisition programs. The high capital requirements of land acquisition could also be reduced by seeking the return of allotted lands through the wills of tribal members and by encouraging the federal government to allocate more public land for tribal use, either through the assignment of title or long-term leases.

Second, greater use of Indian land by Indians will require a change in the lease policies of the tribes and the BIA (Snipp, 1988). In the past, the tribes and the BIA have shown a strong predisposition for leasing tribal lands and natural resources to non-Indians, primarily because the tribes and the BIA have lacked the extensive capital and expertise needed to develop natural resources. For example, tribes with timber frequently opt to sell it to nearby sawmills instead of producing lumber or pulp themselves. Developing mineral and energy resources requires vast amounts of capital, and to date tribal involvement in such activities is virtually nonexistent. Nonetheless, if tribes are to receive a greater share of the total value of their resource base, they must become less dependent on lease agreements for development.

Third, for a few tribes, the settlement of land claims and other lawsuits will provide opportunities for expanding their resource base. These settlements concern the enforcement of treaty rights, the restoration of land seized illegally during allotments, and more recently, mismanaged and inappropriately leased resources under the administration of the BIA. In some cases, these actions entail small amounts, such as a few acres of land seized illegally for taxes. In other cases, the stakes are large, such as in Washington state, where the Lummi and several other Pacific Northwest Coast tribes successfully enforced their claim for fishing rights and have been able to develop a highly successful fishery industry (Olson, 1988). In Wisconsin, the Ojibwa are claiming treaty rights on fish, game, and timber worth possibly millions of dollars.

Policies that increase tribal access to land and other natural resources as a factor of production must take into account several considerations:

1. Reservations are not equally endowed, and natural resource development cannot be viewed as a panacea for expanding opportunities for American Indians. Tribes with little land and few resources will need to depend on other types of development strategies.
2. These resources are finite, and tribes will need to carefully consider not only the rate of their development, but methods for managing their conservation.
3. Extractive industries are not only a declining segment of the American economy, they are cyclical and sensitive to economic booms and busts.

Tribal leaders may be reluctant to become overly dependent on this type of economic activity.
4. Some tribes may find certain types of land use and natural resource development unacceptable. The disruptions and intrusions of tourism have caused some pueblos in the Southwest to be closed to outside visitors. In some tribal cultures, the land is considered sacred, and developments such as mining are viewed as sacrilegious.

Labor

Labor as an income-earning factor of production calls attention to skill, experience, and investment in training and education. The reservations' pool of labor is less skilled than that of the encompassing counties, although it is by no means an unmarketable labor pool (Snipp and Summers, 1989). The same is true of Indians living off the reservations (Snipp, 1989; Snipp and Summers, 1989). Policy instruments that will improve the accessibility of education and training are of utmost importance to achieving social and economic parity.

Self-determination is a place- and people-oriented policy that adopts explicitly the goal of economic development on reservations. Preparing people to emigrate is the older, abandoned policy of assimilation. Self-determination policy takes the position that human capital investments should be made on reservations to increase the employment potential of reservation residents in their local labor markets, on or near the reservation. It also recognizes explicitly that labor demand in the local markets must be increased, and institutionalized barriers to full participation, such as racism, must be removed.

American Indians are divided between those living on and those living off reservations. This fact, and the failures of past assimilation efforts, must be taken into account in considering options. The ideology of self-determination is quite amenable to the interests of all Indians because of its commitment to seeking options which maximize freedom of choice. However, the practical import of the policy bears directly on the locational dimension of human capital investment policy.

Existing legislation clearly establishes the authority of tribal governments to develop education and training systems on the reservations. However, some reservations are limited by insufficient operating funds and physical capital or by small populations. Thus, in some instances success of the self-determination policy may require an increase in federal assistance to support tribal investment in its human capital. For small reservations where operating a separate education and training system is not feasible, support needs to be provided for off-reservation education programs such as those funded by the Johnson-O'Malley Act.

There are two options for structuring federal support for Indian education and training. One option provides support through transfer payments to the student, the student's family, or the tribe. Another provides support through payments directly to the provider, either in the public or private sector. In addition, whether the transfer should be tied to the recipient's place of residence is questioned. The greatest freedom of choice would be achieved by basing the support on need and permitting the recipient to select the education and training service provider. This alternative has two more features that are particularly attractive. It avoids discrimination between reservation and nonreservation Indians because place of residence is deemed irrelevant. It also permits the recipient to select a provider who is believed to be culturally unbiased and free from ethnic or racial prejudice.

Capital

The mere provision of greater access to education and training does not guarantee that American Indians will be better off unless complementary policies are pursued which will provide for more productive employment opportunities for those educated. Thus, the demand for labor needs to be increased, especially through job creation on the reservations.

There is no evidence of any automatic "trickle down" of benefits of regional economic growth. Active and growing economies in the encompassing counties do not result in larger numbers of jobs on the reservations. They do provide some limited opportunities for off-reservation employment, but little else (Snipp and Summers, 1989).

Lack of capital is one reason for the low level of on-reservation development. It also contributes to the generally weak multiplier effects of agriculture and other resource-based industries on reservations. The lack of development of consumer-oriented industries on reservations, even those having substantial income from off-reservation employment, also calls attention to the lack of capital (Murray, 1985; Snipp and Summers, 1989; Vinje, 1988).

Ultimately, for American Indians to achieve social and economic parity they need ownership of a proportional share of the nation's capital assets. However, the immediate need is for policy options that will provide Indians with greater access to finance capital. Two policy options are available to the federal government in this regard. First, it may use tax revenues to finance grants and loans to tribes and individuals for business development projects. Second, it may merely assume the role of guarantor for private sector initiatives to provide business loans and credit. Since the passage of the Self-Determination Act in 1975, both options have been pursued, albeit on a limited scale.

Some reservations are taking advantage of these policy options and are beginning to achieve job creation and capital accumulation (Vinje, 1988). This suggests that an expanded capital fund could permit a wider participation by tribes, Indian business groups, and individuals. One possibility for enlarging the volume of available debt capital would be establishing an American Indian Development Bank that would be open to subscribers from all elements of the public and private sectors. If deposits were guaranteed by the federal government, in the fashion of the Federal Deposit Insurance Corporation, the volume of available debt capital might be substantially increased. Given the aim of increasing Indian ownership of capital, policy options which might encourage non-Indians to take an equity position in business development on reservations would appear to be counterproductive.

Institutions

Limited experience in business management also restricts development. The culture of entrepreneurship which is so vaunted by theorists of economic development is not a familiar element in the culture of many reservation Indians (Highwater, 1981). This is especially so if one takes entrepreneurship to mean individual ownership of land and capital and the use of those resources for personal gain. Because communal concepts are quite strong in many Indian cultures even today, cooperative and collective ventures are attractive organizational tools for development.

Fortunately, business management skills need not be equated with individualistic entrepreneurship. Whether the resources used in business enterprises are communally or privately owned, their effective use depends on the same knowledge and understanding of business activities and principles. Given the cultural heritage of many American Indians, perhaps a better understanding and application of the concepts and techniques of industrial democracy would be more appropriate than those of the private entrepreneur to business development on Indian reservations.

The political autonomy of tribal governments is in some respects greater than that of municipalities. Their limited sovereignty allows them some comparative advantages. Tribal governments, for example, can offer outside investors exemptions from certain types of taxes and regulations. However, these exemptions should be weighed carefully. As Vinje (1988) points out, there would be no benefit in repealing minimum wage rules so tribal members could compete with workers in Third World nations whose wage is 50 cents per hour.

In view of recent administrations' predisposition toward "free enterprise zones," it seems likely that they will remain important as policy instruments. To maximize tribal benefits from enterprise zones several conditions need to be imposed. First, implementation of free enterprise zones must be the decision of the tribal governments. Second, a percentage of the gross business revenues of firms locating on the reservation should be assigned to a Tribal Investment Fund. Third, within a specified number of years (5–10) tribal members should hold a substantial proportion of the management positions of each firm. The costs of training such management personnel should be borne in full by the business firm. Fourth, the tribe should have an equity position in each firm that locates on the reservation. In the case of publicly traded stock companies, this may be done through ownership of stock either by the tribe or by individual tribal members. Size of the reservation population also must be considered in the creation of on-reservation jobs. It is clear that on-reservation employment is proportionally higher on reservations with larger populations. It is equally clear that many of the reservations have resident populations that are too small to provide a large enough on-reservation market to support economic development. Yet one must be cautious about writing off small reservations as having no development potential. Family enterprises can be quite successful in creating jobs and can even become large enterprises. Therefore, very small reservations need to consider the prospects of economic development within the framework of small business development rather than regional or community economic development.

Conclusion

For several hundred thousand Americans, "home" is one of 278 federally entrusted Indian reservations. Since the late nineteenth century, these descendants of "the first of this land" have been subjected to changing federal policy aimed at giving them social and economic equality with other Americans. Yet, nearly 100 years later, they remain among the poorest of Americans.

The Founding Fathers of the United States first attempted to deal with American Indians by isolating them from the onslaught of European settlers desiring tribal lands. When that failed, a policy was adopted which aimed to assimilate them into the mainstream of white society through various programs of education, land tenure reforms, and dissolution of tribal governments. That course, also a dismal failure, led to the adoption of the current policy of self-determination.

Self-determination policy recognizes the legitimacy of tribal governments and calls upon them to become increasingly responsible for reservation administration. It reaffirms the concept of tribal sovereignty, acknowledges the legitimacy of Indian rights granted by treaties negotiated in the nineteenth century, and has brought greater federal support for expanding tribal administrative capabilities, judicial systems, and economic development on reservations. However, the exercise of tribal sovereignty is highly controversial, since it denies the authority of state and local governments to control, regulate, or otherwise intervene in affairs on reservations, which in effect have been granted "home rule" by the federal government.

Political autonomy should not be equated with economic self-sufficiency or viability. Nor should it be viewed as a justification for terminating long-standing federal obligations. The exercise of legitimate decision making is doomed to failure in the absence of essential economic resources. Tribal leaders can achieve social and economic equality with other Americans only when tribes have access to the necessary factors of production—land and other natural resources, fiscal resources, human resources, and institutions for integrating and coordinating their effective management. On many reservations, one or more of these essential ingredients are in short supply or completely lacking. Thus, while some reservations have made measurable gains under the policy of self-determination, others have not.

Limited resources, factional politics, and discrimination are obstacles that must be overcome before economic vitality on Indian reservations can be realized. Federal policy is an indispensable resource for surmounting the barriers to economic development. With some adjustments, the current policy of self-determination should make a strong contribution to Indian economic and social equality.

Notes

Support for this work was provided by grants from the Aspen Institute for Humanistic Studies, the Ford Foundation, and the graduate school of the University of Wisconsin. All opinions expressed herein and any inadvertent errors are the sole responsibility of the authors. We also wish to thank Mary Miron for editorial assistance.

1. This chapter deals only with issues related to American Indians residing on reservations. The great majority of American Indians living in rural areas are situated on reservation land. Furthermore, the special legal and political status of reservations makes development policies for these communities significantly different from the policies that might be used to address the needs of American Indians living outside reservations.

2. Reliable data for American Indians are difficult to obtain. Unfortunately, the 1980 census is the most recent source of social and economic data; more up-to-date information is not available.

3. For a variety of complicated methodological reasons related to procedures and to processes of racial self-identification in 1970 and 1980, some of the improvements between 1970 and 1980 may not be as large as they seem. Nonetheless, most observers agree that while there were significant improvements between 1970 and 1980, the magnitude of these improvements is less certain. For a discussion of the problems in temporal comparisons for American Indians, see Snipp (1986, 1989) and Passell and Berman (1986).

4. We are well aware, of course, that this is an extremely abridged recounting of Indian policy. In reality, its history contains many inconsistencies and complexities that defy simple description. The history of Indian policy more nearly resembles a record of administration by trial and error with fits and starts, not a simple linear progression (see Prucha, 1984). However, given the limitations of space, we have adopted this four-stage perspective for its brevity and heuristic value, even though it exaggerates actors' rationality and clarity of purpose while making history appear to be a monotonic, unidirectional process.

References

Barsh, Russel Lawrence, and James Youngblood Henderson. 1980. *The Road: Indian Tribes and Political Liberty.* Berkeley, Calif.: University of California Press.

Carlson, Leonard A. 1981. *Indians, Bureaucrats, and Land: The Dawes Act and the Decline of Indian Farming.* Westport, Conn.: Greenwood Press.

———. 1988. "Property rights and American Indians: American Indian farmers and ranchers in the late nineteenth and early twentieth centuries." Pp. 107–141 in Frederick E. Hoxie, ed., *Overcoming Economic Dependency: Papers and Comments from the First Newberry Library Conference on Themes in American Indian History.* Occasional papers in Curriculum Series, No. 9. Chicago: Newberry Library.

Clinton, Lawrence, Bruce A. Chadwick, and Howard M. Bahr. 1975. "Urban relocation reconsidered: Antecedents of employment among Indian males." *Rural Sociology* 40(2):117–133.

Deloria, Vine, Jr., and Clifford M. Lytle. 1984. *The Nations Within: The Past and Future of American Indian Sovereignty.* New York: Pantheon Books.

Fixico, Donald L. 1986. *Termination and Relocation: Federal Indian Policy 1945–1960.* Albuquerque, N.Mex.: University of New Mexico Press.

Highwater, Jamake. 1981. *The Primal Mind: Visions and Reality in Indian America.* New York: Harper and Row.

Hoxie, Frederick E. 1984. *A Final Promise: The Campaign to Assimilate the Indians 1880–1920.* Lincoln, Nebr.: University of Nebraska Press.

Institute for Government Research. 1928. *The Problem of Indian Administration [The Meriam Report].* Baltimore: Johns Hopkins Press.

Lewis, David Rich. 1988. "Farming and the Northern Ute experience, 1850–1940." Pp. 142–164 in Frederick E. Hoxie, ed., *Overcoming Economic Dependency: Papers and Comments from the First Newberry Library Conference on Themes in American Indian History.* Occasional papers in Curriculum Series, No. 9. Chicago: Newberry Library.

Murray, James M. 1985. "The economic impact of the Bay Mills and Sault Ste. Marie Indian communities." Mimeograph. Green Bay, Wis.: JMA Inc.

Olson, Mary B. 1988. "The legal road to economic development: Fishing rights in Western Washington." Pp. 77–112 in C. Matthew Snipp, ed., *Public Policy Impacts on American Indian Economic Development.* Albuquerque, N.Mex.: University of New Mexico, Institute for Native American Development.

Passel, Jeffrey S., and Patricia A. Berman. 1986. "Quality of 1980 census data for American Indians." *Social Biology* 33(3–4):163–182.

Presidential Commission on Indian Reservation Economies (PCIRE). 1984. *Report and Recommendations to the President of the United States.* Washington, D.C.: U.S. Government Printing Office.

Prucha, Francis Paul. 1984. *The Great Father: The United States Government and the American Indians.* Lincoln, Nebr.: The University of Nebraska Press.

Snipp, C. Matthew. 1986. "The changing political and economic status of the American Indians: From captive nations to internal colonies." *American Journal of Economics and Sociology* 45(2):145–157.

———. 1988. "Public Policy Impacts and American Indian Economic Development." Pp. 1–22 in C. Matthew Snipp, ed. *Public Policy Impacts on American Indian Economic Development.* Albuquerque, N.Mex.: University of New Mexico, Institute for Native American Development.

———. 1989. *American Indians: The First of this Land.* New York: Russell Sage Foundation.

Snipp, C. Matthew, and Gary D. Sandefur. 1988. "Earnings of American Indians and Alaska natives: The effects of residence and migration." *Social Forces* 66(4):994–1008.

Snipp, C. Matthew, and Gene F. Summers. 1989. "Jobs and income in Indian country." Mimeograph. Madison, Wis.: University of Wisconsin, Department of Rural Sociology.

Sorkin, Alan L. 1978. *The Urban American Indian.* Lexington, Mass.: Lexington Books.

Thornton, Russell. 1987. *American Indian Holocaust and Survival: Population History Since 1942.* Norman, Okla.: University of Oklahoma Press.

U.S. Bureau of the Census. 1937. *The Indian Population of the United States and Alaska.* Washington, D.C.: U.S. Government Printing Office.

———. 1983. *General and Social Economic Characteristics, United States Summary.* PC80-1-C1. Washington, D.C.: U.S. Government Printing Office.

Utley, Robert M. 1984. *The Indian Frontier of the American West 1846–1890.* Albuquerque, N.Mex.: University of New Mexico.

Vinje, David J. 1988. "Economic development on reservations in the twentieth century." Pp. 38–52 in Frederick E. Hoxie, ed., *Overcoming Economic Dependency: Papers and Comments from the First Newberry Library Conference on Themes in American Indian History.* Occasional papers in Curriculum Series, No. 9. Chicago: Newberry Library.

15

The Doubly Jeopardized:
Nonmetropolitan Blacks
and Mexicans

Leif Jensen

Nonmetropolitan (nonmetro) blacks and Mexicans suffer a double jeopardy owing to their geographic location and minority group status. Compared with their metropolitan (metro) counterparts and with nonmetro whites, they have considerably lower median incomes and higher poverty rates (Jensen and Tienda, 1989). The deprived position of rural minorities imposes obvious micro and macro social costs. The poor suffer from inadequate health care, nutrition, housing, and educational opportunities, while societal costs are inherent in outlays for social programs and foregone output. While fluctuating in severity since the 1960s, the comparative economic disadvantage of rural minorities has been sizable and persistent (Jensen and Tienda, 1989). Their plight stands in stark contrast to the value of equal opportunity and constitutes a social problem that demands greater political and academic attention.

From a policy standpoint, little attention is paid to rural blacks and Mexicans, per se, although several programs and policies bear directly on them. This chapter is organized around three areas. First, antipoverty policy is particularly important given the extraordinarily high poverty risks faced by rural minorities. This discussion concentrates on means-tested cash assistance programs. The remaining two areas concern employment policy. Efforts to increase the labor supply among nonmetro minorities are focused on, and then programs to enhance their employability are emphasized. Next, the demand for nonmetro minority labor is addressed by examining local economic development strategies, affirmative action, and immigration policy. I conclude by culling policy recommendations for nonmetro minorities in the 1990s.

TABLE 15.1 Median Family Income and Family Poverty Rates by Race/Ethnicity and Nonmetro Status, 1959–1986 (in constant 1986 dollars)

	Black		Mexican		White	
Year	Nonmetro	Metro	Nonmetro	Metro	Nonmetro	Metro
			Median Family Income			
1959	$ 6,131	$14,034	$10,244	$16,881	$17,710	$24,052
1969	11,469	20,122	14,645	21,378	23,873	32,496
1979	14,964	19,276	17,626	21,771	25,948	33,152
1986	13,182	18,950	13,560	19,764	24,310	34,556
			Percent Change in Median Family Income			
1959–69	87.1%	43.4%	43.0%	26.6%	34.8%	35.1%
1969–79	30.5	−4.2	20.4	1.8	8.7	2.0
1979–86	−11.9	−1.7	−23.1	−9.2	−6.3	4.2
1959–79	144.1	37.4	72.1	29.0	46.5	37.8
1959–86	121.7	35.0	32.4	17.1	37.3	43.7
			Family Poverty Rate			
1959	71.9%	36.3%	57.2%	31.1%	23.0%	9.4%
1969	38.1	20.2	31.5	17.5	9.8	4.6
1979	26.0	20.3	21.3	16.0	6.9	4.2
1986	31.0	23.0	33.5	18.2	9.6	4.7

Source: U.S. Bureau of the Census (1960; 1970; 1980; 1987).

Recent Trends in Relative Economic Status

The economic deprivation of nonmetro blacks and Mexicans is a legacy of profound subjugation in the rural South and Southwest of the United States. Many have sought prosperity in urban areas outside these regions, but today's geographic distribution of nonmetro blacks and Mexicans echoes their historical roots. Recent U.S. Census Bureau data show that 94 percent of nonmetro blacks reside in the South. Within that region they are found largely in Mississippi, Georgia, North and South Carolina, and Texas. These five states account for about 58 percent of all nonmetro blacks. Adding Louisiana, Alabama, and Virginia brings the total to 78 percent. Nonmetro Mexicans are even more geographically concentrated. The Mexican border states of Texas, Arizona, and New Mexico account for about 69 percent of all nonmetro Mexicans (36 percent in Texas alone), and the addition of California, Oklahoma, and Colorado brings the total to 82 percent. The lack of economic vitality in the rural areas of many of these states has important policy implications.

As a point of departure, it is important to document recent trends in the socioeconomic status of nonmetro blacks and Mexicans. As seen in Table 15.1, from 1959 to 1986, nonmetro black and Mexican families made significant economic advances, followed by some deterioration in status. This table shows U.S. Census Bureau data on median family income in 1959, 1969,

1979, and 1986 within categories of race/ethnicity and metro/nonmetro residence. The first panel reveals significant increases in the median incomes of all families during the 1960s and 1970s. However, in part because of their disadvantaged beginnings, the relative increase in family income was greatest for nonmetro black and Mexican families. Particularly impressive was the 144 percent increase among nonmetro blacks from $6,131 to $14,964 (in 1986 dollars) over these two decades.

Of the groups considered in Table 15.1, nonmetro minority families enjoyed the greatest proportionate gains in median income over the 1960s and 1970s. However, the early 1980s were not as kind. While all groups except metro whites witnessed declines in real income between 1979 and 1986, these losses were greater among nonmetro black and, especially, Mexican families. The latter registered income losses of 23 percent over this seven-year period.

This pattern of improvement and deterioration—especially among non-metro blacks and Mexicans—is also observed in poverty rate trends. The improvement over the 1960s has been attributed to a number of factors. Blacks, for example, benefited from their continued movement out of southern agriculture and into northern industries. Also, the civil rights movement began to dismantle institutionalized discrimination (Levy, 1987), and Lyndon Johnson's War on Poverty dramatically increased funding for a wide range of antipoverty programs (Kerbo, 1983). Moreover, the tight labor market of the later 1960s meant that employers hired blacks in greater numbers than they would have otherwise (Levy, 1987). Nonmetro minority median income rose only modestly in the recession-ridden 1970s and deteriorated appreciably between 1979 and 1986. These trends suggest that minorities may be particularly vulnerable in a slack economy and underscore the importance of considering labor market conditions when studying their economic status.

Implications of Antipoverty Programs

The socioeconomic portrait above attests to the doubly jeopardized position of rural minorities. Among government initiatives to ameliorate this situation, foremost in the minds of many are means-tested cash assistance programs. These programs, including Aid to Families with Dependent Children (AFDC), Supplemental Security Income, and general assistance, are referred to as *public assistance.* Existing evidence suggests these programs do help reduce poverty among minority families (Tienda and Jensen, 1988). Accordingly, I consider the interface between antipoverty programs and poor rural minorities.

While many believe that poverty and welfare use go hand in hand, surprisingly few poor families actually receive public assistance—particularly in nonmetro areas. Tabulations of 1987 Current Population Survey (CPS) data show that about 54 percent of poor nonmetro black families received some public assistance as compared with 64 percent among their metro counterparts (see Jensen and Tienda, 1989). The respective figures for poor

Mexican families are 24 percent (nonmetro) and 38 percent (metro), while for whites they are 36 percent and 40 percent.

Nonmetro poor are less likely to receive welfare support because they are less likely to be eligible for AFDC. For example, compared with their counterparts in central cities, poor nonmetro families are more likely to have a working family head, more likely to be headed by a married couple, less likely to have children present, and less likely to live in states that offer welfare benefits to married couples when the breadwinner is unemployed (AFDC-UP) (Jensen, 1988). However, even among those who are eligible, nonmetro minorities remain less likely to receive public assistance than their metro counterparts. Analysis of 1987 CPS data reveals that among the families eligible for public assistance, the metro and nonmetro receipt rates were, respectively, 75.5 percent and 68.0 percent for blacks, 65.8 percent and 56.6 percent for Mexicans, and 51.8 percent and 55.5 percent for whites.

As the most sweeping piece of welfare reform legislation since the early 1980s, the Family Support Act (FSA) of 1988 will gradually revamp AFDC. The FSA seeks to combat welfare dependency by imposing on welfare recipients stronger inducements to work and by more aggressively seeking child support from absent parents. One provision of the act, the nationalization of AFDC-UP, should disproportionately benefit rural minorities. Recent CPS data indicate that while 55.9 percent of poor metro blacks live in AFDC-UP states, only 11.5 percent of their nonmetro counterparts are so situated. The corresponding figures for poor Mexicans are quite similar. The FSA mandates that all states offer AFDC-UP by October 1990. This program will help many additional nonmetro minorities in intact families who must turn to AFDC due to labor market dislocation.

Unfortunately, the FSA does not address other problems with the current welfare system that will continue to leave rural minorities behind. States vary greatly in their ability and desire to provide cash assistance for the poor, and they are given considerable latitude in implementation. As a result, benefit levels vary significantly; as with AFDC-UP, nonmetro minorities tend to be concentrated in those states (primarily in the South) that offer lower welfare payments. Analysis of 1987 statewide data published by the U.S. Department of Health and Human Services reveals that the mean maximum AFDC benefit for one needy adult and two children per month was $317 for poor blacks in metro areas and $201 in nonmetro areas. The corresponding figures for poor Mexicans are $402 and $262, and for whites, $364 and $316.

These inequities in support levels for minority poor give rise to the following policy recommendations. First, an adequate national benefit level needs to be established and enforced as soon as possible for nonmetro minorities. As it is, state benefit levels are well below official poverty thresholds and are insufficient to provide even the most meager basic needs. Second, research is needed to confirm whether needy rural minorities are less likely to receive welfare benefits than their urban counterparts, as was suggested by the preliminary figures above. If so, such policy initiatives as improved promotion and outreach need to be implemented so that rural minorities can be better served. Third, like Social Security, AFDC benefits need to be better indexed to the cost of living so that future inflationary periods will not erode real benefit levels.

Employment Policies

In lieu of a significant increase in viable employment opportunities, changes in welfare policy will do little to raise the average incomes of rural minorities, because many low-income people do not qualify for assistance, and many who do qualify do not receive benefits. Recent U.S. Census Bureau (1987) data indicate that compared with means-tested transfer income, earnings comprise a far greater share of family income, even among the poor. About two-thirds of the total family income among poor nonmetro Mexicans and about half of that for poor nonmetro blacks is accounted for by earnings; public assistance and all other sources account for much smaller percentages. Poor rural minorities make ends meet principally through earnings, not government transfers. Therefore, policies that enhance minority labor force participation and labor market opportunities must be considered.

Employment Characteristics

Auxiliary analyses of 1987 U.S. Census Bureau data (not shown in Table 15–1) were carried out to document the employment characteristics of blacks, Mexicans, and whites in nonmetro and metro areas. Among all individuals aged 14 and over, nonmetro blacks and Mexicans have the lowest employment rates (59.1 percent and 62.4 percent, respectively), which helps explain their comparatively low average income. However, among poor individuals, non-metro minorities have somewhat higher employment rates than their metro counterparts, with the employment rate for poor nonmetro Mexicans (50.3 percent) being the highest among the groups considered. That over 50 percent of nonmetro blacks and almost 60 percent of nonmetro Mexicans are in the labor force (either employed or looking for work) suggests that their deprivation is due less to a lack of work commitment than to a lack of adequate employment opportunities.

Occupational distributions reveal that nonmetro minorities are under-represented in the higher paying professional and managerial occupations and overrepresented in the lower paying service, operative, laborer, and farm laborer occupations. Naturally, this clustering is even more apparent among the poor. Over 73 percent of poor nonmetro blacks report service, operative, or laborer occupations. The distribution of poor nonmetro Mexicans across occupations is somewhat different. They are employed as operatives and laborers, and also as farm laborers—the latter accounting for 28.3 percent of this group.

Finally, even full-time, year-round work does not guarantee an income above the poverty level. Given their clustering in lower paying jobs, this is particularly true of rural minorities. Among those working 48 or more weeks and 35 or more hours per week in 1986, 12.0 percent of nonmetro blacks and 13.8 percent of nonmetro Mexicans were poor. These poverty rates far exceeded those of their metro counterparts and those of metro or nonmetro whites.

Raising the Labor Supply

Other things being equal, employment opportunities for nonmetro minorities will increase in direct proportion to improvements in the human capital they bring to the labor market. Aggregate increases in skill levels and educational attainment should both promote greater labor force participation by increasing the opportunity cost of remaining out of the labor force and improve employability by broadening the pool of jobs for which rural minorities qualify.

Unfortunately, nonmetro blacks and Mexicans are at a decided disadvantage in terms of educational attainment. Compared with their metro counterparts or nonmetro whites, nonmetro blacks and Mexicans have lower high school graduation rates and, on average, have completed fewer grades of school. Nonmetro Mexicans are particularly undereducated, having a mean completed education of less than nine years. Patterns of geographic residence partially explain the educational disadvantage faced by rural minorities. Public schools in the South and Southwest have a history of de jure and de facto segregation of blacks and Mexicans, and public funding of education in these regions has perennially lagged behind national averages (Ross, 1989; San Miguel, 1987).

These inequities must be addressed if rural minorities are to seriously compete for better paying jobs. If state coffers cannot adequately support education, they should be supplemented with federal funds. Targeted to school districts with high dropout rates, this support would necessarily benefit areas with high nonmetro minority populations. In addition, programs to promote high school completion must be improved. Incentives such as open enrollment and reduced tuition to state colleges or vocational schools could be offered to high school graduates in targeted populations. To qualify, high school graduates could be obliged to work in or near their home town for a specified period, thus preventing a rural "brain drain."

In addition to these initiatives, we need programs that enhance the human capital of older adults who have already completed their education. These programs are especially important in view of the ongoing industrial restructuring of both metro and nonmetro America. Current programs are inadequate for nonmetro minorities. For example, the Job Training Partnership Act (JTPA) provides remedial education, vocational training, and on-the-job training. However, rural areas tend to be offered less specialized and more limited services under JTPA (National Commission on Employment Policy, 1988). Similarly, under the FSA, the new welfare system will provide education and training, job search skills, and child care to eligible welfare recipients. However, because they are less likely to receive welfare in the first place, rural minorities are less likely than their urban counterparts to qualify for these benefits. Moreover, the FSA offers no assurance that these services will be provided to more remote rural populations, and it exempts from participation welfare recipients in areas where the program is not available. There is a reluctance to bear the added cost of reaching out to rural populations in need. Policymakers need to be sensitized to this urban bias in social welfare policy.

An issue relevant for nonmetro Mexicans is bilingual education. Bean and Tienda (1987) show that net of other determinants of earnings, there are substantial positive returns to fluency in English for Mexican-American men. (There was little effect for Mexican women, apparently because of their segregation in low-skilled jobs that did not require the ability to speak English.) In addition, the inability to speak English reduces educational attainment as a result of grade retention and higher dropout rates (Valdivieso and Davis, 1988).

U.S. census data for 1980 reveal that about 20 percent of nonmetro Mexican householders speak English poorly or not at all. This figure increases to 28 percent among the poor. While the corresponding percentages for metro Mexicans are actually somewhat higher, even those for nonmetro Mexicans reflect a need for English training. Controversy surrounds how best to teach English. Bilingual education, which blends the use of both English and Spanish in the curriculum, has been preferred by Latino groups and has been part of federal policy since 1968. Evidence on the success of bilingual education is mixed (Baker and de Kanter, 1983), although a recent study offers a positive evaluation (U.S. General Accounting Office, 1987).

Under existing immigration law, the large-scale influx of Mexicans to both rural and urban areas will continue, as will the need to enhance their opportunities through English training. Bilingual education should remain a prominent part of the curriculum in those districts with appreciable Mexican-origin populations. In addition to easing the transition to English, such programs can foster ethnic pride and self-esteem, enhance student performance by allowing greater involvement of Spanish-speaking parents, and decrease prejudice and discrimination against Mexican-Americans by increasing awareness and sensitivity among whites (Simpson and Yinger, 1985).

Efforts to increase the employability and labor force participation of nonmetro minorities will help alleviate their disadvantaged socioeconomic status. However, without policies designed to increase labor demand, education and training efforts might only see the best and brightest rural minorities migrate to urban areas. In at least one instance, existing policy fosters this situation. In some rural service delivery areas under JTPA, officials have "decided that local opportunities were too limited and offered training in occupations that were available in nearby cities" (National Commission on Employment Policy, 1988:120).

enterprises that offer well-paying positions. Rural communities with high minority concentrations face even greater obstacles. Largely black and Mexican towns in rural America are at a competitive disadvantage owing to a comparative lack of investment and human capital. In the context of the Deep South, Colclough (1988) analyzed 1970 and 1980 U.S. Census Bureau data and found that the ecological pattern of industrial restructuring greatly favors predominantly white counties. That is, black counties are far more likely to lose, and white counties to gain, industrial employment. Moreover, gains in black counties and poor counties tend to be in low-wage industries. This scenario is consistent with Falk and Lyson (1988), who report that the rural Black Belt failed to benefit from the "Southern Renaissance" of the 1970s.

It appears that just as discrimination against ethnic minorities continues at the individual level, so too do many businesses avoid locating in areas with high minority concentrations. We need to consider aggressive policies to generate local employment in these places. Tax breaks, local infrastructure development, and other subsidies could be offered to industries that locate in targeted areas. These benefits could be contingent on hiring substantial numbers of local residents. Since these areas are apt to be at a comparative disadvantage regarding financial capital, funding would have to come largely from state and federal sources. Also, matching funds could be offered to minority entrepreneurs who seek to establish local enterprises.

Affirmative Action. The deprived economic position of rural minorities is rooted in a history of subjugation and discrimination. Evidence shows that the disadvantages of color are persistent (Tienda and Jensen, 1988). *Affirmative action* (AA) refers to a wide variety of legal efforts to dismantle institutionalized discrimination against women and minorities in education and employment. With respect to employment, AA efforts range from such relatively benign means as having employers target discriminated groups with job vacancy announcements to more aggressive measures, such as legally imposing numerical quotas. These measures differ in the degree to which they give preferential treatment to discriminated groups. Many persons regard as unfair reverse discrimination against members of dominant groups simply to rectify past injustice. This sentiment became more pervasive over the past decade and buttressed the Reagan administration's attempts to dismantle affirmative action.

Evidence on the effectiveness of AA programs is mixed. Some disappointing efforts reflect poor implementation and lax enforcement of AA guidelines (Leonard, 1985). However, when implemented properly, substantial increases in black employment have been documented (Smith and Welch, 1986). In education, affirmative action has been shown to increase the admissions of blacks and Mexicans to colleges and professional schools (Simpson and Yinger, 1985).

While substantive evidence is lacking, there are two reasons to suspect that affirmative action has been less successful in rural areas than in urban places. First, while AA initially bolstered employment of minorities in low-skilled occupations where rural minorities cluster, recent successes have been seen in high-skilled jobs where they do not. Second, the threshold at which firms must fully comply with federal AA guidelines is 100 employees. Because in rural areas there are proportionately more workers in firms under this threshold, rural minorities are less likely to benefit from affirmative action.

In view of their demonstrated, albeit modest, success, AA programs remain a viable policy response to the acutely disadvantaged position of rural minorities. However, to improve their effectiveness, better enforcement of AA guidelines, stronger penalties for violations, and rewards for exemplary compliance need to be considered. In addition, smaller firms also need to be required to comply with AA guidelines, a policy that would prove especially beneficial for rural minorities.

Immigration Policy. Finally, immigration policy has relevance for labor demand. Since the late 1960s, the United States has been in the midst of a wave of immigration from developing countries in Asia and Latin America. This influx has rekindled old concerns over the macroeconomic impact of immigration. Evidence suggests that, in the aggregate, immigrants are a net economic benefit. However, in this context, it is important to consider the effects of immigrants on selected subpopulations of citizens. If immigrants are similarly skilled and can merely substitute for minority citizens in the labor force, the wages and employment rates of the latter will be attenuated. Empirical evidence is equivocal, although it appears immigrants have a very small negative effect on the wages of native Mexicans and native blacks.

Whether this evidence is compelling enough to call for a more restrictive immigration policy is open to dispute. We need to know more about immigration's impact on rural minorities, particularly those most vulnerable. For example, it seems likely that policies promoting the recruitment of foreign labor by agricultural enterprises in the Southwest and West of the United States can only suppress the wages of an already exceedingly deprived group—Mexican-American farm laborers. Nonetheless, immigration policy continues to promote this stream. The Immigration Reform and Control Act of 1986 made it easier for unauthorized immigrants to gain amnesty (and eventually citizenship) if they were employed as agricultural laborers. Moreover, under the H-2A and Replenishment Agricultural Worker programs, many foreign citizens gain access to the agricultural labor market.

High population growth rates in developing countries guarantee continuing pressure on their citizens to emigrate to the United States. In the 1990s, the United States will face difficult immigration policy decisions. Additional research on the effects of immigration on rural minorities will help inform those crafting policy alternatives.

Last-resort Jobs. Rejuvenated affirmative action measures and efforts to spur economic development in targeted areas are ways to increase the demand for the labor of rural minorities. Even so, not all of those who want and need a job will find one. As Ellwood (1988) suggests, the government should, as a last resort, create and offer jobs at decent wages to the able-bodied poor who simply cannot find other alternatives. While such an approach seems drastic, it is consistent with the nation's value preference for work over welfare.

Conclusion

The outset of this chapter quantified the severe socioeconomic disadvantages faced by rural minorities, highlighting the need for a satisfactory policy response. I conclude by culling policy alternatives for rural blacks and Mexicans in the 1990s. The following list is not exhaustive. To develop additional alternatives, policy formulators must be creative and open-minded. Although many of these policies do not target rural minorities per se, they should benefit blacks and Mexicans disproportionately, given their double jeopardy.

Antipoverty Policy

- Rural minorities tend to cluster in states with more conservative social welfare policies. Fair and adequate national standards for benefit levels and eligibility criteria need to be established and enforced.
- To maintain real benefit levels over time, welfare payments (e.g., AFDC) need to be indexed to inflation.
- Program promotion and outreach in rural areas need to be improved.
- To help the working poor, minimum wages need to be raised to the point where a full-time, full-year worker can earn at least a poverty-level income for a family of four. The national minimum wage should be better indexed to inflation.

Labor Supply Policies

- To improve educational quality and attainment, rural school districts with high minority concentrations need supplemental funding. These funds could be used to improve faculty, curricula, and facilities; to establish incentive schemes to promote high school completion and college attendance (e.g., via tuition assistance); to establish low-cost adult education programs to help local residents learn the new skills needed for restructured labor markets; and to enhance bilingual education programs, in part by offering subsidies to schools that hire bilingual teachers.
- Affirmative action efforts in education have proved successful in the past and need to be increased.
- To prevent a rural "brain drain," programs need to be developed that attract college graduates back to their home communities. For example, reduced tuition or a guaranteed job could be offered to promising young minority teachers if they return after college. This and similar arrangements could be contractual.

- Rural minorities need to be targeted under existing federal programs designed to increase labor force participation. For example, under the FSA the new Job Opportunities and Basic Skills (JOBS) training program must regularly review its list of targeted groups. Rural minorities could easily be added to that list. (If anything, present programs seem to forsake more remote rural areas.)
- Affordable child care needs to be offered to those who want to work but cannot because of child care responsibilities.
- Programs need to be developed whereby those with marketable skills can volunteer their time to teach these skills to rural minorities.

Labor Demand Policies

- Federal and state-supported tax breaks, infrastructure development, and other subsidies need to be offered to industries that locate in areas with high concentrations of rural minorities. These benefits could be contingent on the hiring of a certain percentage of local residents.
- Programs need to be developed that contribute low-cost start-up capital— perhaps via matching funds—to rural minority entrepreneurs who seek to establish promising local enterprises.
- Affirmative action programs need to be enhanced in several ways. Enforcement needs to be improved and both positive and negative sanctions strengthened. The pool of firms that must comply with AA guidelines needs to be broadened by requiring smaller firms to participate.
- Research is needed on immigration's effect on the economic status of rural minorities. Immigration policy should be adjusted if deleterious effects on particular subpopulations are found.
- As a last resort, the government should create and offer jobs at decent wages to the able-bodied poor who cannot otherwise find work.

A number of these suggestions buck recent political trends. Affirmative action, amidst recent Supreme Court decisions that compromise the effectiveness of existing efforts, should be increased. Bilingual education, at a time when states such as Florida, Colorado, and Arizona have declared English their official language, should be enhanced. Finally, greater labor market intervention, despite the popularity of laissez-faire economics, should be called for.

Rebuilding support for preferential measures will be difficult. During the 1960s political backing derived not only from the civil rights movement but from rising real incomes. Subsequently, the pie has stopped growing, and expansion of preferential programs could foment among whites resentment of "undeserving minorities." However, research shows that, other things being equal, whites who recognize the structural barriers faced by minorities are more tolerant of such programs as affirmative action (Kluegel and Smith, 1983). The dissemination of sound empirical evidence on the persisting disadvantages of color could help rekindle support for preferential policies.

In the meantime, it seems pragmatic to initiate policies that are less controversial. Partially subsidized entrepreneurship, targeted economic development and educational assistance, an adequate minimum wage, and volunteerism should be pursued immediately. Unfortunately, however, we have not reached the point where preferential programs are unnecessary (Sandefur, 1988). Without an aggressive and multidimensional effort it is unlikely that the double jeopardy faced by rural minorities will disappear by the year 2000.

References

Baker, K. A., and A. A. de Kanter. 1983. "An answer from research on bilingual education." *American Education* 19(6):40–48.

Bean, Frank D., and Marta Tienda. 1987. *The Hispanic Population of the United States.* New York: Sage.

Colclough, Glenna. 1988. "Uneven development and racial composition in the Deep South: 1970–1980." *Rural Sociology* 53(1):73–86.

Ellwood, David T. 1988. *Poor Support: Poverty in the American Family.* New York: Basic Books.

Falk, William W., and Thomas A. Lyson. 1988. *High Tech, Low Tech, No Tech: Recent Industrial and Occupational Change in the South.* Albany, N.Y.: State University of New York Press.

Jensen, Leif. 1988. "Rural-urban differences in the utilization and ameliorative effects of welfare programs." *Policy Studies Review* 7(4):782–794.

Jensen, Leif, and Marta Tienda. 1989. "Nonmetropolitan minority families in the United States: Trends in racial and ethnic economic stratification, 1959–1986." *Rural Sociology* 54(4):509–532.

Kerbo, Harold R. 1983. *Social Stratification and Inequality: Class Conflict in the United States.* New York: McGraw-Hill.

Kluegel, James R., and Eliot R. Smith. 1983. "Affirmative action attitudes: Effects of self-interest, racial affect, and stratification beliefs on whites' views." *Social Forces* 61(3):797–824.

Leonard, J. S. 1985. "The effectiveness of equal employment law and affirmative action regulation." Working Paper no. 1745. Cambridge, Mass.: National Bureau of Economic Research.

Levy, Frank. 1987. *Dollars and Dreams: The Changing American Income Distribution.* New York: W. W. Norton.

National Commission on Employment Policy. 1988. "Evaluation of the effects of JTPA performance standards on clients, services, and costs." Research Report No. 88-16. Washington, D.C.: U.S. Government Printing Office.

Ross, Peggy J. 1989. "Human resources in the South: Directions for rural sociology in the 1990s." Presidential address at the 1989 annual meeting of the Southern Rural Sociological Society, Nashville, February.

Sandefur, Gary D. 1988. "The duality in federal policy toward minority groups, 1787–1987." Pp. 207–229 in Gary D. Sandefur and Marta Tienda, eds., *Divided Opportunities: Minorities, Poverty and Social Policy.* New York: Plenum.

San Miguel, Guadalupe, Jr. 1987. *Let All of Them Take Heed: Mexican Americans and the Campaign for Educational Equality in Texas, 1910–1981.* Austin, Tex.: University of Texas Press.

Simpson, George Eaton, and J. Milton Yinger. 1985. *Racial and Cultural Minorities: An Analysis of Prejudice and Discrimination.* 5th ed. New York: Plenum.

Smith, J. P., and F. R. Welch. 1986. *Closing the Gap: Forty Years of Economic Progress for Blacks.* Santa Monica, Calif.: Rand Corporation.

Tienda, Marta, and Leif Jensen. 1988. "Poverty and minorities: A quarter-century profile of color and socioeconomic disadvantage." Pp. 23–85 in Gary D. Sandefur and Marta Tienda, eds., *Divided Opportunities: Minorities, Poverty, and Social Policy.* New York: Plenum.

U.S. Bureau of the Census. 1960. Public Use Samples of the *U.S. Census of Population and Housing.* Data base. Washington, D.C.

_____. 1970. Public Use Samples of the *U.S. Census of Population and Housing.* Data base. Washington, D.C.

_____. 1980. Public Use Samples of the *U.S. Census of Population and Housing.* Data base. Washington, D.C.

_____. 1987. *Current Population Survey: Annual Demographic File, 1987.* Ann Arbor, Mich.: Inter-university Consortium for Political and Social Research. Data base.

U.S. General Accounting Office. 1987. "Bilingual education: A new look at the research evidence." GAO/PEMD-87–12BR. Washington, D.C.: U.S. Government Printing Office.

Valdivieso, Rafael, and Cary Davis. 1988. "U.S. Hispanics: Challenging issues for the 1990s." *Population Trends and Public Policy* 17:1–16.

16

Capacity Building and Rural Government Adaptation to Population Change

David L. Brown and Nina L. Glasgow

Fundamental Policy Issues

Change, not stability, is the usual demographic situation for most of rural America. Since change is so endemic, assisting rural communities to adapt to demographic change is a fundamental policy issue for the 1990s. Some demographic changes, like the rural migration reversals of the 1970s and 1980s, are rapid and unpredictable. Others, like aging of the rural population, take longer and can be anticipated with more certainty. Rural areas differ greatly in population size, composition, and in patterns of population change. Some areas have been growing steadily for a long time, while others are characterized by chronic decline or long-term stability. Some rural area populations are growing proportionately older; others are attracting working-age migrants and their families and are not aging at all. Since the demographic situation is so diverse, public policy must be adapted to fit particular types of circumstances. A separate policy to fit every situation is not practical, but distinct types of demographic situations can be identified for policy attention.

Population growth (or decline) affects the local community by altering the supply of workers in the local labor market, by shifting the demand for consumer goods and services, and by changing the demand for public services and infrastructure. Adaptation to population change is affected by the rapidity of the change and whether it was anticipated; by the initial characteristics of the local population such as its size, degree of demographic diversity, and geographic location vis-à-vis other areas; by the fiscal, administrative, technical, and managerial capacity of the local public sector; and by the initial adequacy and characteristics of infrastructure and services provided by the public sector and/or the private sector.

Local government, the institutional nexus through which services are produced and delivered, municipal functions are administered, and development strategies are planned and coordinated, is at the center of the impact of rural population change (Sokolow, 1982). Unfortunately, many local governments lack sufficient technical, managerial, or administrative capacity to guide the local community through its responses to a changed demographic situation. Accordingly, enhancing local government capacity to adapt to demographic change is a high priority for rural policy in the 1990s.

The Changing Demographic Context Affecting Rural Governments

Recent Trends in Rural Population Change

The unprecedented rural and nonmetropolitan population turnaround of the 1970s proved to be relatively short lived. By the end of the decade, the nonmetropolitan net migration surplus had begun to diminish (Richter, 1985), and by 1984 the balance of migration had turned to favor metropolitan growth. Over half of nonmetropolitan counties lost population from 1985 to 1988, compared with only 460 (about 20 percent) that lost population during the 1970s (Brown and Deavers, 1988). The most recent data show that nonmetropolitan growth has begun to recover slightly since 1986 but the growth is still only half as rapid as it is in metropolitan counties (Butler and Swanson, 1990).

While much research emphasizes the nonpecuniary causes of the 1970s turnaround, there is little question that economic forces are associated with the reduction of nonmetropolitan population growth and net migration since 1980. Reduced rural growth is surely associated with a delayed rural area recovery from the 1979–1982 recession, financial stress in agriculture and its linked industries, and slow employment growth or decline in rural manufacturing and natural resource–based industries.

Not all rural areas have shared in this decline. In fact, rural areas that depend on recreation and retirement-based industries have actually grown at a faster rate than metropolitan areas since 1980. In contrast, areas that depend on manufacturing have grown slowly during the decade; farming areas have been nearly stationary or in decline since mid-decade; and mining-dependent areas have experienced population decline since 1983 (Glasgow, 1990; Elo and Beale, 1988). Moreover, rural areas differ in their patterns of growth over time. Some areas have grown (or declined) in consistent and predictable ways during recent decades, some areas have been relatively stable, while others have waxed and waned between unpredictable periods of growth and decline, boom and bust (Brown and Beale, 1982).

Adapting to these unpredictable patterns of change is especially difficult. Differences in the two components of population change, natural increase and net migration, both contribute to these interarea variations in population change, but in recent decades net migration has accounted for most of the difference (Elo and Beale, 1988).

Recent Trends in Population Composition

Changes in population composition have also characterized both urban and rural areas during recent decades and have direct implications for local community adaptation. Changes in age composition, and in the size and structure of households, in particular, have important impacts at the local community level. Broad-based secular changes in these two aspects of population composition have affected communities at all levels of urbanization, yet urban-rural differences persist, as do differences between local areas within both the urban and rural (or metropolitan and nonmetropolitan) sectors. For most aspects of family and household composition the rural and urban populations are following parallel but different courses—moving in the same direction, but remaining on distinctly separate paths (Fuguitt, Brown, and Beale, 1989). Age at first marriage has increased; the number of children couples have persists at a historically low level; household size has declined; single-parent households, especially those maintained by women, are increasingly common; cohabitation of unmarried couples was twice as common in the 1980s as it was a decade before; and almost half of all persons now marrying will eventually divorce (Cherlin, 1981). Both rural and urban areas have experienced these changes, but a more traditional family structure, as indicated by a higher proportion of married-couple households with minor children, a smaller proportion of single-parent families, and a lower proportion of persons living alone, persists in the most rural parts of America (Fuguitt, Brown, and Beale, 1989).

Most communities, regardless of their level of urbanization, have also experienced similar changes in age composition during recent decades, but again, some urban-rural differences persist. The effects of the post–World War II baby boom, the current prolonged period of low fertility, and increased longevity are clearly etched on population structure at all levels of urbanization. Most communities have experienced a decline in the proportion of children, movement of the baby boom cohorts into young adult and middle age, and a swelling of the elderly age groups because of reduced mortality.

In contrast, migration, both internal and international, has influenced urban and rural areas differently. Legal immigration from abroad has had most of its recent impact in highly urbanized areas, while internal migration has transferred millions of young adults from rural to urban areas over time (some even during the rural migration turnaround of the 1970s). Elderly migration, on the other hand, has been toward rural areas since the 1960s. As a consequence, urban areas have a relative surplus and rural areas a relative deficit of persons in the young adult and middle ages, and rural areas have a relative surplus of the elderly (Fuguitt, Brown, and Beale, 1989; Glasgow, 1988).

Population Change and the Demand for Public Goods

Population change affects local governments most directly by shifting the demand for public sector goods and services. Population growth and growth in the number of households translate into increased demand for particular public goods and infrastructure. More households, and by definition more housing units, are directly associated with increased demand for water, sewers, roads, sidewalks, street lights, and other housing-associated infrastructure. Of course, this assumes that the affected communities did not have excess capacity before experiencing growth in the number of households.

Different population groups have different needs, so differential growth rates by age, gender, income level, and household type are likely to affect the changes in the demand for certain types of public goods, services, and infrastructure. In-migration of retirees, for example, has a direct effect on the demand for medical care; growth or decline in the youth population affects the demand for formal educational services and facilities and for law enforcement; more single-parent families with young children influence the need for child care services and welfare assistance; and growth in the number of low-income or unemployed persons is associated with more demand for income transfer and job training programs. Conversely, decline of specific population groups reduces demand for certain public services. Low population growth due to low fertility, for example, reduces the demand for schools, initiates public debate over the allocation of public expenditures for the old and young, and can lead to school closings, consolidations, and unemployed teachers.

Constraints on Adaptation to Population Change

Population-induced changes in public expenditures are not automatic and are not necessarily guided by notions of economic efficiency. As Barkley (1974) points out, markets for public goods are not "tidy." Ordinary markets do not exist for public goods. To a great extent, consumers reflect their preferences through the ballot box, not the cash register. In addition, locality-specific social structure must be taken into account (Deaton, 1983). Many rural areas, for example, resist school consolidation despite clear evidence of the economic benefits of scale in education (Fox, 1980) and general agreement that larger schools deliver more comprehensive, if not better, education. The local school is more than an educational institution. It has cultural and social importance that local residents value and are frequently willing to subsidize through higher than average expenditures per pupil taught. The impact of population change on the market for public goods, then, is mediated through a screen of social and political structures.

The adaptation of local government to population change can be constrained by insufficient capacity and political will. The relationship between governmental capacity and adaptation is intuitively obvious. Population growth is unlikely to result in new or expanded public services, for example, where local governments lack the technical expertise to design and operate programs, where they are inefficient producers and users of public revenues, and where they have limited ability to acquire and analyze new information.

However, as Sokolow (1981:705) points out, "The ability to act in this sense is dependent on the desire to act." Regardless of their level of capacity, local governments will not adapt their production and provision of services in response to population change unless such actions are judged to be politically acceptable. Local governments, especially in small towns and rural areas, tend to be conservative, consensus-seeking, nonconfrontational bodies. Elected or appointed officials are hesitant to risk their political capital unless they believe such actions are consistent with citizens' desires.

Capacity and will are interdependent concepts. While it is true that all of the capacity in the world will not result in innovative new public programs without the political will to take such risks, it is also true that capacity can help build political support for change. The ability to assess changing community needs in response to demographic trends, to acquire and analyze information, and to determine the feasibility of alternatives for provision of service can all be used to mobilize the public in support of new or enlarged programs in growing areas or, conversely, in support of contracting programs in areas experiencing population decline.

Adaptation to population change is especially difficult in rural areas because of their smaller size, lower density, dispersed settlement patterns, and generally lower income levels. These traditional rural attributes constrain resources and options. One outcome is that individual rural communities are seldom able to adopt possible cost-saving economies of scale. Hence, the per unit cost of providing public services can be prohibitively high. In addition, because small economies typically specialize in one industry or in a narrow range of industries, they are more vulnerable to adverse changes in the business cycle, and they have great difficulty adjusting to structural change in the nation's (or region's) economy (Killian and Hady, 1988). As Stinson (1987) has shown in areas experiencing farm financial stress, declining economic fortunes and associated reductions in land values and tax revenues have a direct negative impact on local governments' ability to finance and provide public services.

Increased societal (and global) integration is another contemporary trend that exacerbates local governments' ability to adapt to population change. Local decisions and actions are no longer taken (if they ever were) in isolation or in response to purely local needs and interests. Local government officials must observe extralocal rules, mandates, and regulations. Adaptation is likely to be a complex multistep process requiring technical expertise and a consideration of issues over a long planning horizon.

The number of extracommunity ties is now so large that they can be a source of problems for individual rural governments (Bradshaw and Blakely, 1979). To expand services in reponse to population growth (or contract them in response to decline), for example, local government officials must ask these questions: who is involved? how are the partners linked? what do they expect from each other? and, how long will the relationship remain important? Moreover, since rural governments utilize financial resources from higher levels of the intergovernmental system, these extracommunity relationships frequently entail some degree of economic dependency. While federal resources to local government have diminished since 1979 as a result of the "New Federalism," state government has become a more active partner (National Governors' Association 1988).[1] Local governments have always had some degree of extralocal orientation, but outside ties are now much more continuous and complex, and they circumscribe the autonomy of individual local governments (Sokolow, 1987).

Policy Framework

The policy framework developed here recognizes that local governments in both growing and declining rural areas would benefit from policy assistance. We understand that the simple growth-decline dichotomy oversimplifies the rural demographic situation. Rapidly growing areas, areas of chronic decline, areas in which current growth trends are a reversal from the past, and areas gaining (or losing) particular population subgroups are all legitimate claimants for policy attention. The growth-decline distinction used here only underscores our essential point that local governments can be heavily stressed in growing and declining areas, especially if change is rapid, unanticipated, a break from the past, or if it substantially alters the population composition.

Public policy should be sensitive to the differing needs of growing and declining areas. Community-level responses to growth and decline are not symmetrical (Johnson, 1985). Social systems tend to respond readily to growth, while inertia in social structure tends to constrain adjustments to decline. We are used to thinking about problems associated with decline, but growth can present its own set of problems. In both cases institutional adaptations are necessary, but since the outcomes of growth and decline differ, different adjustment strategies are likely to be followed.

Growth strains existing facilities and services, and it can present a whole set of social and environmental externalities. Local government in growing areas can be pushed to produce new services, but since the property tax base takes several years to adjust, new services will have to be financed out of current revenues. User fees can supplement current revenues during this transition period. Some critics contend that user fees tend to be regressive, especially as a means of financing household and personal services like waste disposal. However, in fast-growth areas like California user fees appear to be viewed as a legitimate way to fund needed public works improvements by having newcomers pay for some of the public costs they generate (Sokolow, 1990). In contrast, population decline typically leads to excess capacity, extra per capita costs because of fewer persons and diminished economies of scale, and lower levels of service (Rogers, 1982). Moreover, areas experiencing population change are likely to have short-run inefficiency problems as they add or delete capacity. Such problems can be expected to be more severe and of longer duration in areas experiencing decline. It is easier simply to add capacity during periods of growth than to withdraw incremental parts of a capital facility from production in response to decline (Coelen and Fox, 1981).

Conventional rural policy in the United States, especially federal-level policy, has focused heavily on declining areas. These policies have taken two forms: development policies designed to retain capital, labor, and other resources in declining areas, or transition policies designed to reduce the costs of resource reallocations associated with ongoing economic and demographic changes (Drabenstott, Henry, and Gibson, 1987). A third category, capacity building, should be added to enhance local government's capacity to plan for and manage service production and provision, basic municipal functions, and development strategies in the face of changing demographic conditions. Capacity building should not be an alternative to transition and development policies; rather, it should be an adjunct that focuses more directly on the public sector and that is directly concerned with individual and household-level quality of life, in addition to economic development.

Capacity Building

Capacity building is an elusive term lacking a rigorous definition. Newland's (1981:iv) definition, "increasing the ability of people and institutions to do what is required of them," guides our thinking. In this case we are concerned with a community's ability to manage its own affairs. Capacity building merits special attention as an aspect of public policy because it is not tied to the local community in a conventional way through capital or labor markets or through individual or household-level income supplementation or service provision.[2] It has a broader orientation to overall governance, resource mobilization, program development, and public management as they are affected by population growth or decline. Both equity and efficiency considerations motivate policies to strengthen local institutions. Enhanced capacity to plan for and manage public services in response to change, for example, can contribute to a more efficient use of public resources, resulting in better quality services at a more affordable price for all citizens. And, while local government's role in nurturing economic development to stem population decline or enhance growth is somewhat debatable, more effective public management, greater technical capacity, and more efficient use of public monies will likely improve an area's competitive position in the national and regional economy.

Both transition and development policies focus on economic development and only incidentally on individual or household-level quality of life— through trickle-down in the case of development policy and through income transfers and training for displaced workers in the case of transition policy. Capacity building, in contrast, explicitly focuses on quality of life issues such as access to essential services, maintenance of both social and physical infrastructure, and more effective, efficient, and responsive public institutions. While development and transition policies focus some attention on the local public sector, they subsidize public infrastructure in support of economic development of, for example, private businesses, financial institutions, and displaced workers. In contrast, capacity building focuses on strengthening the public sector in support of community sustainability.

Local governments with the following attributes are better able to facilitate community social and economic viability and population retention. As

Honadle (1981) points out, capable institutions are forward looking. They anticipate problems and opportunities before they happen and they evaluate alternative strategies for dealing with these situations. Consequently, they are better able to capitalize on opportunities and minimize problems. Key characteristics of capable institutions include technically knowledgeable leaders, efficient administrative and fiscal procedures, access to reliable information with which to make decisions, and an effective framework for involving public opinion in important decisions. While much of this expertise can be secured from outside consultants, the emphasis in capacity building is to lessen dependency on outside experts and institutionalize capacity into the local community's permanent structure.

Some Elements of Capacity Building Policy

The above conceptualization makes it clear that capacity building is more than just obtaining increased support services like engineering, computer, budget and finance, legal, and grants management. It also includes leadership skills, conflict resolution and group processes, governmental organization and procedures, program planning and forecasting, and assessing community needs. Both types of strengthening contribute to local governments' capacity to conduct tactical functions such as promoting economic development, producing and providing public services, and maintaining physical infrastructure in the context of population growth or decline (Russo, Waltzer, and Gump, 1987). What can rural governments do to strengthen their capacities?

Professionalization. Small rural governments frequently depend on part-time volunteer officials who perform many diverse responsibilities. They tend to be so preoccupied with the daily routine that they rarely have time to engage in forward-looking planning, programming, or budgeting activities (Sokolow, 1981). In addition, local officials often lack technical knowledge in critical areas such as powers and duties, budgeting, and leadership and group process skills. These limitations constrain forward-looking planning and impede the provision of daily service.

Most rural government officials would benefit from formal training, but financially strapped local governments may view such training as an unaffordable luxury. State and federal government can fill the gap by providing free or highly subsidized training. To be attractive, such training should be offered locally, since many local officials depend on other jobs for their livelihoods. Moreover, because officials are not likely to respond well to "top down" programs, the substantive focus of the training should be planned collaboratively by the officials themselves and the trainers. Local resource persons such as community college instructors should be involved wherever possible.

Local governments are more than service providers. As Sokolow (1981:704) notes, they are "devices of local democracy, agents through which citizens express, deliberate, and resolve community problems." These nontechnical, process-oriented functions are particularly important in rural areas experiencing in-migration and population growth, since in-migration can be a precondition of conflict between longer-term residents and in-migrants who have different expectations, attitudes, and abilities to pay for public services and infrastructure. Local officials must be able to mobilize others to work together and resolve conflicts between opposing groups while satisfying their respective needs. These types of situations require officials to have leadership skills and knowledge of group processes. Since local officials frequently lack these skills, they would benefit greatly from leadership training, including team management, effective communication, the principles of social action, and conflict resolution.

In addition to other types of technical assistance, local governments need adequate information to anticipate, plan for, and adapt to demographic change. Community-relevant sociodemographic data give local decision makers an accurate picture of community structure and change, and if the data are presented in a comparative framework they can help local officials see the shared nature of their situation or its uniqueness. By pointing to emerging problems and opportunities, these data help local officials appreciate the economic implications of current population trends and changes. Such analyses are useful in choosing from among alternatives for future action.

While many states recognize that small-area data can help rural communities adjust to demographic change, few have invested serious resources in local-area data access. Some states transmit census-type data tables to county extension offices over electronic bulletin boards, but virtually no state has developed innovative training programs to enable local officials to manipulate the data, to display them graphically, or even to recognize why, and in which circumstances, such analysis might be helpful. The Cooperative Extension Service, in cooperation with state-level development agencies and land-grant universities, could take the lead in developing locally relevant data access programs to help local government officials make more effective adjustments to demographic change. Extension would be more than a conduit of census-type data. Local officials would be shown how to manipulate data and why and when such analyses might be useful.

State and federal agencies, universities, associations, private consultants, and part-time contractors are also sources of technical information. In Oklahoma, for example, extension economists work with local officials to help them evaluate the economic feasibility of alternative service provision systems (Nelson, Tweeten, and Doeksen, 1984; Favero and Heasley, 1989). Local officials identify service needs and options. The economists use a budgeting methodology to compare the costs and revenues of alternative systems for providing the needed services. These do-it-yourself feasibility studies help the local officials choose an affordable service-providing option that is appropriate to their community.

Organizational Alteration. Organizational change is another way of enhancing technical and administrative capacity. In the extreme case, a traditional rural government experiencing substantial population change might deal with the situation by creating a chief executive officer position and filling it with a professional administrator. This would simplify lines of authority and add professional expertise, although city council control and citizen access would be reduced (Sokolow, 1982).

Few rural governments can afford this option, even if they have the political will to do so.[3] An altenative is to add professional capacity by joining with neighboring communities to share the services of a circuit-riding administrator. Such arrangements are frequently initiated on a demonstration basis for several years, using state or federal grants (for example, through the OPM Intergovernmental Personnel Act).

Substate Regionalism. Small rural governments can increase their capacity through interlocal cooperation. These arrangements may involve a single function (fire protection), or they may be for general-purpose governance (consolidation of several services). The former case does not usually involve an actual alteration of governmental structure, while the latter case typically does. In either instance boundaries are redrawn and units are consolidated to overcome the limiting conditions of small size, low density, and insufficient revenues that render individual rural governments acting alone inefficient. Technical capacity, administrative effectiveness and efficiency, and individuals' access to services (especially specialized services) are enhanced by reducing governmental fragmentation, avoiding duplication of services, increasing coordination, and achieving territorial adequacy and economies of scale.

Interlocal agreements can be particularly useful among areas experiencing differential rates and directions of population change. Growing communities can "borrow" infrastructure and technical expertise from declining areas where excess capacity is likely to be developing. In contrast, capital is more difficult to transfer. Tax base and bonding capacity are rooted in particular localities. If state law is facilitative and local thinking is supportive, resource transfers can be accomplished expeditiously and do not have to wait for new revenues to be raised, new facilities to be constructed, new grants to be awarded, or new service delivery systems to be organized. Accordingly, effective government and access to a reasonable level of services can be maintained in the face of demographic change.

Substate regionalism takes many forms. For example, the Cooperative Extension Service in Iowa is experimenting with intermunicipal clustering as an integral part of their leadership development program, Tomorrow's Leaders Today. Many other areas have experimented with multicounty planning districts to supply areawide planning for public services, provide a forum where representatives of individual communities can resolve differences and marshal resources in support of common goals, and share the cost of professional and capital resources that no individual community could afford on its own. Similarly, councils of governments provide a mechanism for regional growth management and for planning and coordinating activities that transcend political boundaries. They also help to implement expensive mandated services (Bradshaw and Blakely, 1979). All of these arrangements require a facilitative state policy environment, especially with regard to the legal and tax implications of joint arrangements.

Regardless of its benefits, substate regionalism is often resisted by grassroots officials, who may see it as a threat to local autonomy. A similar antagonistic attitude at the federal level has substantially reduced funding to support areawide planning and coordination. The Reagan administration viewed regionalism as an attempt to wrest control from local elected officials and concentrate authority in larger, nonrepresentative governments. Between 1979 and 1983 funding for virtually all substate regional commissions was terminated or severely reduced (Bender, Browne, and Zolty, 1987). Given these reductions in federal support, the future of regional entities largely depends on state-level encouragement, including financial and technical support and positive attitudes of local officials. The National Governors' Association (1988), in its new publication *New Alliances for Rural America,* explicitly recognizes the importance of facilitating intercommunity cooperation.

Innovative Governance. Local rural governments can use innovative techniques and organizational methods to reduce the costs and increase the efficiency of their service delivery responsibilities. For example, service provision can be concentrated in a central location and transportation ties provided for outlying residents. This type of arrangement can include a sharing of facilities and personnel by several communities, and it can even involve organizational consolidation, as in the case of public education and regional hospital services. In contrast, modern transportation and communication technology make it possible to decentralize services and deliver them to people where they live. The delivery of health services to the elderly and disabled, for example, can use this type of arrangement.

Innovative methods are also being developed to facilitate planning and access to information. Many new methods for assessing community needs, for example, have been developed. Many of these methods use a community development perspective that is predicated on the assumption that usable knowledge is more likely to result from a process that involves local participants. The "action research" technique uses collaboration between residents and specialists to plan, conduct, analyze, and utilize research on issues pertinent to community change, including adapting to population growth and decline (Ryan, 1988).

Local governments can expand their capacity in response to population change by making greater use of volunteers. In fact, since many rural areas are growing by attracting retirees, the pool of potential volunteers is expanding. Retired business persons bring managerial and financial knowledge to the community; clergy bring a thorough knowledge of human relations and group process skills; and engineers, lawyers, doctors, and craftsmen bring technical skills. All these volunteers can benefit their new communities and contribute to lower per unit costs for local government in the face of increasing demands.

Conclusion

Population change creates problems and opportunities for rural areas. Capable local governments can guide communities through these difficult transitions. To do this, rural governments must be forward-looking, able to process relevant information about the merits of alternative options, and technically competent in an array of areas. Adaptation to population growth, decline, and compositional change is especially difficult where change is rapid, unanticipated, and a break with past trends. While most policy discussions focus on situations of decline and population loss, public programs can also make a difference in growing areas or in those that are experiencing compositional changes. It is not easy to rally public support of assistance to growing areas, but publicly supported strengthening of local government can help growing communities both to capitalize on the opportunities associated with growth and to avoid costs. Declining areas will also benefit from enhanced governmental capacity.

The policy framework developed in this chapter contends that local government capacity building should be a coequal element in rural development policy, along with more traditional credit, infrastructure, and human resource programs. Inadequate capacity of local government creates undue hardship and missed opportunities for many rural areas. It seems axiomatic that more capable governments will be better able to adapt to the challenges posed by demographic change.

We have outlined a set of activities that can contribute to local government effectiveness in planning and managing for change and producing and providing public services. These activities include enhancing local officials' level of technical and political expertise, improving access to information and technical assistance, promoting the adoption of innovative technology and organizational arrangements, and encouraging interlocal cooperation.

This last item is especially critical and requires that local areas reconsider community boundaries, at least for some functions and responsibilities. Many rural communities are hesitant to become involved in interlocal arrangements, but we believe that go-it-alone strategies are out of place in an age of increased national and global political, economic, and social integration. The federal government, following the National Governors' Association's lead, should reassert its leadership by encouraging and supporting substate regionalism through financial and technical assistance. In addition, state governments can be more assertive in assisting their communities to cope with growth and decline. As Sokolow (1990) has observed, "States have the ability to expand the revenue powers, organizational options, and regulatory powers available to their local governments."

Finally, the Cooperative Extension Service can play a larger role in providing information, training, and technical assistance to local government. While extension has economic development programs for local officials in many states, the system lacks the resources to be effective throughout rural America. If it is to make a significant contribution to enhancing governmental capacity in rural America, the extension service will have to develop new materials and delivery mechanisms and redirect resources from more traditional programs to rural development. This is an important goal for extension as it renegotiates its social contract for the coming century.

Notes

Discussions with David Allee, Duane Wilcox, and Mike Hattery of Cornell University's Local Governance and Development Project were invaluable in framing our perspective on methods of enhancing local government capacity. Calvin Beale, Beth Honadle, Alvin Sokolow, and Mildred Warner also made helpful comments. Arline Clair did an excellent job preparing the manuscript.

1. Dubin (1989) has shown that federal government grants to state and local governments grew by less than 4 percent between 1981 and 1985, compared with a 29 percent increase in total government expenditures during the period.

2. Our focus is at the village, town, or county level. We recognize that social, political, or economic communities might be somewhat different than governmental jurisdictions, but governmental functions are an important element of most rural communities. Moreover, we believe that local government is the nexus through which community adaptation to demographic change occurs.

3. Sokolow (1982) indicates that the effects of population change do not show up in organizational changes in the cities he studied, even though officials recognized that adaptation to change was made more difficult by their present administrative structure.

References

Barkley, Paul W. 1974. "Public goods in rural areas: Problems, policies, and population." *American Journal of Agricultural Economics*, 56(5):1135–1142.

Bender, Lewis, William P. Browne, and Thaddeus C. Zolty. 1987. "The new federalism and substate regionalism." *Publius* 17(4):159–174.

Bradshaw, Ted K., and Edward J. Blakely. 1979. *Rural Communities in Advanced Industrial Society.* New York: Praeger.

Brown, David L., and Calvin L. Beale. 1982. "Diversity in post-1970 population trends." Ch. 2 in Amos H. Hawley and Sara Mills Mazie, eds., *Nonmetropolitan America in Transition.* Chapel Hill, N.C.: University of North Carolina Press.

Brown, David L., and Kenneth L. Deavers. 1988. "Rural change and the rural economic policy agenda for the 1980's." Ch. 1 in David L. Brown, J. Norman Reid, Herman Bluestone, David A. McGranahan, and Sara Mazie, eds. *Rural Economic Development in the 1980's: Prospects for the Future.* Rural Development Research Report No. 69, Washington, D.C.: USDA, Economic Research Service.

Butler, Margaret, and Linda Swanson. 1990. "Nonmetropolitan population growth recovering after mid-decade slump." *Rural Conditions and Trends.* Washington, D.C.: USDA, Economic Research Service.

Cherlin, Andrew. 1981. *Marriage, Divorce, and Remarriage.* Cambridge, Mass.: Harvard University Press.

Coelen, Steven, and William Fox. 1981. "The provision of community services." Ch. 15 in Amos H. Hawley and Sara Mills Mazie, eds., *Nonmetropolitan America in Transition.* Chapel Hill, N.C.: University of North Carolina Press.

Deaton, Brady J. 1983. "New institutional arrangements for supplying local public services under new federalism with special reference to education." *American Journal of Agricultural Economics* 65(5):1124–1130.

Drabenstott, Mark, Mark Henry, and Lynn Gibson. 1987. "The rural economic policy choice." *Economic Review: Federal Reserve Bank of Kansas City* January:41–58.

Dubin, Elliott J. 1989. "Geographic distribution of federal funds." *ERS Staff Report.* AGES 89-7. Washington, D.C.: USDA, Economic Research Service.

Elo, Irma T., and Calvin L. Beale. 1988. "The decline in counterurbanization in the 1980's." Paper presented to the annual meeting of the Population Association of America, New Orleans.

Favero, Philip, and Daryl K. Heasley. 1989. *Cooperative Extension and New Alliances for Rural Development: Five Case Studies.* Publication No. 58. University Park, Penn.: Northeast Regional Center for Rural Development.

Fox, William F. 1980. *Relationships between Size of School and School Districts and Cost of Education.* ESCS Technical Bulletin No. 1621. Washington, D.C.: USDA. April.

Fuguitt, Glenn V., David L. Brown, and Calvin L. Beale. 1989. *Rural and Smalltown America.* New York: Russell Sage Foundation.

Glasgow, Nina. 1988. *The Nonmetro Elderly: Economic and Demographic Status.* Rural Development Research Report No. 70. Washington, D.C.: USDA, Economic Research Service.

————. 1990. "Attracting retirees as a community development option." *Journal of the Community Development Society* 21(1):102–114.

Honadle, Beth Walter. 1981. "A capacity building framework: A search for concept and purpose." *Public Administration Review* September/October: 575–580.

Johnson, Kenneth M. 1985. *The Impact of Population Change on Business Activity in Rural America.* Boulder, Colo.: Westview Press.

Killian, Molly Sizer, and Thomas F. Hady. 1988. "The economic performance of rural labor markets." Ch. 8 in David L. Brown, J. Norman Reid, Herman Bluestone, David A. McGranahan, and Sara M. Mazie, eds., *Rural Economic Development in the 1980's: Prospects for the Future.* Rural Development Research Report No. 69. Washington, D.C.: USDA, Economic Research Service.

National Governors' Association. 1988. *New Alliances for Rural America.* Washington, D.C.: National Governors' Association.

Nelson, James R., Luther Tweeten, and Gerald Doeksen. 1984. "The economics of rural community services in the United States." Ch. 4 in Richard Lonsdale and Gyorgy Enyedi, eds., *Rural Public Services: International Comparisons.* Boulder, Colo.: Westview Press.

Newland, Chester A. 1981. "Local government capacity building." *Urban Affairs Papers* 3(1):iv–v.

Richter, Kerry. 1985. "Nonmetropolitan growth in the late 1970's: The end of the turnaround?" *Demography* 22(2):245–263.

Rogers, David L. 1982. "Community services." Ch. 14 in Don A. Dillman and Daryl J. Hobbs, eds., *Rural Society in the U.S.: Issues for the 1980s.* Boulder, Colo.: Westview Press.

Russo, Philip A., Herbert Waltzer, and W. Robert Gump. 1987. "Rural government management and the new federalism: Local attitudes in southwestern Ohio." *Publius* 17(4):147–158.

Ryan, Vernon D. 1988. "The significance of community development to rural economic development initiatives." Ch. 16 in David L. Brown, J. Norman Reid, Herman Bluestone, David A. McGranahan, and Sara Mazie, eds., *Rural Economic Development in the 1980's: Prospects for the Future.* Rural Development Research Report No. 69. Washington, D.C.: USDA, Economic Research Service.

Sokolow, Alvin. 1981. "Local governments: Capacity and will." Ch. 19 in Amos H. Hawley and Sara Mills Mazie, eds., *Nonmetropolitan America in Transition.* Chapel Hill, N.C.: University of North Carolina Press.

_____ . 1982. "Population growth and administrative variations in small cities." Ch. 8 in William P. Browne and Don F. Hadwiger, eds., *Rural Policy Problems: Changing Dimensions.* Lexington, Mass.: Lexington Books.

_____ . 1987. "Introduction: Small governments as newcomers to American federalism." *Publius* 17(4):1–14.

_____ . 1990. Personal communication.

Stinson, Thomas F. 1987. "The farm crisis and the future of rural local governments." *Publius* 17(4):175–188.

17
Rural Transportation

Ronald C. Wimberley

Characterized by their remoteness from urban concentrations, rural areas are distinctive in their transportation requirements. Policy issues include the deteriorating conditions of rural transportation infrastructure and how to pay for its improvement, the federal financial responsibility for rural transportation, and eliminating negative impacts of transportation deregulation on rural areas to promote rural economic and social viability.

Without sufficient external linkages for transporting people, goods, and services, rural communities would be unable to achieve or maintain their social and economic well-being. Rural places also may improve their quality of life by improving internal linkages within the locality. But while internal linkages are better than no linkages at all, it is not clear that internal linkages alone are sufficient to reach community goals. As an analogy, it is not easy to lift one's self without external leverage. Outside linkages are needed to get a person or a community moving. Internal, local linkages are needed to help them keep going.

Infrastructure Policy Context for Rural Transportation

The early twentieth century sociologist Charles Horton Cooley made an almost casual generalization that cities develop at breaks in the transportation system. If that is the case, rural areas represent a transportation system's beginnings and endings. Access to, from, and within rural areas is essential for a two-way physical linkage with the outside world. When access is used—when people commute or when they, their products, and services move—linkages are established. Still, rural transportation is just one element of the larger complex of rural infrastructure and policy.

Infrastructure and Transportation

In its report to the President and Congress, *Fragile Foundations* (1988:1), the National Council on Public Works Improvement finds "convincing evidence that the quality of America's infrastructure is barely adequate to fulfill current requirements, and insufficient to meet the demands of future economic growth and development." The Council gives the grade of "a scant C" to the nation's infrastructure.

Rural transportation-related infrastructure is considered as bad or worse. Rural economic decline aggravates the situation. The National Council on Public Works Improvement (1988:6) states that the "needs of most rural and smaller [highway] systems exceed available resources." And the shift of responsibility from federal and state levels to local areas for financing infrastructure casts a third strike against rural localities.

With specific reference to transportation, Aschauer (1988:3) concludes, "A root cause in the decline in the competitiveness of the United States in the international economy may be found in the low rate at which our country has chosen to add to its stock of highways, port facilities, airports, and other facilities which aid in the production and distribution of goods and services."

These national transportation assessments support what rural analysts have been saying. Kaye (1982:158), for instance, notes that social scientists now recognize "that a rural region injures its potential for development if its basic economy lacks competitive transportation for inputs and outputs and if a significant percentage of its population lacks access to job sites, basic services, and social interaction." Unfortunately, however, rural infrastructure, including transportation systems, did not keep pace with population growth during the 1980s. Wardwell (1986) argues that if rural population growth of the 1970s were to continue, the current infrastructure would not be able to support it.

Rural Social Interaction: Symbolic and Physical

Of course, the transportation system is not the only linkage through which rural America's social interactions take place. Information can be either directly exchanged orally and through other symbols transmitted in face-to-face relationships or sent indirectly through media such as print, telephones, radio, television, and computer networks. But people, food, fiber, and minerals cannot be moved electronically as if they were abstract, symbolic messages. And, for that matter, neither can printed information. For people and tangible items, their actual transportation is the vital linkage.

Rural areas and transportation remain inseparable in today's society and world economy. Given the distances between rural natural resources and the places where the bulk of the population lives, rural transportation must work effectively. Rural transportation systems, however, do not always work without problems. It is these problems that we must examine objectively.

Agriculture and Rural Transportation Policies

Over a decade ago, a U.S. Department of Agriculture (USDA) and Department of Transportation (DOT) rural transportation task force report, *Transportation Services to Meet Growing Needs in Agriculture* (USDA and USDOT, 1979:8), summarized the transportation problem this way:

Changes and deficiencies in the transportation system now take place against a background of uncertainty. Inflation, the energy crisis, and the Nation's need to increase exports pose policy questions for all segments of the economy, but particularly for transportation and agriculture. The U.S. agricultural community can produce more food than the Nation needs, but it can export the surplus only if there is an adequate and reasonably predictable supply of transportation equipment and service. Both the long-term transportation problems of agriculture and the larger economic issues affecting transportation and agriculture demand solutions.

Not only does this assessment describe the situation for agricultural transportation, the report also shows that the problem has been around for a while.

This account also illustrates the traditional policy emphasis on agriculture in particular rather than on rural transportation in general. When rural roads are considered, for example, there is a tendency to think of them in the context of the farm-to-market roads that Congress initiated in a 1944 policy and revised in 1976 (Berg, 1986). The policy assumption that meeting farm needs will satisfy the rural nonfarm sectors, as well, was never entirely sound and is less valid today than ever.

Agricultural transportation continues to be a major component of rural transportation policy, but there is much more to rurality than farming. Rural nonfarm residents outnumber rural farm residents by a ratio of more than ten to one (Wimberley, 1986). While many rural nonfarm people depend directly or indirectly on agriculture for their livelihoods, a majority rely on other natural resources, manufacturing, tourism, or businesses and services. Agriculture remains a primary rural enterprise in general, although many rural places are not particularly agricultural.

Social Interdependence and Responsibility

Goods and services as well as rural and urban people cross the boundaries of such governmental units as communities, cities, counties, states, and nations. These movements, plus communications, among different social units make our society complex. Social units—rural, urban, or otherwise—are interdependent.

Due to these interactions of persons and groups across territorial and social boundaries, the responsibility for what happens in even the most remote and sparsely populated areas—which produce goods and services for others and which consume goods and services from elsewhere—is the collective responsibility of all. This interdependence implies federal as well as state and local responsibility for rural areas and communities.

Options

Major transportation linkages correspond to lines of social and economic inputs to and outputs from localities. These become linkages for individuals, households, firms, institutions, communities, and for the larger society. It is easy to take for granted that the complex of social and economic linkages that sustain rural areas and their interdependence with other places will not fail. Rural transportation translates into trips for local people and visitors, goods for local consumers and firms, and markets for rural products.

Ways and Means

Transportation options may be considered as ways and means. *Ways* represent routes along highways, bridges, railways, airways, and waterways. *Means* of conveyance are autos, trucks, buses, trains, planes, and boats. Alternatives among the ways and means are important for those who use rural transportation.

Roads. A major part of the rural transportation system is roads. The 3.9 million miles of roads and streets in the United States are more than can be found in any other country. Rural areas disproportionately claim nearly 3.2 million miles, or 82 percent, of this system. Of the rural miles, over 2.2 million are controlled by local governments, 0.7 million by state governments, and 0.2 million by the federal government (U.S. Bureau of the Census, 1989; USDOT, 1988).

Of the total urban and rural mileage, 0.3 million miles are part of the federal-aid highway system which supplements state matching funds for planning, rights-of-way, engineering, construction, resurfacing, restoration, rehabilitation, and reconstruction. States and localities, however, are responsible for maintaining and patrolling federal-aid highways. The complexities of this financing system are described elsewhere (Walzer and Chicoine, 1989a; Walzer and McFadden, 1989; Marathon and Norton, 1988; and USDOT, 1988).

The federal-aid system includes the 44,000 miles of interstates completed since 1956 with more to be finished by 1991. Interstates directly connect 42 percent of the nation's counties, reach 31 percent of the nonmetropolitan counties (Marathon and Norton, 1988), and represent major linkages for nearby rural areas. During the 1970s, after completion of most of the interstate system (U.S. Bureau of the Census, 1989) and when migration to rural areas was high, nonmetro counties on interstates experienced greater in-migration and employment growth (Lichter and Fuguitt, 1980).

Although there is still some demand for building major highways to access rural areas of some states and for constructing new local streets and roads, there appears to be greater interest in road quality. The Federal Highway Administration (USDOT, 1988) makes present serviceability ratings (PSR) for rural roads. These include interstate highways, principal arterial roads which provide interstate and intrastate connections among larger cities, minor arterial roads for other intrastate and intercounty connections, major collector roads for other county seats and towns, and minor collector roads for developed areas and small communities (Walzer and McFadden, 1989).

The PSR scale ranges from 0 for very poor to 5 for very good pavement conditions and excludes unpaved roads. Serviceability ratings below 3.5 occur for 42 percent of the rural interstate highways and about 50 percent of the arterials. Sixty-seven percent of the major collectors and 83 percent of the minor collectors fall below this level. Another 12 percent of the major collectors and 36 percent of the minor collectors are unpaved (USDOT, 1988). Although ratings are not reported for local roads beyond the minor collectors, these data show that noninterstate road surfaces worsen as they stretch into local and rural destinations.

Further research indicates that road quality is of particular concern at the community level, where federal and state resources for roads are limited and where maintenance has been deferred to finance other needs during local fiscal crises. In their national study, for example, Reid and Sullivan (1984; Reid et al., 1984) found that 58 percent of the rural communities are at least partially responsible for road and street maintenance and construction. Also, they found some of the worst roads in unincorporated communities. Large community road problems include narrowness, resurfacing, weight limits, and unpaved roads subject to closing from floods and weather conditions in the smallest communities. Their survey suggests the desire for new roads is due to growth and crowding.

Physical and social conditions contribute to the danger of rural roads. Physical factors include rough terrain, poorly paved surfaces, inadequate engineering, lack of signs and markings, types of vehicles, and poorer conditions of vehicles. Social factors include mail delivery, school bus operation, the movement of farm equipment, closeness of large freight or passenger vehicles, driver fatigue, more older drivers with visual restrictions, unfamiliarity with roadways, speeding, not using seat belts, and intoxication (Bearer, McWilliams, and Stommes, 1989; Southern Rural Development Center, 1989).

Due to such factors, rural accidents are nearly twice as likely to be fatal as are urban accidents. Rural fatality rates are higher than urban rates regardless of highway or road type. Fatality rates per vehicle miles traveled become worse as one moves from interstates to noninterstates, from federal-aid to nonfederal-aid highways, from arterial to collector roads, and from collectors to local roads (U.S. Bureau of the Census, 1989).

Bridges. According to the Federal Highway Administration's National Bridge Inventory of bridges at least 20 feet long, 81 percent of the nation's 578,000 bridges are classified as rural (USDOT, 1988; Marathon, 1989). Nearly one-half of the rural, or 35 percent of the total, bridges are on rural local roads.

The quality of bridges, as with roads, can restrict or prohibit heavily loaded trucks as well as passenger traffic. According to DOT's National Bridge Inventory (Marathon, 1989), rural bridges average 37 years in age and are older than the urban bridges by six years. Half of the rural bridges were built before 1957. Forty-six percent are either structurally deficient or functionally obsolete as compared to only 31 percent of the urban bridges. Of the obsolete or deficient rural bridges, over three-fourths need replacement and the remainder need rehabilitation or widening.

Who is responsible for maintaining rural obsolete and deficient bridges? Counties care for 63 percent, 30 percent are the responsibility of states, and

6 percent are local. The federal government maintains less than 1 percent (Marathon, 1989). Through the National Bridge Inventory, however, those with low ratings may qualify for federal Highway Bridge Replacement and Rehabilitation Program funds, which are administered by the states or counties.

In data compiled for the National Association of Counties, Walzer and McFadden (1989) report that among bridges controlled by counties, sometimes with state or federal assistance, 45 percent are eligible for replacement and another 30 percent qualify for rehabilitation. For all rural bridges in 1988, regardless of county, state, or federal control, the figures are similar. Twenty-eight percent qualify for replacement while 31 percent merit rehabilitation (Marathon, 1989).

Reid and Sullivan's (1984) USDA survey provides additional information on conditions of rural bridges. They report that about half of the rural communities in their study had bridges with weight limits so low they could not be used by heavy farm equipment or large delivery trucks. One-fourth of the communities had one or more bridges that were too narrow. One-third had deferred maintenance on one or more bridges for a year. In each case, the smaller, unincorporated communities were among the most deficient. According to a rural Virginia study (Taylor, Johnson, and Lammivaara, 1986), weight or size restrictions, surface conditions, and poor construction or design had to be met by reducing the weights or sizes of loads, rerouting, delays, extra truck maintenance, and greater costs. Johnson (1989) explains how road and bridge deficiencies handicap rural businesses. These descriptive data and analytic findings signal a crisis for rural bridges.

Railroads, Air Service, and Waterways. Rural rail service around the country has its deficiencies as well. These include abandonment of certain lines by rail companies, seasonal shortages of rail cars, deterioration of track beds, mismanagement, labor costs, and, ironically, the existence of captive users of rail shipping in some communities without alternative carriers. In recent decades, many railroads have gone bankrupt and have left certain areas stranded. Although rail passenger and freight services in rural areas have declined significantly, railroads remain an important element in the rural, agricultural, and natural resource transportation system. In particular, short-line railroads seem to hold promise for economic development in some rural areas. Small railroads have increased mileage since 1985 and are beginning to offset the abandonment of some lines by major carriers (Batson and Bearer, 1989).

Ports, certain portions of their business, and the opening of waterways come about through policy decisions. Many exist largely to ship rural products. That New Orleans is a major world port for exporting wheat, corn, and rice may be surprising. Business through this port is heavy since the Mississippi River links the Gulf of Mexico to farming areas of the Delta, Midwest, Plains, and Great Lakes. The Mississippi and other waterways such as the Tennessee-Tombigbee also provide upstream supplies of materials, fertilizers, and fuels. Problems faced by shipping on waterways include canal construction, channel dredging, the operation of locks and dams, and port facilities. Waterways, of course, must link with rail and truck lines.

The role of air service in rural development appears to be increasing (Stommes and Beningo, 1989). However, small communities seldom qualify for commercial passenger service and federal Airport Improvement Program funding unless they can count on 2,500 to 10,000 passengers annually. Airports in small places, where they exist, serve local firms and private pilots and offer economic linkages, diversification, and business expansion. Presently, however, there is little policy basis for using rural air facilities as a tool for rural development.

When roads, bridges, railways, or other ways of rural transportation become obsolete or dysfunctional, the costs of rural exports and imports increase. Rural business becomes not only more costly and less profitable, but it is less competitive. In some cases, an obsolescent infrastructure can prohibit enterprises from operating at all and therefore obstructs rural economic viability.

Automobiles, Vans, and Buses. For rural passenger transportation, automobiles are the mainstay. With distance a fact of life for rural residents, auto use has become a necessity. Nationally, about nine out of ten households have one or more autos, with an average of 1.6 per household. Over half of those without vehicles live in the largest cities (Stommes, 1989) where there are alternative means of transportation.

Many rural people, however, do not have cars or other viable options for public transportation. The Transportation Task Force (1985) of the Extension Committee on Organization and Policy reports that 15 percent of the rural families do not own vehicles. This figure grows to 45 percent of the elderly and 57 percent of the poor. Another 52 percent of all rural households own only one auto. Furthermore, the task force finds public transportation available to fewer than 1 percent of the work force in rural areas.

Obviously, alternatives to automobile ownership are needed for many rural persons and families. Reliance upon rides from neighbors and friends is an inadequate option. At minimum, local public transportation systems are required for those who cannot drive due to age, health, or impoverishment and for capable, working-aged residents who cannot afford their own vehicles. Otherwise, many of these people become immobilized and less self-sufficient. They are unable to obtain available jobs, unable to participate in educational programs that would provide employment skills, unable to use any day care services for dependent children or adults so they can work, and unable to properly benefit from health-care services.

Various service agencies offer demand-based transportation for their clientele and are located in rural areas (Fountain and Doeksen, 1985). Although about one-fourth of our population—including disproportionate shares of the elderly and low-income populations—lives in rural areas, and despite the distances to be traversed by rural people for work and service needs, rural mass-transit vehicles, mostly vans, amount to only 12,142. This is barely more than one-tenth of all mass-transit vehicles (National Council on Public Works Improvement, 1988).

Trucks. Regardless of the potential for rural rail, water, and air freight, trucking plays the dominant economic role. Trucking becomes even more necessary for communities losing rail freight services. In addition to carrying goods to and from local areas, trucking normally connects with other truck terminals, railroads, airports, and waterways to bring consumer items, equipment, and supplies to their final commercial outlets. In turn, local trucking connects the rural origins for raw and locally processed products to other freight carriers.

Trucking is especially important for moving perishables such as fresh fruits, vegetables, milk, eggs, livestock, poultry, and grains. In addition, parcel delivery has become a supplement to rural mail delivery. Given the heavy dependence on trucking, rural places, as well as the urban places they serve, are vulnerable to transportation conditions and fuel shortages. Just as important is vulnerability to breakdowns in the fragile set of social conditions—including regulations and labor-management issues—which sustain timely trucking services.

Deregulation of Transportation Services

A new turn for rural transportation policy, deregulation, appeared in the 1980s. In one form or another, deregulation influences passenger and freight service on bus, rail, air, and trucking lines. Its overall effects are somewhat sketchy but reveal a pattern of disadvantage to rural areas. Since deregulation, for example, truck and rail freight rates can vary and are open to contract negotiation. The result is often higher costs to rural people and firms.

Impacts on passenger service are summarized by the USDA's Office of Transportation (Stommes, 1989:3, 25) as follows:

> Substantial loss of air, rail, and intercity bus services during the past decade has left many rural communities with limited access to any form of public transportation.
> While the benefits nationally outweigh the costs, those costs are falling disproportionately on small communities and rural areas. On a national scale, the magnitude of these costs is relatively small, but they are significant to those rural areas losing their transportation service.

Furthermore, the repercussions of deregulation persist and continue to influence rural life and business.

Stommes and Beningo (1989) point out that communities of less than 25,000 had nearly three-fourths of the losses of air service and places under 5,000 had one-third of the service terminations during the first decade of deregulation ending in 1987. They observe that air fares increased in medium and small markets. However, they also suggest that the real cost of air service for small communities—at least for those that still have air service—has declined, although not as much as for larger airports. Shifts to smaller aircraft, commuter lines, fewer flights, and safety questions are associated with deregulation.

In a twelve-state study on the impacts of the Airline Deregulation Act of 1978 and the Bus Regulatory Reform Act of 1982, Oster (1988) found that within two years after deregulation, bus service ceased in 20 percent of the communities previously served. Three-fourths of the bus providers had been terminating lines prior to deregulation. Similarly, Oster's research on airlines shows that 17 percent dropped airports following deregulation. However, he doubts that this decline was directly related to deregulation, since nearly all the terminations were by commuter airlines exempt from deregulation. Instead, the decline is attributed to the 1980–1982 economic recession. He concluded that while those losing air service have alternative means of transportation, those without bus service—the poor, young, and elderly living in the smallest communities—do not.

Since the 1970 Rail Passenger Services Act, commercial passenger service essentially has been assumed by Amtrack. Yet the federal subsidy for Amtrak remains problematic, and fewer rural towns receive service. Just as rural rail freight has tended to shift to trucking, rural rail passengers have shifted to other means, including intercity buses, which have declined as well. From the 1982 bus deregulation until 1986, 896 communities gained bus service while 3,763 lost it. Among the losing communities, 3,432 had fewer than 10,000 residents. Another 751 places experienced reduced service according to an Interstate Commerce Commission report (Stommes, 1989).

Research that completely evaluates the effects of deregulation on rural transportation remains incomplete. But whether as a result of deregulation or economic conditions, it is obvious that many rural communities have lost services. The net effects of rail, air, and bus deregulation have reduced services to rural places while increasing their costs. No doubt deregulation intensified the impact of economic decline in rural places. Overall, deregulation policies have not improved transportation in rural areas; if anything, they appear to have had the opposite effect.

Financing Rural Transportation Infrastructure

The federal funding system for rural transportation and infrastructure in general underwent changes in the 1980s. Federal revenue sharing ceased in 1987 and other federal programs diminished throughout the decade. Greater responsibility shifted to states and localities. This shift corresponded with a rural and agricultural crisis that put many communities in an additional bind. Only about one-fifth of rural road mileage now qualifies for federal assistance (Marathon and Norton, 1988).

The retreat in federal funding has been duly noted by a number of public interest organizations. As summarized by Busson and Hackett (1987:2) for the Council of State Governments, "Since 1982 when federal grants-in-aid for public works began to decline in real dollars, the role of state vis-à-vis the local government has undergone a gradual change." An exception to the federal aid decline is a fairly stable level in federal trust funds for transportation.

In a report for the National Association of Counties, Walzer and McFadden (1989) show that from 1977 to 1986 and prior to the end of revenue sharing, county highway financing had already begun to dwindle from such sources as property taxes, federal and state intergovernmental aid, and in real dollars of federal highway aid per mile. On the other hand, reliance on bonds, notes, and state highway aid per mile had increased. Busson and Hackett (1987) similarly show a trend for most states to increase their gasoline or fuel taxes along with other auto and truck fees to pay for bridge costs and other public works. In addition, they find that bond and loan programs have been initiated to help localities with roads and bridges.

Without sufficient funding from federal or state sources, such as revenue sharing, Walzer and Chicoine (1989b) found that a national sample of county officials ranked higher property taxes and postponement of new construction as their top strategies for funding road and bridge improvements. These were followed by deferring maintenance and reducing equipment purchases. Although none of these options seems highly desirable, they are choices that often must be made.

States and local governments do have an assortment of customary tax, fee, and bond techniques for replacing or supplementing federal funds for rural transportation. Creativity is needed. Innovations should include financing for the social components of local transportation infrastructure—public administration and management—as well as the physical infrastructure itself. Most states and localities require additional federal assistance as well.

Rural Policies on Purpose

The ways and means of rural transportation can be affected by national or special interest transportation policies, whether they are designated as rural policies or not. It is doubtful that policymakers paid sufficient attention to deregulation's effects on rural America. With the scheduled completion of the interstate highway system in 1991, national transportation policy faces new directions and new legislative objectives (Office of Transportation, 1989; Bearer, McWilliams, and Stommes, 1989).

New national transportation policies should explicitly take into account the needs of rural areas, communities, and their people. Appropriations, financing, regulations, and deregulations must include a rural dimension. Otherwise, well-intended policies oriented to the interests of urban population centers or policies designed exclusively to aid agriculture can be ineffective and inequitable due to unintended and undesirable effects on rural transportation.

Conclusion

Rural transportation is a crucial variable for helping to achieve equality and efficiency for rural places across our country. By their nature, rural areas are dispersed geographically. With favorable communication and transportation systems, rural Americans do not have to be socially isolated. Better communication systems will readily permit symbolic social interactions to take place. However, people and other physical objects must be physically transported. Rural transportation is required to move rural people, the items they consume, and the goods they extract or process.

As things now stand, and according to various assessments, much of our rural transportation infrastructure needs to be improved. Policy issues and actions fall into at least two general dimensions. One is to provide financial support for improving the ways—roads, bridges, railroads, airways, and waterways—of rural transportation. Another policy dimension is to establish regulations which allow rural areas and communities to improve their transportation means—autos, buses, trucks, trains, planes, and ships—in order to improve unfavorable rural economic and social conditions which have been compounded by recent transportation deregulation policies.

Essentially, rural transportation policies need to finance the ways and regulate the means. Specific policy actions at issue entail the following:

- Rural roads and bridges should be maintained, replaced, or constructed in order for rural places to be externally linked. Priorities should be established. Conditions of rural bridges are critical.
- Streets and roads within rural communities and their surrounding areas require improvement for local transportation needs, which include daily commuting for work, for services, and leisure.
- In some places, ports and waterways should be considered to enhance the shipping of agricultural products and other raw materials or manufactured goods.
- Innovative and equitable ways of financing rural transportation facilities should be developed along with an innovative social infrastructure for managing transportation needs.
- Federal financial support for rural transportation infrastructure should be increased to further supplement that of states and, especially, localities.
- Van or bus services should be established or reinstated, as well as subsidized, to serve rural people and to provide an alternative to auto transportation within and between communities.
- Rural areas must have adequate and competitive trucking and delivery services, especially where other freight options have been curtailed.
- Some rural areas would be better served by rail transportation for passengers and shipping rather than exclusive reliance on autos and trucks.
- Air service is needed to quickly link rural communities and regions with distant communities to serve employers, economic development, passenger transportation, and emergency needs. Policy and financial support should be established.
- Energy needs for transportation are subject to crises and, if there are shortages, rural areas are most vulnerable. Effective energy policies should be in place for services and rural products.

- Although the availability and conditions of rural transportation command immediate attention, improving the safety of rural transportation remains an important concern and should be addressed through policies.
- More comprehensive, systematic, and timely data on rural transportation conditions are needed to assess conditions and changes. Deregulation's impacts need to be evaluated so that policies may be revised in order to respond properly to rural transportation problems.

The network of social and physical transportation infrastructure sustaining rural America and linking it to other places which rely on its people and products is complex and vital. Yet this infrastructure is chronically vulnerable. Strengthening the rural transportation system against its vulnerabilities becomes an important route to other forms of economic and social viability in rural America.

Notes

This chapter is a contribution to USDA-CSRS Regional Project S-246 through the North Carolina Agricultural Research Service, North Carolina State University. Comments from Tom Johnson, Claude Allen, Gerald Doeksen, Bob Tosterud, and Neal Flora on an earlier draft are appreciated and Ruth McWilliams and Eileen Stommes are thanked for providing information. The author is responsible for the views expressed here. A detailed draft of this chapter is available from the author.

References

Aschauer, David Alan. 1988. "Rx for productivity: Build infrastructure." *Chicago Fed Letter* (September):1–3.

Batson, John, and Martha Bearer. 1989. *Importance of Small Railroads to Agriculture and Rural America.* Washington, D.C.: USDA, Office of Transportation.

Bearer, Martha A., Ruth T. McWilliams, and Eileen S. Stommes. 1989. *Beyond Isolation: The Future of Rural Transportation as Described at the Transportation 2020 Forums.* Washington, D.C.: USDA, Office of Transportation.

Berg, George L., Jr. 1986. "Rural roads and bridges." Pp. 396–402 in R. C. Wimberley, D. Jahr, and J. W. Johnson, eds., *New Dimensions in Rural Policy.* Washington, D.C.: Congress of the United States.

Busson, Terry, and Judith Hackett. 1987. *State Assistance for Local Public Works.* Lexington, Ky.: The Council of State Governments.

Fountain, E. A., and G. A. Doeksen. 1985. "Public transit systems for rural Oklahoma." *Current Farm Economics* 58(December):28–30.

Johnson, Thomas G. 1989. "State rural transportation programs in an era of contraction: Background paper." Washington, D.C.: National Governors' Association.

Kaye, Ira. 1982 "Transportation." Pp. 156–163 in D. A. Dillman and D. J. Hobbs, eds., *Rural Society in the U.S.: Issues for the 1980s.* Boulder, Colo.: Westview Press.

Lichter, Daniel T., and Glenn V. Fuguitt. 1980. "Demographic response to transportation innovation: The case of the interstate highway." *Social Forces* 59(December): 492–512.

Marathon, Nicholas. 1989. *Rural Bridges: An Assessment Based upon the National Bridge Inventory.* Washington, D.C.: USDA, Office of Transportation.

Marathon, Nicholas, and Jerry D. Norton. 1988. *Rural Highway Finance: Federal Funding for Interstate and Non-Interstate Highways in Rural Areas.* Washington, D.C.: USDA, Office of Transportation.

National Council on Public Works Improvement. 1988. *Fragile Foundations.* Washington, D.C.: NCPWI.

Office of Transportation, USDA. 1989. *Reconnecting Rural America: Recommendations for a National Strategy.* Washington, D.C.: USDA, Office of Transportation.

Oster, Clinton V., Jr. 1988. "Is deregulation cutting small communities' transportation links?" *Rural Development Perspectives* 4(June):13–16.

Reid, J. Norman, Thomas F. Stinson, Patrick J. Sullivan, Leon B. Perkinson, MonaCheri P. Clark, and Eleanor Whitehead. 1984. *Availability of Selected Public Facilities in Rural Communities: Preliminary Estimates.* Washington, D.C.: USDA, Economic Research Service.

Reid, J. Norman, and Patrick J. Sullivan. 1984. "Rural infrastructure: How much? How good?" *Rural Development Perspectives* 1(October):9–13.

Southern Rural Development Center. 1989. "Roads offer threatening conditions." *Capsules* 9(January):2.

Stommes, Eileen S. 1989. *Reconnecting Rural America: Report on Rural Intercity Passenger Transportation.* Washington, D.C.: USDA, Office of Transportation.

Stommes, Eileen S., and Steve Beningo. 1989. *Rural Air Service: Its Importance to Rural Communities, Its Status since Deregulation.* Washington, D.C.: USDA, Office of Transportation.

Taylor, Daniel B., Thomas G. Johnson, and Sari Lammivaara. 1986. *Virginia Agri-Access Network Pilot Study: Final Report.* Blacksburg, Va.: Virginia Cooperative Extension Service.

Transportation Task Force. 1985. *Rural Transportation Education: Challenges for Cooperative Extension.* Washington, D.C.: NASULGC, Extension Committee on Organization and Policy.

U.S. Bureau of the Census. 1989. *Statistical Abstract of the United States, 1989.* Washington, D.C.: U.S. Department of Commerce.

U.S. Department of Agriculture and U.S. Department of Transportation (USDA and USDOT). 1979. *Transportation Services to Meet the Growing Needs of Agriculture: A Preliminary Report of the Rural Transportation Task Force.* Washington, D.C.: USDA, Office of Transportation.

U.S. Department of Transportation (USDOT). 1988. *Highway Statistics, 1987.* Washington, D.C.: U.S. Department of Transportation, Federal Highway Administration.

Walzer, Norman, and David L. Chicoine. 1989a. *Rural Roads and Bridges: Federal and State Financing.* Washington, D.C.: USDA, Office of Transportation.

———. 1989b. *Rural Roads and Bridges: A Dilemma for Local Officials.* Washington, D.C.: USDA, Office of Transportation.

Walzer, Norman, and Claudia McFadden. 1989. *Linking America: The County Highway System.* Washington, D.C.: National Association of Counties.

Wardwell, John M. 1986. "Public policy and rural infrastructure." Pp. 380–387 in R. C. Wimberley, D. Jahr, and J. W. Johnson, eds., *New Dimensions in Rural Policy.* Washington, D.C.: Congress of the United States.

Wimberley, Ronald C. 1986. "Agricultural and rural transition." Pp. 39–45 in R. C. Wimberley, D. Jahr, and J. W. Johnson, eds., *New Dimensions in Rural Policy.* Washington, D.C.: Congress of the United States.

18
Family Planning and Fertility in International Context

Gretchen T. Cornwell and C. Shannon Stokes

Although interest in the components and consequences of world population growth has been evident in intellectual circles since the time of Malthus, it has only recently become a topic for policy debate. In the past few decades, demographers have increasingly recognized that the classic model of the Western demographic transition that described some of the historical experiences of the West is not being replicated in much of the developing world. The demographic transition model suggests that the dramatic decline in mortality associated with improved standards of living, stable supplies of food, and improved public health would soon be followed by a compensating decline in fertility. Fertility declines in many nations have been slow, resulting in persistently high rates of population growth in many Third World countries that are striving to raise living standards and promote economic development.

Well-known responses have ranged from the pessimistic views popularized in such books as *The Population Bomb* (Ehrlich, 1968), *Famine 1975!* (Paddock and Paddock, 1967), and *The Limits to Growth* (Meadows et al., 1972) to the optimistic perspective presented by Julian Simon in *The Ultimate Resource* (1981). Less familiar to the public, yet more influential in determining U.S. policy, have been analyses supported by the United Nations, the World Bank, the U.S. Agency for International Development (USAID), and the National Academy of Sciences.

For many years, U.S. policy emphasized the importance of slowing population growth through active family planning programs as key elements of development strategies and assistance. The United States emphasized this position at the 1974 United Nations Population Conference in Bucharest. The United States had been a staunch supporter of the development of the United Nations Fund for Population Activities (UNFPA), at that time, providing about half of UNFPA's budget. At the Bucharest meeting, many Third World delegations attacked the U.S. position as imperialistic and genocidal. The conference largely rejected the U.S. position and emphasized the need for a new international economic order and the primacy of development assistance over family planning and population control. Indeed, the notion that "development is the best contraceptive" received widespread acceptance by a coalition of less developed countries and Eastern bloc delegations. Ironically, among those nations opposing the U.S. position were the People's Republic of China and host country Romania, each of which was actively engaged in far-reaching, if not unprecedented, attempts to implement population control policies (Berelson, 1979; Greenhalgh and Bongaarts, 1987).

Over the next ten years, shifts in domestic U.S. politics (including the 1984 presidential election, which represented the perspective of the New Right) led to changes in the U.S. position. Consequently, by 1984, the U.S. delegation to the Mexico City conference took the position that population growth, by itself, was a neutral phenomenon and that families have an absolute right to determine their family size. The U.S. delegation emphasized the importance of removing barriers to economic development as the primary factor promoting economic growth and leading to lowered fertility and slower population growth (Finkle and Crane, 1985). Since that time, this position has been articulated in condemnation of China's one-child policy and its associated coercive activities, particularly abortion. As a result, USAID stopped supporting the UNFPA in 1985 (Crane and Finkle, 1989).

The debate surrounding the change in the U.S. position has heightened awareness of the need for an objective appraisal of the links between population growth and economic development. It is widely assumed that rapid population growth in Third World nations retards development by impeding capital accumulation, depressing wage levels, slowing improvements in health and education, and contributing to resource depletion and widespread poverty. However, systematic evidence supporting this assumption is surprisingly scarce.

This chapter addresses three questions concerning U.S. development assistance policy: (1) Should continued population growth in developing countries be a topic of policy concern? (2) Will primary reliance on family planning programs, the major emphasis of past U.S. policy, slow population growth significantly? (3) How can the United States assist developing nations that wish to lower fertility and slow population growth?

Population Growth and National Development

The Working Group on Population Growth and Economic Development, formed under the auspices of the National Academy of Sciences, issued the report *Population Growth and Economic Development: Policy Questions* in 1986. This group contrasted the probable consequences of rapid growth and slower population growth for their effects on exhaustible and renewable resources, environmental degradation, capital investment and worker output, per capita income and income distribution, schooling and health, unemployment, and urban growth. This analysis has generated considerable debate within the population and development community and appears likely to stimulate needed additional research.

The Working Group notes that, although some population growth has positive consequences for economic development and some growth has a neutral effect, overall "slower population growth would be beneficial to economic development for most developing countries" (Working Group on Population and Development, 1986:90). Growth is defined as desirable because a growing population not only assures availability of a labor pool, it stimulates capital formation, investment, and output. Concern with the effects of population growth on the depletion of resources is viewed as overstated because most resources are consumed in industrialized countries. Moreover, as resources become scarce, prices rise, thereby stimulating conservation or substitution. In addition, population growth has spurred agricultural intensification and technological innovation in both the agricultural and industrial sectors (Boserup, 1965, 1981).

However, development encompasses more than economic growth. The report does not address the effects of population growth on education, health, and income distribution as convincingly as it does the consequences for economic growth. The World Bank report (1984:79) states that "the goal of development extends beyond accommodation of an ever larger population; it is to improve people's lives." When the rate of population growth equals or exceeds the rate of economic growth, finding the resources to improve education and health systems is difficult, if not impossible. Wealthy countries can redistribute resources to meet new priorities. Most Third World countries lack this margin of flexibility. The report emphasizes that countries characterized by low income and low levels of education also experience the most rapid population growth; yet they are least well equipped to adapt to it.

While generalizations about the aggregate-level relationship between population growth and economic development remain elusive, for individual countries the evidence is clearer that rapid population growth has had negative effects on wage rates and thus has contributed to greater income inequality. Preston (1986:73) cites research suggesting that real agricultural wages in Bangladesh in the 1970s were lower than they were in the 1830s. Moreover, much of the decline occurred after 1950, the period of most rapid population growth.

Densely settled agrarian nations appear to face particularly acute problems in this regard. Rapid population growth rates, by depressing rates of return to labor relative to other factors of production, increase income inequality and the percentage of people living in poverty. Slowing population growth in such countries would appear to be consistent with development assistance programs aimed at "the poorest of the poor."

Increasing school enrollment and raising educational levels are widely held policy goals of developing nations. Somewhat surprisingly, using cross-national data, the Working Group found no association between growth in the school-age population and school enrollment rates. However, the association between population growth and expenditures per child was strong and inverse. To the extent that expenditures per child reflect the quality of schooling received, rapid growth is likely to impede the quality of schooling, even if it does not reduce the rate of enrollment.

The argument that it is difficult to achieve significant economic and social progress while sustaining high fertility rates receives varying degrees of support from other quarters (see World Bank, 1984; Horlacher and MacKeller, 1987; Mason et al., 1986; Demeny, 1984; McNicoll, 1984). However, there is some consensus that the consequences of rapid population growth differ greatly among countries. Additionally, while slowing population growth in and of itself would not solve development problems, it would allow enough time in which issues of agricultural and economic productivity, as well as levels of education and health, could be addressed. If the proposition that rapid population growth hinders development is accepted and governments opt to lower fertility rates and slow population growth, the question remains: What can governments do to encourage slower population growth?

Family Planning and Fertility

Family planning has been the most popular policy response to slow population growth. USAID has actively supported family planning programs, directly as a development strategy and indirectly through funds to other organizations, most notably the UNFPA. As indicated earlier, USAID currently does not support UNFPA, but it does endorse family planning, as seen in its own activities and in its support of other organizations such as the Population Council. Family planning, which helps families realize their desires for family size, is politically viable. Family planning provides many benefits, such as improved maternal and child health, beyond fertility control. Because of these benefits, countries have been able to establish family planning programs without emphasizing their potential for reducing fertility, a particularly important issue in rural areas, where children contribute greatly to a farm's household economy. Family planning programs are essential to the health and welfare, as well as the demographic, goals of all countries. This chapter confines the discussion to the impact of family planning on fertility.

In considering the contribution that family planning may make to slowing rapid population growth, we turn to Africa. Africa is the world's poorest continent and also the fastest growing. Of the 21 poorest countries in the world, countries with a per capita gross national product in 1985 below $300, 16 are African (World Bank, 1987). These countries have agricultural-based economies, and, averaging across countries, over 70 percent of the labor force works in the agricultural sector. With a single exception, each of these countries has a total fertility rate (TFR) greater than 6.0 births per woman, implying very high fertility and the potential for continued rapid population growth. Recognition of a direct relationship between extreme poverty and high levels of fertility has been emerging slowly among developing countries. In 1985, only 10 out of the 48 sub-Saharan countries had national development plans which emphasized the need to reduce or stabilize rates of population growth (Heckel, 1986). Support for family planning is much broader, with over three-fourths of sub-Saharan governments supporting family planning, often as part of integrated maternal-child health programs in which the emphasis is placed on birth spacing and maternal health, not family size limitation (World Bank, 1986).

This emphasis on family planning suggests that rates of contraceptive use would be substantial, even in high-fertility countries, if contraception were widely available. However, this is clearly not the case. For example, Kenya is one of three African countries that articulated slower growth policies as early as 1967 (World Bank, 1984). In spite of this demographic policy and public commitment to family planning, Kenya's TFR increased from 7.1 in 1971 to 7.8 in 1985, one of the highest rates in the world (Safilios-Rothschild, 1985; World Bank, 1987). The projected TFR of 6.0 for the year 2000 indicates that Kenya's rapid population growth is likely to continue. In contrast, over this same 15-year period, Thailand's TFR of more than 6.0 decreased to its 1985 level of 3.2 (Mason et al., 1986). Current projections indicate that Thailand will achieve replacement-level fertility around the year 2000 (Zachariah and Vu, 1988).

The above data provide a reference point from which to examine the conditions under which we might anticipate family planning to have a substantial impact on fertility. Fertility has been conceptualized as being the outcome of three factors—the supply of children, the demand for children, and the costs of regulating fertility (Easterlin, 1975). The *supply of children* is the number of children a woman would have if she made no deliberate attempt to limit births (i.e., a natural fertility regimen). The direct effect of family planning on fertility reduces the supply of children by reducing the costs of fertility regulation and increasing contraceptive use.

Family planning has also been viewed as having an indirect effect on fertility through its potential for reducing the demand for children. Demand for children is determined, in economic terms, by their costs relative to their benefits. In traditional subsistence societies, the costs of children are low relative to their immediate and long-term contributions, resulting in high demand. Children are valued for their labor contributions, for the anticipated security that they provide to aging parents, as well as for the hard-to-define satisfactions that parenting provides. In many cultures, women's status in the family and in the community is largely determined by whether they have children, particularly sons. Children may be the guarantee of access to resources such as agricultural land, which is particularly crucial in economies where women are the primary farmers. In these cultures, the demand for children can actually exceed the supply; that is, women are not able to have as many children as they would like to have. The demand for children may also be great under conditions of high infant and childhood mortality, when "extra" births are viewed as a necessary buffer against childhood mortality (Rizk, Stokes, and Nelson, 1982).

Implicit in the transition from high to low fertility is a transformation in the benefits and costs of children, with the outcome being an excess of supply relative to demand. This transformation is a necessary precondition to the widespread adoption of contraception. When the supply of children is greater than the demand, there is motivation and a need for contraception that family planning can satisfy. Analyzing data from the Demographic and Health Survey studies for Peru, Brazil, the Dominican Republic, and Liberia, Westoff (1988:232) concludes, "The overwhelming majority of women who want no more children or who want to postpone fertility . . . are behaving in a manner consistent with that goal." This is consonant with Frank's (1985:39) observations on sub-Saharan Africa: "For the region as a whole, a 'take-off' in the adoption of modern contraception will probably not occur until there is an underlying shift in the demand for children."

Family planning proponents have argued that family planning programs go beyond helping women to plan births. They feel that family planning also contributes to a decrease in the demand for children by inducing or motivating women to want to limit family size, resulting in increased acceptance of contraception. Sherris (1985:762) evaluated the impact of family planning programs on fertility, concluding, "As virtually all studies have found, family planning programs work best where socioeconomic status is relatively favorable." In other words, family planning programs are effective when socioeconomic and cultural circumstances predispose families to want fewer children, that is, when the potential supply of children exceeds demand for children. This is the point at which "low-cost" fertility regulation—that is, available, accessible, and affordable family planning—can make a critical contribution to slowing population growth.

U.S. Policy Options

Access to affordable, modern family planning should be considered essential to the health and welfare of women and their families, regardless of the level of economic development and population growth. Family planning deserves support for many reasons, including its potential for improving equity for poorer families (Preston, 1986) and for enhancing women's ability to control their lives. According to Davis (1967:737), "The need is not to abandon family planning programs but to put equal or greater resources into other approaches." The following section focuses on the importance of policies that support an integrated approach to population/development questions. This approach emphasizes factors that reduce the demand for children and encourage the adoption of contraception but that also contribute to social and economic development. We focus on two of the many factors that are particularly relevant to the rural agricultural sector, women's status and agricultural development. Particular reference is made to rural areas in Africa.

Status of Women

The U.N. Decade for Women, 1975–1985, spurred interest in the status of women as a means to and goal of socioeconomic development. Frank and McNicoll (1987) argue that in the Kenyan context, typical of much of Africa, fertility rates remain high because access to resources is uneven, with control of some basic resources remaining the province of men. Programs directed at incorporating consideration of gender have had many positive consequences for the social and economic well-being of women, their families, and their countries. The extent to which these programs have had concomitant impacts on reproductive behavior is not as easy to assess. As Mason (1984) emphasizes in her seminal monograph, "status" has been defined and measured in many ways, thus limiting generalizations. There appears to be a consensus that, conceptually, women's status refers to gender equality/inequality (Mason, 1984; Oppong, 1985; Powers, 1985). Access to and control over valued resources is seen as fundamental, influencing autonomy and dependency.

Education and paid employment are the most frequently used indicators of access to resources. In a study based on data from 75 countries, Safilios-Rothschild (1985) concludes that there is a direct relationship between fertility control and access to resources, as indicated by survival (health and nutrition), education, and paid employment. National investment in education results in a more skilled work force, providing an edge in the international market arena. At the individual level, education expands economic and noneconomic opportunities, enhancing access to resources.

Providing women with access to education has several implications for fertility, one of which is that women who have more education marry later. In most contexts, this also means that they begin having children at a later age, thus shortening the time span during which childbearing is possible (Smith, 1983). Education exposes women to new ideas and values as well as knowledge. It equips women with skills that enable them to seek out and use new information, increasing the likelihood of effective contraception (Hermalin, 1983; Jain and Nag, 1985). Education can also influence motivation to limit family size through its effect on employment. Women who are better educated generally earn higher wages in the formal labor market; thus, they stand to lose more income by devoting time to childrearing (Standing, 1983). Clearly, efforts that establish mandatory minimum levels of education, build the quality of education, and, very important in rural areas, ensure universal access to education have benefits in many domains. As Caldwell reminds us (1982:43), "The educated provide a window to the modern world and a means of sampling its pleasures."

U.S. development aid policy recognizes the importance of improving women's access to resources, although the commitment as measured in dollars is modest. Congress has stressed, in addressing USAID, "the great importance that they attach to ensuring that AID's development assistance programs actively incorporate women" (Congressional Record, September 26, 1988). Women in Development monies are to be used to develop and expand efforts, not as a substitute for other funds that might have been used for women-oriented activities.

Agricultural Development

Safilios-Rothschild (1985) and others emphasize that in order for policies and programs addressing issues of women's status to have an affect on fertility, these efforts must extend into rural areas, where the vast majority of women live. With over three-fourths of the population in many less developed countries living in rural areas and earning their livelihood from agriculture, and with women doing most of the farming in many of these areas, changes in agricultural organization and production can have substantial impacts on fertility.

Farm households make both food production and family size decisions. Agricultural development policies aimed at altering agricultural production practices, family labor allocation, and technology packages can be expected to influence family size decisions by changing the costs and benefits of children to the household. Agricultural growth is a major development objective for most developing countries, because agricultural commodities provide access to the international economy. Agricultural growth is doubly important when population growth creates an escalating need for additional food supplies. Policies related to food production are among those most critical for countries striving to attain economic self-sufficiency. Research from the last ten years indicates that in rural households, decisions affecting agricultural production and family size are interrelated (see Stokes and Schutjer, 1984; Boserup, 1985).

Factors determining agricultural production are land, labor, and capital/technology. Access to and control of these factors are the basic assets of farm households. Within a given level of technology, the ways in which land and labor interact to influence fertility may be specified. Systems of land tenure vary widely, ranging from all land being owned communally (traditional tribal societies), to ownership being vested in a few owners (plantations and haciendas), to land being divided into individually owned plots. When farmers do not own the land they cultivate, the household must depend on family labor to maintain or improve its economic condition. Research indicates a consistent, positive association between tenancy and fertility (Stokes and Schutjer, 1984; Cornwell and Robinson, 1988).

Research also indicates that the association between landownership and fertility varies, depending on the size of the landholding. Larger family farms require more labor, supporting high fertility. However, in the long run, landownership can substitute for children as a source of old-age security by guaranteeing an income when the owner can no longer work and manage the land and thus receive a labor or management return. The land-fertility relationship is further complicated in areas of Africa in which women are responsible for subsistence production, yet their husbands are the landowners, producing and controlling the revenue from cash crops. Even though technically the farm is family owned, in practice the wife cannot assume that it will provide her with long-term security, and it remains in her best interests to bear many children (Frank and McNicoll, 1987; Boserup, 1985). In such a context, the access women have to resources is critical.

Technology is obviously important to household production and its relationship to fertility. Technology can substitute for land or labor, supporting increased output on a given plot of land with less labor. However, in the context described above, for a variety of reasons, labor-saving technologies may not be available to the women responsible for family food production. New technologies may be inappropriate as development tends to focus on cash-generating production. When appropriate technologies are developed, women farmers may not be able to purchase them because, lacking title to the land they farm, they do not have adequate collateral to obtain credit (Boserup, 1985). Given this scenario, women are likely to rely on children for their labor contributions and long-term security, supporting continued high fertility.

Agricultural development programs can help countries meet the dual goals of increasing agricultural production while slowing population growth. Given the real constraints on U.S. aid funding, it is rational to selectively support programs that explicitly consider the linkages of these goals. For example, land reform programs that increase operator ownership of agricultural land may interact with programs promoting adoption of new technologies, leading to a decline in the need for family labor and smaller desired family size. However, programs that emphasize new technologies in a context in which a large proportion of operators are not owners may have disappointing effects on production and reinforce support for high fertility. Other program goals can be evaluated similarly, including the development of and access to credit and markets, off-farm employment opportunities that can supplement marginal farm-derived income, technologies appropriate for subsistence farming, and education and extension efforts targeted to the farm operator, regardless of gender. Consideration of the interface between the socioeconomic and demographic contexts in which development programs are implemented is consistent with USAID Women in Development directives. Although agricultural policies can have a significant impact on fertility over the long run, comparatively little empirical research has been devoted to these connections.

Conclusion

This chapter addresses issues surrounding U.S. policy concerning rapid population growth in developing nations and suggests five goals for U.S. policy efforts.

First, there is a general consensus that slowing population growth by reducing family size would enhance the capacities of developing nations to achieve economic development, while meeting basic needs and improving quality of life. U.S. policy responses to this concern have concentrated on provision of family planning services, assuming that people are having larger families than they want and that if contraception were available, family size would be reduced. This policy has had relatively little impact on fertility in the many regions of the world where the benefits of large families are great. The persistence of high fertility in these regions, in combination with other social and economic goals, suggests that we need to examine policies that can influence women to accept family planning.

Second, in considering U.S. policy options that could assist countries in slowing population growth, it is important to maintain a focus on rural households and families. In many countries experiencing high rates of population growth, over three-fourths of the population live in rural areas. Rural women who live in predominantly agricultural households will bear most of the world's children in the next few decades. These women usually have a major responsibility to provide for their families' economic welfare, yet their limited resources constrain their capacity for satisfying this responsibility. Within this context, children are valued highly both for their labor contributions and for the security they may provide women in the long run. The resources available to women, particularly opportunities for education, determine the extent to which they can control and improve their personal and familial economic and social well-being. This transformation must occur before we can expect women to limit family growth.

Third, because of the centrality of agriculture to rural households, support of development programs that enhance equity in access to land, new technologies, credit, and markets can increase production for consumption and export, while reducing reliance on children as a form of security. In many rural societies, women have access to land as producers but do not have control as owners. Under such conditions, family labor is the primary productive resource under the control of women. Programs that broaden the resource base controlled by women, through support of gender-neutral resource policies such as landownership, have the potential for lowering fertility. Improved access to appropriate technologies, credit, and markets has a similar impact.

Congress has directed USAID to recognize the role of women in its development assistance programs. USAID's Women in Development mandate articulates such a position for the United States and provides an institutional base for supporting integrated development/population programs. Congress has directed USAID "to seek to ensure that the percentage of women participants will be in approximate proportion to their traditional participation in the targeted activities or their proportion in the population, whichever is greater" (Congressional Record, September 26, 1988).

Fourth, a vigorous, sustained commitment to development programs directed toward women, combined with continued support of family planning, directly and through other institutions such as UNFPA, is consistent with helping developing countries slow their rates of population growth.

We conclude that rapid population growth in less developed countries continues to impede development and should be a focus of U.S. policy. Although family planning programs are important and deserve support for a variety of reasons, they should not be viewed as a panacea for the problem of rapid growth. An array of policy options make support of slower population growth compatible with economic development assistance. Policies that improve the status of women and provide them with greater access to and control over productive resources seem particularly important. Similarly, agricultural development policies directed toward improving farm households' access to land, new technology, credit, and markets have the potential to increase equity and household income, while reducing the demand for children.

Finally, an integrated, broad-based U.S. population and development policy that emphasizes factors affecting the demand for children as well as more narrowly focused approaches such as family planning appears to have the best chance of success.

References

Berelson, B. 1979. "Romania's 1966 anti-abortion decree: The demographic experience of the first decade." *Population Studies* 33:209–222.

Boserup, E. 1965. *The Conditions of Agricultural Growth.* London: Allen and Unwin.

———. 1981. *Population and Technological Change.* Chicago: University of Chicago Press.

———. 1985. "Economic and demographic interrelationships in sub-Saharan Africa." *Population and Development Review* 11:383–397.

Caldwell, J. C. 1982. *Theory of Fertility Decline.* London: Academic Press.

Congressional Record. 1988. U.S. House of Representatives. September 26. Washington D.C.: U.S. Government Printing Office.

Cornwell, G. T., and W. C. Robinson. 1988. "Fertility of U.S. farm women during the electrification era, 1930–1950." *Population Research and Policy Review* 7:277–291.

Crane, B. B., and J. L. Finkle. 1989. "The United States, China, and the United Nations Population Fund: Dynamics of U.S. policymaking." *Population and Development Review* 15:23–59.

Davis, K. 1967. "Population policy: Will current programs succeed?" *Science* 158:730–739.

Demeny, P. 1984. "A perspective on long-term population growth." *Population and Development Review* 10:103–126.

Easterlin, R. A. 1975. "An economic framework for fertility analysis." *Studies in Family Planning* 6:54–63.

Ehrlich, P. R. 1968. *The Population Bomb.* New York: Ballantine Books.

Finkle, J. L., and B. B. Crane. 1985. "Ideology and politics at Mexico City: The United States and the 1984 International Conference on Population." *Population and Development Review* 11:1–28, 166, 168.

Frank, O. 1985. "The demand for fertility control in sub-Saharan Africa." Working Paper No. 117. New York: Center for Policy Studies, The Population Council.

Frank, O., and G. McNicoll. 1987. "An interpretation of fertility and population policy in Kenya." *Population and Development Review* 13:209–243.

Greenhalgh, S., and J. Bongaarts. 1987. "Fertility policy in China: future options." *Science* 235:1167–1172.

Heckel, N. I. 1986. "Population laws and policies in sub-Saharan Africa." *International Family Planning Perspectives* 12:122–124.

Hermalin, A. I. 1983. "Fertility regulation and its costs: A critical essay." Pp. 1–53 in R. Bulatao and R. D. Lee, eds., *Determinants of Fertility in Developing Countries.* New York: Academic Press.

Horlacher, D. E., and F. L. MacKeller. 1987. *Population Growth Versus Economic Growth.* New York: United Nations Population Division.

Jain, A. K., and M. Nag. 1985. "Female primary education and fertility reduction in India." Working Paper No. 114. New York: Center for Policy Studies, The Population Council.

Mason, A., D. B. Suits, S. Y. Koo, N. Ogawa, M. Phananiramai, and H. Sigit. 1986. *Population Growth and Economic Development: Lessons from Selected Asian Countries.* New York: United Nations Fund for Population Activities.

Mason, K. O. 1984. *The Status of Women.* New York: The Rockefeller Foundation.

McNicoll, G. 1984. "Consequences of rapid population growth: Overview and assessment." *Population and Development Review* 10:177–240.

Meadows, D. H., D. L. Meadows, J. Randers, and W. W. Behrens III. 1972. *The Limits to Growth.* New York: Universe Books.

Oppong, C. 1985. "Links between women's work activity, education and motherhood in developing countries: A conceptual and methodological approach." Paper presented at the Workshop on Women's Status and Fertility, New York, Rockefeller Foundation.

Paddock, W., and P. Paddock. 1967. *Famine 1975!* Boston: Little, Brown and Co.

Powers, M. G. 1985. "Measuring the situation of women from existing data." Paper presented at the Workshop on Women's Status and Fertility, New York, Rockefeller Foundation.

Preston, S. H. 1986. "Are the economic consequences of population growth a sound basis for population policy?" Pp. 67–95 in J. Menken, ed., *World Population and U.S. Policy.* New York: W.W. Norton and Co.

Rizk, I. A., C. S. Stokes, and M. R. Nelson. 1982. "The influence of individual and community-level child mortality on fertility in Egypt." *Studies in Comparative International Development* 17:74–86.

Safilios-Rothschild, C. 1985. "The status of women and fertility in the Third World in the 1970–80 decade." Working Paper No. 118. New York: Center for Policy Studies, The Population Council.

Sherris, J. D. 1985. "The impact of family planning programs on fertility." *Population Reports* (Series J) 29:733–771.

Simon, J. L. 1981. *The Ultimate Resource.* Princeton: Princeton University Press.

Smith, P. C. 1983. "The impact of age at marriage and proportions marrying on fertility." Pp. 473–531 in R. A. Bulatao and R. D. Lee, eds., *Determinants of Fertility in Developing Countries.* New York: Academic Press.

Standing, G. 1983. "Women's work activity and fertility." Pp. 517–536 in R. A. Bulatao and R. D. Lee, eds., *Determinants of Fertility in Developing Countries.* New York: Academic Press.

Stokes, C. S., and W. A. Schutjer. 1984. "Access to land and fertility in developing countries." Pp. 195–215 in W. A. Schutjer and C. S. Stokes, eds., *Rural Development and Human Fertility.* New York: Macmillan.

Westoff, C. F. 1988. "Is the KAP-gap real?" *Population and Development Review* 14:225–232.

Working Group on Population Growth and Economic Development. 1986. *Population Growth and Economic Development: Policy Questions.* Washington, D.C.: National Academy Press.

World Bank. 1984. *World Development Report 1984*. New York: Oxford University Press.
_____. 1986. *Population Growth and Policies in Sub-Saharan Africa*. Washington, D.C.: The World Bank.
_____. 1987. *World Development Report 1987*. New York: Oxford University Press.
Zachariah, K. C., and M. T. Vu. 1988. *World Population Projections, 1987–88* Edition. Baltimore: The Johns Hopkins University Press.

19

Water Quality and Agriculture

Stephen B. Lovejoy and Jerald J. Fletcher

Water, the elixir of life, is one of the resources we abuse most. Water is essential for human life. We drink it, bathe in it, and use it for thousands of production purposes including producing food. Throughout most of our history, we have utilized easily captured water on the surface or in free-flowing springs. The discovery of underground deposits of water, called *aquifers*, has allowed settlement of areas far removed from rivers and lakes. We have also become quite creative in our uses of water. We use it for cooling, for heating, for cleansing, and as a means of waste disposal.

While some people and some communities are extremely concerned about the availability of water, the largest problem facing everyone is the degradation of our water supplies. We dump millions of tons of pollutants into our rivers and streams every year. In the past, our vast water supplies assimilated these compounds. Now, many of our rivers and streams have become cancer-causing waste dumps. Our plentiful supplies of groundwater were once capable of diluting and rendering harmless the small quantities of pollutants leaking into them. No more! Similar aquifers now contain traces of the chemicals we have been using to build a better life.

Water quality has emerged as a major policy issue for the United States, especially for the agricultural sector. Many policies and programs are being advocated as means to clean water goals. The policy challenge is to develop policies and programs that achieve clean water goals, while maintaining a prosperous agricultural sector that satisfies our food and fiber needs. This chapter presents some of these issues, offers a framework for analysis of the external or off-site costs of agricultural production (e.g., water quality degradation), and discusses a few of the policy alternatives.

Specifically, the following issues need to be addressed: (1) How much water is needed and how do we as a society allocate it among competing uses? (2) How clean must our water be? Does all water need to be clean enough for its highest valued use? (3) What causes degradation of our water supplies? and (4) How do we achieve our goals (using efficiency and equity arguments)? How do we balance competing interest groups? What should be the role of government?

Background

The 1960s and 1970s exhibited a major turning point in environmental affairs in the United States. Public concern about the protection and preservation of the environment was illustrated by the passage of the National Environmental Protection Act and the authorization of the Presidents' Council on Environmental Quality, the establishment of the Environmental Protection Agency, and the nationwide observance of the first Earth Day. Public concern has increased over the availability of clean environmental amenities. A 1988 Roper survey found that, in 1987, 54 percent of Americans thought we were spending too little money on improving and protecting the environment and only 7 percent said that we were spending too much on environmental quality. In the same poll, 58 percent of Americans said that we should sacrifice economic growth in order to preserve and protect the environment.

Since the early 1970s, the number of Americans suggesting that we spend too little on environmental protection and improvement has remained between 48 and 61 percent (Dunlap, 1987). Sixty-six percent of Americans suggest that protecting the environment is so important that requirements and standards cannot be too high, and continuing environmental improvements must be made regardless of cost (Dunlap, 1987).

In 1982, despite the general trend toward deregulation of our economy, 35 percent of Americans suggested that there was not enough government regulation of and involvement in environmental protection (Dunlap, 1987). By 1986, 59 percent of Americans said that the government needed to be more involved in environmental protection and regulation (Dunlap, 1987).

In general, the high levels of concern about the environment first evidenced in the 1970s are still viable and, in some cases, growing. A majority of Americans feel that more environmental protection is desirable, and most are willing to make some sacrifices for such protection. A major responsibility for policy analysts is to provide estimates of the sacrifices required for alternative levels of environmental protection. This information can then be used as the basis for public decisions.

Many of these initial environmental protection programs were primarily concerned with point sources of pollution. Point sources were easier to identify and probably gave society the largest payoff for each tax dollar expended. The early water quality programs concentrated on industrial waste and municipal waste, as made evident by the programs on municipal waste treatment plants and the constraints imposed on industrial processors in terms of their treatment and disposal of the waste from their production process. As a result of these programs, major reductions in water pollutants have been achieved.

As the programs have made progress in controlling these point sources of pollution, the role of nonpoint sources has been highlighted. With air pollution, we soon recognized that just controlling industrial sources of pollution alone would be ineffective since nonpoint sources, primarily automobiles, were such major contributors. This early recognition and development of programs may be why we have seen major improvements in air quality in the past decade, while the improvements in water quality have been considerably less. Part of the problem is that the nonpoint sources of water pollution are more difficult to identify than are the nonpoint air sources, and they have greater variability (e.g., an individual car will pollute the air just as much in New Jersey as it will in Colorado, while a bare field's impact on water quality will depend on such things as the topography, the slope, and the land uses in surrounding fields).

From previous research, we know that agricultural production is a major source of nonpoint source water pollution. Clark (1985) estimates that the off-site cost of agricultural production is between $3 and $13 billion per year with a point estimate of $6 billion. Damages to biological systems, which were not estimated, could add $1 to $2 billion per year. These costs include recreational, navigation, and water treatment costs as well as flood damages. Clearly the off-site impacts are not inconsequential. Rural nonpoint source water pollution emanating from cropland, forests, pastures, and ranges constitutes the major impairment of many water bodies in the United States. Nonpoint source pollutants are among the primary causes of impairment in 76 percent of the lakes, 65 percent of the rivers and streams, and 45 percent of the estuaries. Evidence suggests that 50 to 70 percent of surface water quality problems caused by nonpoint sources result from agriculturally related activities. Agricultural contamination of surface water is expected to prevent achievement of society's water quality goals even after completion of planned point source controls.

To reduce the contribution of farmland or cropland to water degradation, farmers and ranchers must alter their cropping patterns and their production practices. Specifically, some land is not well suited to some crops (e.g., soybeans on highly erosive land, particularly near a water body), some areas may be particularly vulnerable to agricultural chemical degradation and therefore should rely on rotations that minimize the environmental costs of agricultural production, and animal production activities may have serious external environmental effects. In general, public agencies (federal, state, and local) must influence farmers to use production practices, crop rotations, chemical applications, and animal production practices that maximize production of food and fiber but minimize the impacts on environmental resources.

The tremendous quantity of conferences and papers on environmental issues illustrates the increasing importance attached to water quality and the charge to all of us to find methods to produce the food and fiber desired by consumers and to provide the high-quality soil and water resources demanded by our citizens. In the Environmental Protection Agency's comparative risk project, agriculturally related risks were among the largest outstanding risks confronting the agency and society.

These issues are especially difficult for many rural communities and their citizens. While agriculture and forestry constitute a significant part of many rural economies, rural residents face a higher risk from consumption of chemicals in their water. Nearly 90 percent of rural Americans use groundwater for drinking. While many residents of urban America receive their drinking water (from surface or ground supplies) after extensive testing and treatment by a sophisticated water utility, many rural water utilities do little more than keep the pumps running and maintain the distribution system. In addition, the millions of rural residents supplying their water needs with private wells have few if any safeguards against poor quality drinking water. This situation has led some observers to propose legislation to protect drinking water supplies, especially those vulnerable to contamination from agricultural chemicals.

These problems, however, do not easily lend themselves to regulatory actions. First, several million farmers on hundreds of millions of acres would have to be regulated. Second, there are major problems of measuring and identifying specific pollutants from individual farms resulting from specific production practices. In addition, present agricultural conservation programs are not structured to deal effectively with the water quality problem. There are two major problems, temporal inconsistencies and site specificity, with present agricultural and soil conservation programs and their ability to secure environmental benefits.

While programs like the Conservation Reserve are excellent for promoting goals like soil conservation and protection of future productivity, they are less effective for addressing other environmental concerns. A *reserve*, by definition, implies something held back for use at a later time. However, if certain activities (e.g., use of certain agricultural chemicals on sandy soils where there is a high water table) have substantial negative environmental consequences, these activities must be stopped permanently, not for one year or ten years. This illustrates a major problem with the use of the conservation programs promulgated by the Food Security Act of 1985 for improving the quality of environmental amenities. If we want to protect the quality of an environmental good, we want it protected indefinitely. It may take several years for some surface waters and decades for some groundwater resources to show improved quality after a change in agricultural production activities. Wildlife will return to an area of improved habitat within a few years but will disappear quickly when the habitat is again used for crop production. The impacts of such sudden ecological shocks are difficult to evaluate but are definitely negative. In short, the protection of environmental amenities is not a temporary issue that can be solved with short-term programs. Institutional mechanisms need to be established to provide for the protection of these resources for a very long time, if not indefinitely.

The other problem with environmental protection under the Food Security Act of 1985 is the spatial consideration. The occurrence of water quality problems or other environmental degradation from agricultural production is not uniform. Some areas exhibit little or no environmental degradation from agricultural activities while other areas experience significant levels of degradation. Thus, changes in agricultural production to achieve environmental goals should not be identical in all areas of the country. Rather, these changes should be targeted to those areas where the production activities impose significant environmental costs (e.g., degraded water quality). Targeting based on environmental criteria is essential for meeting the goals of an improved environment. Several observers have suggested that the targeting of regions, even microtargeting of specific acres in a watershed, is essential for meeting water quality goals, especially if those goals are to be achieved efficiently (Lee, Beasley, and Lovejoy, 1985).

However, targeting must be conducted on the basis of actual environmental degradation and the costs that are associated with a particular production practice in a specific locale, not on the basis of gross erosion rates. High rates of erosion on cropland far from a water body may have little or no effect on water quality while low erosion rates near a water body may have significant impacts. In addition, the uses and valuation of the water must be examined. Sites should be evaluated and compared with one another to see where intervention would yield the greatest social benefit at the least cost. However, a conceptual means of evaluating the impacts of agricultural production costs on water quality and other environmental amenities is essential. While many observers have examined a particular production practice and attempted to estimate a cost, a more general conceptual scheme for organizing these empirical examinations or for suggesting productive areas for future examination is lacking. However, this does not preclude policy decisions being made on the basis of whatever information is available.

With the emergence of legislation by federal and state governments to reduce the impacts of agricultural production on other citizens, we may be on the verge of significant constraints to property rights in agriculture (Lovejoy and Potter, 1986). In the past, producers have not had to consider the environmental costs of their production decisions. Agriculturalists managed their property in whatever manner they selected with little or no consideration of the impact of those management decisions on the general public or on other agricultural producers. One of the major difficulties of policymaking in this area is estimating the costs and benefits of alternative courses of action, both to the individual and to the general public. In fact, much of the policy is enacted without a full understanding of the problem or even an analytical framework to make the problem comprehensible.

For many rural areas, the choice between water quality and agricultural production levels is not clear cut. While nearly all rural residents would forego income instead of injuring themselves, their children, or their neighbors, the effects of agricultural chemicals are not completely understood. Risk of contamination or risk of health effects is difficult to comprehend, let alone make intelligent trade-offs with jobs, income, and economic well-being. In addition, many analysts present an unclear picture of the linkages between changes in land use and changes in individuals' or communities' well-being.

This chapter describes a framework for the analysis of the effects of various physical, management, sociodemographic, and economic factors on off-farm costs of agricultural production activities, including water degradation. While some of the relationships are accepted fact, this conceptual framework provides a convenient framework for integrating a number of these common-sense ideas. This framework was formulated as part of an examination of the various determinants of off-farm costs of production and was also intended to dispel some of the potential misconceptions related to the development of appropriate cost estimates. Without a conceptual framework to link agricultural production practices and social costs, policy-makers may formulate inefficient and overly burdensome policies and regulations.

An Outline of the Conceptual Framework

The framework developed in this chapter links a number of different factors that determine the societal costs resulting from agricultural production (e.g., off-site costs of erosion or water quality costs of waste management or agricultural chemicals). This framework is described below and outlined graphically in Figure 19.1. While this framework is useful for analyzing a number of categories of off-site costs, it is illustrated with the off-farm sedimentation process since we have developed better indicators of surface movement of chemicals and soil particles, the process involved, and the relationship to management practices. Analysis of other types of environmental degradation, such as degradation of groundwater supplies, would follow the same logic but with a somewhat different set of explanatory factors and processes.

Sedimentation, as a natural phenomenon, is ubiquitous but highly variable. Major determinants of the quantity of soil and attached chemicals leaving a parcel of land are the physical characteristics of that parcel and the environmental factors impinging on it. The major physical factors influencing the rate of sedimentation or the amount being transported off the farm include climatic conditions that determine the quantity, intensity, and temporal distribution of wind and rainfall; soil properties that determine soil erodibility or the susceptibility of a particular soil to erosive forces; and topographic variables such as the length and steepness of a field slope, distance to concentrated flow areas, and drainage characteristics that affect the likelihood that detached soil particles reach ditches or drains and become sedimentation.

In addition to the influence of the physical factors, the amount being transported off the farm is affected by land use characteristics. For cropland, the primary characteristics are the practices related to agriculturally induced sedimentation, including crop and tillage selection, as well as alternative means of controlling sediment movement off-farm, such as terraces, grassed waterways, and other structures. These factors are related to both the original detachment of soil particles from their original location (erosion) and the movement of sediment into off-farmland sites and water bodies.

Once the appropriate physical factors and management characteristics are recognized, the effects of these factors on erosion and sediment transport

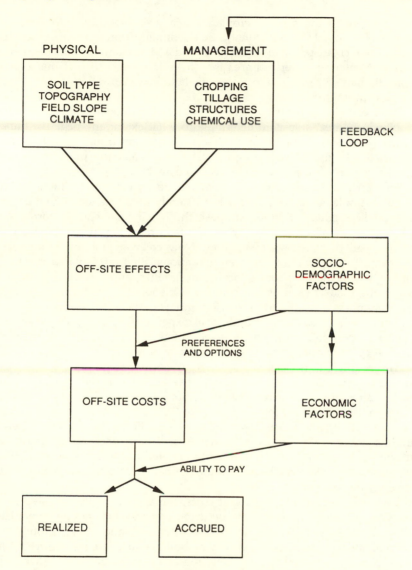

Figure 19-1 Framework for the Analysis of Off-Site Costs of Agricultural Production

at the farm level can be estimated. However, the actual effects that occur when sediment leaves the farm depend on the characteristics of the surrounding area and community; not on farm-level attributes. For example, sediment that enters a large river system immediately after leaving the farm boundary will not affect roads or drainage, although the effect on water quality may be substantial. The quantity of roads, ditches, and total land area relative to the area of cropland in a given locality may serve as a reasonable proxy for the likelihood that sediment from farms in a particular locality will create problems relative to road and ditch maintenance. Likewise, sediment entering a wetland area may have less effect than if the sediment were discharged directly into a river or lake because wetlands can serve as a sediment sink or filter.

After estimating the physical effects of the sediment or chemicals from cropland, the next step is to determine to what extent any negative impacts matter. The costs of the off-farm effects of sediment from agricultural lands are related to the physical effects, but the actual costs perceived depend on the preferences and options available to both the farm and nonfarm communities and how various alternatives are affected by sediment buildup.

For example, suppose a farmer has recently plowed a steep field adjacent to a public roadway. Further, suppose that an intense spring storm causes a high rate of soil detachment from this field resulting in sediment buildup on the road that restricts traffic flow. Now consider the costs imposed by sediment buildup for two different situations. First, an isolated rural community where the road serves local farm families, and second, a community where the road is used as the primary transportation route by a relatively large number of individuals on a regular basis with alternative routes available only at substantial additional expense. Obviously the urgency of a cleanup operation would be perceived differently in each of these situations, but the costs to society can also be seen to differ.

This example illustrates that a variety of sociodemographic factors related to individual and community preferences as well as the availability and type of alternatives influence the perception of off-farm costs in a particular situation. Measures that may reflect these factors include population density, the ratio of urban to rural population, education, and income levels in addition to any information on the tastes and preferences of the potentially affected population. These measures are related to the characteristics of the affected community which determine whether these effects actually impose costs on the community.

Even after estimating the social costs, there is an additional step in the analysis. Once off-farm costs have occurred, the costs may not be immediately realized but may be left to accrue for future attention (e.g., groundwater contamination). Consider the sediment buildup in a drainage ditch. While the sediment is deposited over time, the actual costs are not realized until either the sediment buildup impairs the ability of the ditch to perform its usual function or the ditch is cleaned and cleaning charges are paid. While this point is obvious when considered, there may be long periods between the deposition of sediment in roadside ditches or large drains and actual sediment removal operations or other maintenance costs. In addition, the buildup may occur so slowly that it goes unnoticed. For example, many roads in Indiana were originally constructed with roadside ditches far deeper than are apparent today. It may well be that the appropriate action today is not to rebuild such ditches but to maintain them sufficiently to fulfill their primary function. However, it should be realized that an initial investment in the ditch has been depreciated and that maintenance costs will tend to rise as the usefulness of the original structure deteriorates.

The division between realized and accrued costs depends on a variety of economic and social factors. The ability of a county and its taxpayers to pay for maintenance—as reflected in assessed valuation, tax revenues, road expenditures, and other relevant measures—may dictate the proportion of costs that are accrued for future payment. Both the willingness and ability to pay influence the allocation between accrued and realized costs.

The type of framework presented in this paper is certainly not static but, rather, extremely dynamic. In addition, the linkages discussed are not one way; there are continuous feedback loops. Economic factors affect the preferences the public holds and the options that may be exercised. In addition, both economic and sociodemographic factors affect both individual management decisions and the concerns society expresses about those decisions. In the past, society's role in management decisions was primarily through cost-sharing programs and the provision of technical assistance. As the relationships between these factors change, society may choose to establish different types of policies or regulations (e.g., more stringent or less stringent) that could directly affect management decisions related to cropping choices, use of chemicals, and production practices. These changes will ultimately affect the off-farm costs of agricultural production.

The conceptual framework developed here describes the types of relationships generally believed to exist in a variety of analytical circumstances. Given that these relationships are reasonable approximations of the actual processes involved, we feel that this diagrammatic approach should assist citizens, program officers, and policymakers in understanding how this complex agricultural-ecological system operates. In addition, it should provide a convenient framework for empirical analysis of the costs, realized and accrued, as well as for analysis of the benefits of alternative policies.

Proposed Policy Options

Spatial and temporal factors need greater attention in developing agricultural programs and evaluating their impact on environmental amenities. Since protection of environmental amenities is spatially varied, some allowance needs to be made for spatial variation for the program. At the same time, specific environmental amenities need protection now (e.g., Chesapeake Bay or a community's water supply), and they will likely need protection in the future. While short-run programs like the Conservation Reserve Program (CRP) may assist in achieving soil conservation goals, protection of water quality and other environmental goods requires programs with much longer time horizons.

While some groups are looking toward the state's assessment and management plans (mandated by Section 319 of the Water Quality Act of 1987) to steer states and farmers into more environmentally sensitive behaviors, without funding from federal or state sources, these plans may do little good. There are, however, programs that could have significant impacts on agricultural land use in many locations.

If these programs are to be effective in achieving water quality goals, they will require greater coordination between the Environmental Protection Agency, the Department of Agriculture, and the Fish and Wildlife Service. However, states must also take a more proactive role in coordinating with federal agencies and taking on more of the responsibility for ensuring that programs have water quality as an objective within their states.

The states should identify the cropland acres and practices producing the greatest degradation, especially in those watersheds identified in their Section 319 assessments and management plans. They then need to target these cropland acres for participation in USDA programs (e.g., CRP) and, if necessary, supplement federal funds with state funds to ensure enrollment in state and local units of government. Also, interested citizens need to encourage participation and implement programs to inform and assist farmers in identifying acres, filling out forms, and so on to reduce the hassle (e.g., reduce transaction costs) of enrolling their acres in these programs.

State and local governments need to promote strict interpretation of conservation compliance rules even though that may not be popular with some agricultural interests within the state. Conservation compliance will not be popular with those interests that are prohibited or penalized from traditional production practices. State Soil Conservation Service (SCS) and Agricultural Stabilization and Conservation Service (ASCS) officials need to be encouraged to consider the water quality implications, not just soil conservation and farm finances, in their decision making. This is especially important in areas where there is significant degradation of environmental amenities from agricultural production activities. Water quality should be initiated as a goal of individual farm conservation plans, not just for those farms with highly erodible lands. Farmers should be encouraged to make greater use of soil testing for nutrient recommendations and greater use of integrated pest management. By proper use of agricultural chemicals, farmers can ensure minimum input costs as well as environmental protection. These activities might be accomplished by each state's Cooperative Extension Service, land-grant university, and so forth. Activities may also include research on economic thresholds for pesticides, provision of scouting services by the Cooperative Extension Service, or research on the role of manure in nutrient management.

ASCS should be encouraged to target Agricultural Conservation Program (ACP) funds to those areas with the largest problem and to those practices which will have the most significant impact on water quality. States could also be more proactive about buffer strips for protection of surface water quality. Enrollment of additional acres along water edges would be beneficial. Also, easements or other tools should be considered to protect streambanks, lake borders, and the like. States should examine the experiences of other state programs, such as Minnesota's RIM program, Missouri's and Indiana's taxation cost-share programs, Iowa's and Illinois's regulatory approach, and Nebraska's fertilizer management program. This examination could also include other states' experiences with attempts to reduce water quality degradation from animal waste. We need further examination of regulatory and nonregulatory approaches to animal waste management, storage, and disposal, including potential assistance to new businesses that use animal waste in a less resource-degrading manner (e.g., dried and sold for home gardens). There is a definite need for long-term solutions to the agricultural nonpoint source water quality problems. We need creative policy options and good analysis of the impacts and costs of alternatives.

The framework presented in this paper is an appropriate conceptual device for initiation of the analysis of policy options. State and local governments, as well as groups of private citizens, can use this conceptual framework in their attempts to meet their demands for reduced degradation of water resources and other off-site costs of agricultural production.

Conclusion

To reduce agricultural production's negative effects on water quality, farmers and ranchers must alter their cropping patterns and their production practices. Public agencies (federal, state, and local) must encourage farmers to use production practices, crop rotations, chemical applications, and animal production practices that maximize food and fiber production but minimize the impacts on environmental resources, including water quality.

A major source of potential water quality improvements are the conservation programs within the U.S. Department of Agriculture. The conservation provisions of the Food Security Act of 1985 offer considerable potential for improved water quality. However, these programs need to be refocused to supply both soil and water protection.

Protection of our water resources will require us to alter our soil and water conservation programs. First, we must target our efforts and resources to those regions, counties, and acres where agricultural production imposes unacceptable damage to environmental resources. Second, we must develop programs and mechanisms that permanently alter damaging production patterns. Third, we must carefully examine proposed production changes for their impact on food supplies, prices, local communities, and farm families as well as their impact on environmental amenities, health risks, or ecology.

References

Batie, S. S. 1983. *Soil Erosion: Crisis in America's Croplands?* Washington, D.C.: The Conservation Foundation.

Clark, E. H., II. 1985. "The off-site costs of soil erosion." *Journal of Soil and Water Conservation* 40(1):19–22.

Conservation Tillage Information Center. 1985. *1984 National Survey Conservation Tillage Practices.* Fort Wayne, Ind.: National Association of Conservation Districts.

Dunlap, R. E. 1987. "Public opinion on the environment in the Reagan era." *Environment* 29(July/August):6–11, 32–37.

Fletcher, J. J., and W. D. Seitz. 1986. "Information needs for conservation decisions." Pp. 55–70 in S. B. Lovejoy and T. L. Napier, eds., *Conserving Soil*. Ankeny, Ia.: Soil Conservation Society of America.

Lee, J., S. B. Lovejoy, and D. Beasley. 1985. "Soil loss reduction in Finley Creek, Indiana: An economic analysis of alternative policies." *Journal of Soil and Water Conservation* 40(1):132–135.

Lovejoy, S. B. and H. Potter. 1986. "Changing agricultural property rights in the environmental era." Pp. 160–170 in American Society of Agricultural Engineers, *Water Resources Law: Proceedings of the National Symposium on Water Resources Law*. St. Joseph, Mo.: American Society of Agricultural Engineers.

20
Soil Conservation

Ted L. Napier

Soil conservation emerged as a significant environmental issue in the 1930s when several million acres of land in the Midwest were severely damaged by wind erosion. Inappropriate farming practices, combined with highly arid conditions, produced dust storms which emphatically demonstrated that abuse of land resources could not continue without serious environmental consequences.

The Dust Bowl had a nationwide socioenvironmental impact. Land operators lost future productivity, national supplies of food and fiber were threatened, deposition of displaced topsoil created problems for urban dwellers, and the loss of farms due to extensive soil erosion exacerbated the impacts of the depression for many landowners (Napier, 1990b).

Environmental concern during the Dust Bowl era generated considerable political support for government intervention to resolve erosion problems. The U.S. Congress responded by authorizing the formation of federal conservation agencies and by allocating economic resources to cost-share soil conservation programs at the farm level.

Vast resources have been devoted to soil erosion control efforts during the past five decades; however, many of the environmental problems identified in the 1930s persist (Halcrow, Heady, and Cotner 1982; Lovejoy and Napier, 1986; Napier, 1987; Napier, 1990a; Napier and Camboni, 1988). While cost-sharing and technical assistance have encouraged the adoption of soil conservation practices, such incentives have forced many landowners to depend on state and federal governments to solve erosion problems. Research suggests that individual landowners are not motivated to adopt soil conservation practices without government subsidies (Napier, 1987). Such findings suggest that government policies have become extremely important factors in determining how farmers use soil resources.

This chapter identifies some of the most important policy issues associated with soil conservation in the United States. Research results that focus on soil resource problems will be discussed in the context of the policy issues noted.

Soil Resource Policy Issues

The following policy issues will be discussed:

1. What is the primary purpose of soil conservation programs in the United States?
2. What level of soil erosion is socially acceptable in the United States?
3. What should be the government's role in protecting soil resources?
4. What should be the individual landowner's role in protecting soil resources?
5. What policies need to be formulated to implement effective soil conservation programs?
6. What priority should be placed on policy consistency among government programs?

Discussion of Policy Issues

Purpose of Soil Conservation Programs

Implementation of conservation efforts will remain fragmented, inconsistent, and ineffective unless the primary goal of conservation programs is determined. Soil conservation legislation enacted before 1985 emphasized control of agricultural production and maintenance of farm income rather than the conservation of soil resources (Harmon, 1987; Napier, 1990b; Rasmussen, 1982). Given these uses of conservation funding, it should not be surprising that soil erosion is still a problem after decades of conservation efforts. Even the Conservation Title of the Food Security Act of 1985, which has been acclaimed to be revolutionary environmental legislation, was authorized to address at least three agricultural issues simultaneously. The legislation was enacted to reduce soil erosion, enhance farm income, and control commodity supplies.

While these are worthy objectives, it is highly doubtful that they are compatible. Research has shown that the adoption of many soil conservation practices is not profitable in the short run and is probably not profitable in the long run (Ervin and Washburn, 1981; Korsching and Nowak, 1980; Lovejoy and Parent, 1981; Mueller, Klemme, and Daniel, 1985; Putman and Alt, 1988; Swanson, Camboni, and Napier, 1986). These findings suggest that adoption of soil conservation practices will not facilitate maintenance of farm income unless large federal subsidies are provided to producers. Also, use of soil conservation resources to retire highly erodible land from production will not benefit many commercial farmers, who often operate farmland that is less subject to erosion.

The use of conservation resources to control commodity supplies could easily relegate soil conservation to a minor role in Conservation Title efforts (Napier, 1988). Much of the most productive farmland in the United States is being eroded at very low levels and the future productivity of these soil resources is not threatened (Crosson, 1984). The use of limited conservation resources to retire highly productive land with low erosion potential via Conservation Title programs would reduce substantially the effectiveness of soil conservation efforts to divert highly erodible farmland from crop production.

Decision makers must determine what needs to be accomplished by soil conservation policies and they must recognize that multiple objectives will be very difficult to achieve. Soil conservation policies can either emphasize conservation and reduce damages associated with erosion or they can enhance farm income and stabilize commodity prices. It is unrealistic to expect soil conservation policies to address multiple agricultural problems simultaneously (Napier, 1988).

Determination of the Socially Acceptable Level of Soil Erosion

Once decisions have been made about the objectives to be achieved by soil conservation efforts, policymakers must determine what level of agricultural soil loss can be tolerated. Decision makers should assume this role because they are in the most appropriate position to synthesize information from a variety of sources and to establish erosion levels that are equitable for all interest groups. They are also in an excellent position to assess what is achievable in the context of available economic and human resources to address erosion problems.

The most important considerations in establishing a socially acceptable level of soil erosion are the social, economic, and environmental costs and benefits associated with reducing soil erosion (Eleveld and Halcrow, 1982). If soil erosion is confined to cultivated land with deep topsoils and to areas where soil displacement would have few adverse effects on people living downstream, soil loss above replacement levels may be acceptable. Under these conditions, chemical additives could be used to maintain agricultural productivity, and off-site costs would be relatively inconsequential. Large investments of economic and human resources in soil conservation programs would not be justified.

While a large proportion of cultivated land in the United States is being eroded at very low rates, approximately 25 percent of all cultivated farmland is eroding at twice the tolerance level (Sampson, 1985). Of particular concern is the 10 to 15 percent of cultivated farmland which is contributing 80 to 90 percent of all water-related soil erosion (Gardner, 1985). Such levels of soil loss will result in degradation of land resources (Lal, 1984; Larson, 1981; McCormack, Young, and Kimberlim, 1982; Pimentel, 1987). These data suggest that future productivity on some cultivated farmland in the United States is being adversely affected (Swanson, Camboni, and Napier, 1986). Application of inorganic fertilizers cannot offset productivity losses on farmland being eroded at this magnitude.

Soil erosion significantly contributes to off-site damages. Some of the most common off-site costs of soil erosion are loss of recreation opportunities, degradation of fish and wildlife habitat, reduced aesthetic quality of land and water resources, disruption of rail and highway transportation systems, and increased costs of making water potable (Halcrow, Heady, and Cotner, 1982; Lovejoy and Napier, 1986; Napier, Scott, Easter, and Supalla, 1983). Off-site damages have been shown to be extremely high (Easter, Leitch, and Scott, 1983; Miranowski, 1983), and they must be considered when developing a national soil loss standard.

In the past, socially acceptable levels of soil loss were determined primarily on the basis of on-site damages associated with lost agricultural productivity. It was reasoned that land resources should be protected to ensure future food supplies. While this objective is highly desirable, there is little evidence that our food and fiber production is threatened by present rates of soil loss. Recent research suggests that on-site damages will be relatively inconsequential during the next century (Crosson, 1984; Eleveld and Halcrow, 1982; Nelson and Seitz, 1979).

In sum, the existing literature suggests that a socially acceptable level of soil erosion can be determined, but we must consider both on-site and off-site damages. Research indicates that off-site damages should be considered more heavily when determining socially acceptable levels of soil erosion.

The Role of the Government in Soil Conservation

To date, government involvement in soil conservation efforts has been justified primarily on the basis of protecting future agricultural productivity; recent consideration has also been given to off-site damages. Farmers, who are often concerned about short-run profits, are sometimes willing to degrade land resources to maximize profits. Consequently, government has been forced to assume the role of protector of future productive capacities of land resources. One means of accomplishing this goal is through soil conservation programs.

Concern for off-site damages associated with soil erosion has also encouraged government involvement in soil conservation efforts. Nonfarm people affected by off-site damages want to distribute the costs of mitigating erosion damages among as many members of society as possible. One method of accomplishing this goal is to make government responsible for amelioration of damages caused by soil erosion. Given the difficulty and cost associated with identifying specific agricultural polluters, farmers are seldom forced to pay for off-site damages. It is less expensive in the long run for the government to pay farmers to use conservation practices which will keep the soil and farm chemicals on the land.

Government intervention is expected when existing institutional structures fail to protect a significant portion of the population from some externally imposed damage. The present farming system has failed nonfarm populations because most land operators treat soil erosion as an externality of production, and nonfarm populations have been forced to assume the major portion of the costs (Halcrow, Heady, and Cotner, 1982; Lovejoy and Napier, 1986;

Napier, Scott, Easter, and Supalla, 1983; Swanson, Camboni, and Napier, 1986).

The government's role in the development and implementation of soil conservation programs during the next decade needs to be determined. Government involvement in soil conservation efforts in the past has relied on voluntary adoption of soil conservation practices (Harmon, 1987; Napier, 1987; Napier, 1990b; Napier and Forster, 1982; Rasmussen, 1982). Government agencies have used economic subsidies in the form of cost-sharing assistance to motivate land operators to implement recommended soil conservation programs at the farm level (Camboni, Napier, and Lovejoy, 1989). Education and technical assistance have also been used extensively.

While considerable progress was made in reducing erosion rates observed during the Dust Bowl years, many scholars have been questioning the return to investment in conservation efforts during the past 50 years. Much of the concern has been focused on the strategies employed by government agencies commissioned to implement conservation efforts. Reliance on voluntary adoption of soil conservation practices has been extensively challenged (Lovejoy and Napier, 1986). Strategies that emphasize education have had relatively little effect on adoption of soil conservation practices without significant monetary subsidies (Korsching and Nowak, 1980; Lovejoy and Napier, 1986; Napier, Thraen, Gore, and Goe, 1984; Napier, Thraen, and McClaskie, 1988; Napier and Forster, 1982; Swanson, Camboni, and Napier, 1986). Continued reliance on these methods is probably not justified. The government's role in educating farmers on soil conservation practices will probably be less important in the future.

Since research has shown that off-site damages of soil erosion are so significant and that farmers tend to treat soil erosion as an externality of production, it is highly likely that the role of state and federal governments in controlling soil erosion will be substantially greater in the future. The nature of that role will be significantly affected by the response of individual landowners to resolve soil erosion problems. If farmers assume greater responsibility, state and federal governments will probably continue to play the traditional role of facilitator and provider of technical and economic assistance. If land operators continue to ignore pollution caused by technology-intensive farming practices, it is likely that the government will assume a much more coercive role.[1]

Government coercion can take many forms, such as restricting fertilizer and pesticide applications, prohibiting the production of erosive crops on certain types of cropland, requiring that specific soil conservation practices be used on certain types of cropland, and a host of other restraints. While farm operators will resent government intervention in farm-level decision making, the role will probably be forced on state and federal governments by nonfarm populations, which constitute the vast majority of the society.

The Role of Landowners in Soil Conservation

Bromley (1982) suggests that only individuals, not society, have rights to land resources and that these rights are protected by the state. While

Bromley's position is probably somewhat overstated, he is correct that landowners possess extensive rights to land resources in the United States.

Traditionally, property owners have been able to use land resources in any manner which they deem appropriate, unless they create a nuisance for others. Unfortunately, nuisance laws are extremely difficult to enforce because the plaintiff must prove that a specific landowner is responsible for his or her damages. Given that a large number of farmers are contributing the same or similar pollutants, securing conclusive evidence that a particular land operator is the sole contributor to the plaintiff's problem is problematic and expensive.

Since it is very difficult and costly to identify how much pollution has been contributed by a specific agriculturalist, land operators know it is unlikely that they will ever be penalized for erosion-related pollution. Farmers are also aware that the economic returns to the adoption of soil conservation practices are relatively low compared to other investment options. Thus, farmers are not motivated to adopt soil conservation practices voluntarily (Napier, 1987).

To date, farmers basically have been exempt from existing environmental regulations because it has been less costly for society to mitigate the off-site damages of agricultural pollution (Napier, 1989). Also, the federal government has been reluctant to examine seriously the property rights of landowners because agricultural pollution is a politically sensitive issue. However, increasing costs of agricultural-related pollution, combined with an expanded awareness among nonfarm populations of the environmental degradation generated by farmers, will probably result in significant mod-ifications of property rights in the future. It is highly probable that property owners will be constrained in the use of land resources. Society will probably assume the right to control land use and cultivation practices on highly erodible land in order to reduce off-site damages.

Batie (1986) summarizes the situation well when she observes that future property rights to agricultural land will reflect the public's concern that natural resources should be protected. Her argument strongly suggests that the era of absolute rights of landowners is drawing to a close. Regulated use of land resources to prevent environmental degradation is quite possible and is probably required to prevent abuse of land resources. The nature of the regulations will depend heavily on society's values, which will be reflected in the policies established by decision makers. Bromley's (1982) observation that society does not have rights to land resources will no longer be correct.

The policy issue which must be addressed in the future is the determination of property-owner rights to land resources. Protection of land resources will probably be extended beyond nuisances created for other members of society to include protection of future use of the resource by subsequent generations and owners. Future property rights will undoubtedly reflect society's concern for off-site damages from agricultural sources.

Policies to Guide the Development
of Soil Conservation Programs

Assuming decision makers determine that conservation is the primary objective of soil conservation efforts, policies must be created to facilitate the implementation of programs to accomplish this goal. Some of the policy goals might be to maximize soil loss savings, wildlife benefits, recreation benefits, and benefits to specific nonfarm groups and to minimize economic costs, on-site and off-site damages, adverse impacts on land operators, and land retirement.

Objectives used to guide implementation of conservation efforts can affect outcomes. Recent research shows that implementation of the Conservation Reserve Program (CRP) using a least-cost approach probably lessened its effectiveness as a soil-saving program (Reichelderfer and Boggess, 1988). The establishment of low bid levels during the initial enrollment periods of the CRP precluded enrollment of highly erodible farmland that was also highly productive. Much of the land initially enrolled in the program was in the arid regions of the West. Reichelderfer and Boggess (1988) suggest that alternative policies probably would have resulted in greater soil savings with minor changes in the cost of the program.

The distribution of human and economic resources among potential program participants must be determined before soil conservation programs can be developed. Before the 1980s soil conservation resources were available to any landowner who asked for assistance, as long as resources were available (Kleckner, 1988). This policy resulted in the use of soil conservation resources on land that had relatively few erosion problems.

A major policy shift was the introduction in the 1980s of "targeting," whereby limited soil conservation resources were designated for use on highly erodible land (Napier, 1987; Swanson, Camboni, and Napier, 1986). It was reasoned that concentration of limited conservation resources on highly erodible land would maximize soil loss savings. Evidence suggests that this assumption was correct, especially when microtargeting was employed (Lovejoy, Lee, and Beasley, 1986).

Targeting was incorporated into the CRP, and eligibility to participate in the program was primarily determined by erosion potential of land resources. Only highly erodible land could be enrolled. Subsequently, a large proportion of agricultural landowners were excluded from participating in the CRP because they did not own land that qualified for enrollment. Many landowners resented being excluded from the CRP, and they applied considerable political pressure on policymakers to change CRP participation criteria. Over time, the criteria for participation have been modified. As a result, soil conservation agencies' abilities to target conservation resources on highly erodible land have been reduced considerably.

The role of targeting needs to be clarified in the process of developing future soil conservation programs. While it is politically expedient for funding to be made available to all landowners who apply for assistance, the goal of optimum soil loss reduction cannot be achieved with such a policy.

Policymakers must also address the role of coercion in program implementation strategies. Before the Conservation Title of 1985 was introduced, soil conservation programs were totally voluntary. Property owners could enter land resources in soil conservation programs, implement conservation practices on enrolled land using government subsidies, and eliminate the conservation investments when contracts were completed. Government agencies could not force farmers to continue use of soil-conserving practices when participation in conservation programs was terminated. However, elements of coercion were incorporated into the Conservation Title via cross compliance associated with the CRP, sodbuster, swampbuster, and the conservation compliance (CC) components of the legislation (Napier, 1990b). Land operators who violate any of the Conservation Title components may forfeit eligibility for participation in a number of federal farm programs. Violation of CRP contracts will also result in similar penalties (Napier, 1990a).

The right of property owners to put land into agricultural production has been substantially constrained by the Conservation Title. The conversion of land to agricultural production is permissible only under specific conditions outlined in the legislation. Also, conservation plans are now required for all highly erodible cropland. A conservation farm plan must be developed by 1990 and be fully implemented by 1995. Access to government programs will be forfeited until the conservation plan is fully implemented.

The most coercive element of the Conservation Title as it was originally conceived was conservation compliance, which established very specific criteria for implementing conservation plans at the farm level. The intent was to reduce soil erosion to T (replacement level) by 1995. Land operators were compelled to comply or they would lose access to government programs. Political pressure was exerted from many segments of the agricultural system to modify the intent of the legislation. Action taken by the chief of the Soil Conservation Service (SCS) in response to these efforts has substantially reduced the potential effectiveness of the CC (Napier, 1990b).

The level of coercion that may legitimately be applied to landowners to protect soil resources also needs to be determined. If landowners are unwilling to reduce soil loss to socially acceptable levels and if nonfarm populations become more reluctant to assume the costs of mitigating the off-site damages of soil erosion, more coercive approaches will probably be implemented.

Assuming coercion is used more frequently to reduce soil loss to socially acceptable levels, policymakers must determine which social organization within the federal government should assume primary responsibility for administering conservation efforts. Recent experience associated with changing the criteria of the conservation compliance components of the Conservation Title suggests that the SCS of the U.S. Department of Agriculture (USDA), as it is presently constituted, is not the appropriate agency to implement coercive conservation programs (Napier, 1990b). Policymakers must also provide the necessary authority for the selected agency to perform its designated tasks. The U.S. Environmental Protection Agency (EPA) should be considered a strong candidate for assuming this role, since it has a history of coercive implementation of environmental regulations. Delegation of the administration of soil conservation programs to the EPA would free SCS/USDA to emphasize its educational-technical support role, which it performs so well.

Policy Consistency and Soil Conservation

The effectiveness of soil conservation programs in the United States is significantly influenced by a variety of federal policies that are designed to accomplish objectives not directly related to the protection of soil resources (Swanson, Camboni, and Napier, 1986). Some federal policies facilitate soil conservation efforts, while many others impede achievement of soil conservation objectives. For example, national policies that encourage farmers to maximize farm output will almost always exacerbate soil loss on cultivated fields.

Policy consistency at the federal level needs to be examined. National farm programs which encourage land operators to maximize short-run profits often conflict with efforts to divert highly erosive agricultural land from production. Commodity programs impede adoption of soil conservation practices because farmers must continually maximize production to keep payments as high as possible. Most soil conservation practices do not contribute to such an objective.

A number of options are available to policymakers that will affect soil conservation behaviors of landowners. We need to consider the development of policies that reduce agricultural output on highly erodible land (Sampson, 1985). Removing economic incentives to keep highly erodible cropland in production will facilitate soil conservation efforts. The following are other policy options which should be examined: (1) revising tax regulations to encourage farmers to invest in technology-intensive farming practices; (2) developing tax incentives to reward landowners who adopt soil conservation practices; (3) gradually eliminating many commodity programs that encourage maximum production of food and fiber on land resources; and (4) directing soil conservation subsidies to land operators who employ sustainable farming systems, which are not as profitable as technology-intensive production systems.

Conclusion

Research shows that national agricultural and environmental policies are closely linked to soil conservation efforts. It is becoming more evident that degradation of land resources will not be significantly reduced until a number of policy issues are addressed at the national level.

Policymakers must examine the objectives to be achieved by soil conservation efforts and establish priorities. They must determine what level of soil loss is socially acceptable and outline the roles to be played by public and private sectors. Policies must be enacted to guide the development and implementation of soil conservation programs. Last, policymakers cannot ignore the linkage between national agricultural and environmental policies. The desirability of achieving consistency of national policies is becoming increasingly evident.

The role of state and federal governments in soil conservation efforts will likely become increasingly important during the next several decades. It is also quite probable that the role will become more regulatory unless landowners assume greater responsibility for reducing off-site damages associated with agricultural production. If these predictions are shown to be correct, the success of government participation in soil conservation efforts will be significantly influenced by the type of policies created to facilitate involvement. Since policy deliberations are time consuming, it is imperative that the decision-making process begin soon and that all interests be represented. Without good policies to guide program development and implementation, the relevance of future soil conservation efforts will be jeopardized.

Notes

Salaries and research support which made this chapter possible were provided by the Ohio Agricultural Research and Development Center of The Ohio State University and the Soil Conservation Service of the United States Department of Agriculture. The statements made in this manuscript are solely those of the author and do not represent official positions of the funding organizations.

1. Coercion refers to government intervention into farm-level decision making via legislative action. Land operators who violate environmental regulations can be subject to penalties that may vary from fines to loss of rights to engage in production agriculture on highly erodible land.

References

Batie, Sandra S. 1986. "Why soil erosion: A social science perspective." Pp. 3–14 in Stephen B. Lovejoy and Ted L. Napier, eds., *Conserving Soil: Insights From Socioeconomic Research*. Ankeny, Ia.: Soil and Water Conservation Society of America Press.

Bromley, Daniel W. 1982. "The rights of society versus the rights of landowners and operators." Pp. 219–232 in H. G. Halcrow, E. O. Heady, and M. L. Cotner, eds., *Soil Conservation Policies, Institutions and Incentives*. Ankeny, Ia.: Soil and Water Conservation Society of America Press.

Camboni, Silvana M., Ted L. Napier, and Stephen B. Lovejoy. 1989. "Factors affecting participation in the CRP in a micro-targeted area of Ohio." Pp. 205–222 in Ted L. Napier, ed., *Implementing the Conservation Title of the Food Security Act of 1985*. Ankeny, Ia.: Soil and Water Conservation Society of America Press.

Crosson, Pierre. 1984. "New perspectives on soil conservation policy." *Journal of Soil and Water Conservation* 39(4):222–225.

Easter, K. William, Jay A. Leitch, and Donald F. Scott. 1983. "Competition for water, a capricious resource." Pp. 135–153 in Ted L. Napier, Donald Scott, K. William Easter, and Raymond Supalla, eds., *Water Resources Research: Problems and Potentials for Agriculture and Rural Communities*. Ankeny, Ia.: Soil and Water Conservation Society of America Press.

Eleveld, Bartelt, and Harold G. Halcrow. 1982. "How much soil conservation is optimum for society?" Pp. 233–250 in H. G. Halcrow, E. O. Heady, and M. L. Cotner, eds., *Soil Conservation Policies, Institutions and Incentives*. Ankeny, Ia.: Soil and Water Conservation Society of America Press.

Ervin, David, and R. A. Washburn. 1981. "Profitability of soil conservation practices in Missouri." *Journal of Soil and Water Conservation* 36(2):107–111.

Gardner, B. Delbert. 1985. "Government and conservation: A case of good intentions but misplaced incentives." Pp. 8–16 in *Soil Conservation: What Should Be the Role of Government?* West Lafayette, Ind.: Indiana Cooperative Extension Service.

Halcrow, H. G., E. O. Heady, and M. L. Cotner, eds. 1982. *Soil Conservation Policies, Institutions and Incentives*. Ankeny, Ia.: Soil and Water Conservation Society of America Press.

Harmon, K. W. 1987. "History and economics of farm bill legislation and the impacts of wildlife management and policies." Pp. 105–108 in J. E. Mitchell, ed., *Impacts of the Conservation Reserve Program in the Great Plains*. Denver, Colo.: U.S. Forest Service.

Kleckner, D. 1988. "Conservation programs: Mandatory or voluntary?" *Journal of Soil and Water Conservation* 43(5):358.

Korsching, Peter F., and Peter Nowak. 1980. "Sociological factors in the adoption and maintenance of best management practices." Journal paper number J-10148. Ames, Ia.: Iowa State University Experiment Station.

Lal, Rattan. 1984. "Productivity assessment of tropical soils and the effects of erosion." Pp. 70–94 in F. R. Rijsberman and M. G. Wolman, eds., *Quantification of the Effect of Erosion on Soil Productivity in an International Context*. Delft, Netherlands: Delft Hydraulics Laboratory.

Larson, W. E. 1981. "Protecting the soil resource base." *Journal of Soil and Water Conservation* 36(1):13–16.

Lovejoy, Stephen B., and Ted L. Napier, eds., 1986. *Conserving Soil: Insights from Socioeconomic Research*. Ankeny, Ia.: Soil and Water Conservation Society of America Press.

Lovejoy, Stephen B., and Dale Parent. 1981. "The sociological study of soil erosion." West Lafayette, Ind.: Department of Agricultural Economics (mimeograph).

Lovejoy, Stephen B., John G. Lee, and David B. Beasley. 1986. "Integration of social and physical analysis: The potential for micro-targeting." Pp. 121–129 in Stephen B. Lovejoy and Ted L. Napier, eds., *Conserving Soil: Insights from Socioeconomic Research*. Ankeny, Ia.: Soil and Water Conservation Society of America Press.

McCormack, D. E., K. K. Young, and L. W. Kimberlim. 1982. *Current Criteria for Determining Soil Loss Tolerance*. Madison, Wis.: American Society of Agronomy.

Miranowski, John A. 1983. "Agricultural impacts on environmental quality." Pp. 117–134 in Ted L. Napier, Donald Scott, K. William Easter, and Raymond Supalla, eds., *Water Resources Research: Problems and Potentials for Agriculture and Rural Communities*. Ankeny, Ia.: Soil and Water Conservation Society of America Press.

Mueller, D. H., R. M. Klemme, and T. C. Daniel. 1985. "Short- and long-term cost comparisons of conventional and conservation tillage systems in corn production." *Journal of Soil and Water Conservation* 40(5):466–470.

Napier, Ted L. 1987. "Farmers and soil erosion: A question of motivation." *Forum for Applied Research and Public Policy* 2(2):85–94.

———. 1988. "Anticipated changes in rural communities due to financial stress in agriculture: Implications for conservation programs." Pp. 84–90 in J. E. Mitchell, ed., *Impacts of the Conservation Reserve Program in the Great Plains.* Denver, Colo.: U.S. Forest Service.

_____. 1989. "Farmer adoption of soil conservation practices: Lessons for groundwater protection." Office of Technology Assessment report under contract number J3-4810.0.

_____, ed. 1990a. *Implementing the Conservation Title of the Food Security Act of 1985.* Ankeny, Ia.: Soil and Water Conservation Society of America Press.

_____. 1990b. "The evolution of U.S. soil conservation policy: From voluntary adoption to coercion." Pp. 627–644 in John Boardman, Ian Foster, and John Dearing, eds., *Soil Erosion on Agricultural Land.* London: John Wiley.

Napier, Ted L., and D. Lynn Forster. 1982. "Farmer attitudes and behavior associated with soil erosion control." Pp. 137–150 in H. G. Halcrow, E. O. Heady, and M. L. Cotner, eds., *Soil Conservation Policies, Institutions and Incentives.* Ankeny, Ia.: Soil and Water Conservation Society of America Press.

Napier, Ted L., Donald Scott, K. William Easter, and Raymond Supalla, eds., 1983. *Water Resources Research: Problems and Potentials for Agriculture and Rural Communities.* Ankeny, Ia.: Soil and Water Conservation Society of America Press.

Napier, Ted L., Cameron S. Thraen, Akia Gore, and W. Richard Goe. 1984. "Factors affecting adoption of conventional and conservation tillage practices in Ohio." *Journal of Soil and Water Conservation* 39(3):205–209.

Napier, Ted L., and Silvana M. Camboni. 1988. "Attitudes toward a proposed soil conservation program." *Journal of Soil and Water Conservation* 43(2):186–191.

Napier, Ted L., Cameron S. Thraen, and Stephen L. McClaskie. 1988. "Adoption of soil conservation practices by farmers in erosion-prone areas of Ohio: The application of logit modeling." *Society and Natural Resources* 1(2):109–129.

Nelson, Mack C., and W. D. Seitz. 1979. "An economic analysis of soil erosion control in a watershed representing corn belt conditions." *North Central Journal of Agricultural Economics* 1(1):173–186.

Pimentel, David. 1987. "Soil erosion effects on farm economics." Pp. 217–241 in J. M. Harlin and G. M. Barardi, eds., *Agricultural Soil Loss: Processes, Policies and Prospects.* Boulder, Colo.: Westview Press.

Putman, John, and Klaus Alt. 1988. "Erosion control: How does it change farm income?" *Journal of Soil and Water Conservation* 42(4):265–267.

Rasmussen, W. D. 1982. "History of soil conservation, institutions and incentives." Pp. 3–18 in H. G. Halcrow, E. O. Heady, and M. L. Cotner, eds., *Soil Conservation Policies, Institutions and Incentives.* Ankeny, Ia.: Soil and Water Conservation Society of America Press.

Reichelderfer, K., and W. G. Boggess. 1988. "Government decision making and program performance: The case of the conservation reserve program." *American Journal of Agricultural Economics* 70:1–11.

Sampson, R. Neil. 1985. "Government and conservation: Structuring an improved public role." Pp. 1–6 in *Soil Conservation: What Should Be the Role of Government?* West Lafayette, Ind.: Indiana Cooperative Extension Service.

Swanson, Louis E., Silvana M. Camboni, and Ted L. Napier. 1986. "Barriers to adoption of soil conservation practices on farms." Pp. 108–120 in Stephen B. Lovejoy and Ted L. Napier, eds. *Conserving Soil: Insights from Socioeconomic Research.* Ankeny, Ia.: Soil and Water Conservation Society of America Press.

21

Farmland Tenure Policy

Patrick H. Mooney and Jess Gilbert

Policy Issues

Over 40 years ago land economist Leonard Salter (1943:317–320) raised the question: "Do we need a new land policy?" He pointed to some of the mistaken assumptions about the "colossal experiment" of land policy in U.S. history. He argued that the mistake was not in "trying to establish a system of independent land ownership with a high degree of freedom for the owners of land." Rather, the mistake was to assume that the system would work automatically, without state intervention. Salter also pointed out that "when the ownership of land is purely a commercial transaction," we do not have "a self-perpetuating system, but a self-destructive system" in which farmers lose equity in the land they work, as well as security in the society in which they live, while the wealth of the soil itself is continually depleted. He argued that the real question is whether we can find ways to assure farm people of the "right to find economic opportunity and equality and security in the holding of their land." At the same time, we must also find devices "that will protect our land and the people who work it from these cumulative and self-destructive tendencies which operate when private ownership of the soil is interpreted to mean the right to use land titles as financial playthings."

Salter's concerns are still appropriate today. Policy questions always assume particular values that inform declared goals. With respect to farmland tenure, one general issue is whether we want an agriculture in which land is owned and controlled by people who live near and work on that land. The traditional alternative is an agriculture in which nonproducers enjoy some control over the land as well as a share of the income produced by those who do work that land. Are there options developed by other Western nations that we in the United States can adapt? A second issue is society's interest in the long-term protection of land as a valuable natural resource. The major value dilemma here is who should have the primary responsibility for ensuring land stewardship: private property owners, some level of government, or another social institution?

Policy Context

Thomas Jefferson and other founding fathers believed that a wide dis-tribution of productive property was essential to political democracy. They therefore sought to institute public policies favoring owner-occupied settle-ment. After early domination by speculators, agrarian interests won passage of the 1862 Homestead Act, which offered land to settlers at low cost. Yet the first U.S. census to include land tenure data, in 1880, revealed that one-fourth of all farmers were full tenants (i.e., they owned none of the land they operated). The proportion of tenant farms continued to grow through the 1930s, when it reached almost half of all U.S. farms. The Jeffersonian goal of establishing owner-operators on the nation's farms had seemingly failed.

Around 1920, the goal of agricultural policy changed from the earlier advocacy of wide landownership to a narrower focus on higher farm commodity prices (Salter, 1943). This new emphasis on price supports was incorporated in the New Deal's major agricultural policy. However, another New Deal policy, embodied in the Farm Security Administration (FSA), continued the more egalitarian effort to distribute land. This federal agency had a number of experimental programs, including cooperative farms, rural community development projects, and long-term farm leases. The FSA offended some powerful agricultural interests, however, and during World War II, the agency was gutted and replaced by the less threatening Farmers Home Administration (FmHA).

Since the late 1940s land tenure issues have not been squarely on the national policy agenda. Salter's (1943) analysis of agricultural policy between the world wars became even more appropriate for the post–World War II era: commodity price-support programs dominated policy discussions, and the landownership goal was downplayed. Lip service was paid to the values of owner-operatorship, while most farm policy paved the way for continued concentration of production and landownership.

Based on conventional land tenure categories, 1982 data reveal that full owners accounted for 42 percent of all commercial farmers, part owners for 43 percent, and tenants (nonowners) for 15 percent. This classification, however, ignores two major actors of the land tenure system: landlords and creditors. For example, in 1978 (the latest available data), over 25 percent of all U.S. farmland was owned by nonoperator landlords (Gilbert and Harris, 1984). They have legal claim to substantial portions of the income produced by their tenants. Similarly, credit relations lurk in the shadows of "ownership." In 1987, creditors held $143 billion in farm debt, about one fifth of all farm assets (USDA, 1988; USDA, 1989). The 1980s dem-onstrated the importance of credit to a complete analysis of the land tenure system, as thousands of farmers lost ownership of their farms.

This crisis is only the most recent in a long history of sudden devaluations of inflated land prices. Such crises, fueled by credit, transform the agricultural structure and thereby increase tenancy and concentration of landownership

(Mooney, 1986). While lending institutions held much of this appropriated land in the mid-1980s, in 1988 and 1989 this land was dumped on the market. The quasi-public Farm Credit System (FCS), which in 1986 held more acquired property than any other lender, sold nearly one million acres in the first six months of 1988. Much of this land was sold for cash, implying that the wealthy (whether farmers or outside investors) are consolidating landholding. This trend, in turn, implies yet another phase of increasing tenancy or concentration.

Such cycles of tenancy and indebtedness are part of larger economic cycles. Economic theorists of both the right and the left suggest that capitalist economies are characterized by cycles of economic development (capital accumulation) and stagnation/devaluation. Agricultural policies affect the land tenure system within the context of such economic cycles. For example, New Deal policies provided a basis for the phase of capital accumulation that arose from the last major downturn (the Great Depression). However, policies appropriate to an expansionary phase cannot offer feasible solutions to the current crisis.

The Reagan administration's lack of a coherent policy has left many of the same policy issues that were being discussed in the late 1970s and early 1980s (e.g., USDA, 1981; Rodefeld, 1982; Brown, 1982). This failure makes those questions all the more urgent today. In the 1970s and 1980s the rapid inflation and deflation of farmland prices precluded distribution of rights to the use of land in an orderly way, which, according to Wunderlich and Chryst (1958), is the function of a land tenure system.

Policy Assumptions

Contemporary value preferences suggest three different policy directions: "free market," "liberal," and "progressive." Although we present these as three analytically distinct options, they are often blurred in practice. The assumption that guides the free market policy option is that competition among producers will reward efficiency, defined as *profit-maximization*. All other substantive values (e.g., autonomy in one's labor and management, environmental protection, intergenerational transfer of land) are assumed to result from successful profit-maximization—or else are subordinated to free market values. The assumption of liberal proponents is that technocratic solutions are possible within existing governmental institutions. They believe that corporate and state experts can better evaluate the consequences of land tenure and land use policy than can local communities.

The assumption of the progressive position is that as long as land is a commodity, cyclical crises will be inevitable. Therefore, the progressive reform position focuses on transforming the commodity status of farmland. As both Mooney (1986) and Strange (1988) note, the recent crisis afforded an opportunity for this transformation because much agricultural land was confiscated by federal agencies and other lenders. For instance, in 1987 the quasi-public FCS and USDA's FmHA held over four million acres of re-possessed farmland. Although some of this land has already been sold to the highest bidder, this property could still provide a pilot project in true land banking such as exists in Canada and Western Europe (Strong, 1979; see below). Land banking could work against increased concentration if offered to beginning and low-net-worth farmers, targeted to those committed to environmentally sound production practices.

In the 1970s, tax and credit policies strongly influenced land tenure. Inheritance taxes, for example, reinforced the concentration of ownership (Strange, 1988). FmHA's original goal of providing access to farm ownership through subsidized credit to low-net-worth and beginning farmers was increasingly displaced by its rural industrialization efforts. By the mid-1970s, the question of who owns the land began to resurface among political activists, government researchers, and academicians. In turn, they examined the role of other policies concerning land tenure consequences. In 1978, for the first time since 1946, USDA conducted a national study of landowners, which remains the latest ownership data available (Gilbert and Harris, 1984). The following year, USDA Secretary Bob Bergland initiated a research effort on the changing structure of agriculture, including landownership (USDA, 1981). In the 1980s, these issues were again pushed to the side by policy influentials. Thus, in the absence of an explicit land policy, the farm commodity, tax, and credit policies will continue to structure land tenure. Even many of the most liberal farm organizations have ignored land tenure structure per se and have directed their attention toward production control programs, tax relief, and credit reforms.

In the United States, state and local governments have major authority over private landownership and use (Boxley, 1979). While the federal government has no explicit land tenure policy, 15 states have some restrictions on corporate landownership and farm operation. The states with the strongest restrictions are all in the western Corn Belt and Great Plains. However, none of these state-level policies effectively direct land tenure patterns. State laws grant many exceptions and are often aimed at peripheral issues (e.g., foreign landownership). Only 11 states even require businesses to report their landholdings.

Local governments, of course, control property zoning and other means of land use planning. Very few planning techniques challenge private property rights to land but instead rely on incentives and voluntary approaches (Boxley, 1979). One exception is the Community Land Trust (CLT), which leases land to farmers under long-term, renewable, and inheritable leases. This form of mixed ownership gives title to the land to a nonprofit corporation (the CLT), while the ownership of buildings and other improvements belongs to the leaseholder (e.g., a person, family business, or another CLT). Since the leaseholder is guaranteed equity in the improvements, sellers do not profit from unearned increases in market value. In exchange for the security that this tenure form provides, the leaseholder must practice environmentally and socially responsible agriculture, as defined by the democratically elected local board of trustees. This form of land tenure recognizes the legitimate interests of the entire community in this basic resource, while no party holds the land itself as a commodity (Institute for Community Economics, 1982; Buttel, 1983). Davis (1984:210) contends that the CLT is "able to achieve a just and lasting reallocation of equity between individual lease-holders and the local community . . . to reverse the worst effects of land speculation. It has the potential of altering, quite fundamentally, the ways in which local lands are held, used and developed." Further, the CLT can meet the demands of both the agricultural interest groups for new forms of beginning-farmer assistance programs as well as the environmental lobby's demands for greater protection and conservation of our land and water.

Policy Options

The assumption underlying the free market option is that market forces will allocate resources most efficiently and equitably. Free marketeers assume that landownership will fall to those (regardless of occupation or residence) most capable of optimally using the resource. The cycles of boom and bust are seen as restoring equilibrium to the market. Further, this position assumes that environmental problems in agriculture are best solved by supply and demand. The difference between owning and renting land is reduced to the cost of capital (i.e., interest vs. rental payments). Qualitative distinctions between these forms of access to land are irrelevant.

The assumption underlying the liberal model is that the state can protect the long-term interests of the larger society in land resources. Market forces are endorsed but they need occasional state direction. In the post–World War II era this philosophy has primarily meant facilitating the use of credit to buy land. This position developed in accord with New Deal concerns regarding the problems of poverty, soil erosion, and social unrest associated with tenancy in the 1930s (National Resources Committee, 1937).

Progressive reformists believe that both free market and liberal options will result in continued periodic crises for farmers, landowners, and the natural environment. The progressive reforms would alter the process of land concentration by more equitably redistributing property rights. At the heart of such reforms is the notion that some farmland must be removed from the market so that it can no longer be an object of speculation; that is, it must be "decommodified." Decommodification of land through more economically democratic investment will permit more stability in access to land for producers in exchange for more socially and ecologically responsible production. The assumption is that land tenure and land use have societywide effects. Progressives assume that farmers with long-term interests in the land are more conservation-minded than are short-term tenants. An isolated piece of research (Albrecht and Thomas, 1986) that has recently questioned this assumption is believed to be historically and regionally contingent, requiring further examination and explanation.

The reaction against such intrusions on the farmers' so-called freedom will be strong. A critical assumption, then, is that the farm family's real choice in the free market solution is to submit to control by credit institutions

TABLE 21.1   Land Tenure Policy Options

Policies Favoring	Free Market	Liberal	Progressive
Absentee ownership/ tenancy	1	2	3
Credit dependency	1	2	3
Nonfarm employment	1	1	2
Production control	3	1	2
Progressive property taxation	3	2	1
Decommodification of land	3	3	1

1 = Primary policy proposal.
2 = Acceptable policy proposal with modification.
3 = Unacceptable policy proposal.

or nonoperating landlords, or to vertical integration with processors through contract production. In the liberal solution, the choice is to become overly dependent on government, which supports prices and subsidizes credit. Progressive alternatives such as land trusts and land banking (described below) ask farmers to surrender their false sense of autonomy—not to the banker, landlord, processor, or state but to their own community in the form of democratic control over land use and (re)distribution. The farm family would gain a long-term lease with a rent based on the productive value of both the farmland and farmers' labor, rather than a rent based on the highly variable and speculative value of the land as a commodity. In exchange, society gains greater influence over its long-term interest in the protection of natural resources.

Where Are We Going?

Clearly the federal government is hesitant to deal directly with the land tenure question. Rather, the structure of land tenure is determined indirectly by other policies (e.g., policies for commodities, taxes, and credit). Free market and liberal reformist options are the most likely policy directions. (See Table 21.1.) The dominant framework within which these policy alternatives are cast provides a rather narrow range of options. Direct intervention is impeded by the sanctity of private property and its exclusion from societal control. The lack of success with liberal agricultural policy as a means of securing stable owner-operatorship is often used to advocate free market noninterventionism, as though that were the only other possible solution.

U.S. Senator Jesse Helms (1987:382) holds that the 1985 Farm Bill "signals the intention of Congress to make a decisive transition to a market-oriented farm policy." The spirit of such a shift implies, of course, that land tenure patterns will also be subject to purely market forces. One criticism of the current forms of intervention is that they lead to further concentration of landownership. Thus, within the narrow range of political debate, the choice is between more or less rapid concentration, while the redistribution of wealth is a nonissue. As former USDA Secretary Bob Bergland wrote in 1981, "It may not be possible, given our strong feelings about private ownership in the United States . . . to radically alter the trends toward greater separation of ownership and operation, [and] increased concentration of ownership. . . . However, we should correct [i.e., change] policies that accelerate rather than retard these trends" (USDA, 1981:148).

In a related vein, responses to the credit crisis of the 1980s often tend to fall back on tenancy as an acceptable form of production. Boehlje and Pederson (1988), for example, criticize farmers' lack of acceptance of leasing assets as a means of expanding agriculture's "narrow capital base." These proposals sometimes advocate liberal reforms by encouraging policies that would facilitate longer-term leases or compensation to tenants for improvements made on the property under their tenure. A free market solution to the current credit crisis is to sell limited partnership interests in farmland to outside investors (e.g., Boehlje and Pederson, 1988). This practice would subvert owner-operatorship and provide a portion of the value produced by the operator to the outside investor. Another common alternative in the free market vein is to facilitate an explicit commodification of the farmer's or the farm family's labor through off-farm employment. This off-farm work is seen as a means of subsidizing high costs of credit and as providing a temporary shelter from the process of concentration. Proponents of these schemes often express surprise at farmers' reluctance to engage in such relations and imply that resistance is irrational.

Cochrane (1986) proposes a liberal solution in which government intervenes with a "whole new agency" specifically devoted to assisting part-time farmers with low-cost credit and managerial/technical advice, funded with money saved from abandoning the old commodity programs. Other liberal reforms include demands for the state to facilitate production control. Senator Tom Harkin's Save the Family Farm Act, an alternative which lost to the free market policy, was clearly intended to defend owner-operatorship by means of attacking the overproduction problem by restricting supply. Thus, increasing commodity prices would allow farm families to continue to own the land they farm. Harkin (1987) argues for a new direction in farm policy, but the program is limited to market intervention and does not directly confront the question of transforming the property rights in land. Other liberal measures are directed at reforming the credit system (e.g., liberalizing foreclosure laws for renegotiation of loans and subsidizing interest rates) (Cochrane, 1986). Clearly, such reforms are designed to salvage production based on credit, not to go beyond it. At most, they deal with symptoms rather than root causes of the problem.

What Should We Do?

Although a combination of free market and liberal policies is most likely to occur at this time, it is important to propose other, more creative options, such as reforms that begin to erode the commodity character of land. This position is based on the empirical observation of the cyclical depressions tied to the commodity status of land. At a minimum, temporary reforms should be undertaken to ease the burden on farm people. In the meantime, we hope that more progressive ideas—common in most advanced Western nations, but excluded from the mainstream of public debate in this country—can be the basis for a new land policy. We will first outline a few moderate reforms and then discuss progressive agenda items around which a land policy might be developed.

At the state level, the 1975 Iowa Family Farm Protection Act provides a model that could be extended to impede some of the worst effects of corporate ownership and limited partnerships. The act places an acreage limit on farm units in which none of the partners are actually engaged in day-to-day farm work. States can also act, through local Soil and Water Conservation District personnel, to supervise more closely the use of inventory land currently held by lending institutions. They could thus protect this land from the abuse that accompanies short-term profit-seeking.

At the federal level, there is a serious need for basic data collection. We simply do not know very much about landownership in this nation. Such lack of knowledge impedes our ability to develop a land policy. A replication of the USDA's 1978 Land Ownership Survey will tell us much about the effects of the recent crisis on land tenure patterns. Legislation requiring nonfamily-farm corporations to report their landholdings would help separate myth from reality on this question of corporate farming. Finally, the 1980s farm crisis revealed a shocking lack of reliable, comprehensive data on foreclosures, debt-related transactions, and indicators of farm financial stress.

To turn more directly to farm policy, expanding conservation reserve programs could supply management that would facilitate stewardship by landowners. The FmHA should retain its original mission of providing low-interest loans for farm ownership to beginning, low-net-worth farmers. The federal government could also ensure that inventory land, especially that held by the FCS and FmHA, is sold with low-interest, long-term, lease-purchase agreements to re-entering, beginning, or minority farmers. The practice of selling to the highest bidder will only refuel the fires that led to the 1980s crisis.

Among the more bold policy initiatives set forth from the progressive camp is Marty Strange's (1988) recent book *Family Farming* (cf. Mooney, 1986). Strange recalls Thomas Jefferson's argument that "legislators cannot invent too many devices for subdividing property" (1988:274). He holds further that if the government is "going to regulate the price (or supply) of commodities, it should be willing to intervene in the land market as well" (1988:198). Indeed, regulating commodity pricess indirectly affects land markets. He argues for a state-level progressive property tax. Such a tax, however, might encourage further tendencies toward mixing of ownership and tenancy, a development that would increase the amount of land under tenancy. Strange also suggests strong state inheritance and federal estate taxes to break up large holdings, pieces of which could then be reintroduced into the market. That market, however, would also be modified by eliminating the advantages that corporate organizations have over working farmers.

Strange then calls for new forms of land tenure such as the CLT. Another option is the land bank, a common practice in most advanced Western societies. *Land banking* is "public, or publicly authorized, acquisition of land to be held for future use to implement public land use policy" (Strong, 1979:2). Land banking can take on a wide variety of specific forms within this broad definition. Strong (1979) believes that the French experience is the most appropriate model for the United States, since France recently came to land banking and has a similar perspective of landownership.

Canadian land banking could also be a model for the United States. While land banks can be directed to redistribute land to private ownership, "most American commentators argue that leasing is preferable to sale" (Strong, 1979:280). In agriculture, the price of rent could be based on the productive value of the land (i.e., based on average returns to farm commodities produced in the region within the past several years). This approach would impede speculative overpricing of farmland. Any subsidy of agricultural production incurred by such a program could be viewed by society as a cost, not only for food security, but also for soil and water conservation. In other nations' experiences, one of the most serious obstacles to land banking is the initial acquisition of land. As noted above, the FmHA and the FCS have acquired substantial inventories of land in the 1980s that could be used in land banking pilot projects.

Like the CLT, the land bank "substitutes the value of equity for the prevailing American value of speculative opportunity" (Strong, 1979:268). Individuals reap the rewards of their own labor, while the larger community retains the social increment in land prices. This is quite unlike the current system, which "holds the public sector accountable for losses in value of private land but does not credit it with gains" (Strong, 1979:39). Insofar as these more progressive proposals restrict the unearned gains of the speculator, derived from public investment and the labor of others, they will be undoubtedly opposed by the wealthy and powerful minority.

Yet Strange (1988) contends that such programs are no longer considered so radical as they once were. They provide farmers with long-term leases to land owned by communal or public entities and also preserve the fundamental character of family farm agriculture—owner-operatorship. What the farmer owns is "not the land, but the long-term right to use it" (1988: 276). Thus, we propose, with Strange (1988), a national land policy that includes the social responsibility of using land well.

Conclusion

We conclude by returning to Leonard Salter's 1946 question: "Do we need a new land policy?" Our answer is indicated by the plight of a farm family we recently interviewed. The father labored for thirty years to repay the Federal Land Bank for his land. When his children came of age to farm in the late 1970s, he mortgaged some land to accommodate his sons' participation. Within a few years after the decline of commodity and land prices, they were forced into foreclosure, declared bankruptcy, and were reduced to renting the very farm they had "owned" the past three decades. Now the sons are *again* buying the home farm through the Federal Land Bank. Land is too valuable to be treated as a mere commercial transaction or financial plaything (Salter, 1946), and public policy should reflect this value.

The commodity status of land, along with its naturally limited character, gives rise to cycles of speculation and devaluation. We have just experienced another downturn in land markets, a crisis of tremendous consequence to our farm population and our rural communities. These crises threaten the value of owner-operatorship, a value long held in the United States.

The options to remedy such crises are to (1) once again rebuild the structure of credit dependency, (2) return to a new phase of tenancy, or (3) break these cycles by undermining the commodity character of land that lies at the heart of speculation. The first option promises that we will sooner or later find ourselves in the same trouble we are presently in. The second option presents a socially and environmentally unstable form of production that encounters resistance from farmers who aspire to long-term rights to use the land. The third option demands some hard choices and sacrifices. Land banking and land trusts require that farmers recognize the myth of independent ownership that derives from early U.S. history. If farmers want to farm as families, without the exploitative relations of tenancy and indebtedness, without intervention by bankers and absentee landlords, the land trust and land bank models should be introduced into the policy arena. The question of who owns the land is too important to be resolved by default through other policies. The values that will inform a land policy must be derived from public debate among those who work the land and those who consume its produce. We all have a stake in this vital natural resource; future generations, too, must be made secure. We need a land policy.

References

Albrecht, Don E., and John K. Thomas. 1986. "Farm tenure: A retest of conventional knowledge." *Rural Sociology* 51(1):18–30.

Boehlje, Michael, and Glenn Pederson. 1988. "Farm finance: The new issues." *Choices* 3(3):16–19.

Boxley, Robert F. 1979. "Ownership and land use policy," Pp. 161–167 in *Structure Issues in American Agriculture*. Agricultural Economic Report Number 48. USDA: Economics, Statistics, and Cooperatives Service.

Brown, David. 1982. "Land use." Pp. 373–381 in Don A. Dillman and Darryl J. Hobbs, eds., *Rural Society in the U.S.* Boulder, Colo.: Westview Press.

Buttel, Frederick H. 1983. "Beyond the family farm." Pp. 87–107 in Gene F. Summers, ed., *Technology and Social Change in Rural Areas*. Boulder, Colo.: Westview Press.

Cochrane, Willard W. 1986. "A new sheet of music: How Kennedy's farm adviser has changed his tune about commodity policy and why." *Choices* (Premier Issue): 11–15.

————. 1987. "Saving the modest-sized farm or the case for part-time farming." *Choices* (2nd Quarter): 4–7.

Davis, John Emmeus. 1984. "Reallocating equity: A land trust model of land reform." Pp. 209–232 in Charles C. Geisler and Frank J Popper, eds., *Land Reform, American Style*. Totowa, N.J.: Rowman and Allanheld.

Gilbert, Jess, and Craig Harris. 1984. "Changes in types, tenure, and concentration of U.S. farmland owners." Pp. 135–160 in Harry K. Schwarzweller, ed., *Research in Rural Sociology and Development*. Vol. 1. Greenwich, Conn.: JAI Press.

Harkin, Tom. 1987. "The save the family farm act." Pp. 388–397 in Gary Comstock, ed., *Is There a Moral Obligation to Save the Family Farm?* Ames: Iowa State University Press.

Helms, Jesse. 1987. "The 1985 farm bill." Pp. 381–387 in Gary Comstock, ed., *Is There A Moral Obligation to Save the Family Farm?* Ames, Iowa: Iowa State University Press.

Institute for Community Economics. 1982. *The Community Land Trust Handbook*. Emmaus, Penn.: Rodale Press.

Mooney, Patrick H. 1986. "The political economy of credit in American agriculture." *Rural Sociology* 51(4):449–470.

National Resources Committee. 1937. Farm tenancy: Report of the president's committee. Washington, D.C.: U.S. Government Printing Office.

Rodefeld, Richard. 1982. "Who will own and operate America's farms?" Pp. 328–336 in Don A. Dillman and Darryl J. Hobbs, eds., *Rural Society in the U.S.* Boulder, Colo.: Westview Press.

Salter, Leonard A., Jr. 1943. "Farm property and agricultural policy." *Journal of Political Economy* 51(1):13–22.

————. 1946. "Do we need a new land policy?" *The Journal of Land and Public Utility Economics* 22(4):309–320.

Strange, Marty. 1988. *Family Farming: A New Economic Vision*. Lincoln, Nebr.: University of Nebraska Press and San Francisco: Institute for Food and Development Policy.

Strong, Ann. 1979. *Land Banking: European Reality, American Prospect*. Baltimore: Johns Hopkins University Press.

United States Department of Agriculture (USDA). 1981. *A Time to Choose*. Washington, D.C.: U.S. Government Printing Office.

————. 1988. *Agricultural Income and Finance: Situation and Outlook Report*. Washington, D.C.: USDA, Economic Research Service. AFO-31. December.

————. 1989. *Agricultural Income and Finance: Situation and Outlook Report*. Washington, D.C.: USDA, Economic Research Service. AFO-32. February.

Wunderlich, Gene, and Walter E. Chryst. 1958. "Farm tenure and the use of land." Pp. 295–301 in *Land: The Yearbook of Agriculture*. Washington, D.C.: USDA.

22
Forest Resource Policy

Louise Fortmann and Sally K. Fairfax

Forests and what we do with them are not the concern of foresters alone; nor of the bushworkers; nor of the paper-makers; sawmillers and board-makers; nor of the scientists; nor of the water supply authorities; nor of picnickers and tourists; nor of the fauna; nor of the environmentalists. All have a stake. So have the next and future generations. Moreover, . . . they form part of a global resource. (Westoby, 1987)

The history of forest policy and management in the United States can be viewed in terms of a gradual and hotly contested expansion of the definition of what forests are and what they are good for. This chapter explores previous perceptions of forests as barriers to what we depict as the next step in the process. It notes the nearly total absence of social scientists in the past and their centrality to the development of future forest resource policy.

Forests were once viewed as a resource to harvest and replant to provide a stable timber supply, and therefore employment, for small logging communities. Today, forests are understood to be complex ecosystems. This view has been enhanced by an increasingly multifaceted appreciation of forest productivity. For example, fisheries may provide a more stable resource base than timber; recreation may be an ecologically less destructive and economically more productive use of forests; and the death, accident, and seasonal unemployment rates of the logging industry may be so high and the wages so low that even if logging is an economically optimal use, the social costs to the labor force, their families, and the local communities are unacceptable. Just as the idea of the forest ecosystem has overtaken the notion of the forest as an aggregate of trees and logs, so has the concept of forest resource-dependence supplanted the old familiar timber-dependent community.

The progression of ever-broadening forest resource-policy frameworks from trees to ecosystems and from timber dependence to resource dependence must lead to another phase in which policy moves beyond the forest boundary to encompass the rural region. Policy for the 1990s must involve plans for forest resources wherever and in whatever context they occur rather than for discrete national or industrial forests.[1] The focus must be on rural regions and how forest resources contribute to regional economic and social well-being. This shift from a biological to a social planning context will accompany the shift from a focus on outputs to a focus on process. It is the formulation of a process which includes and responds to the full diversity of institutions and actors concerned with forest resources and which is crucial to the essential agenda of the next decade. The emerging role of social science will be not one of filling some "social data gap" but, rather, one of redefining the substance and parameters of the policy process.

A new process is important because forest goods and services are produced not merely in ecologically diverse forest types, but in socially and economically disparate settings under a diversity of ownerships, thus complicating forest use and management. Having achieved a more refined understanding of forest policy's regional context, the need to come to grips with this social diversity is immediate and pressing. For example, the public owns 28 percent of the nation's forest land (20 percent is held by the diverse agencies of the federal government) while the forest industry owns 14 percent, farmers own 24 percent, and the remaining 34 percent is held in other nonindustrial private ownerships (USDA, 1982). These different forest ownerships face different constraints, have different goals, and have been addressed in different ways. Public interest groups—local, state, and national—play an increasing role in decision making on both public and private forest lands. They too have different claims and diverse mechanisms for implementing those claims on the various ownerships.

This multiplicity of actors and perspectives is a major component of our emphasis on the evolution of a new process. A political maturation is necessary for the evolution of a regional and social context for forest policy. That is, the evolution of a more comprehensive process will have to overcome vestiges of a deeply held presumption that whereas the people control their own federal and state-owned lands, they do not have a clear grip on privately held lands. Environmental lawyer Joseph Sax (1984) observes, quite correctly, that the notion that public values or political decisions dominate on federal forests while private and personal decisions control industrial and privately owned lands is nonsense. Federal management of federal lands is no more subject to congressional and political direction than are privately held lands, which are increasingly regulated by diverse federal, state, and local planning and environmental protection programs as well as by tax policies.[2]

Moreover, the evolution of a new process will have to overcome a presumption—rampant in the forestry profession and widely shared in the general public—that resource management is a technical, not a social, undertaking. This notion too is currently being challenged (Burch, 1971, 1988). Under the impetus of strong local and national environmental movements, the nature of the production process itself has become as salient a policy issue as the nature and quantity of the products that ought to be provided. For example, the acceptability of using pesticides (particularly when aerially sprayed), from both environmental and health perspectives, continues to be questioned. Debate continues on clearcuts and the amount of land that ought to be set aside for nontimber uses such as recreation, grazing, and preservation of pristine areas and rare and endangered species. The individuals and groups raising these issues are by no means unified. State and national environmental organizations, on the one hand, and a myriad of highly localized protesting groups and individuals, on the other, often question forest policy for very different reasons, using very different repertoires of protest (cf. Fortmann, 1988).

These broad social changes presage the evolution of a regionally and socially based process for forest policy debte. However, such a change will not come easily. The intellectual and political history of the forestry profession and the history of forest management in this country suggest that the next decade will witness battles over this evolution and, in particular, the nature of the process itself.

Legacies of the "Forest as Log Factory" Era

The heritage of the forestry profession has left many foresters peculiarly maladapted to respond productively to changing social organization and values.[3] We have discussed this problem elsewhere (Fortmann and Fairfax, 1985; Fortmann, Kusel, and Fairfax, 1989) and will make only two observations here to point to the source of the resistance and hence the debate over any new policy process. First, fiercely independent agencies, well established and apparently successful, will fight to retain control over "their" land. Second, antilocal bias continues within the professional forestry culture.

Agency Resistance

Forest policy questions arise in the context of a natural resource sector that has been dominated by a single federal bureaucracy of enormous cachet and impact. The U.S. Forest Service is, for many, the very model of a modern major bureaucracy. Clarke and McCool (1985), for example, appropriately characterize it as a "bureaucratic superstar." Evolving a regional decision-making structure and rural development perspective will, if they appear threatening to the U.S. Forest Service, be no small task. The other major federal agency in the resource management field that controls considerable land necessary for implementing a rural regional policy focus, the Bureau of Land Management (BLM),[4] has long labored in the shadow of the Forest Service and is likely to continue to do so. Its lack of power is somewhat compensated for by the support of the range livestock industry, which has long enjoyed an influence in Washington that surpasses its economic import. This powerful constituency has no particular reason to welcome an opening of the policymaking process. In addition, BLM's 1976 authorizing statute, the Federal Land Policy and Management Act (FLPMA), so carefully ties BLM real estate transactions to complex planning and public interest determinations that BLM objections to (or organizational inability to implement) a regional perspective would also be formidable barriers.[5]

Professional Resistance

Forestry professionals in federal agencies are likely to object to submerging "their" lands into a regional decision-making process for diverse reasons. Principal among them is the intellectual history of the Progressive Era conservation movement. According to Samuel P. Hays (1959:267), "Social and economic problems, [Theodore] Roosevelt believed, should be solved, not through power politics, but by experts who would undertake scientific investigations and devise workable solutions."

The crux of the gospel lay in a rational and scientific method. Hays (1959:276) concluded that the conservation movement raised a fundamental question in American life: "How can large-scale economic development be effective and at the same time fulfill the desire for significant grassroots participation?" The emphasis on socially based regional rural development that is evolving in forest policy poses precisely the same question. But this emphasis runs directly counter to the traditions of the Progressive Era foresters and their present-day successors. From reading Hays we can conclude that the Forest Service straddled the gap between technical expertise and grassroots participation by assuming and asserting that the locals wanted what the foresters could produce: timber to keep local mills supplied. Thus, it embraced the most technically grounded and politically powerful segment of the local users as an antidote to political or nontimber-oriented decision making. Although the agency is now able to think of outputs other than timber, controlling the grassroots in order to achieve technically sound forestry is still a dominant theme in agency thought.

Segueing into a New Era[6]

Two interrelated phenomena seem to be pivotal in overcoming these barriers to a new process-focused debate. They are the simultaneous rise of administrative law concepts in resource management and the evolution of new social science approaches to resource management.

The Rise of Administrative Law

This is a familiar concept frequently discussed under the acronyms of EIS and NEPA (environmental impact statements as required by the National Environmental Policy Act) and need not be elaborated here. Suffice it to say that the resource management professions have been caught up short on two basic concepts of administrative law: public hearings and the need to provide a record of decision making. "Public involvement," the bureaucratic response to the Administrative Procedures Act's requirements for "some kind of hearing," as amplified, albeit slightly, in NEPA, has obliged the Forest Service to be uncharacteristically formal in its efforts to involve the public in its internal procedures. Ritual public involvement, no panacea, has nonetheless forced the agency to expand its "key man list" beyond the timber industry. A record of decision making, now manifest in totally unmanageable documents known as forest plans, may have had even more severe impacts. The planning process has revealed, among other things, the difficulties the agency has in telling anyone in advance what it will do on any piece of land except those areas congressionally designated as basically nonmanagement zones.[7]

As a result of the litigious era of the environmental movement, these administrative law concepts were written into major Forest Service and BLM authorizing statutes. In response to major substantive issues which it could not or would not resolve, Congress designed procedures for planning (cf. Fairfax, 1978). Because these new planning regimens have, not surprisingly, failed to quiet the substantive disagreements, the process itself is already a target of major dissension.

Dismal Data. One reason why the process is controversial is that the Forest Sevice (and, to a lesser extent, the BLM) has been exposed in public with its data in disarray and its models for analysis open to piercing critique. Social scientists accustomed to hearing that their concerns are "soft," grounded in mushy feelings and social preferences, may be surprised to hear that the major component of a successful attack on the resource management professions and the hegemony of site-specific manipulations will be superior data and concepts.

Nevertheless, experience suggests that for all its vaunted expertise, the Forest Service's claims to authority are most likely to be weakened by its data and concepts. Perhaps surprisingly, the chief avenue of attack against the technical soundness of forestry and Forest Service policy has not come on the moral issue of who should decide. Rather, the agency has been vulnerable to increasingly well-documented charges that it manipulates its data and muddles its models to maintain its long-standing preference for timber as opposed to other uses.

Environmentalists are not the first to point to inadequacies in Forest Service data. In *Fire and Water* (1962), Ashley Schiff documents beyond cavil that the agency had concealed for decades growing evidence that fire suppression was ecologically unsound, albeit politically attractive. More recently, the forest planning process has demonstrated that foresters know surprisingly little, or at least less than they thought, about how tree growth responds to different treatments and how different management regimens affect other resources. Less surprisingly, perhaps, we know almost nothing about the impact on the forest of diverse users, their interactions, and how to balance them all in a management regimen once glibly proffered as "multiple use." Who wins and who loses under various combinations of multiple uses remain largely unanswered questions. However, this is not to suggest that what is needed is a social science that pigeonholes the actors in the forestry sector; rather, we need for social science to address fundamental questions about the nature and outcomes of the policymaking process.

The Role of Social Science
in a New Forest Resource Policy

For most of this century explicitly forest-oriented social science research has been, at best, on the edge of the formation of forest policy (which in most states has meant Forest Service policy). Political scientists have a long tradition of breathless admiration for the Forest Service as a bureaucracy (cf. Gulick, 1951; Kaufman, 1960) that pays relatively little critical attention to larger issues. When forest policymakers have reached out to sociologists, they have largely limited their participation to addressing details of recreation management or the agency's self-defined people problems (either controlling obstreperous users or selling the Forest Service line to a skeptical public). As the agency was forced both by national legislation, such as the 1969 National Environmental Policy Act, and by local uproar to adopt more participatory decision-making processes, it tried to engineer "public involvement," a manipulative "participatory" process intended to elicit public ratification of agency decisions. By so narrowly framing their need for social science input, forest policymakers cut themselves off from at least three relevant bodies of social science research.

First, even within their restricted focus on public involvement, forest policymakers might have benefited from the massive literature on participation. For example, familiarity with the work of Arnstein (1969) would have warned them that their proposals were nonparticipatory or, at best, tokenism and hence not likely to subdue the demons with which they were wrestling. Perusal of Jacobs' (1978) critique of public participation in natural resource planning in a neocolonial setting in the Southwest would have alerted them to the pitfalls of ignoring ethnic and cultural diversity. Voices were even raised within the agency itself. Blahna and Yonts-Shepard (forthcoming) criticize policymakers for losing issues as a result of eliciting public input too late in the planning process, using an overly narrow base for solicitation of input, developing poor analytical procedures, and deliberately suppressing the issues.

Second, attention to nonagency social scientists would have identified pressing issues in the relationships among those who regulate forest use and management, foresters, and local communities. Such social scientists have illuminated the basic tensions in forest policy. Studies by West (1982), Knowlton (1972), Kelly (1974), Jordon (1983), and Ives (forthcoming) suggest that the relationship of the government forestry, the Forest Service in particular, to local communities has often been remarkably similar to that of a colonial or occupying power (cf. Guha, 1985). Communities have often been frustrated by the Forest Service's interpretation of local control as devolution of decision-making power to the ranger district rather than to local communities. These communities have occasionally acted on their frustration, sometimes violently.

A third body of literature, the development literature on social forestry and forest bureaucracies, has the most useful social science research to apply to the future forest policy. Social science research on forestry for development has illuminated not the specifics of new policies but, more important, the process by which such policies might be developed.

One of the most useful insights to devising an appropriate process for the formulation of forest policy stems from the concept of "bureaucratic reorientation," first proposed by Korten and Uphoff (1981).[8] Bureaucratic reorientation is an iterative process intended to enable bureaucracies to use their own technical training to become more responsive to their clientele and to learn to use the knowledge of that clientele. Peluso and Poffenberger (1989) describe the application of bureaucratic reorientation to the forest bureaucracy in Indonesia, an example worth considering in detail.

The first phase of the process, diagnostic research, involved establishing a team of researchers (ecologists, social scientists, forestry planers, and policymakers) from both universities and departments of forestry who, with the assistance of graduate student field researchers, undertook a year-long study of forest resource conflicts. Training in how to collect sociological data was provided. According to Peluso and Poffenberger (1989:337), involvement in this research and "the expectation that it would benefit both the forest and the rural poor" accomplished three things: it created solidarity among the researchers (and therefore provided cross-institutional links); it created a "positive identification with the people they studied"; and it provided baseline data on the local social organization of forest and land use and management and identified the sources of conflicts between foresters and local villagers.

It is not hard to imagine how such a process might work in forming forest policy in the United States. Players might include not only universities and the Forest Service but also members of state and national environmental and commodity organizations, state resource and rural development agencies, ethnic organizations, and private community development groups. Issues might involve the following:

1. social, economic, and ecological trade-offs between consumptive and nonconsumptive commodity uses of natural resources;
2. social, economic, and ecological trade-offs between commodity uses and the view of the forest as an alluring aesthetic backdrop for resource-independent activities;
3. conflicting definitions of and claims (including both extralegal and illegal usufructuary claims) to forest resources;
4. social and economic effects of varying policies of forest resource use and management on different economic and cultural groups;
5. means of sustaining the value of forest products; and
6. means of encouraging investment in the regeneration of forest resources.

Diagnostic research would have a considerable positive effect on forest policy formulation in a number of ways. Social science expertise in the Forest Service has traditionally been weak. A cross-institutional team would strengthen Forest Service expertise by allowing personnel to interact with social scientists and would establish links to experts in other institutions. Second, cooperation in a research project could result in a common understanding of field conditions by diverse actors in the forest policy arena. Third, active involvement in a research team would provide bureaucrats with a better understanding of field conditions than that provided by the current practice of simply contracting out for a study. Fourth, field data would dispel many of the myths under which forest policy is made. One myth, equivalent to Indonesian foresters' concept of rural people as "ignorant of the meanings and functions of the forest" (Peluso and Poffenberger, 1989:338), is U.S. foresters' equally negative conceptualizations of environmentalists and of loggers. A second myth is the belief that nondeclining, even-flow yield (i.e., a constant flow of logs to the local mill) will result in community stability (i.e., well-being) (cf. Fortmann, Kusel, and Fairfax, 1989).

In the Indonesia project, once a common understanding and documentation of the field context had been established through a discussion of the research findings, the second phase, pilot projects, was begun. Given the vast array of participants in forest policymaking and the possibility of foundation funding, pilot projects which might increase local control over forest resources and return the profits of forest industries to communities for investment in the resource[9] could be established. Contrary to the Progressive Era notion of the virtue of centralization, such projects would be highly decentralized and localized, meeting the diversity of local conditions with a diversity of local policy prescriptions formulated in the context of national economic, social, and environmental concerns. Mistakes will inevitably be made, but there is little to suggest that virtue exists in the center's reserving for itself alone the right to make mistakes.

Conclusion

The past century of national forest policy has focused largely on the trees within the boundaries of national forests. State forest policy has largely provided diverse subsidies to encourage and facilitate fire suppression, pest control, and private reforestation and, in a few states, to regulate the terms of the forests' use. Now, however, not only forests but the communities within and around them are increasingly being seen as parts of larger social, economic, and ecological systems. The interdependence between the condition of natural resources and the well-being of human communities noted by Firey (1978) and forcefully articulated by Blaikie (1984) is now coming to be generally recognized. As a consequence, forest policy will, we are suggesting, recede and will increasingly be perceived as simply a part of more general rural policy. The questions for the 1990s will center around the nature of the relationship between forest resources and regional rural economic and social well-being as well as the processes by which the decisions affecting that relationship are made. We expect that the answers to both questions will differ widely by locality. Thus, in the next decade, policymaking in forestry will place forest resources in their social context, even as the efforts of the last half century have placed the log in its ecological setting. In the forest resource policy of the 1990s, process will be the most important product.

Notes

The research assistance of Sheila Seshan is gratefully acknowledged. Writing was facilitated by the support of the University of California at Berkeley Survey Research Center.

1. An issue that may be expected to emerge in the 1990s is the importance of urban forest resources for microclimatic and aesthetic enhancement. We do not address that issue here, not only because of their urban location but because such resources rarely affect human livelihoods.

2. Note also the argument of Robert Nelson (1986) that the political power of various environmental groups has enabled them to establish de facto private property rights to federal lands.

3. One encouraging exception to this general point is a movement within the Society of American Foresters to restate the national society's formal principles of forestry professionalism to include social dimensions. A second, at the state level, is the integrated regional social and biological policy analysis of California's forest and range resources produced by a team headed by a sociologist (Ewing et al., 1988).

4. Although associated primarily with grazing lands, the BLM in fact also holds forest land and hence is of interest here.

5. The potential for difficulties is demonstrated by *National Wildlife Fund v. Burford.* Allegations concerning inadequate BLM procedures have delayed and confused thousands of diverse real estate transactions for more than four years.

6. *Segue* is the transition from one musical number or sound effect to another.

7. Indeed a whole new literary genre of critiques of the forest planning process has recently arisen (cf. Ramig, 1989).

8. Goldenberg's (1984) commentary on public participation in North America makes many points similar to those of Korten and Uphoff (1981). However, for our purposes Korten and Uphoff's treatment of the issues has the advantages of being not only diagnostic but also prescriptive and of having been field tested in both Sri Lanka and Indonesia.

9. Twenty-five percent of the revenues received from timber harvesting by the U.S. Forest Service are already returned to the counties as a payment-in-lieu of taxes. These funds are currently restricted for use in schools and roads.

References

Arnstein, Sherry R. 1969. "A ladder of citizen participation," *AIP Journal* 35:216–224.

Blahna, Dale J., and Susan Yonts-Shepard. Forthcoming. "Preservation or use? Confronting public issues in forest planning and decision making." In John Hutcheson, Frank Noe, and Robert Snow, eds., *Outdoor Recreation Policy: Preservation and Pleasure.* Westport, Conn.: Greenwood Press.

Blaikie, Piers. 1984. *The Political Economy of Soil Erosion.* New York: Longmans.

Burch, William R. 1971. *Daydreams and Nightmares.* New York: Harper and Row.

_____. 1988. "Gods of the forest." *Farm Forestry News* 2(3):1–3.

Clarke, Jeanne Nienaber, and Daniel McCool. 1985. *Staking Out the Terrain. Power Differentials Among Natural Resource Management Agencies.* Albany, N.Y.: State University of New York Press.

Ewing, R. A., N. Tosta, R. Tuazon, L. Huntsinger, R. Marose, K. Nielson, R. Motroni, and S. Turan. 1988. *California's Forest and Rangelands: Growing Conflict Over Changing Uses.* Sacramento, Calif.: California Department of Forestry and Fire Protection, Forest and Rangelands Resource Assessment Program.

Fairfax, Sally K. 1978. "A disaster in the environmental movement." *Science* 199(February):743–748.

Firey, Walter. 1978. "Some contributions of sociology to the study of natural resources." In M. Barnabas, S. K. Hulbe, and P. S. Jacob, eds., *Challenges of Societies in Transition.* Delhi: Maxmillian Company.

Fortmann, Louise. 1988. "Predicting natural resource micro-protest." *Rural Sociology* 53(3)357–367.

Fortmann, Louise, and Sally Fairfax. 1985. "American forestry professionalism in the Third World: Some preliminary observations on effects." Pp. 105–108 in R. S. Gallin and A. Spring, eds., *Women Creating Wealth: Transforming Economic Development.* Selected papers and speeches from the Association for Women in Development Conference, April 25–27, Washington, D.C.

Fortmann, Louise, Jonathan Kusel, and Sally Fairfax. 1989. "Community stability: The foresters' figleaf." In Dennis LeMaster and John Beuter, eds., *Community Stability in Forest-Based Communities: Proceedings of a Conference on Forestry and Community Stability.* Beaverton, Oreg.: Timber Press.

Goldenberg, Sheldon. 1984. "Organizational responses to issues concerning the delegation of authority in situations involving public participation." *Culture* IV(1):33–42.

Guha, Ramachandra. 1985. "Forestry and social protest in British Kumaun, c. 1893–1921." In Ranajit Guha, ed., *Subaltern Studies IX.* Delhi: Oxford University Press.

Gulick, Luther. 1951. *American Forest Policy: A Study of Government Administration and Economic Control.* New York: Duell, Sloan, and Pearce.

Hays, Samuel. 1959. *Conservation and the Gospel of Efficiency: The Progressive Conservation Movement 1890–1920.* Cambridge, Mass.: Harvard University Press.

Ives, Edward D. Forthcoming. *George Magoon and the Down-East Game War: A Study in History, Folklore and the Law.* Urbana, Ill.: University of Illinois Press.

Jacobs, Sue-Ellen. 1978. "'Top-down planning': Analysis of obstacles to community development in an economically poor region of the southwestern United States." *Human Organization* 37(3):246–256.

Jordon, James William. 1983. "Frontier culture, government agents and city folks." In Allen Batteau, ed., *Appalachia and America: Autonomy and Regional Independence.* Lexington, Ky.: University of Kentucky Press.

Kaufman, Herbert. 1960. *The Forest Ranger: A Study in Administrative Behavior.* Baltimore: The Johns Hopkins University Press.

Kelly, James F. 1974. *The Skoglund Loggers.* Unpublished Ph.D. dissertation. University of California at Riverside.

Knowlton, Clark. 1972. "Culture conflict and natural resources." In William R. Burch, Jr., Neil H. Cheek, and Lee Taylor, eds., *Social Behavior, Natural Resources and the Environment.* New York: Harper and Row.

Korten, David C., and Norman T. Uphoff. 1981. "Bureaucratic reorientation for participatory rural development." NASPAA Working Paper No. 1. NASPAA and USAID.

Nelson, Robert H. 1986. "Private rights to government actions: How modern property rights evolve." *University of Illinois Law Review* 1986:361–386.

Peluso, Nancy Lee, and Mark Poffenberger. 1989. "Social forestry in Java: Reorienting management systems." *Human Organization* 48(4):333–344.

Ramig, John. 1989. "The failure of the federal forest planning process." *Natural Resources and Environment* 3:31–33, 60–61.

Sax, Joseph. 1984. "The claim for retention of the public lands." In Sterling Brubaker, ed., *Rethinking the Federal Lands.* Washington, D.C.: Resources for the Future.

Schiff, Ashley L. 1962. *Fire and Water: Scientific Heresy in the Forest Service.* Cambridge, Mass.: Harvard University Press.

U.S. Department of Agriculture (USDA), Forest Service. 1982. *An Analysis of the Timber Situation in the United States 1952–2030.* Forest Resource Report No. 23. Washington, D.C.: U.S. Government Printing Office.

West, Patrick C. 1982. *Natural Resource Bureaucracy and Rural Poverty: A Study in the Political Sociology of Natural Resources.* Monograph #2. Ann Arbor, Mich.: University of Michigan Natural Resource Sociology Research Lab.

Westoby, Jack. 1987. *The Purpose of Forests: Follies of Development.* Oxford: Basil Blackwell.

23

The Waste Management Problem

Steve H. Murdock, Rita R. Hamm,
Edli Colberg, and F. Larry Leistritz

Reducing and safely storing or disposing of wastes will be a major concern of both rural and urban residents in the United States during the 1990s (Murdock, Hamm, and Leistritz, 1987). The U.S. population, which is expected to be nearly 270 million (Spencer, 1989) by the year 2000, has a growing waste problem. Currently, we are producing more than 1,200 pounds of municipal and solid wastes per person each year (U.S. EPA, 1988). In addition, existing high-level nuclear wastes (including more than 360,000 cubic meters of high-level wastes from defense programs and nearly 18,000 cubic meters of spent fuel rods from nuclear reactors), low-level radioactive wastes in excess of 3.8 million cubic meters, more than 96 million cubic meters of radioactive tailings from uranium mining and processing activities (U.S. Department of Energy, 1988; League of Women Voters, 1985), and other chemical and toxic wastes exceeding 263 million metric tons per year (Weber, 1988) have yet to be adequately managed or safely stored.

Per capita production of wastes and our use of toxic substances are not only large but are continuing to increase. For example, the production of municipal solid wastes increased by 37 percent from 1960 to 1984, and the amount of pesticides used increased by more than 90 percent between 1960 and 1985 (U.S. EPA, 1987). Finally, the pervasiveness of the problem is evident from the fact that the Environmental Protection Agency's (EPA's) national priority list of superfund sites requiring cleanup included more than 760 sites as of June 1988 (U.S. EPA, 1988).

For the nation as a whole, then, the policy issues related to wastes involve obtaining answers to the following questions: How can the United States reduce its production of waste products? Moreover, how can waste products be safely, equitably, and efficiently stored and managed? Whereas each of these issues involves numerous dimensions, this chapter focuses on the socioeconomic aspects of waste management.

The Policy Context

As America enters the 1990s, it has a legacy of unresolved problems related to waste management and few established sociopolitical mechanisms for resolving these problems. The policy context is primarily determined by three factors: the characteristics of the waste materials being handled, stored, or destroyed; the history of the management of wastes and the siting of waste storage and disposal facilities; and the public awareness of and reaction to wastes and their storage or disposal. Each of these is briefly described below.

The Characteristics of Wastes

Wastes are a source of fear because of what is both known and unknown about them. One unknown is the sheer magnitude of wastes. As noted above, the volume is large and growing. Images of barges of unwanted municipal wastes, the growth in the volume of high- and low-level nuclear wastes, and the emerging range and volume of chemical wastes have led to a widespread perception that even the extent of the problem is not well known (Lake, 1987).

Coupled with concerns about the magnitude of wastes are those questions related to their health and environmental effects and the length of time over which these effects are likely to occur. Nuclear wastes emit radiation for thousands of years and thus entail risks that last for generations (Murdock, Hamm, and Leistritz, 1983). For other wastes, such as many chemical wastes, substances once thought to pose no danger have been found to have carcinogenic properties, and in still other cases products which are not harmful on initial storage have become dangerous after being exposed to environmental conditions (Henstock, 1983). Consequently, residents who live close to waste storage or disposal sites are concerned about their own health and safety. They also have strong fears that, although they themselves may not be affected, future accidents or the gradual degradation of the waste storage structures may contaminate the environment and thus create health problems for future generations (Peters 1981, 1988). In addition, residents have strong concerns about the contamination of groundwater and soils (Murdock and Hamm, 1986) and the subsequent increase in exposure to toxic or radioactive substances (Albrecht and Chadwick, 1980).

The History of Waste Management and Storage

In the past, problems such as those at Three Mile Island, Chernobyl, Love Canal, and Times Beach have created a public distrust of technology and industry and of governments' honesty and capability for managing technology and its wastes (Gladwin, 1980). Even when steps to enact systematic siting and management procedures have been attempted, subsequent policy decisions have often led to extensive management difficulties and public opposition. For example, although the intent of the 1982 Nuclear Waste Policy Act was to establish an objective, deliberate process for establishing sites for housing high- and low-level nuclear wastes, its implementation has been problematic. The congressional actions, in designating a single site for storing high-level nuclear wastes in Nevada, failed to follow the evaluative procedures established in the act. As a result, the high-level nuclear waste site in Nevada is beset by legal, equity, and technical issues (Frishman, 1988). In like manner, the numerous compacts formed to locate sites for the disposal of low-level nuclear wastes have been unable to arrive at a group consensus, and many are in danger of collapsing. None has yet succeeded in obtaining a fully licensed site (Bullard, 1987).

Management is also concerned about the institutional arrangements for managing wastes and waste sites (Peelle, 1980; Peelle and Ellis, 1987). How secure are these sites from natural or man-induced events and from simple human carelessness that could lead to soil or water contamination? Recent information about groundwater contamination at nuclear sites in Nevada and Utah and at Three Mile Island has increased this concern and caused people to question whether even the best available techniques can predict long-term impacts for the most dangerous wastes (Albrecht and Chadwick, 1980; Sorenson et al., 1987). Other questions include how these facilities will be controlled during the long periods in which there may be risks, and how wastes will be transported and handled (Schilling et al., 1979; Murdock, Hamm, and Leistritz, 1986).

In addition, there is often regulatory confusion. Citizen groups and industry are faced with a myriad of federal, state, and local agencies that have some regulatory authority related to waste management. In the federal sector, for example, the EPA, the Department of Energy, the Nuclear Regulatory Commission, the Department of Commerce, and the Department of Transportation are just a few of the agencies with authority over the transportation of wastes and the location of waste sites. State and local health agencies, local planning commissions, local water authorities, as well as state and local elected officials may also have varying levels of jurisdiction. For many, it appears that the bureaucracies responsible for managing wastes have come to inhibit rather than enhance the process of locating waste sites and reducing waste production.

Public Reaction

Because waste disposal sometimes involves the handling and storage of dangerous materials and because of the highly publicized nature of recent events related to some wastes (Cook, 1982; Freudenburg and Rosa, 1984; Sorenson et al., 1987), residents are apprehensive about having storage facilities in their areas (Hebert et al., 1978; Freudenburg and Rosa, 1984; Gladwin, 1980). There is growing public sentiment to resist any development that involves taking responsibility for problems created outside of a community's immediate jurisdiction (for a discussion of this "not in my back yard" perspective, see Peelle and Ellis, 1987), and even when the wastes are of local origin, intracommunity conflicts often emerge between the community as a whole and those residents in the neighborhoods most directly impacted (Bullard, 1983).

Another major public issue is that of equity. Residents in potential siting areas may not like being forced to receive an unwanted facility that may store the wastes of an entire nation (Cluett et al., 1979; Peters, 1981, 1988), an entire state (Murdock and Hamm, 1986), or even the wastes of other areas of the same city (Bullard, 1983). These perceptions of inequity may be particularly strong in rural areas whose citizens have long felt exploited by urban residents and urban areas. In addition, questions have often been raised about the equity of one generation's leaving a legacy of unearned risks for future generations (Peters, 1988).

Finally, residents of potential waste-storage sites generally believe that they will have minimal involvement in the management and, particularly, the process of siting a waste facility. They are apprehensive that the major decisions affecting such facilities will be made by others and that local residents' involvement will occur only late in the process—a token level of activity (Albrecht and Chadwick, 1980; Peelle and Ellis, 1987). In addition, residents are concerned that these projects may not be adequately or carefully monitored, particularly in relation to risks within local areas (Halstead et al., 1982, 1984).

In sum, as America enters the last decade of this century, it is faced with a massive waste problem and an atmosphere of public distrust and cynicism. The public is fearful, distrustful, and opposed to any solution that requires them to host a site for waste storage and that does not provide "absolute" safety. Government agencies charged with waste management and storage perceive no way to obtain public support for waste siting and thus assume that the public will be opposed to any project (Kovalick and Newton, 1988). Finally, private industries increasingly fear that they will be faced with unlimited liabilities if they develop and apply new, untested technologies which subsequently are found to be dangerous, even if the information establishing that danger is not revealed for decades after the technology is developed (Deisler, 1988). It appears that there is little opportunity for the United States to resolve its immense waste problems of the 1990s without major changes in existing waste management policies.

Policy Options for the 1990s

What are the options for addressing waste issues in the coming decade? We can substantially restructure the system by using government powers to mandate waste reduction; alternatively, we can largely maintain the existing system while attempting to alter public perceptions and to streamline the management and siting processes contained within it. The option of restructuring the system has numerous possibilities. Some authors (Murdock, Hamm, and Leistritz, 1983; Deisler, 1988) believe that a stronger role should be taken by the central government in mandating waste management and siting decisions. They maintain, for example, that if the political structure were to show greater resolve, it could simply override local and provincial concerns related to siting and follow actions aimed at ensuring societal security. The decisions could be made entirely on rational, technical grounds, and wastes would be managed and stored in the "safest" and least dangerous locations (from the standpoint of proximity to the largest population concentrations).

Unfortunately, we believe this option is no longer possible because of the past history of waste management and siting and because the location of storage facilities nearly always contains a political element (Lake, 1987). There is now simply too little public trust for such a policy to be implemented, and public sentiment is too strong for elected officials to ignore. This option, although intuitively appealing, is no longer feasible, if it ever was.

The option of reform is more feasible and appropriate. It is unlikely that the basic management responsibilities that have been established over more than two decades of environmental activity could or should be altered, but it is equally clear that unless public support can be increased, the problems of reducing, disposing of, and storing wastes cannot be adequately resolved. We thus maintain, with Peelle and Ellis (1987:74), that "what is needed [is] to create a different climate. Participation, opportunities to share and test information, negotiations (and possibly mediation) between affected parties, and economic incentives all must play a role in a new, more open, institutional framework." Given these conditions, the following policy changes should provide a means for the United States to improve its ability to manage its wastes: (1) Policymakers should recognize the commonality of issues underlying the management of different forms of wastes and should reduce or more effectively coordinate the number of agencies with responsibilities for waste management. (2) Policymakers must encourage waste reduction through incentives or by mandated waste reduction. And, (3) Legislators should consider establishing a common process for the siting of waste management facilities. The rationales for these recommendations, the social science research base supporting them, and their likely consequences are presented below and summarized in Table 23.1.

Recognizing Commonalities and Reducing Bureaucratic Involvement

An increasing body of literature (see Murdock, Hamm, and Leistritz, 1986; Freudenburg, 1987) points to a commonality of reactions related to waste management, the location of sites for toxic waste storage, and the central importance of social concerns to the siting process. Although public reactions to waste management and storage may vary depending on the wastes being managed (Halstead et al., 1984) and on the specific area being impacted, (Murdock, Hamm, and Leistritz, 1983, 1986), reactions of fear of uncertainty, of concern about equity, and of mistrust of waste management are relatively pervasive (Lake, 1987).

Whereas different types of technical expertise may be required to analyze the engineering and biological impacts of different forms of wastes, and

TABLE 23.1   Waste Problem Policy Alternatives

Revise the current system to:

1. Recognize the commonality of issues underlying the management of different forms of waste and reduce the number of agencies with responsibilities for waste management.
2. Encourage, promote, and mandate waste reduction in a limited set of areas.
3. Implement legislation to establish a common process for the siting of waste management and/or disposal facilities which should involve:

   - simultaneous consideration of multiple sites.
   - the early formation of a governing board composed of representatives of parties of interest to manage the siting process.
   - an agreed-upon process with specified steps and a commitment to completing all steps and to reaching a decision.
   - an open process with sharing of information and peer review of the technical analysis.
   - negotiation of a "contract of risk" that identifies those responsible and liable for costs for various types of risks and limits the extent and duration of responsibility and liability.
   - provision of compensation and mitigation for the siting area and joint monitoring by federal, state, industrial, and local parties at interest.
   - immutability of selection—that is, assurance that once the process has been fully and completely adhered to, the decision is essentially final.

numerous yet unresolved technical problems remain, the responsibilities of most agencies charged with overseeing waste management are primarily social and political in nature. Therefore the type of wastes to be disposed of and the technical analysis that must be completed during the siting process should not necessarily dictate what organization should be responsible. Policymakers should grant a limited number of agencies the responsibility for waste management to reduce problems of communication and responsiveness. The present system of overlapping, and in some cases (from the public's perspective) nearly indistinguishable, areas of responsibility, slows the process of resolving waste management issues and frustrates the public's desire to be involved in management decisions.

Promoting Waste Reduction

Researchers have extensively analyzed waste reduction methods, including recycling, to determine their impact on the public (see for example, Hazardous Materials Control Research Institute, 1983; Henstock, 1983) and private (see Campbell and Glenn, 1982) sectors in the United States and internationally (Cointreau et al., 1984). Although the U.S. population is growing relatively slowly, past patterns of growth in per capita waste production and the still expanding world population clearly suggest that the waste problem is unlikely to be resolved if the quantity, or at least the rate of growth, of wastes is not reduced. Since ongoing surveys show extensive public support for waste reduction (Lake, 1987), we should implement waste reduction measures.

Two alternatives should be evaluated. Studies on the use of water, energy, and other resources show that increasing costs can lead to conservation. Incentives to recycle (e.g., to sort wastes by type) can be created by either increasing costs for not recycling or reducing costs for recycling. A second option is to mandate waste reduction. Given the magnitude of the waste problem, legislation similar to that used to mandate standards for air emissions and automobile safety may be appropriate.

Establishing a Process for Siting Waste Storage and Disposal Facilities

Socioeconomic research on the siting of waste storage and disposal facilities shows that the process (rather than the type of project, characteristics of the area, etc.) is the key to resolving siting problems (Halstead et al., 1984; Lake, 1987). The *how* may be as important as *what* is to be done in determining whether or not waste sites can be obtained. Research in the areas of hazardous waste siting and socioeconomic impact assessment (Lake, 1987; Halstead et al., 1984; Murdock, Hamm, and Leistritz, 1986) suggests that many of the social conflicts surrounding the siting process may be addressed by increasing the participation of affected individuals.

Legislation should establish a procedure for selecting waste sites that addresses three key questions: Who should be involved? How should they be involved? And, what should be the elements of the process? We believe that, in general, this process should:

1. involve evaluation of multiple sites that are initially equally acceptable;
2. involve all known parties of interest from the very beginning and throughout the siting process;
3. be managed by a governing board composed of representatives of the parties of interest and given authority to locate a site;
4. require as a first step that the governing board establish a siting process with agreed-upon steps, specify time schedules for each step, and make a commitment that the process will result in a siting decision;
5. require close interaction between technical analysis staff and members of the board, open and complete sharing of all information produced at all stages of analysis, and peer review of the technical analysis by persons from outside the agency or entity doing the technical assessment;
6. ensure that the process includes procedures to establish responsibility for each potential area of risk associated with a site and to fix the time period over which liability and responsibility will be maintained; and
7. recognize that both long-term monitoring of the site and compensation and mitigation assistance for the residents living in the immediate area surrounding the site are likely to be necessary.

Analysis of other types of projects clearly shows (Murdock, Hamm, and Leistritz, 1983; Peelle and Ellis, 1987) that participation must involve all parties of interest from the very beginning and that the involvement must allow participants in the siting process to have a direct role in determining its results. Participants must be involved while there are still decisions to be made and alternatives to be considered, not after the fact as a justification for bureaucratic decisions already made. Although additional technical analysis conducted during the siting procedure may lead to the disqualification of some sites, the process should be established after an initial technical screening has been completed. In nearly all cases, even an initial screening is likely to identify several feasible alternatives. Limiting the process to evaluating a single site or using "strawmen" alternatives will likely lead to the failure of the process.

It is equally critical to ensure that all the parties of interest, including representatives from industry, federal and state agency personnel, local citizens from siting areas, owners of land in the siting areas, and others, be involved. To ensure participation, groups with proven abilities to sponsor involvement must be remunerated for expenses. The board may also need to assist in organizing some groups with direct concern for the siting area but who are inexperienced in interest-group politics.

The process must be an open one that has clearly specified steps. Technical and lay persons must share all, even preliminary-stage, information. Attempts to hold technical data until the plan is final inevitably lead to the perception that information is being withheld. On the other hand, sharing information not only leads to increased trust but also, because local persons often have thorough knowledge of the siting area, to valuable information for site evaluation and design (Peelle and Ellis, 1987).

The process must have an agreed-upon set of steps, but it must also be one that all parties know will proceed to a final decision. Perceptions that all steps have not been adequately completed (as in the case of the Nevada high-level nuclear waste decision) can undermine the process. In like manner, the inevitability of the decision must be maintained both to ensure that the process can be completed in a timely manner (and that a decision is made at all) and to ensure concerted involvement by all participants (Halstead et al., 1984).

The process must establish accountability for risks and for costs associated with risks. Different kinds of risks should be negotiated to determine who is responsible, for what period, and for what types of costs. Whether industry or local, state, or the federal government or other interests should be responsible should be negotiated among the members of the governing board. Discerning responsibility and liability both helps to assure that responsibility will be assumed and establishes limits that allow industry and government to assess their corporate or public risks and costs.

Finally, it is critical for participants to recognize that usually a waste disposal site will require long-term monitoring because some impacts are difficult to determine at a given time. They must also recognize those producing the wastes will likely be required to pay compensation and mitigation for those living in the immediate siting area. Past siting processes have usually required residents of a siting area to establish the need for mitigation and compensation. Reversing the expectation, such that compensation and mitigation would be considered as rights that must be shown not to be applicable, could help alleviate residents' concerns that their assumption of risks would not be recognized (Halstead et al., 1984).

In sum, policymakers must implement a new siting procedure in which all interested parties can fully participate and negotiate from the outset. Some may object to this process as too costly and time consuming. However, when we consider the total costs and time involved, including the extensive litigation resulting from the present process, we may find them to be less than those presently incurred. This process simply allows different parties to negotiate in a context where the expectations are clear, where compensation and monitoring are expected, and where good faith negotiations are required.

Conclusion

Waste management will be a major concern for the United States during the 1990s. Because of past waste management problems, residents generally distrust those who manage wastes and lack faith in the process of siting waste storage and disposal facilities. Thus, ways to reduce waste production and to store existing and future wastes without disproportionately and inequitably impacting rural and other groups disadvantaged by geographic location, population, or socioeconomic characteristics have become important issues. To address these issues, policies to reduce wastes and to reduce the number of agencies responsible for waste management must be a priority. Additionally, the management process should be made more accessible. It is also essential to establish a site selection process for waste storage and disposal facilities; the process must be fully participatory and must require good faith negotiations by all interested parties.

Congressional, state, and local legislative action is required to implement such changes. However, even larger changes in perspective may be necessary at the societal level. Managing wastes must become a concern of all society, not just federal, state, and local agencies or private concerns. Officials in agencies and industries involved in waste management and waste facility siting must recognize the legitimate right of others to become fully involved in both the management and the siting processes. Persons and groups with concerns about wastes must also be willing to become involved. A new agency may need to be established to provide the impetus and ongoing expertise to ensure that the agreed-upon procedures for the siting process are properly implemented.

In sum, the policy options presented here are both ambitious and idealistic. Because the present system is largely failing to resolve our waste problem, such options must be explored if we are to rebuild the public will to resolve the waste management problem in the United States.

References

Albrecht, S., and B. Chadwick. 1980. *Sociocultural Analysis for the Proposed Waste Isolation Pilot Plant.* Albuquerque, N.Mex.: Adcock and Associates.

Aldrich, H. E., and P. V. Marsden. 1988. "Environments and organization." In N. J. Smelser, ed., *Handbook of Sociology.* Beverly Hills, Calif.: Sage.

Bullard, C. W. 1987. "Issues in low-level radioactive waste management." *International Journal of Air Pollution Control and Hazardous Waste Management* 11(37):1337–1341.

————. 1988. "Management and control of modern technologies." *Technology in Society* 10:205–232.

Bullard, R. D. 1983. "Solid waste sites and the black Houston community." *Sociological Inquiry* 53(2–3):273–288.

Campbell, Monica E., and H. M. Glenn. 1982. *Profit from Pollution Prevention.* Toronto: Pollution Probe Foundation.

Cluett, C., C. Sawyer, M. Olsen, and D. Manninen. 1979. *Social and Economic Aspects of Nuclear Waste Management Activities: Impacts and Analytic Approaches.* Seattle: Battelle Human Affairs Research Center.

Cointreau, S. J., C. G. Gunnerson, J. M. Huls, and N. N. Seldman. 1984. *Recycling from Municipal Refuse.* Washington, D.C.: The World Bank.

Cook, E. 1982. "The role of history in the acceptance of nuclear power." *Social Science Quarterly* 63:3–15.

Deisler, P. 1988. "Hazardous waste facilities: Issues and concerns confronting the private sector user." Paper presented at the Houston Area Research Conference on New State Roles: Environment, Resources and the Economy. The Woodlands, Tex., November 13–16.

Freudenburg, W. R. 1987. "The density of acquaintanceship: An overlooked variable in community research." *American Journal of Sociology* 92(July):27–63.

Freudenburg, W. R., and E. A. Rosa. 1984. *Public Reaction to Nuclear Power: Are There Critical Masses?* AAAS Selected Symposium. Boulder, Colo.: Westview Press.

Frishman, S. 1988. "The federal nuclear waste policy act—Siting policy experiment gone astray." Paper presented at the Houston Area Research Conference on New State Roles: Environment, Resources and the Economy. The Woodlands, Tex., November 13–16.

Gladwin, T. N. 1980. "Patterns of environmental conflict over industrial facilities in the United States, 1970–78." *Natural Resources Journal* 20(April):243–274.

Halstead, J. M., R. A. Chase, S. H. Murdock, and F. L. Leistritz. 1984. *Socioeconomic Impact Management: Design and Implementation.* Boulder, Colo.: Westview Press.

Halstead, J. M., F. L. Leistritz, D. G. Rice, D. M. Saxowsky, and R. A. Chase. 1982. "Mitigating socioeconomic impacts of nuclear waste repository siting." A report to the Office of Nuclear Waste Isolation. Fargo, N.Dak.: North Dakota State University.

Hamilton, L. C. 1985. "Concern about toxic wastes: Three demographic predictors." *Sociological Perspectives* 28(4):463–486.

Hazardous Materials Control Research Institute. 1983. *Proceedings of the National Conference on Municipal and Industrial Sludge Utilization and Disposal.* Silver Spring, Md.: Hazardous Materials Control Research Institute.

Hebert, J. A., W. L. Rankin, P. C. Brown, C. R. Schuller, R. F. Smith, J. A. Goodnight, and H. E. Lippek. 1978. *Nontechnical Issues in Waste Management: Ethical, Institutional and Political Concerns.* Seattle: Battelle Human Affairs Research Centers.

Henstock, M. E. 1983. *Disposal and Recovery of Municipal Solid Waste.* London: Butterworths.

Kovalick, Walt, and M. Newton. 1988. "A practitioner's model for allocating environmental management responsibilities among levels of government." Paper presented at the Houston Area Research Conference on New State Roles: Environment, Resources and the Economy. The Woodlands, Tex., November 13–16.

Lake, Robert W. 1987. *Resolving Locational Conflict.* New Brunswick, N.J.: Rutgers University Press.

League of Women Voters. 1985. *The Nuclear Waste Primer: A Handbook for Citizens.* New York: Nick Lyons Books.

Murdock, S. H., and R. R. Hamm. 1986. "An assessment of the social and special effects of siting a low-level radioactive waste disposal facility in Texas: Phase II: County and community leader and resident analysis." A report to the Texas Low-Level Radioactive Waste Disposal Authority. College Station, Tex.: Texas Agricultural Experiment Station.

Murdock, S. H., R. R. Hamm, and F. L. Leistritz, eds. 1983. *Nuclear Waste: Socioeconomic Dimensions of Long-Term Storage.* Boulder, Colo.: Westview Press.

Murdock, S. H., R. R. Hamm, and F. L. Leistritz. 1986. "The state of socioeconomic impact analysis in the United States of America: Limitations and opportunities for alternative futures." *Journal of Environmental Management* 23:99–117.

_____. 1987. "The social and special effects of siting high-level and low-level radioactive waste disposal facilities in rural areas." Paper presented at the Conference on Health and Behavioral Impacts of Environmental Hazards. University of California Symposium on Environmental Psychology, May 14-15.

Peelle, E. 1980. *Social Impact Mitigation and Nuclear Waste Repository Siting.* Testimony before the Senate Subcommittee on Rural Development of the Committee on Agriculture, Nutrition, and Forestry. Washington, D.C.

Peelle, E., and R. Ellis. 1987. "Beyond the 'not-in-my-backyard' impasse." *Forum for Applied Research and Public Policy* (Fall):68–77.

Peters, T. 1981. "Ethical considerations surrounding nuclear repository siting and mitigation: A background paper." Prepared for Office of Nuclear Waste Isolation. Battelle Laboratories: Columbus, Ohio.

_____. 1988. "Whole and part: The tension between the common good and individual freedom." Paper presented at the Houston Area Research Conference on New State Roles: Environment, Resources and the Economy. The Woodlands, Tex., November 13–16.

Schilling, A. H., A. Harris, M. Lindell, A. Marcus, R. Perry, and M. Selvin. 1979. *Emergency Response in Transportation of Radioactive Materials: An Evaluation Methodology.* Seattle: Battelle Human Affairs Research Center.

Sorenson, J., J. Soderstrom, E. Copenhaver, S. Carnes, and R. Bolin. 1987. *Impacts of Hazardous Technology: The Psycho-Social Effects of Restarting TMI-1.* Albany, N.Y.: State University of New York Press.

Spencer, G. 1989. "Projections of the population of the United States, by age, sex and race: 1988 to 2080." In *Current Population Reports: Population Estimates and Projections*, P-25(1018). Washington, D.C.: U.S. Bureau of the Census.

U.S. Department of Energy. 1988. *Spent Fuel and Radioactive Waste Inventories, Projection and Change.* Washington, D.C.: U.S. Government Printing Office.

U.S. Environmental Protection Agency (U.S. EPA). 1988. *National Priorities List Fact Book.* Washington, D.C.: U.S. Government Printing Office.

_____. 1987. *Characterization of Municipal Solid Waste in the U.S., 1986 to 2000.* Prairie Village, Kans.: Franklin Associates, Ltd. (1986). Cited in U.S. Bureau of the Census, Statistical Abstract of the United States. Table 335.

Weber, Susan, ed. 1988. *USA by Numbers: A Statistical Portrait.* Washington, D.C.: Zero Population Growth, Inc.

24
Telematics and Rural Development

Don A. Dillman

The major telematics policy issues facing rural America are, first, developing a telematics infrastructure that will adequately support job creation and other rural development goals and, second, encouraging use of that infrastructure to improve the economic and social well-being of rural people. To not accomplish these goals virtually assures further, and perhaps unnecessary, rural population decline as well as decline in many rural people's incomes and life chances.

Telematics is the joining together of telecommunications, broadcast media, and computer technologies into a single infrastructure for developing, sending, receiving, sorting, and utilizing information. This convergence of technologies, made possible by revolutions in computer power and transmission technologies, in combination with the increasing digitization of information, is one of the great macrotrends of our time.

We use the term telematics, rather than telecommunications, telephones, or computers, because of the blurring of distinctions that results from progressive digitization.

> Digitization makes communication from persons to machines, between machines, and even from machines to persons, as easy as it is between persons. Also blurred are the distinctions among information types; numbers, words, pictures, and sounds, and eventually tastes, odors, and possibly even sensations. . . .
> In this way digitization promises to transform current diverse forms of information into a generalized medium for processing and exchange by the social system, much as, centuries ago, the institution of common currencies and exchange rates began to transform local markets into a single world economy. (Beniger, 1986:25–26)

To focus on either telecommunications or computerization without the other is similar to discussing freeways although ignoring cars and trucks. The full meaning of the technological developments relating to one of them can only be expressed in conjunction with developments relating to the other. Digitization is the common language that increasingly makes tele-communications and computerization operable and inseparable in their practical application.

Telematics is important to rural development because the object of its development is a resource (i.e., information) that is increasingly being substituted for energy, labor, natural resources, and time in the production of goods and services, as well as consumption activities (Dillman, 1985). An example is the computer-aided design that allows production of auto-mobiles that are hundreds of pounds lighter, far more fuel-efficient, and less likely to break down than previous models and that indicate via digital displays and sounds when servicing is needed. Telematics makes possible instant air travel reservations and seat assignments because thousands of fares can be processed quickly; the programs assure full loads and therefore more efficient airline operations. Telematics also undergirds development of the global economy, allowing businesses in dozens of countries to compete for U.S. customers. Telematics is both the originator and controller of just-in-time delivery and outsourcing (purchase of components, even very complex ones for which there is little tolerance for error from external suppliers) that replace warehouses and in-house production. Telematics allows the use of remotely located software to retool machines for producing very small production runs on a demand basis, thus eliminating the resource-consuming need for warehouse storage and transfers.

Telematics is having an impact on rural America because it is changing the rules governing who can produce what and where. A downward trend in the proportion of our labor force needed in traditional rural occupations, such as agriculture and manufacturing, and an increase in the proportion involved in information-based services are a result of the application of telematics (Cleveland, 1985). Telematics also makes possible *telework*, that is, work performed occasionally or entirely away from the office or factory that utilizes the output of one's work. It also changes opportunities for farmers from the mass production of undifferentiated commodities to the possibility of tailoring production for niche markets (Dillman, 1990; Kenney et al., 1989).

Until recently, rural development professionals have mostly ignored tel-ematics as an important issue for rural development (Dillman and Beck, 1988). There are several reasons. First, the traditional jobs in resource extraction and utilization were thought to be relatively unaffected by tel-ematics developments. The growing and harvesting of mass-produced com-modities, from corn to wheat, were seen as not subject to much change that might result from the use of computers, better telephone lines, or faster access to information. In a sense, this position is correct, so long as all farmers attempt to grow the same commodity in the same unchanging way; however, that presumption no longer seems true (Dillman, 1990).

Second, service jobs were perceived as unimportant or impractical in rural areas unless they served locally based industries and people. The idea that services could export to other regions of the country, or even the world, was thought to be unrealistic, especially if it relied on the untested concept of working long distance, that is, through telecommuting. This assumption has also been questioned (Beyers et al., 1986).

Third, rural development professionals have focused their attention on other more visible kinds of infrastructure deficits. Rural communities have the country's worst roads, poorest bridges, most inadequate sewage systems, poorest medical services, and most limited access to capital. Continued population decline threatens the existence of school districts and often restricts the available educational opportunities to high school or less.

Fourth, telematics were viewed as a private sector issue. Inadequate or broken-down telephone lines are seen as the problem of the telephone company and not of local, state, or even national officials.

Finally, rural development professionals' concerns about problems such as the static on telephone lines, which restricts their use for facsimile messages, and the lack of computers and computer skills seem minor when compared to the highly visible and far more understandable concerns of rural communities. While washed-out bridges are clearly visible, poor quality telephone lines requiring that facsimile communication proceed at a very low rate (which is more costly and impractical) and the lack of digital switching (which prevents advanced telecommunication activities) are mostly invisible and, to many, incomprehensible.

Prior to 1989, telematics had not surfaced as a rural development issue for national debate. However, in 1989 the U.S. Senate approved a bill (S.1036) known as the Rural Partnership Act that had at its core a number of telematics issues. Although not yet acted on by the House of Representatives, this bill will expand the mission of the Rural Electric Administration (REA) to include more responsibility for rural telephone system improvements; will provide REA-administered incentives for telematics development for rural schools, universities, hospitals, physicians, and business telecommunications centers in order to improve the quality of telecommunications service and computer networks; and will address the continuation of toll-rate averaging as a cornerstone of universal service. This bill stands as important recognition that telematics makes a difference to rural development. This national effort follows a number of state policy efforts whereby states have examined the effects of telecommunications issues on rural communities (see Niles, 1989).

The Policy Context

A number of considerations have coalesced to give impetus to concern about the development and utilization of telematics for rural development. Individually and collectively these issues are giving rise to the deliberate consideration of telematics-based rural development efforts.

Rural Areas Are in Decline

In 1950, about half of the U.S. population lived on farms, in rural open country, and in towns of less than 2,500 persons beyond the suburban fringe. By 1987 that percentage had dropped about in half to 28 percent. In the 1970s, rural growth was temporarily renewed as some retirees, back-to-the-land urban refugees, and others moved to small towns, but that trend was short lived. This migration to rural areas slightly exceeded out-migration at the beginning of the 1980s, broke even in 1982/83, and has since reversed. Net migration to urban areas was over 600,000 in 1985/86 and close to 1,000,000 in the next year (Brown et al., 1988).

The decline in agriculture has been most persistent and significant. From 1945 to 1970, 120,000 farms were lost per year, with a farm population loss of 600,000 people per year. The proportion of the rural population consisting of farmers and their families declined from 15 percent in 1950 to less than 2 percent in 1987. Less than 500 of the nation's 2,443 rural counties are now considered farming dependent, that is, counties where farming is the source of 20 percent or more of labor and proprietor income (Parker et al., 1989).

Rural areas of the United States were settled precisely because natural resources (i.e., farmland, forests, and minerals) were located there. Industries in agriculture, forestry, and minerals have benefited greatly from mechanization. Significant portions of the nation's labor force no longer need to be located near these resources. In essence, U.S. job creation has become unhooked from natural resources (Drucker, 1986). Manufacturing, which once spilled over into rural areas in search of lower wages, has declined from 50 percent of the labor force in 1920 to approximately 20 percent today.

Indicative of the changing fortunes of rural America is the recent proposal in *Planning* magazine to deprivatize the Great Plains from North Dakota to Texas and create a public commons, based on the belief that much of the Great Plains will become nearly totally deserted over the next generation. For environmental and economic reasons, the authors recommend recreation of the nineteenth century "buffalo commons" (Popper and Popper, 1987). Similarly, according to a *Wall Street Journal* article, a Kansas State University team has recommended a "triage" that would gradually write off many small towns (Farney, 1989).

Desirability of Rural Growth

Prediction of the inevitable decline of rural places, especially those farthest from the urban rings of growth that now encircle America's major cities, has not been well received by many. This too is an important contextual factor for the use of telematics to accomplish rural development. Some residents of small communities hang on tenaciously, hoping that a means of revival will be found. This reaction is understandable, considering their limited resources, low property values, and lack of explicit alternatives. Representative Glen English has voiced a frequently offered concern that all U.S. citizens will be forced to live in metropolitan areas if action is not taken (Associated Press, 1989). Although polls show that people prefer to live in more rural areas than they currently do, population distribution has not been a priority for public policy debate (Dillman, 1979).

Whether it is desirable to intervene in order to maintain the existence of a rural population and where that population should be located are major policy issues that are unlikely to emerge in the near future. Yet, the specter of urban pollution, traffic congestion, cities with marginal water supplies, and related concerns makes desirability of rural growth an issue that remains just below the surface of what many would describe as a simmering kettle; these urban problems could muster interest in the telematics approach to rural development.

The desirability of rural growth has also been questioned. Providing services (e.g., mail delivery, water lines, fire protection, and telephones) to people who live in rural areas probably costs more than providing service to residents in medium-sized cities. In addition, the labor of people located far from metropolitan labor markets is less valuable to employers than if employees were to move to an urban location. Thus, it can be argued that protecting people's rights to live in rural areas is economically inefficient and, therefore, undesirable.

Requirements for Rural Job Growth

Agriculture employs only a small minority (9 percent) of rural people, while manufacturing employs 17 percent. Surprisingly, nearly two-thirds of the rural workers are employed in services. For the U.S. economy as a whole, all the net growth since 1979 has occurred in the service sector. Despite the stagnation in population growth in rural areas, some two million service jobs have been created in rural regions since 1979. Between 1979 and 1986, rural service jobs increased by 14 percent, while jobs decreased in the agricultural (13 percent), mining (13.9 percent), and manufacturing (7.1 percent) sectors (Parker et al., 1989).

Porat estimates that for the U.S. economy as a whole in the year 2000 information, knowledge, and education jobs will exceed two-thirds of the labor force; other services will comprise another 10 percent; and manufacturing, commerce, and agricultural jobs will decline to perhaps a fourth of the total (Cleveland, 1985). The inevitable implication is that if rural areas are to grow, they must capture service and information-intensive jobs at an increasing rate.

Underlying these changes is yet another macrotrend, the evolution away from a nationally oriented, mass-production economy toward a globally oriented, consumer-driven economy. This trend has enormous implications for virtually all U.S. business enterprises (Dillman and Beck, 1988). American business of the midtwentieth century succeeded by learning to produce and distribute the same product throughout the U.S. economy. The mass production of thousands, even millions, of nearly identical standard products, from Ford cars to Kleenex, resulted in low prices for U.S. consumers. Competition from other countries for U.S. consumers was minimal. The economic efficiencies which resulted from mass production of standardized products made it possible to build a production-marketing-consumption structure that gave consumers little choice, unless they were willing to pay extremely high prices for customized designs.

The global economy, in which companies from many countries compete to sell similar products and services throughout the world, places a premium on responding to specific consumer desires and niche markets. Telematics is both the precursor and the glue that holds together our post-mass-society economic system. Computers, facsimile machines, and the ability to send software instructions by telephone lines make possible the outsourcing of component parts from dozens of countries and their just-in-time delivery to assembly plants anywhere in the world. Telephone orders are connected to computer-driven production equipment that can be retooled through software instructions to make efficient production runs of a few identical products. Such retooling can sometimes be done at less cost per unit of production than it once could be done for hundreds of identical products.

Just as important, countries have learned to export services from one region of the country to another. Companies use overnight delivery, computer networks, and facsimile machines to obtain data processing, legal assistance, travel agent services, credit consultation, and other services from distant locations as easily as they once obtained these services locally. For example, it is estimated that 75 percent of Washington state's businesses have foreign competitors (Washington State Economic Development Board, 1988).

Long distance communication between computers is as much the signature of modern business as the moving assembly line and its fine division of labor were of the mass production era. Whereas in 1981 the United States had 5.9 million computer workstations, that number increased to 33 million in 1987 and will likely be 60 million by the mid-1990s (Adler, 1988). This transition carries with it the implication that nine out of ten white-collar jobs will have computer workstations in the mid-1990s. Far more workers now know the difference between data base and word processing programs than know the difference between socket and crescent wrenches.

We are approaching a time when businesses that are not electronically connected to other businesses will not be competitive. Just as important, a company's telephones and computers must be hooked into the telecommunication network. A company providing goods under contract for other companies will be unable to compete if it is not accessible by error-free transmissions via facsimile machines and, perhaps, by even more advanced services like 24-hour voice mail. The archetype of business of this new economic order takes small orders and uses software to retool equipment quickly to produce small production runs that can be shipped in small quantities, often overnight, to multiple destinations. In fact, the products being shipped are often services rather than manufactured goods (Dillman, Beck, and Allen, 1989).

So long as natural resources provided the employment base of rural communities there was little choice of location. It was necessary to bring to that rural community whatever resources were needed to grow crops, mine minerals, and cut trees. If rural communities are to prosper in the information age, they will need both the materials to be processed (which may be information) and the tools needed to do that. There is no inherent reason these "new" raw materials and the means for their processing should flow to rural communities (Dillman, Beck, and Allen, 1989).

Emergence of a Telematics-based Theory of Rural Development

In a seminal article on the emergence of the global information society, Harlan Cleveland holds out the tantalizing possibility that the telematics revolution will end the tyranny of rural space. He describes the passing of remoteness as one of the great unheralded macrotrends of our extraordinary time: "Distant farmsteads can be connected to the central cortex of their commodity exchanges, political authorities, and global markets. The fusion of rapid microprocessing in global telecommunications presents nearly all of us with the choice between relevance and remoteness" (1985:27).

While no systematic theory of the connection between telematics and rural development has been put forth, five important elements have been articulated. One element is recognition of the increasing substitution of information for other resources in the production and distribution of goods and services (Dillman, 1985). A second is the increased reliance on service jobs as a source of rural employment and the fact that services can be exported from a region (Beyers et al., 1986).

A third is the long-term trend of declining transmission costs for telecommunications and the ease of inexpensively expanding capacity for such connections through fiber optics (Pool, 1980). It can now be argued that the telecommunications distance between an urban office building and a remote rural community is no greater than the distance between adjacent office buildings. Not since the advent of the voice telephone has there been such an increase in our potential for overcoming the friction of rural space (Dillman, 1985).

A fourth element is the development of overnight package delivery services that reach virtually all regions of the United States, thereby complementing the telematics delivery of information with the physical delivery. This capability is now being expanded to second-day delivery throughout much of the world.

A fifth element is the observed trend toward greater job creation by small, rather than large, businesses (Birch, 1987). One reason offered for this trend is the enhanced ability of small organizations through telematics to obtain and utilize information. Small businesses can fit into small rural communities without changing the fundamental character of such communities or creating unrealistic demands on the infrastructure.

That these potential elements of a telematics theory of rural development can be systematically integrated is given credence by the increasing number of examples of information-intensive work being located in rural places (Niles, 1989). Examples include the headquarters of a national food store chain in Park City, Utah; national software and consulting firms in Ketchum, Idaho; and a telemarketing firm in Breda, Iowa.

An integrated theory of telematics-based rural development remains to be accomplished. Yet, there is sufficient promise of its development and application that policy discussions are occurring in state agencies and legislatures throughout the United States.

Inadequate Telecommunications Infrastructure

Rural America does not have the telecommunications infrastructure to ensure rural development (Dillman, Beck, and Allen, 1989; Parker et al., 1989). Residents of the rural countryside are significantly more likely to have party lines, which prevent operation of computer modems, than are residents of towns and cities, and they are less likely to have computers (Dillman, Scott, and Allen, 1987). In some counties, as many as half of the farmers have party lines, and conversion to private lines often requires much higher rates.

Digital switching, the basic technological requirement for computers to talk to one another (modems, facsimile machines, etc.), is not available in many rural communities, a situation that, although changing rapidly, will not be entirely overcome for many years. Regardless of the presence of digital switching, many rural areas are served by old telephone lines and equipment, which cause noisy connections and interference with data transmission. Poor lines and equipment can delay transmission for facsimile machines or computer modems and therefore increase costs.

Trunkline connections, the long distance path out of a community, sometimes are a bottleneck. The design of these connection points may limit the effectiveness of locally available modern equipment and restrict the quantity and quality of long distance calls below what is actually demanded.

From insurance agencies to car repair, services available via routine local calls in metropolitan areas often require long distance calls from rural communities. In Washington State, for example, a fourth of the residents in the rural countryside must make long distance calls to reach the community they depend on most for goods and services.

People and businesses can access more and more national data networks and services to obtain useful information. Such networks typically provide access through local calls made within major cities. However, rural residents usually must make a long distance call to access networks not offering toll-free lines, increasing their cost by several times.

In addition, rural communities are substantially less likely to have access to alternative long distance carriers, which may result in higher telephone service costs. The cellular telephone, now available in most cities, is not yet available in most rural areas and, because of the cost, is unlikely to be available in some locales for many years. Other advanced services, like voice mail and video conferencing, are far from becoming a reality for most rural Americans.

Policy Questions

Development of a rural telematics infrastructure that will adequately support rural job creation and other rural development goals involves a number of more specific considerations. Each of these areas of concern involves choices, posed here as specific policy questions.

What Is an Acceptable Level of Telematics Infrastructure?

When the telephone came to rural America, attaining inexpensive universal coverage rather than quality service was emphasized (Pool, 1980). Much of that infrastructure is now antiquated, with lines too noisy to carry facsimile messages. The lack of digital switching prevents the availability of advanced telephone services and computer-to-computer transmissions that are increasingly important to their operation. An emerging market orientation, which implies that each user of telecommunications services should provide full cost of those services, threatens subscribers in rural areas, where the density of users is far less than in cities. For example, in Washington state "suburban mileage" charges cause single-party service to cost many times what subscribers within the city limits pay for a similar service (Washington Utilities and Transportation Commission, 1989). At the same time, it is not reasonable to assume that the advanced services available in downtown Chicago, where there are thousands of subscribers, can be made available immediately to every remote rural subscriber. The policy question is, What minimal standard of service should be available?

Parker et al. (1989) have identified 10 policy goals for the provision of rural telephone service:

1. Make voice telephone service available to everyone.
2. Make single-party access to the public switch telephone network available to everyone.
3. Improve the quality of telephone service sufficiently to allow rapid and reliable transmission of facsimile documents and data.
4. Provide rural telephone users with equal access to competitive long distance carriers.
5. Provide rural telephone users with local access to value-added data networks.
6. Provide 911 emergency service with automatic number identification in rural areas.
7. Expand mobile (cellular) telephone service.
8. Make available touchtone and custom calling services, including such services as three-way calling, call forwarding, and call waiting.
9. Make voice message and other services available via local phone calls.
10. Enable rural telephones as carriers to provide the telecommunications and information services that become generally available in urban areas.

Other problems also exist, such as the necessity of calling long distance to access most community services and value-added data networks. It is less a single telecommunications problem that threatens rural America than the cumulative deprivation of a number of deficiencies, all of which must receive attention (Dillman, Beck, and Allen, 1989).

However, the improvement of a rural telecommunications system can only be accomplished over a long time. Reasonable short-term goals are to complete universal service and single-party service, install digital switching, and provide basic touchtone service to all rural households. Rural communities also need access to fiber optics and other capabilities now becoming standard for urban businesses.

What Is Needed to Assure That a Rural Telematics Infrastructure Will Be Utilized?

It is one thing to have an information gateway with instant access to anywhere in the world; it is quite another to use this gateway for a business or consumer purpose. Discussion of what level of services to provide to rural places is inevitably sobered by the prospect of providing services that no one is likely to use. An example of the dilemma is where to provide access (points of presence) for fiber optic lines. Even regional centers of 20,000 or more people may not economically justify the cost of these expensive connections. Yet rural communities already find that they cannot compete for new businesses which require direct access to fiber optic telephone lines.

This issue is especially problematic for rural communities. The use of telematics in business involves fundamentally new ways of making a living and managing a business with which rural people and places have little experience, such as relying on the selling of services to distant locations as a means of making a living. Working on a computer workstation at a remote site and accessing information and market opportunities from data banks (i.e., telecommuting) are also strikingly unusual behaviors for most rural people. In communities where success has been associated with farming, mining, and logging, these business activities may indeed seem strange. Local people lack the experience as well as the daily exposure to innovative entrepreneurs from whom they might learn how to make a living in these new ways. Traditionally, rural communities and people have been slower to adopt new technologies and behaviors than have urban ones (Fisher, 1978), and it would be surprising if telematics proved to be an exception.

One way of increasing the likelihood that rural people and places benefit from telematics is to create demonstration products on the economic and social uses of telematics, much as field demonstration projects were used earlier in this century to encourage farmers to adopt new crop production methods. Such an approach has already been used in remote Scandinavian communities where "telecottages" were established to provide people with learning opportunities on a personal computer and to demonstrate how telecommuting could be utilized to earn a living (Qvortrup, 1989).

Fundamentally, the issue of encouraging economic use of advanced telecommunications may be more of a problem than is the actual installation of digital switching, clean lines, and universal touchtone service in rural communities.

What Are the Limitations of Telematics in Rural Development?

We are well beyond the question of whether telematics makes a difference for rural development. Telemarketing jobs are now located in rural Maine, Iowa, Nebraska, and other states. Farmers use telematics to check yields of just-completed harvests of commodities in other countries in order to make immediate planting decisions. Rural druggists are required to order their supplies through computers. Software development firms, telephone order companies, and insurance firms, all highly dependent on telecommunications, exist in many rural locales. These businesses leave little question that high-quality telematics is essential to many rural businesses. Still unanswered is the question of how critical telematics is for the full array of rural businesses. This question needs to be answered in order to make national decisions on telematics investment.

What Institutional Barriers Need to Be Removed?

A number of institutional barriers hinder improvement of rural telematics infrastructure. For example, it would likely be much cheaper to provide remote rural households with radio-based telephone service rather than stringing ground connections to them. Yet current regulatory structures may discourage telephone companies from using that approach. For example, "rate of return" regulations may encourage larger costs in order to have a larger investment upon which to base profit calculations.

In addition, relatively few rural homes outside of incorporated areas have cable television, an important part of a comprehensive telematics infrastructure. Currently, telephone companies in most locations are prevented by law from providing both telephone and television service. That makes it impossible to realize the savings that would result from running only one set of line connections, rather than two separate ones, to peoples' homes. Learning and business video conferencing applications might also be increased through shared connections.

Yet another issue is the effect of large, urban-based corporations bypassing the public network. Rural people and small businesses seem unlikely to get access through bypass and in the long run will be dependent on the public network. The more that prime accounts of large companies switch to private networks, a trend that could be encouraged by current regulatory practices, the more likely the public access network will lack capital to upgrade its infrastructure.

Resolving these issues will be time consuming and difficult. Only since 1984 has a major move toward deregulation of the nation's telephone system been in force, and many regulatory issues are yet to be addressed adequately.

What Is an Appropriate Balance Between Telematics-based Rural Development and Place Development?

Telematics strategies for development can be created that encourage people to remain in rural places and be economically productive. Alternatively, it is possible to emphasize improving people's knowledge and work skills and to facilitate their movement to urban locations where the work they do will contribute more to the country's economic production and, individually, they will receive higher pay.

A human capital improvement strategy that is nonplace-oriented will likely emphasize bringing telematics to rural schools and improving training opportunities. A place-oriented strategy, on the other hand, would help businesses learn to use telematics to be more productive and would encourage the decentralization of job opportunities in the United States. The two strategies are not mutually exclusive. However, it is clear that one can be emphasized more than the other.

What Are the Linkages Between Telematics and Other Rural Development Prerequisites?

Telematics alone will not solve the development problems of rural America. Water, sewers, airports, financial services, venture capital, and numerous other needs affect the ability of rural places to grow and prosper. It is difficult to imagine telematics investment having a major effect unless overnight delivery services and access to investment capital are available.

A recent European study suggests that telecommunications investment will make a greater difference in moderately rural areas than in the most rural areas (Analysys, Ltd., 1989). In this study involving several European countries, rural was defined both in terms of remoteness and peoples' income levels. We need to learn how telematics investment interfaces with other kinds of investments and the relative emphasis that should be placed on each.

Can Market Forces Be Relied on to Encourage Rural Telematics Investment?

Earlier in this century the Rural Electric Administration (REA) was created to provide electricity to rural areas. Utility companies, at the time, felt there was little likelihood of gaining an adequate return on their investment, which was required for bringing electricity to sparsely located rural households and businesses. It remains to be seen whether a similar situation will face telecommunications companies challenged with modernizing the rural telecommunications system.

The heart of this issue is what policies will encourage or discourage rural investment. On the one hand, toll-rate averaging favors rural areas. Suburban mileage charges for the installation of equipment, on the other hand, penalize rural areas. As the march toward deregulation of the nation's telecommunications continues, new policies will inevitably emerge. Differential rural versus urban effects therefore need to be examined.

Are Telematics-based Rural Growth Strategies Consistent with Residential Preferences?

Examples abound of individuals choosing rural places to live and then using facsimile machines, modems, and overnight delivery to do work that could not have been done from such remote locations in the past. The examples include small businesses, telemarketers, consultants, newsletter editors, and library indexers. Medium-sized enterprises ranging from the Rocky Mountain Chocolate Factory in Durango, Colorado, to Mrs. Fields' Cookies in Park City, Utah, have found it possible to operate their far-flung businesses from rural places where key personnel prefer to live.

For the first time in this century it seems plausible that residential preferences can drive the locational decisions of many individuals. This raises the prospect of rural community development organizations seeking new residents who will bring their jobs with them.

The possibility of residential preferences having an increased influence on such decisions also raises the prospect of a mismatch between certain declining rural areas and growth prospects. Rural seashores, mountains, forests, and lakes seem, on the surface, to be attractive locations for new residents. Traditional farming regions and the great plains seem, on the surface, less attractive.

We know relatively little about residential preferences and how to capitalize on them for rural development purposes. The precise policy issue involves first understanding preferences and then determining whether they might be capitalized on in designing rural development strategies.

Conclusion

Many, if not most, advocates of rural development have been used to thinking of rural development infrastructure in terms of such physical facilities as highways, airports, industrial parks, bridges, and sewers. It represents a substantial leap to think of elements of a telematics infrastructure—for example, digital switches, fiber optics, and facsimile machines—as having similar relevance. Both sets of factors can make a substantial difference in the creation of jobs and the quality of life in rural America.

A book sponsored by the Rural Sociology Society, *Rural Society in the U.S.: Issues for the 1980s* (Dillman and Hobbs, 1982), did not mention telecommunications or telematics as an important issue for research. As an editor of that volume, I can recall no suggestion by any chapter authors or reviewers that such issues should be included. Now, ten years later, telematics has emerged as an important aspect of understanding the future prospects for rural America. The overriding policy issues are whether rural America gets an adequate telecommunications infrastructure and whether this infrastructure will be used for rural development.

Notes

Appreciation is expressed to Edwin Parker and John Niles for their comments on an earlier version of this chapter.

References

Adler, Richard. 1988. "The importance of communications and information systems to rural development in the United States." Background paper for Aspen Institute Conference, Aspen, Colorado, July 24–27, 1988. Menlo Park, Calif.: Institute for the Future.

Analysys, Ltd. 1989. "A study of the economic implications of stimulating applications of IT&T in rural areas." Report No. 89271. Brussels, Belgium: Analysys, Ltd.

Associated Press. 1989. "Rural America struggling to survive." *Daily News.* Pullman, Wash., August 19.

Beniger, James R. 1986. *The Control Revolution.* Cambridge, Mass., and London: Harvard University Press.

Beyers, William, John Tofflemire, Harriet Stranahan, and Erik Johnsen. 1986. "The service economy: Understanding growth of producer services in the Central Puget Sound region." Seattle: Central Puget Sound Economic Development District.

Birch, David. 1987. "The rise and fall of everybody." *INC.* September.

Brown, David, J. N. Reid, H. Bluestone, D. A. McGranahan, and S. M. Mazie. 1988. *Rural Economic Development in the 1980's: Prospects for the Future.* Washington, D.C.: U.S. Department of Agriculture.

Cleveland, Harlan. 1985. "The twilight of hierarchy: Speculations on the global information society." *Public Administration Review* 45:20–29.

Dillman, Don A. 1979. "Residential preferences, quality of life, and the population turnaround." *American Journal of Agricultural Economics* 61(5):960–966.

———. 1985. "The social impacts of information technologies in rural North America." *Rural Sociology* 50(1):1–26.

———. 1990. "Information technologies in agriculture: The United States experience." In M. Harkin, ed., *Information Technology in Agriculture, Food and Rural Development.* Luxembourg: Commission of the European Communities.

Dillman, Don A., and Donald M. Beck. 1988. "Information technologies and rural development in the 1990s." *The Journal of State Government* 6(1):29–38.

Dillman, Don A., Donald M. Beck, and John C. Allen. 1989. "Rural barriers to job creation remain, even in today's information age." *Rural Development Perspectives,* pp. 21–27.

Dillman, Don A., and Daryl J. Hobbs. 1982. *Rural Society in the U.S.: Issues for the 1980s.* Boulder, Colo.: Westview Press.

Dillman, Don A., Lesli Peterson Scott, and John Allen. 1987. Telecommunications in Washington: A Statewide Survey. Technical Report. Pullman, Wash.: Washington State University, Social and Economic Sciences Research Center.

Drucker, Peter F. 1986. "The changed world economy." *Foreign Affairs* 64:764–791.

Farney, Dennis. 1989. "On the Great Plains, life becomes a fight for water and survival." *Wall Street Journal,* August 16, p. 1ff.

Fisher, Claude. 1978. "Urban-to-rural diffusion of opinions in contemporary America." *American Journal of Sociology* 84(1):151–157.

Kenney, Martin, et al. 1989. "Midwestern agriculture and U.S. Fordism." *Sociologia Ruralis* 29(2):131–148.

Niles, John. 1989. *Advanced Telecommunications for Economic Development.* A report prepared for the Washington State Economic Development Board. Olympia, Wash.: WSEDB.

Parker, Edwin B., Heather E. Hudson, Don A. Dillman, and Andrew D. Roscoe. 1989. *Rural America in the Information Age: Telecommunications Policy for Rural Development.* Lanhorn, Md.: The Aspen Institute and University Press of America.

Pool, Ithiel de Sola. 1980. "Communication technology and land use." *Annals of the American Academy of Political and Social Science* 451(September):1–12.

Popper, Deborah Epstein, and Frank J. Popper. 1987. "The Great Plains from dust to dust." *Planning,* pp. 12–18.

Qvortrup, Lars. 1989. "The Nordic telecottages: Community teleservice centers for rural regions." *Telecommunications Policy* (March).

Washington State Economic Development Board. 1988. *Washington Works Worldwide: Positioning Ourselves to Compete in the New Global Economy.* Olympia, Wash.: WSEDB.

Washington Utilities and Transportation Commission. 1989. *The status of telecommunications infrastructure in Washington state industry.* Vol. 2. Olympia, Wash: WUTC.

25

Rethinking Biotechnology Policy

Frederick H. Buttel

Less than a decade ago biotechnology was virtually an unknown notion in the rural policy community. Since that time, biotechnology has become one of the major modalities through which policy toward rural and agricultural America is being formed. Current policy approaches to biotechnology are very limited. These policies are largely confined to how to best encourage as much public and private biotechnology research and development (R&D) as possible in order to enhance national economic competitiveness and to help states and other subnational units capture high-technology investment and employment. More fundamental policy issues must be addressed before the academic and national policy communities can be assured that current approaches are appropriate. These issues include the following:

1. What are our national goals in the agricultural, food, and fiber sectors, and how can R&D, in general, and biotechnology R&D, in particular, contribute to meeting these goals?
2. What has been (or must be) sacrificed in order to pursue biotechnology R&D for the food, agriculture, and fiber sectors, and with what consequences?
3. How are public agricultural R&D priorities determined? What are likely to be the major agricultural biotechnology R&D priorities of private sector firms? What are the implications of private R&D priorities for public research institutions?
4. What are likely to be the social impacts of new biotechnologies in the food, agriculture, and fiber sectors and on rural America? What are the implications of these social impacts for research policy and priorities?

The Policy Context

Biotechnology has become the classic case of means-ends confusion in policy discourse. Biotechnology, which logically should be a *means* for achieving particular goals, is typically seen as an end in itself; in a strong sense, biotechnology is a solution in search of problems. For example, a recent policy statement by the Joint Council on Food and Agricultural Sciences (1987:vi), the major agricultural research policymaking body in the U.S., included "expand biotechnology and its applications" as the second most important of eight major priorities of U.S. public agricultural research. Others listed were maintenance and preservation of water quality, sustenance of soil productivity, and preservation of germ plasm and genetically improved plants. Earlier, in 1984, basic biotechnology research was considered by the Joint Council to be the number one priority for the food and agricultural sciences (1984:iv).

The Joint Council's prioritization efforts typify the policy confusion that abounds in the agricultural research and science policy communities—a belief that biotechnology is an end in itself. Means-ends confusion in biotechnology R&D policymaking is by no means confined to the Joint Council. The stated aims of the land-grant universities (LGUs) and state agricultural experiment stations that have established major biotechnology research programs lead one to believe that their major reason for establishing such programs is, simply, to have them (Buttel, 1986a).

Social Forces Affecting Biotechnology R&D Policy

Why has there been such means-ends confusion in agricultural policymaking? Among the factors involved have been a number of material and ideological trends that have combined to displace social goal discourse with technical and ideological discourse. Several of the more important trends are examined below.

First, the rise of biotechnology in agricultural research occurred at a distinctive moment in the development of the U.S. agricultural research system. As the biotechnology era began, the U.S. land-grant system had just begun to experience a decline in the real value of its public research funding, and land-grant research administrators were keen to restore their funding levels to those enjoyed in the early and mid-1970s. Biotechnology seemed especially promising for doing so, since it offered opportunities for expansion of both public and corporate research funding. Also, beginning with the Pound Report in the early 1970s (National Research Council, 1972), the land-grant system had been on the defensive for its lack of basic biological research. The potential of biotechnology in agricultural research presented an attractive opportunity to address the basic science critics of the land-grant system. Finally, the early 1980s were a period of considerable hype of biotechnology and other high technologies. While some of this hype was a sincere expression of scientific excitement about the potentials of this new technology, much of it consisted of self-interested public relations activities by biotechnology firms directed toward selling stock and attracting investors and by scientists and research administrators seeking to attract funding. In sum, the conditions were propitious for a massive shift of LGU research resources into biotechnology (e.g., as documented by Hansen et al., 1986).

Second, there has been a discernible trend over the past two decades toward greater international competition via technological R&D. Gilpin (1987) stresses that technological competition is one of the defining features of what he calls the "emergent international economic order." Accordingly, in biotechnology and other high-technology areas, such an ideology of national competitiveness has developed that other potential considerations, especially those of a social equity nature, have become secondary to bolstering the U.S. competitive position.

But as Gilpin (1987) stresses, the very uncertainties engendered in the new era of international technological rivalry virtually guarantee the elaboration among major industrial states of competition-limiting strategies—for example, increased sectoral protectionism and increased regionalization of the world economy—in order to counter the dislocating impacts of this new order. Gilpin also stresses that new high technologies tend to be so rapidly diffused because of rapid interstate flow of information that international technological leadership through R&D policy is very difficult to achieve. Also, the fact that much of global high-technology trade is in military hardware reflects more on national strategic ties than on industrial competitiveness. Thus, the basic imagery of increasingly global, competitive markets and international economic integration through market-driven, high-technology competition is an incomplete ideology. Yet this same ideology has been the underlying parameter of biotechnology R&D policy discussions, enabling policy discourse to focus on biotechnology development as an end in itself. The ideology of national competitiveness in a global high-technology economy has also contributed to an aura surrounding such areas of R&D as biotechnology, microelectronics and informatics, and new materials.

Third, biotechnology has tended to be seen as the magic bullet that will make possible revolutionary increases in productivity and be a driving force for revitalizing whole sectors and national economies. In part, this imagery of biotechnology has derived from the milieu of international technological competition and high-technology hype discussed earlier. This imagery has been reinforced by a number of studies (OTA, 1986) in which very substantial agricultural productivity increases (along with socioeconomic dislocations) were estimated for such new agricultural biotechnologies as bovine growth hormone (bGH) (see Buttel and Geisler, 1989).

Fourth, in the midst of very powerful pressures directing the LGU system toward increased emphasis on biotechnology, a significant coalition of groups opposing biotechnology has emerged. These groups and individuals, ranging from urban-based public interest and lobbying groups to concerned social scientists, have resisted the market-driven nature of biotechnology R&D, urged that there be stricter environmental regulation of new biotechnology innovations, argued for alternative research priorities in public biotechnology R&D, opposed patenting of novel life forms, and argued for social control over potentially dislocating biotechnologies such as bGH. This oppositional subculture is quite diverse; some of its major groups (e.g., Jeremy Rifkin and his Foundation for Economic Trends) oppose biotechnology research per se, while others (e.g., the Committee for Responsible Genetics) argue for more socially responsible and equitable applications of this technology.

Perhaps most significant, however, the biotechnology opposition coalition involves two dimensions that have been unprecedented since World War II. One is that this coalition has occasionally included farmer groups (e.g., the Wisconsin Family Farm Defense Fund, which has been a major critic of bovine growth hormone technology, and of the role of the University of Wisconsin in developing the technology). This trend may be particularly threatening if biotechnology engenders resistance to the LGU system from the system's major class of presumed beneficiaries. The second dimension is that opposition to a technology (or technologies) several years before commercial application is very unusual.

Fifth, the biotechnology opposition, despite its relative weakness in influencing policy, has engendered very strong reactions by private firms and public research institutions. Private firms' major trade groups (the Association of Biotechnology Companies and the Industrial Biotechnology Association, along with related groups such as the Animal Health Institute) have devoted much of their efforts to countering opposition to biotechnology. Public agricultural research institutions have generally embraced the industry position in these debates; in part, this has been because major regulatory restrictions on agricultural biotechnologies would reduce the ability of these institutions to move discoveries from their biotechnology programs to the market and, ultimately, to farmers' fields and feedlots.

Sixth, it is important to stress that biotechnology was prematurely commercialized. That is, the private biotechnology industry was initiated at a point when major product revenues from biotechnology innovations were 10 to 15 years away. Even today, most new biotechnology start-up companies operate with large balance sheet losses. This premature commercialization was based largely on unrealistic assumptions about the speed of R&D and regulatory circumstances. Also, the climate of biotechnology hype at the time when most new and established companies moved into biotechnology (1980 to 1984) contributed to this early pattern of very large investments.

The most significant policy impacts of rapid, premature commercialization of biotechnology are twofold. First, because of most new and established biotechnology firms having made large investments in product lines that, under the best conditions, will not yield positive balance sheets for several years, any barriers to commercialization—regulatory barriers, public interest group opposition, and so on—raise the stakes for the industry and are consequently resisted vigorously by trade groups. Second, with the biotechnology industry already overcrowded, with as many as 400 U.S. start-up companies and an additional 50 established American multinational companies involved as of late 1987 (OTA, 1988), there is virtually no room for new companies. Thus, the many state governments that have made major investments in biotechnology premised on attracting new start-up firms to their states are likely to be disappointed with the results from these investments.

In sum, because biotechnology policy has become a politicized arena where discourse is particularly ideological—and often very symbolic and emotional—in nature, a sober assessment of policy issues is lacking. The massive levels of public and private investment in the technology (see, e.g., OTA, 1988) now tend to lock private firms, the national and state governments, public research institutions, and other entities into particular positions on issues that are not readily changed by new policy-relevant knowledge. Also, as is the case in most other areas of technology innovation, precise (usually *ex ante*) data on which to base policy assessments are thin and subject to considerable error.

What Has Been Sacrificed in Order to Pursue Biotechnology R&D? The rise of biotechnology in the LGU system has occurred during a period in which total funding and faculty full-time equivalent (FTE) levels have declined modestly in real terms. This suggests that the increased level of biotechnology research resources, especially faculty research FTEs, has come at the expense of other programs. Which programs have been sacrificed, and with what consequences?

Again, precise data on these issues are not readily available. Our best source of data, the Hansen et al. (1986) study of plant breeding and biotechnology, suggests that additional biotechnology FTEs have tended to come at the expense of applied research, in general, and applied plant breeding, in particular. Put somewhat differently, state funds have been shifted from applied research geared to the technical needs of farmers in the state to biotechnology research, most of which is generic (or nonlocally adapted) research.

While it is premature to draw any conclusions about the consequences of these shifts, one potential consequence does suggest itself. The LGU system, especially since the 1950s, has been largely a state-supported system, based on the rationale that it is in the interest of the farmer groups and the legislature of a state to allocate that state's funds to its agricultural experiment stations so that the state's farmers can compete with farmers in other states (Buttel and Busch, 1988). Accordingly, the research portfolio of the experiment stations has historically tended to emphasize applied, locally adapted research that benefits the state's farmers. If it has been the case that experiment station biotechnology research FTEs have been mainly funded with state monies, and if the bulk of biotechnology research mainly serves clientele other than the state's farmers, the expansion of biotechnology may make the state funding base of the experiment station system more problematic in the future.

Public Biotechnology Research Priorities and the Division of Labor Between Public and Private Research. The rise of biotechnology in the 1980s has two important implications for research priority determination. First, biotechnology greatly expands the options available to agricultural researchers by providing new tools to pursue goals (e.g., herbicide-tolerant crop varieties, use of genetically modified bacteria that inhibit ice nucleation on high-value horticultural crops, salt-tolerant crop varieties, and extensive use of growth hormones in livestock) that were difficult to accomplish with traditional research methods. Biotechnology is especially malleable with respect to the interests of the various groups that struggle for the attention of the land-grant system. For example, biotechnology can be employed to reinforce or substitute for the use of agricultural chemicals, or it can be applied to benefit either large- or small-scale farmers. Second, the stagnation of public agricultural research funding, and especially the declining real value of "formula" funding has led LGU researchers to depend more heavily on externally funded projects (Lacy and Busch, 1989).

Each factor has major implications for determining research priorities in LGU biotechnology programs. On one hand, biotechnology in principle provides a wide range of research alternatives among which scientists and administrators can choose. On the other, the decline of formula funding implies that biotechnology researchers will mainly look to external funding sources and, accordingly, the work they pursue will be shaped by the priorities of external agencies and corporations. Also, research regarding the goals of LGU administrators who established biotechnology programs suggests that one of their most important considerations was the ability of biotechnology researchers to attract external research support (Buttel et al., 1986).

Unfortunately few data exist regarding how research priorities in LGU biotechnology programs and faculties are being determined. We can, however, venture some educated guesses, based on the three major sources of funding: federal competitive grants, state grants and special state appropriations, and corporate funding.

For most biotechnology researchers, especially those who work at a relatively basic level, federal competitive grants (from NSF, NIH, USDA, DOE, and so on) are a preferred form of research funding. These grants encourage fundamental or basic research of the sort that enables publication in major scientific journals, are considered by peer scientists to be the most prestigious, and provide a high degree of flexibility about the timing of publication. There are no data that indicate the nature of the agricultural biotechnology research priorities that are shaped by federal granting agencies and the implications of these priorities for the types of agricultural technologies that will be developed. Nonetheless, given that federal funding of agricultural biotechnology is less than $100 million (and perhaps as little as $75 million) annually and is exhibiting only modest growth, the rapidly expanding cadre of land-grant biotechnology researchers has had to look elsewhere for most of their support.

As noted earlier, state grants and appropriations have been pivotal in the establishment of LGU agricultural biotechnology programs. In the case of the experiment stations, which had relatively little basic research expertise in the early 1980s, state funds (both reallocated funds and special appropriations) have constituted most of the program support. Most state biotechnology funding programs were premised on attracting high-technology investment and employment to the state (Buttel et al., 1986). Accordingly, state biotech-

nology programs have generally encouraged—and in many cases have required—active collaboration with the private sector (Lacy and Busch, 1989;
OTA, 1988). Thus, the basic thrust of state government support of LGU
biotechnology programs may be to direct land-grant biotechnology researchers
to emphasize the technical goals of interest to private sector firms.

Evidence on private sector research priorities in agricultural biotechnology
firms is no less sparse, in part because of corporate secrecy. Also, agricultural
biotechnology firms are relatively diverse, ranging from multinational be-
hemoths such as Monsanto, du Pont, and American Cyanamid to large (e.g.,
Genentech and Agracetus) and small (e.g., Crop Genetics International) start-
up firms. Accordingly, one would expect heterogeneity of research priorities
as a concomitant of the niche-seeking strategies of the roughly 50 American
start-up and 15 U.S.-based multinational agricultural firms in the already
overcrowded agricultural biotechnology sector.

The relationship between biotechnology and agricultural chemicals is the
most important criterion for assessing biotechnology research priorities. In
this regard, available information about private research priorities—as revealed, for example, in major trade publications—suggests a mixed picture.
On one hand, the development of crops tolerant of widely used herbicides
(e.g., glyphosate and triazine) represents the most common research program
in private firms (Buttel, 1986a; OTA, 1984). Other research priorities involving
packaging of new crop varieties and chemicals (e.g., encapsulated horti-
cultural-crop embryos containing pesticides and some fertilizer) are also
common. On the other hand, private biotechnology firms, both large and
small, have done some significant research on bioinsecticides (e.g., Crop
Genetics International's InCide corn borer bioinsecticide), biofertilizers, and
other technologies that will substitute for the use of traditional agricultural
chemicals. Also, it is widely held that biotechnology will make possible a
new generation of pesticides that are more environmentally benign than
those currently used (OTA, 1986).

This complex pattern may be accounted for by the following factors.
First, the substantial emphasis given to biotechnologies that substitute for
chemicals may, in part, reflect the fact that these are technically straight-
forward, single-gene traits that help firms get products on the market as
soon as possible. Second, over the longer term, private firms' research
priorities will revolve around expansion of farmers' demands for purchased
inputs, both chemicals and seeds. Third, this pattern will become clearer
as start-up companies become increasingly linked to multinational chemical
companies through stock ownership, joint ownership, joint ventures, contract
research, and licensing of technology. Nonetheless, these points are still
largely conjectures, and the collection of more comprehensive data on private
sector, agricultural biotechnology research priorities remains an important
gap in social science research.

The research priorities that are being pursued in private R&D have several
crucial implications. First, industrial sponsorship accounts for between 12.5
and 20 percent of LGU agricultural biotechnology research funding; the future

prospect is for stagnant or declining public funding and an increased need for scientists to depend on the external funding environment. Thus, private priorities will tend to become public priorities as a result of the need of university scientists to position themselves to attract industrial funding. Accordingly, this trend may deepen the privatization of public agricultural research that has increasingly occurred in this decade. Second, private research priorities will be the fundamental determinant of the social impacts of agricultural biotechnologies in the future. Third, "orphan" biotechnologies (that is, technologies that are socially useful but not privately profitable for R&D) will need to be emphasized in the LGU system. As I will note later, these factors also have implications for LGU biotechnology transfer policy.

The Social Impacts of New Agricultural Biotechnologies. The key question has been whether agricultural biotechnologies have distinctive characteristics that will accelerate the decline in the number of farms, the demise of the family farm, and the concentration of agricultural assets and sales. At present, there are no conclusive data on which to base definitive judgments. There are several reasons why such data either do not exist or are equivocal. First, agricultural biotechnology products, like the methods used to develop them, are an extremely diverse set. Biotechnologies such as bGH, herbicide-tolerant crop varieties, bioinsecticides, and "ice-minus" bacteria, have, on the surface, little in common. Second, current biotechnology products are not necessarily representative of those that will be developed over the next two or three decades. As noted earlier, current commercial developments tend to focus on technically simple, single-gene traits rather than on polygenic traits and far more complex research methods. Third, it is not yet clear the degree to which new biotechnology products will be capital-intensive and will increase output, two major factors that shape farm structural consequences. Fourth, ex ante data inherently have a large error term.

Most data and the debate over the farm structural consequences of agricultural biotechnologies have focused on bGH, a naturally occurring hormone that can now be produced in large quantities by genetically modified bacteria containing a gene that codes for the hormone. Shortly after the technical properties of the hormone were understood, two major socioeconomic studies of bGH technology (Kalter et al., 1985; OTA, 1986) were conducted. Both studies assumed large revenue-over-cost returns to farmers from using bGH and large per-cow increases in milk production due to the hormone. Each suggested that bGH would very rapidly be adopted, result in large increases in productivity, lead to sharp declines in the number of dairy farmers, and accelerate the trend toward concentration in the dairy sector. More recently, however, several studies and critiques (Buttel, 1986b; Buttel and Geisler, 1989) have suggested that the output and socioeconomic impacts of bGH may have been exaggerated in previous research.

While this debate cannot be resolved here, I wish to make several observations that have implications for how we conceptualize the social impacts of biotechnologies. To the degree that bGH will ultimately result in large immediate increases in output and productivity, bGH will very likely prove to be an atypical agricultural biotechnology. It is increasingly apparent that the more common pattern will be that biotechnologies will tend to lead to incremental production gains—with the long-term aggregrate pattern being, at most, a continuation of the post–World War II pattern of 2 to 3 percent annual gains in productivity and output. Thus, we should be cautious in assuming that ex ante data on bGH have much applicability to assessment of the farm structural consequences of at least the first generation of agricultural biotechnologies. There are good reasons to believe that to the degree that biotechnology inputs lead to incremental gains, their farm structural impacts may not be qualitatively different from those of biochemical technologies after World War II.

Even for biotechnologies involving substantial productivity increases, the degree to which these new biotechnology inputs will lead to the demise of family farming is limited. To be sure, large immediate increases in productivity and output would lead to major social dislocations, especially on the part of smaller or less profitable operations. But increased output in a mature sector such as milk and milk products (characterized by low price elasticities of demand and market saturation) will tend to reduce product prices, and probably profits as well, making the sector unattractive to large-scale capital. Thus, while productivity-increasing biotechnologies will lead to increased concentration (most likely by encouraging "larger-than-family"farms), they will be unlikely to lead to an industrial farm structure.

Furthermore, biotechnologies are very likely to be biased toward larger farmers and their technical needs, but the basis of this technical bias will probably differ from that of post–World War II agricultural technology. Previous technologies tended to revolve around mechanization (Cochrane, 1979; LeVeen, 1978), to involve lumpy investments and scale economies, and to be most useful to large operators with sufficient investment capital and farm scale to be able to make use of them. Most biotechnologies, however, will in principle be divisible inputs. But these biotechnology inputs are very likely to require high levels of management skill and, in many cases, the ability to purchase and use computers and expert systems (e.g., the expert system for bGH that has been developed at Cornell University with funding by one of the major prospective manufacturers of bGH). These management skills are most common among large operators (Kalter, 1985) and will represent a new type of factor bias and a new basis for conferring the benefits of new technologies on larger operators.

Finally, it should be stressed that social scientists and agricultural research administrators should not succumb to agricultural fundamentalism in pondering the socioeconomic impacts of biotechnology. While most observers of agricultural biotechnology tend to focus on plant and animal improvement and other inputs into production agriculture, more fundamental long-term impacts may come from a very different application of biotechnology: the use of modern industrial bioprocessing techniques in food processing, which will increasingly sever the direct link between agricultural commodities and final food and fiber products (Goodman, Sorj, and Wilkinson, 1987). Ironically, the biotechnology debate in the U.S. dairy sector has totally ignored the possibility that industrial biotechnology is being applied to developing techniques to convert cheaper vegetable (e.g., rapeseed) proteins into substitutes for the milk protein casein (van den Doel and Junne, 1986). The development of industrial substitutes for casein and other agricultural raw materials may have a greater long-term impact on farm structure than will new agricultural biotechnology inputs.

Policy Options

The foregoing has identified several of the issues and problems surrounding biotechnology policy, focusing primarily on the LGU system. Following are a number of policy options for rationalizing LGU biotechnology programs and increasing their contributions to citizen welfare.

Increase the level of policy-oriented biotechnology research. Public agricultural biotechnology R&D policy is currently being formulated in a virtual vacuum of policy-oriented social science research information, mainly by recourse to such ideological "black boxes" as national competitiveness, university-industry cooperation, and so on (see National Research Council, 1987, for a representative example of policy recommendations based on these and other pervasive ideological appeals). There is, however, virtually no satisfactory research information on these and other research policy black boxes and on the degree to which they are relevant to agriculture and food and its various subsectors; hence, they remain black boxes.

It is unclear whether biotechnology will affect farmers and farm structure differently than did previous agricultural technologies. Nonetheless, it is very clear that biotechnology has become a lightening rod for concerns about distributional issues. As Ruttan (1987) has noted, land-grant scientists are "reluctant revolutionaries"; they wish to revolutionize the conditions of agricultural production, but they shy away from recognizing the ways they revolutionize rural and agricultural life. More often than not, these scientists disavow that such social considerations should bear on their work. Ruttan (1987) makes it clear that the days are gone when this posture can be maintained. The controversial nature of biotechnology makes it all the more imperative that research administrators and scientists have available as much information as possible—including ex ante assessment data—on which to base decisions. Policy research on biotechnology should therefore include (but not be limited to) impacts on farm structure and distribution. Information on prospective social impacts of new technologies should also be systematically included in research priorities during the decisionmaking process at the federal and LGU levels.

Assess the extent and implications of external determination of the LGU research agenda. The rise of agricultural biotechnology appears to have reinforced the longstanding trend of the decline of intramural funding and the increase of extramural funding of research. This trend suggests that LGU research, in general, and biotechnology research, in particular, will be strongly shaped by the priorities of external groups, especially corporations and federal granting agencies. Unfortunately, there exists little information on the consequences of this pattern and on desirable alternatives. Ruttan (1982), for example, has provided some preliminary evidence to suggest that the advantages of project funding (grant and contract) and the disadvantages of institutional funding (Hatch or formula) of agricultural research have been exaggerated. New initiatives for agricultural research funding tend to be developed by officials from the largest agricultural experiment stations, which are in the best position to obtain competitive research grants, and by basic science-oriented institutions such as the Board on Agriculture of the National Research Council. As a result, these initiatives have stressed competitive grants for basic research and expressed ambivalence about institutional funding of agricultural research. But there has been virtually no subsequent research on the benefits and costs of institutional versus project funding of agricultural research.

Increase the orientation of LGU biotechnology programs to state-level farmer needs. LGU biotechnology programs, which have been heavily state funded, must be concerned with both their long-term viability and the viability of the larger LGU institutions within which they are located. One of the most important means for doing so is to shore up their state funding base, especially by increasing the emphasis on locally adapted research relating to the technical needs of state-level farmer groups. This has been the mechanism by which support for state agricultural experiment stations has been traditionally generated in state legislatures. It seems plausible that experiment stations' identification with pursuing high technology to meet state needs will be an effective budget appeal to state governments.

Improve the integration between basic biotechnology research and applied, locally adapted research and extension. In order for a significant share of basic biotechnology research to lead to locally adapted technology of relevance to a state's farmers, this research must be closely linked with the applied LGU research program.

Diversify the basic research portfolio of experiment stations. Two of the unfortunate consequences of the biotechnology boom in LGUs have been that biotechnology has been seen as coterminous with basic research in agriculture and that other basic biological sciences with strong potential for application to agriculture have been ignored. Other biological disciplines with potential applications to agriculture include agroecology and evolutionary biology, both of which are especially relevant to solving the environmental problems of agriculture (Gould, 1988). In particular, such fields as microbial ecology, in which the basic sciences of ecology and molecular biology can be combined to yield new leverage on solving agricultural problems, have strong potential.

Reevaluate opportunities for transfer of biotechnology and other technical information. Whereas several decades ago extension and other public or quasipublic institutions (e.g., seed improvement cooperatives) were the focal technology transfer institutions for public agricultural research, LGUs have shifted toward private sector firms as the major modalities of technology transfer. Extension has been largely relegated to the role of providing farmers with advice on which commercial inputs sold by private firms should be used, and the role of seed improvement cooperatives has declined as LGUs have reduced their traditional plant breeding and varietal release programs (Hansen et al., 1986). The potentials of biotechnology and other basic research methods in agriculture suggest that LGUs should reconsider their approaches to technology transfer. Many socially desirable applications of new basic research methods, particularly those that promise to significantly reduce chemical usage, will not likely be privately profitable. LGUs will accordingly need to rethink their reliance on technology transfer to the multinational agricultural inputs sector and consider alternatives such as restoring their applied plant breeding programs and increasing their emphasis on public domain varietal release.

Increase extension's emphasis on improving farmer management capacity. Evidence suggests that new agricultural biotechnology products are likely to be management intensive. Accordingly, if extension is to make possible a relatively equitable transfer of these inputs to farmers, there must be an increased focus on improving the management capacity of farmers, especially on the part of smaller farmers who would otherwise be less able to use the new technologies effectively.

Ensure the perception and reality of LGU institutional neutrality on the contentious issues relating to biotechnology. Biotechnology has become a controversial technology. LGUs have responded to this controversy by promoting biotechnology and, in general, embracing the industry position in various debates (e.g., over release of modified organisms, bGH, industry-university linkages; Buttel, 1989). LGUs must recognize the risks involved in such a posture. Continued opposition to biotechnology is likely on a number of grounds: its impacts on farmers, on the environment, and on the impartiality of the LGUs themselves. Institutional neutrality may be wise not only politically, but also in terms of making decisions on research priorities that ensure broad benefit from the technology.

References

Buttel, F. H. 1986a. "Biotechnology and public agricultural research policy." Pp. 123–156 in V. J. Rhodes, ed., *Agricultural Science Policy in Transition*. Bethesda, Md.: Agricultural Research Institute.

––––––. 1986b. "Agricultural research and farm structural change: Bovine growth hormone and beyond." *Agriculture and Human Values* 3(Fall):88–98.

––––––. 1989. "Theoretical issues in the regulation of genetically engineered organisms: A commentary." *Politics and the Life Sciences* 7(February):135–139.

Buttel, F. H., and L. Busch. 1988. "The public agricultural research system at the crossroads." *Agricultural History* 62(Spring):303–324.

Buttel, F. H., and C. C. Geisler. 1989. "The social impacts of bovine somatotropin: emerging issues." Pp. 137–159 in J. J. Molnar and H. Kinnucan, eds., *Biotechnology and the New Agricultural Revolution*. Boulder, Colo.: Westview Press.

Buttel, F. H., M. Kenney, J. Kloppenburg, J. T. Cowan, and D. Smith. 1986. "Industry/land-grant university relationships in transition." Pp. 296–312 in L. Busch and W. B. Lacy, eds., *The Agricultural Scientific Enterprise*. Boulder, Colo: Westview Press.

Cochrane, W. W. 1979. *The Development of American Agriculture*. Minneapolis, Minn.: University of Minnesota Press.

Gilpin, R. 1987. *The Political Economy of International Relations*. Princeton, N.J.: Princeton University Press.

Goodman, D., B. Sorj, and J. Wilkinson. 1987. *From Farming to Biotechnology*. Oxford: Basil Blackwell.

Gould, F. 1988. "Evolutionary biology and genetically engineered crops: Consideration of evolutionary theory can aid in crop design." *BioScience* 38:26–33.

Hansen, M., L. Busch, J. Burkhardt, W. B. Lacy, and L. R. Lacy. 1986. "Plant breeding and biotechnology." *BioScience* 36(1):29–39.

Joint Council on Food and Agricultural Sciences. 1984. *FY 1986 Priorities for Research, Extension, and Higher Education*. Washington, D.C.: Joint Council on Food and Agricultural Sciences.

———. 1987. *FY 1989 Priorities for Research, Extension, and Higher Education*. Washington, D.C.: Joint Council on Food and Agricultural Sciences.

Kalter, R. J. 1985. "The new biotech agriculture: Unforeseen economic consequences." *Issues in Science and Technology* 2:125–133.

Kalter, R. J., et al. 1985. "Biotechnology and the dairy industry: Production costs, commercial potential, and the economic impact of bovine growth hormone." A. E. Research 85-20. Ithaca, N.Y.: Cornell University, Department of Agricultural Economics.

Lacy, W. B., and L. Busch. 1989. "The changing division of labor between the university and industry: The case of agricultural biotechnology." Pp. 21–50 in J. J. Molnar and H. Kinnucan, eds., *Biotechnology and the New Agricultural Revolution*. Boulder, Colo.: Westview Press.

LeVeen, E. P. 1978. "Small scale farming in an industrial society: A critical appraisal of *Small is Beautiful*." In R. C. Dorf and Y. L. Hunter, eds., *Appropriate Visions*. San Francisco: Boyd and Fraser.

National Research Council (NRC). 1972. *Report of the Committee on Research Advisory to the U.S. Department of Agriculture*. Washington, D.C.: National Academy of Sciences.

———. 1987. *Agricultural Biotechnology*. Washington, D.C.: National Academy Press.

Office of Technology Assessment (OTA). 1984. *Commercial Biotechnology*. Washington, D.C.: OTA.

———. 1986. *Technology, Public Policy, and the Changing Structure of American Agriculture*. Washington, D.C.: OTA.

———. 1988. *New Developments in Biotechnology, 4: U.S. Investment in Biotechnology*. Washington, D.C.: OTA.

Rockefeller Foundation. 1982. *Science for Agriculture*. New York: Rockefeller Foundation.

Ruttan, V. W. 1982. *Agricultural Research Policy*. Minneapolis, Minn.: University of Minnesota Press.

———. 1987. "Agricultural scientists as reluctant revolutionaries." *Choices* Third Quarter, p. 3.

van den Doel, K., and G. Junne. 1986. "Product substitution through biotechnology: Impact on the third world." *Trends in Biotechnology* 4:88–90.

26

International Development

Conner Bailey

Sustainability, equity, and participation are the three policy goals addressed in this chapter, which focuses primarily on rural development and natural resource management in Third World nations. The emphasis here on rural development is justified because most people in the Third World live in rural areas. Problems of resource depletion often reflect the desperation of people marginalized by agricultural and industrial development. Those who remain in rural areas often are forced into patterns of resource use that provide short-term subsistence but are not sustainable in the long run. Many threats to resource systems, however, are caused not by the poor but by members of elite classes who use their position to gain control over lands, forests, and water resources.

Development is defined here as a process of change through which environmentally sustainable and socially equitable improvements are made to the quality of life for all or most members of a society. Development efforts should be judged on their contribution toward these broad criteria. Economic growth may be a part of development, but is not the same thing as development. Indeed, unsustainable or inequitable forms of economic growth that significantly heighten inequalities in wealth, income, or political power should be recognized as the antithesis of development. Policies and programs that treat intended beneficiaries as objects of, rather than participants in, development often lack detailed local information that is necessary to recognize and minimize negative social or environmental consequences of induced change. Participatory approaches are more likely to support equitable and sustainable development than are strategies based on external planning and direction from above (Korten and Siy, 1988).

Consistent with the larger purpose of this volume, emphasis here is placed on international development policy options available to decision makers in the United States who represent government as well as nongovernment organizations (e.g., foundations, private voluntary organizations, and universities). Without de-emphasizing the important roles played by other countries in promoting international development, it is fair to say that since the 1950s the United States has performed a leading role in setting the development agenda. Until 1988, the United States had the largest bilateral development assistance budget of any bilateral donor, although in that year Japan's total funding was larger. The U.S. Agency for International Development (USAID) continues to have a larger and more experienced staff than any other bilateral agency, a factor that will tend to maintain USAID influence (Koppel, 1989). Moreover, the United States continues to wield considerable power in formulating policies of the World Bank and the International Monetary Fund (IMF), organizations that can be characterized as the carrot and stick, respectively, of development agencies.

The U.S. influence in the development community extends beyond bilateral and multilateral agencies. Major private foundations (e.g., Ford and Rockefeller) and nongovernment organizations (e.g., CARE, Heifer International, and Catholic Relief Services) are based in and staffed largely by citizens of the United States. Agricultural scientists and private foundations from the United States continue to play major roles in work of the international agricultural research centers from which sprang the Green Revolution (e.g., the International Maize and Wheat Improvement Center in Mexico, the International Rice Research Institute in the Philippines, and the International Potato Center in Peru). USAID provides a large portion of the core budget for these centers, which also are heavily influenced in structure and staffing patterns by the agricultural research system of the United States.

Given the breadth of this involvement, the influence of the United States on setting the agenda for development discussions is likely to remain quite strong. The United States, however, cannot retain a leadership role in international development during the 1990s by resting on its laurels. This is especially true in view of domestic pressures to reduce funding for international development. The challenge facing policymakers in this country is how best to contribute to the development process in an era of serious budget constraints.

The Policy Context

Geopolitics and Development

U.S. international development policy is the product of a complex interplay of humanistic and geopolitical impulses. In 1987, Israel and Egypt received half of all U.S. foreign assistance expenditures, which totaled $10.8 billion in that year (*Wall Street Journal*, June 1, 1989). The next six-largest recipients of USAID funds also are countries of geopolitical importance to the United States: Pakistan, Turkey, El Salvador, the Philippines, Greece, and Honduras. In 1987, these countries accounted for an additional 25 percent of total expenditures. Half of all bilateral development aid is in the form of military assistance. To turn an old saw on its head, development aid often is war by other means.

These figures clearly indicate the strong geopolitical nature of U.S. development policy. Political allies and strategically placed nations are the primary beneficiaries of our assistance. Unfortunately, the history of U.S. involvement in the internal political affairs of developing countries often has been in support of anticommunist dictators. As a consequence, the United States frequently has forefeited the moral high ground, extending a bayonet rather than the hand of development. This has not always been the case, however. The role of the United States in removing the dictators Marcos of the Philippines and Duvalier of Haiti allied this country with the forces of reform.

As we enter the 1990s, geopolitical conditions are changing rapidly. From the 1950s to the mid-1980s, fear of aggressive communist expansion provided the United States with a major incentive for development assistance. In the past few years this fear has begun to dissipate, providing opportunity to reflect and act upon a new development agenda, one that is consistent with the best impulses of the United States and its citizens. Development policy that supports corrupt regimes for reasons of geopolitical advantage cannot be expected to gain lasting approval from the citizens of the United States. Policies that reflect national ideals of social justice, political freedom, and concern for the environment provide a more solid base of public support for funding international development efforts.

The Debt Crisis

The Third World's foreign debt crisis of the 1980s has seriously distorted development policy. During the 1970s, the gradual decline in the value of the dollar and negative real interest rates made borrowing for development a smart decision. Commercial banks in the United States and Europe promoted taking on debt as a means of absorbing surplus liquidity caused by the flow of dollars from OPEC nations. Rising real interest rates, combined with declining prices of primary commodities in the early 1980s, dramatically altered the fiscal condition of many Third World nations (Flora, 1989). Moreover, increasing values first of the dollar and later of the Japanese yen had a major impact on the outstanding debt principal in terms of local currencies.

The debt crisis has put tremendous political pressure on Third World leaders. External agencies such as the IMF and the World Bank push for fiscal reforms, including the removal of subsidies for fuel and food or the shrinking of a government's bureaucracy, as a condition for desperately needed funds. Countries become more dependent on the IMF and the World Bank because these agencies influence commercial banks, and commercial banks will limit their dealings with countries that refuse to adhere to policies promoted by the World Bank and the IMF. Foreign exchange shortages also generate internal pressures on political leaders from business and industrial interests, which depend on imports of spare parts as well as raw and finished materials.

The need to expand foreign exchange earnings at a time of declining commodity prices has encouraged short-term solutions with the potentially heavy long-term costs associated with environmental degradation and resource depletion, as will be discussed below. In addition, export-oriented development typically benefits urban elites rather than the rural poor. Most of the profit from this export trade is gained by urban processors, shippers, and bankers. This is particularly true of agricultural, forestry, and fisheries commodities. Efforts to promote exports often deflect limited staff and funding away from pressing domestic needs and from opportunities for alternative development strategies.

Policies and programs designed to meet the challenge of debt repayment are likely to be incompatible with the broader development needs of Third World countries. Current U.S. policy promotes a plan to write off part of the outstanding Third World debt in return for fiscal and trade reforms, which often have immediate negative consequences for the poor. This plan may temporarily reduce the pressure of the debt crisis, but it does not significantly alter the Third World countries' basic need to expand foreign exchange earnings. Problems of debt repayment are real and cannot be wished away. Neither can they be solved by further limiting the opportunities of the poor. Projects designed primarily to support export-oriented development are likely to have negative social, economic, and resource system consequences (as discussed in the next section). Because of its influence on multilateral development agencies, the United States can play a key role in decoupling issues of development and the Third World debt crisis. Development is a bigger and more complex issue than the debt crisis.

Policy Goals

U.S. government and nongovernment development assistance agencies should support the policy goals of equity, sustainability, and participation.

Equity

Distributional equity is not the same thing as equality. What constitutes an equitable distribution of development benefits can only be defined in terms of culture, and therefore it involves subjective values. Despite the diversity of human cultures, it is nonetheless true in most parts of the Third World that the rapid penetration of global market forces has disrupted the complex fabric of social and economic relationships which once held whole societies together. Where wealth once may have been redistributed, acting as a kind of sociopolitical cement, today's economic opportunities are more likely to be viewed from the perspective of individual advantage. As traditional redistributive norms break down, certain classes of people are likely to be systematically disadvantaged, even by well-meaning development efforts. Under these conditions, judgments regarding equity can and should be made.

Concerns regarding distributional equity have not always featured prominently in development literature. During the 1950s, emphasis was placed on accumulation of capital. The rural poor were seen as contributing little to a nation's progress toward economic "take-off." The role of agriculture was to produce food for the urban sector and generate economic surplus, which could be siphoned off to promote industrial development, the primary path toward capital accumulation. Over time, the farm sector would benefit from expanded employment opportunities in the industrial sector. In short, the benefits of development would trickle down.

In the 1960s and 1970s, agricultural development became recognized as valuable in its own right due to significant advances in production technologies, causing the period to be known as the Green Revolution. For many, the Green Revolution represented scientific domination over nature. The role of science was to defeat pests and drought with chemicals and canals as well as to alter the genetic structure of major food crops to fit the model of high-input agriculture established in the United States.

Simultaneously embraced as both a means of feeding a rapidly growing world population and a strategy for putting agriculture on a commercial rather than a subsistence basis, the Green Revolution frequently resulted in increased inequality of income and wealth within the agricultural sector. At a regional level, Green Revolution–inspired development efforts focused on areas where soil fertility and the availability of irrigation were necessary conditions for successful introduction of high-yielding varieties of wheat, corn, and rice. Regions where these conditions did not exist were ignored, creating regional imbalances in development. In areas where the Green Revolution was introduced, the primary beneficiaries often were landowners (Cohen, 1975). Tenants and landless agricultural laborers, on the other hand, sometimes suffered declining fortunes (Scott, 1985). In many areas, mechanization of land preparation and harvest reduced employment opportunities for landless agricultural laborers. In some cases, tenants lost access to land as owners took advantage of new opportunities for profit.

The Green Revolution did not always create such problems, and it did lead to impressive increases in food production in many countries. Nonetheless, it is true that the changing structure of agriculture in tropical Third World countries has marginalized large numbers of landless agricultural laborers. Many of these people have moved to urban areas, swelling the slum population and posing serious social and political threats to the state. Others forced out of farming have moved into ecologically fragile uplands and forest lands, which have limited capacity to support agricultural production. Yet others have moved to the coast, where fish stocks and other coastal resources already are heavily exploited. In short, the gains of the Green Revolution often carried social costs that only now are being realized.

Sustainability

Sustainable development depends on more than the wise use of natural resources, although this is a concern of central importance. Programs of agricultural or industrial development that require substantial subsidies or protection may prove to be economically and politically unsustainable, just as surely as overfishing and overgrazing are unsustainable in biological terms. For present purposes, however, discussion will be limited to problems of ensuring sustainable use of natural resource systems.

A long-held view regarding development was that Third World nations were endowed with abundant labor and natural resources. The key problem was to marshal these forces of production for the national cause of economic progress. Natural resource systems, in particular, were seen as storehouses of wealth which could be used to generate investment capital. There was, initially, little appreciation for the finite nature of these systems or how vulnerable they were to overexploitation. The view that development is the same thing as increased production resulted in policies that emphasized exploitation instead of management. This approach continues to be favored by Third World policymakers, who are struggling to unburden their nations of large foreign debts by exporting minerals, timber, beef, fish, and other primary commodities. External donor agencies such as USAID and the World Bank are sympathetic to this need, as are a number of large commercial banks which have a stake in the outcome.

The need to expand foreign exchange earnings has encouraged short-term solutions with potentially heavy long-term costs from environmental degradation and resource depletion. This preoccupation with foreign exchange has led governments to emphasize production of cash crops for export in countries where available food is limited. Similarly, fisheries development projects frequently lead to exports of fish from Third World nations to Japan, the United States, and Western Europe. Rapid denudation of tropical forest lands by commercial loggers and cattle ranchers also is a result of the pressure to expand exports.

Four decades of development effort suggest that external intervention into established systems can lead to disaster. Livestock development projects in Africa, for example, have led to serious problems of overgrazing. Similarly, development efforts aimed at increasing marine fisheries production frequently have exacerbated problems of resource depletion and have led to serious, widespread problems of social disruption in coastal communities. Problems of resource degradation are also affecting coastal ecosystems, upland areas, and tropical rain forests. Coastal ecosystems are experiencing a variety of threats, including pollution and the destruction of mangrove forests for pulpwood or conversion to shrimp ponds. In many upland areas, migration of landless people has set in motion a destructive cycle of shifting cultivation that, without adequate fallow, depletes the soil through leaching and/or erosion. Similar problems of deforestation and soil depletion are caused by logging of tropical rain forests and the expansion of both small- and large-scale farming and ranching activities into these agriculturally marginal lands.

Beyond these immediate impacts, resource depletion limits or even eliminates future development options. Recognition that development efforts may pose serious threats to natural resource systems has spurred a reorientation away from projects designed purely to increase production and toward those which improve the long-term productive capacity of the resource base. Good examples of this direction are agroforestry projects (designed to reduce erosion while providing income and other incentives to farm households in upland communities) and coastal resource management projects (aimed at improving institutional capacity to manage these complex ecosystems). USAID supports both types of projects and has identified natural resource management as a central theme of its efforts. Moreover, the United States has been instrumental in pushing environmental reforms within the World Bank, which now considers a project's environmental impact in its funding decisions.

Participation

The advantage of public participation in development has been recognized since at least the 1950s, when community development programs were initiated. These programs were based on the recognition that the intended beneficiaries of development knew what their needs were and could be organized to help achieve these goals. Such an approach would contribute to cost-effective implementation and a sense of pride and ownership by project participants. However, early community development efforts were prone to a number of serious limitations (Korten, 1980). Organizers sent into target communities saw their task as assisting in the creation of local consensus on "felt needs." Where communities were divided along lines of class, caste, or faction, consensus formation tended to be limited to non-controversial matters of peripheral importance. Further, community development organizers generally lacked the resources necessary to implement projects that were agreed upon, undermining their credibility with local residents. Community organizers had limited ability to influence expenditure of government public works funds or the activities of important government agencies. Heads of departments of agriculture, for example, were intent on implementing their own programs and had little incentive to respond to requests forwarded by community organizers not associated with (and who had no authority over) their particular agency.

Unable to deal effectively with local conflicts or affect the flow of government resources, community development gradually declined in popularity during the 1960s. About this time, there emerged important advances in agricultural technologies which captured the attention of those responsible for development policy. The Green Revolution provided something that community development did not: a specific focus for practical action. Among the changes brought about by the Green Revolution was an enhanced role for scientific experts as leaders in the development process. Indigenous knowledge systems were discounted as relics from the past that should be abandoned. Government-built and -managed irrigation systems determined the timing of the cropping cycle, and hence dictated the pace of life and even the types of crops that could be grown (Bailey, 1983). In sum, the Green Revolution represented a move away from local participation and toward scientifically rational direction from above.

In recent years, however, the pendulum of participation has begun to reverse direction. Evidence of the positive benefits of participation in the development process is growing, and this approach is being incorporated in projects supported by USAID, the World Bank, and Third World governments (Korten and Siy, 1988; Uphoff, 1985; Salmen, 1987). However, participation is not universally embraced as the favored approach to development. This is particularly true where popular participation challenges vested bureaucratic and class interests.

Policy Options

Focusing on the three development goals outlined above (equity, sustainability, and participation), this section draws attention to policy options available to decision makers in the United States. The policy options discussed below are divided into two categories: those based on strengthening the capacity of central government to direct development, and those that focus on decentralization of development planning and implementation.

Whether to promote centralized or decentralized authority to design and implement development projects is a fundamental problem. In some countries national authorities need to be strengthened to counterbalance local elites who, through ownership of land or control over local militias, can sidetrack development programs. Under these conditions, government and nongovernment policymakers in the United States should concentrate their efforts on strengthening agencies of the central government. In other countries, entrepreneurial and political elites at the national level use their position and power to capture the bulk of development benefits. Under these conditions, the United States should support strategies based on decentralization of decision-making authority.

Centralization and decentralization are not mutually exclusive choices. More often, a mix of strategies may be preferable, supporting a strong central government and at the same time encouraging grassroots participation, both as a means to enlist local energies in the development process and to act as a democratic counterweight to centralized power.

Strengthening Government Agencies

As used here, development involves a sustainable process leading to improvements in human standards of living. Changes that are not socially or environmentally sustainable over time do not fit this definition of development. A major constraint to sustainable development is the inability of Third World governments to manage effectively their natural resource base. Causes of this inability include but are not limited to technical and administrative weaknesses. Because there is no one cause, there is no one solution. Consequently, several nonexclusive options are proposed below to deal with this problem.

One way for USAID to promote sustainable and equitable development is to increase the capacity of government agencies to meet this need. The form of development known as "institution building," involving training of staff and provision of necessary facilities and equipment, is a prime example of external efforts designed to enhance development planning and organizational capabilities in Third World nations.

The guiding assumption behind institution building is that governments ultimately are responsible for ensuring that a society's resource base is protected for future generations. In most Third World nations, the ability of central governments to control what happens in the provinces is distinctly limited. The newly independent states of Asia and Africa inherited natural resource agencies that were oriented primarily toward extractive activities, not resource management. Indeed, with the exception of areas directly affected by cash crop production, the role of colonial governments in rural areas usually was quite limited. The natural resource agencies of newly independent nations have limited experience in attempting to manage remote forests, grazing lands, or fishing grounds. The constraints to a country's establishing adequate management capabilities include the lack of scientific understanding of complex tropical ecosystems and inadequate funding for staff and equipment. Thus, both research and administrative capacities need to be strengthened.

Quite often, Third World policymakers do not fully understand the dimensions or dynamics of the problems they face. Most countries in which USAID operates have a shortage of funds available for research and, in some cases, a shortage of trained individuals to do the necessary work. USAID support for local research, backed up where needed by researchers from universities or research institutions in the United States or elsewhere, can have a major impact on strengthening the ability of government agencies to make wise decisions regarding resource use. The costs to support these efforts need not be great.

Other approaches to strengthening organizational capacity within government agencies include educational and training opportunities and the provision of buildings and equipment. Efforts of this kind are a familiar part of many development programs. Education and training programs usually involve sending people to universities in the United States, while providing buildings and especially equipment may lead to procurement of materials in the United States. Both activities tend to increase political support for USAID budget requests to Congress. Government leaders in recipient nations also favor these types of programs. Able young staff are given the opportunity to further their education, and facilities are built and equipped. Project outputs of this type are tangible and easily quantifiable evidence of development. The link between these activities and the broader definition of development used here, however, is an issue that needs critical evaluation.

Promoting development through established government agencies can neither be ignored as an option nor embraced uncritically. Government agencies (e.g., ministries of agriculture) control budgetary and staff resources of enormous value for development purposes. The argument can be made that government agencies are the only way to reach large numbers of people. Under certain circumstances, frequently associated with the presence of a strong leader (Korten, 1980), it is possible to reorient government agencies to play a progressive role in development. However, in some situations elite domination of the development process persists, despite recognition that top-down strategies of development planning and implementation have frequently led to project failure (Kottack, 1985). Some national elites are more interested in personal enrichment than in development. Under these conditions, alternative, nongovernment approaches must be adopted.

Decentralization of Authority

The decision to decentralize resource management authority either to local governments or to community organizations has the advantage of allowing private individuals and communities to participate in the development process. Decentralization is likely to result in greater opportunities for local participation. In addition, decentralization allows people who understand local conditions to be in a decision-making position. This is important because the complexity of tropical resource systems makes it impossible to propose a single solution of universal applicability; the management of diversity does not easily lend itself to centralized decision making.

Decentralization will take some mental adjustment. National government agencies are staffed with experts who have been socialized into believing they are the vanguard of development. Embracing a truly participatory approach means that government officers must relinquish their leadership roles and suffer some diminution of power over institutional resources. Members of the economic elite at the national level also may be opposed to, or seek to limit, popular participation in development planning and implementation. Changes that significantly threaten domination by entrepreneurial and political elites will meet predictable opposition.

Similarly, broadly based public participation in development may be counter to the interests of local elites outside of the national capital. Simply turning over power to local leaders and organizations is not always a viable approach because it cannot be assumed that they represent community or broader social interests. Local elites may be inclined to line their own pockets and enhance their own power and prestige by controlling the flow of development resources. Even where self-aggrandizement is not a problem, local organizational capacity to take part in planning and implementing development activities may lack experience in dealing with government agencies or other powerful outsiders. Questions of participation, like those of sustainability and equity, are fundamentally political.

Two focal points for action are proposed for situations when conditions warrant the decision to promote decentralization.

Promote Involvement of Nongovernment Organizations. The USAID and other United States–supported development agencies could further promote the involvement of nongovernment organizations (NGOs) in grassroots organizational efforts. NGOs have proven to be effective conduits for external assistance, and USAID currently channels considerable assistance through NGOs. Most of this collaborative effort has been in the form of project implementation. However, much more could be done through NGOs to increase the capacity of local organizations to play a larger part in development planning and implementation. More broadly, a strong NGO movement promotes political pluralism by helping the poor find their voice. Until they do so, many Third World governments will be less than adequately responsive to their needs, partly out of ignorance and partly because no political pressure exists to do otherwise.

From the perspective of USAID, NGOs provide an important degree of flexibility and a shield from charges of political interference in domestic matters of aid recipients. NGOs typically are structured so that they can more quickly respond to new conditions or opportunities than relatively cumbersome government bureaucracies (including USAID). NGOs also insulate USAID from direct involvement in building local organizational capacity, a politically touchy issue in many countries.

Promote Community-based Common Property Systems for Resource Management. The inability of most Third World governments to manage their natural resource base limits future development options. The absence of clear and enforceable property rights and the consequent open access nature of many natural resource systems is the major reason for these management problems.

Many external development experts have promoted privatization as the most effective and efficient means of limiting access to, and therefore managing, a resource. Their basic rationale is the view that, under open access conditions, individuals inevitably seek to maximize their own benefit even at the expense of the common good (Hardin, 1968).

During the past decade, however, a wealth of information has become available which shows that we should not accept the universality of a moral order based exclusively on individual rationality. There is a growing literature which documents the ability of communities in the Third World (as well as in Japan, Europe, and the United States) to effectively manage natural resource systems in a communal fashion (National Research Council, 1986). A growing trend in development projects involving natural resource systems is the attempt to empower local people through creation of community-based common property systems.

Resource depletion frequently occurs under conditions of open access, defined as the absence of property rights. Under open access it is impossible to allocate a resource among users or to limit levels of exploitation. Under common property systems, however, property rights are created which allow for such restraint. Common property systems are based on group or community rights over property and have proven successful in the management of irrigation systems, forest resources, fishing grounds, and other group-managed resource systems. As such, they provide an alternative to individual ownership, government ownership, or open access. Runge (1986) argues that common property systems support the equity and sustainability criteria of development. Because management takes place at the local level, informal social sanctions are available to enforce community norms of fairness. Intimate knowledge of fishing grounds, grazing lands, and forest resources provides the basis for management decisions carefully fitted to the local system, while community dependence on the resource strongly guarantees that it will be managed on a sustainable basis for generations to come.

In addition to promoting equity and sustainable management of natural resources, common property systems also promote participatory development. Local knowledge is a key ingredient in the effective design and management of irrigation systems (Korten and Siy, 1988). For people to participate actively in the development process, they must be able to exert some control over decisions which directly affect their lives. Power to control access to and allocate use of resources upon which a community depends is the raison d'être that will attract strong grassroots participatory support.

Promoting common property as a development model poses the risk of romanticizing rural communities as bastions of harmony and open-handed goodwill. Reality is far more complex. Often, personal and ideological factions or divisions based on class or caste make it difficult for users of a particular resource to act collectively. However, the opportunities for strengthening local organizational capacity should not be ignored. Only when small-scale producers are able to act collectively will they be able to participate effectively in the development process. Only as an organized group will they be able to exert sufficient political pressure to ensure that their interests are considered when policies and programs are established.

Conclusion

The United States will continue to play a major role in international development during the 1990s, for geopolitical as well as humanitarian reasons. Given budget limitations and the foreign trade deficit, however, static United States funding for foreign assistance is likely to continue. As a consequence, Japan and other donor countries will gradually increase their influence in shaping the development agenda. Nonetheless, the United States has unique organizational capacities and a large number of experienced individuals committed to development. Future leadership requires progressive vision, not just dollars. A strong argument can be made that the first order of business for development policy is the assurance of sustainable patterns of natural resource use. Many past development projects negatively affected natural resources and the environment. Widespread concerns over rapid deforestation in Brazil and desertification in the Sahel, among other examples of resource depletion, have made the development community sensitive to the need for biological sustainability. Growing environmental concern within the United States has led to significant reorientation of development policy toward sustainability in agricultural and natural resource systems. USAID has identified natural resource management as a central agency concern. The United States plays a leading and progressive role in promoting environmentally sound development policies within multilateral agencies and, through bilateral ties, in nations which are aid recipients.

The United States is doing less than it could or should in promoting equity and participation. These two goals, along with that of increasing sustainablility, are closely related. Public participation in development planning and implementation is cost-effective and enhances the likelihood that projects will be successful. Participatory strategies of development are not a universal panacea for solving development problems, but there are clear advantages to local participation in fostering effective, equitable, and sustainable development. Most important, however, organization provides political influence for people who are typically on the political and economic margins of society.

The political content of participatory development initially may make some Third World governments reluctant to take this path. But the advantages in terms of equity and sustainability of development efforts are such that these governments should take this risk. The United States can play a progressive role in Third World development by promoting development policies and programs that center on people-oriented issues of equity, sustainability, and participation.

References

Bailey, C. 1983. *Sociology of Production in Rural Malay Society.* Kuala Lumpur: Oxford University Press.

Cohen, J. 1975. "Rural change in Ethiopia: The Chilalo agricultural development unit." *Economic Development and Culture Change* 22:580–614.

Flora, C. B. 1989. "Presidential address." Annual meetings of the Rural Sociological Society, Seattle, Washington, August 5.

Hardin, G. 1968. "The tragedy of the commons." *Science* 162:1243–1248.

Koppel, B. 1989. "Applied American rural sociology and USAID in Asia: What future?" *The Rural Sociologist* 9(2):32–40.

Korten, D. C. 1980. "Community organization and rural development: A learning process approach." *Public Administration Review* 40:480–511.

Korten, F. F., and R. Y. Siy, Jr. 1988. *Transforming a Bureaucracy: The Experience of the Philippine National Irrigation Administration.* West Hartford, Conn.: Kumarian Press.

Kottack, C. P. 1985. "When people don't come first: Some sociological lessons from completed projects." Pp. 325–356 in M. M. Cernea, ed., *Putting People First: Sociological Variables in Rural Development.* New York: Oxford University Press.

National Research Council. 1986. *Common Property Resource Management.* Washington, D.C.: National Academy Press.

Runge, C. R. 1986. "Common property and collective action in economic development." *World Development* 14(5):623–636.

Salmen, Lawrence F. 1987. *Listen to the People; Participant-Observer Evaluation of Development Projects.* New York: Oxford University Press.

Scott, J. C. 1985. *Weapons of the Weak.* New Haven, Conn.: Yale University Press.

Uphoff, N. 1985. "Fitting projects to people." Pp. 359–395 in M. M. Cernea, ed., *Putting People First: Sociological Variables in Rural Development.* New York: Oxford University Press.

27

A Rural Policy Agenda
for the 1990s

James A. Christenson and Cornelia B. Flora

Rural America has much to offer the social, cultural, and economic structures of the United States. The values of the rural way of life have been espoused since the founding of our country. While many urbanites enjoy the amenities of city life, they also desire the open spaces and environmental integrity of rural living for aesthetic, recreational, and sociocultural reasons. Rural America generates raw goods and materials that help to balance the national deficit. It also generates food, fiber, and natural resources for our everyday use. It is the source of abundant water, the purifier of our air, and the habitat for our wildlife. With so much to offer to society, then why is it that all is not well in the hinterlands of America?

The social and economic problems in rural areas differ in degree and in kind from those in urban areas because of geographical isolation, decaying infrastructure, and limited governmental capacity. The statistics presented in this book show a systematic gap between rural and urban areas in the United States. Rural areas have higher rates of poverty, unemployment, and mortality; lower levels of educational attainment, employment skills, and vocational training; and more limited access to health care, social services, public water systems, and a modern telecommunication system. For example, in 1987 rural poverty rates were 50 percent higher than metro poverty rates; and rural rates were even higher than inner-city poverty rates. The situation for rural Native Americans, blacks, and Hispanics is even more alarming.

Should rural America be treated like a Third World country? In many ways, the social, economic, and cultural problems that many rural Americans face are similar to those faced in less developed countries. The authors document some of the biases and blind actions of current national and state policies that tend to treat rural America in this way. Issues challenging rural America that are similar to those affecting less developed nations include a high level of poverty, isolation from economic opportunities, limited access to credit and technical assistance, governmental incapacity, an inadequate infrastructure, garbage disposal, toxic waste, substandard schools, health

333

care, isolation of certain groups (especially the elderly), and discrimination against many other special groups. In short, rural areas are beset with many social, economic, and environmental problems of Third World countries but are part of a major first world society. Rural America lacks the resources and political benefits to which urban areas have access to address such issues. Rural America is becoming a separate impoverished "outland" within American society.

The world economy has changed and it continues to change rapidly. Most national policies view the United States as a homogeneous unit, with rural problems seen as minor variations of urban problems. Policies that are implemented to alleviate urban problems are assumed to treat the same problems in rural areas. But, rural problems are not the same, nor are the consequences of policies developed for urban populations of the U.S. experienced in the same way by rural populations.

The United States is a multiple sector society, regionally diverse, and segmented with strong ties to a global marketplace. Policies that affect one part of the U.S. economy do not necessarily affect others. The trickle down effect is a myth. A coherent set of policies that recognizes differences needs to shape the future of all segments of the United States, including the rural hinterland. As noted in Chapter 2, the rise of the Far East, glasnost, the changes occurring in Europe, and the sleeping giant of South America, combined with the precarious nature of oil production, the power of multinational corporations, and environmental concerns set a new stage for policy decisions. If the United States does not try to maximize the potential for all sectors of our society, it will no longer drive the world's political, social, and economic forces. For example, the rural labor force is languishing. Demographics suggests that there will be a major shortage of young skilled workers by the year 2000. Rural youth are not being educated to participate in the new highly skilled labor force. A major human resource is being wasted.

Many unsubstantiated assumptions have guided policy decisions to the detriment of rural areas. These assumptions include, but are not limited to, (1) all communities have equal opportunities to generate economic growth; (2) economic growth benefits all; (3) industrial policies and human resource policies are unrelated; (4) jobs are a function of the marketplace, not the government; and (5) workers have appropriate skills and are mobile. In addition, national policies relative to rural populations in the rest of the world influence the social and economic conditions of our country.

The rural economy is very uneven, manifesting a quiltlike pattern of strengths and weaknesses. Historically, rural America was considered relatively homogeneous, dominated by agriculture. This is no longer true, except in a few counties scattered throughout the United States. Segments of the rural economy are more closely integrated in the global economy than they are in the national economy. As noted by the contributors to the first part of this book, rural America remains a separate and unequal partner because of state and national policies, specifically farm and financial policies, but also those related to the working poor, families, and special targeted groups and populations.

Fairness and equal opportunity mandate appropriate treatment of rural America. For example, poverty often is seen as an urban problem, particularly an inner-city problem. As noted in Chapter 8, if one only looks at urban poverty, policy and programs will be directed toward female-headed non-working households. A very different situation exists in rural areas, with the dominant model being a family in which both the husband and wife hold jobs, each often holding more than one, but who still live in poverty.

Fairness demands that federal, state, and local programs look to the diversity of situations throughout the United States and for particular peoples to develop the policies and programs that eliminate biases and provide equal opportunity. In relation to the policies on work and the working poor, policies should "make work pay."

Fairness also requires that the large variations in benefit levels which exist from state to state and region to region be minimized. Small variations may be warranted based on given living conditions, but support programs for children, the elderly, and other targeted groups should be fairly applied across the United States.

The uniqueness of various regions and conditions must be recognized. Public policies should encourage activities in rural America to be ecologically responsible, socially acceptable, and economically viable. For example, public agencies should influence farmers' production practices to maximize production of food and fiber but minimize the impact upon environmental resources, including water quality, air quality, and soil conditions. In short, we must examine proposed changes in light of their impact on food supplies, prices, local communities, and families, as well as their impact on environmental amenities, health risks, and ecological systems. National policies could be developed that reflect farmland tenure ideas as proposed in Chapter 21, or forest resource policies as proposed in Chapter 22, or waste management policies as proposed in Chapter 23. The 1990s will be consumed with policy questions related to waste management, water quality, and the environment.

We want to call special attention to the fact that local, state, and federal leaders, along with the private sector, all have a role to play and a vested interest in rural America. Decisions cannot be made in isolation of consequences. Nor can decisions be made based on aggregated information that does not acknowledge the unique conditions and situations of particular groups and geographical areas. America is proud of its heterogeneous population and its wide variety of ecological conditions. It is somewhat surprising that, despite this pride in our diversity, we have yet to design government policies that acknowledge the consequences and implications of this diversity.

The conclusion of this book is inescapable. Severe poverty, human capital underutilization, environmental degradation, and deterioration of both the physical and social infrastructure cannot be overcome in rural America without government assistance in terms of policies, programs, and funds.

TABLE 27.1   Rural Policy Issues for the 1990s

1. Policies attuned to unique rural conditions (Chapter 1).
2. National public works investment policy (Chapter 2).
3. National industrial policy (Chapter 2).
4. Secondary market for rural business loans (Chapter 3).
5. Technical assistance for rural financial programs (Chapter 3).
6. Community Reinvestment Act for nonbank financial institutions (Chapter 4).
7. Community-oriented financial institutions (Chapter 4).
8. Competition for existing economic activities (Chapter 5).
9. Increased rural development programs with which to decouple the farm sector (Chapter 6).
10. Farm labor safety for handling of chemicals, equipment, and biotechnological innovations (Chapter 7).
11. Uniform Supplemental Security Income (SSI) benefit levels across states (Chapters 8 and 11).
12. Federal minimum SSI payment at least equal to the poverty level (Chapters 8 and 9).
13. Make work pay (Chapters 8 and 9).
14. Skills development of rural people (Chapters 9 and 10).
15. National youth service program (Chapter 9).
16. Equity of access to supporting services (Chapter 10).
17. Jobs programs and community development activities targeting the elderly (Chapter 11).
18. Model programs of senior entrepreneurship and volunteerism (Chapter 11).
19. Employment of elderly (Chapter 11).
20. Resource-based relative-value scale reimbursement policy (Chapter 12).
21. National health insurance (Chapter 12).
22. Environmental contamination originating in urban areas (Chapter 12).
23. Education and training programs (Chapter 13).
24. Educational attainment and poverty (Chapter 13).
25. Free-enterprise zones for American Indians (Chapter 14).
26. A national minimum wage indexed to inflation (Chapter 15).
27. Capacity building of rural institutions (Chapter 16).
28. Reconstruction of the infrastructure of rural America (Chapter 17).
29. Broad-based U.S. population and development policy (Chapter 18).
30. Water quality as an objective of all funded programs (Chapter 19).
31. Buffer strips for protection of surface water quality (Chapter 19).
32. Tax incentives for soil conservation practices (Chapter 20).
33. Subsidies for sustainable farming systems (Chapter 20).
34. Land trusts to facilitate long-term family farming (Chapter 21).
35. Policy to address complex forest ecosystems (Chapter 22).
36. Siting process for waste storage and disposal facilities (Chapter 23).
37. Waste reduction (Chapter 23).
38. Telematics infrastructure for job creation (Chapter 24).
39. Privatization of research enterprise (Chapter 25).
40. Integration between biotechnological research and Cooperative Extension programs (Chapter 25).
41. Community-based common property systems for resource management (Chapter 26).

The private sector will never provide leadership to overcome these "people" and ecological problems.

Much of the current legislation and programs were developed at a time when rural and urban people were more separate, when people were less mobile, when the pace of technological change was a bit slower, when the infrastructure was new and appropriate, and when the global transformation of the world was not even a factor. Legislation and funds are needed to deal with today's issues in an appropriate and relevant maner.

Thus, this book has laid out research-based options to deal with rural issues. We realize that rural people, poor people, and the conditions of our hinterland are not popular issues. If American society is to prosper, then all segments of society need to be respected and appropriate problems addressed. Fairness and equity in rural programs will result in a stronger, more vibrant, more economically viable United States.

In Table 27.1, we highlight some of the many policy recommendations presented in this book. This table shows in what part of the book different subjects are treated. It lists some of the most important issues and represents a range of policy options presented in the various chapters. We want it to encourage you to explore in more depth the critical issues confronting national, state, and local decision makers. Our hope for the next decade is that rural America will be treated fairly, and that the unique contributions that rural areas and rural people make to U.S. society will be reflected in thoughtful legislation.

About the Book

Crisis in rural America is by now an all too familiar complaint, yet the problems presented by changing demographics, economic decline, and increasing poverty persist. They have not vanished with a new administration. However, with a new farm bill in the offing, now is the time for a fresh initiative to assess the difficulties facing nonurban America and to offer positive solutions.

Rural Policies for the 1990s, written by some of the foremost experts on rural America, focuses on policy-relevant research. Within a carefully crafted framework, the contributors present stimulating discussions on resolving problems and improving the situation in rural areas. Looking at the crucial issues of employment, demographics, environment, technology, and the global impacts of national and international policies, they offer a broad analysis that is neither regionally based nor biased. The result is not an advocacy book, but one that effectively enhances our understanding of the problems facing rural America and presents concrete proposals for revitalizing it.

Cornelia B. Flora is professor and head of the Department of Sociology at Virginia Polytechnic Institute and State University. **James A. Christenson** is associate dean of the College of Agriculture and director of Cooperative Extension at the University of Arizona.

About the Editors
and Contributors

Conner Bailey is associate professor of rural sociology at Auburn University. He has lived in Southeast Asia nine out of the past twenty-two years, while conducting research on upland and lowland agriculture and on coastal aquaculture and marine fisheries. His research interests are the political economy of international development and the sociology of natural resources and the environment. Among his publications are *The Sociology of Production in Rural Malay Society* (1983); *History of the Malay Kingdom of Patani* (translation with J. N. Miksic, 1985) and *Indonesian Marine Capture Fisheries* (1987).

Janet L. Bokemeier is professor and associate chair of sociology at Michigan State University. As a rural sociologist, she studies farm families; gender differences in labor market experiences; labor utilization within the household, with a focus on multiple jobholding; and career advancement and burnout among professionals. Her articles have appeared in the *Journal of Marriage and the Family, Rural Sociology, Sociological Quarterly, Personnel Psychology,* and the *Journal of Extension.* She is coauthoring a book on contemporary farm family issues with Lorraine Garkovich.

David L. Brown is associate director for research at the New York State Agricultural Experiment Station, professor of rural sociology at Cornell University, and acting director of Cornell's Community and Rural Development Institute. He administers and conducts social science research and policy analysis on such topics as population change, distribution, and composition; community and economic development; organization of services; and land use.

Frederick H. Buttel is professor of rural sociology and a member of the Program on Science, Technology, and Society at Cornell University. He also serves as president of the Rural Sociological Society and as chair of the biology and society major at Cornell. His major research interests are the relationships among technological change, rural social change, and the environment. He has coauthored several works, including *Environment, Energy, and Society* (1982), *Rural Sociology of Advanced Societies* (1980), and *Labor and the Environment* (1984).

James A. Christenson is associate dean and director of Cooperative Extension, College of Agriculture at the University of Arizona. He has served as editor of *Rural Sociology* and president of the Rural Sociological Society. He has coauthored or coedited four books, including *The Cooperative Extension: A National Assessment* (with Paul Warner, 1984).

Edli Colberg is a research analyst with the Texas Department of Human Resources in Austin, where he identifies human service needs in rural and urban areas of Texas. He has published several works on the demographic and social dimensions of development in rural areas.

Gretchen T. Cornwell is adjunct assistant professor of rural sociology and a research associate in the Population Issues Research Center at The Pennsylvania State University. Her research interests include the relationship between women's status and roles and their demographic behavior.

Kenneth L. Deavers serves as director of the Agriculture and Rural Economy Division, Economic Research Service, U.S. Department of Agriculture. He has written extensively about policy issues related to rural development, including rural poverty policy.

Don A. Dillman is director of the Social and Economic Sciences Research Center and professor of sociology and rural sociology at Washington State University–Pullman. He is also past president of the Rural Sociological Society and a fellow in the American Association for the Advancement of Science. His recent works include the book *Rural America in the Information Age: Telecommunications Policy for Rural Development* (1989) and several other policy-oriented publications on rural telecommunications issues.

Mark Drabenstott is assistant vice president and economist with the Federal Reserve Bank of Kansas City, where he heads the regional economics group in the economic research department. He also serves as chairman of the Federal Reserve System Committee on Agriculture and Rural Development. He has authored numerous articles on such subjects as farm policy, rural development, farm exports, and agricultural finance.

Cynthia M. Duncan is assistant professor of sociology at the University of New Hampshire, where she teaches stratification, political sociology, and social change and development. She has written a review article with Ann Tickamyer on rural poverty in the 1990 *Annual Review of Sociology*.

Sally K. Fairfax is professor of natural resources law and policy in the Departments of Forestry and Resource Management and Environmental Planning at the University of California–Berkeley. Her most recent work concerns state school lands and the notion of a beneficial trust as an antidote to vacuous multiple-use concepts. She is coauthor with Carolyn Yale of *The Federal Lands* (1987).

William W. Falk is professor and chair of sociology at the University of Maryland–College Park. He has been editor of the journal *Rural Sociology*. His most recent books are *High Tech, Low Tech, No Tech: Recent Industrial and Occupational Change in the South* (1988) and *Research in Rural Sociology and Development: Rural Labor Markets* (1989), both written with Thomas A. Lyson.

Jerald J. Fletcher is associate professor of resource management at West Virginia University. His research focuses on the economic factors related to water quality problems from nonpoint pollution. He has also served as a consultant to the U.S. Environmental Protection Agency, the Environmental Law Institute, the Conservation Technology Information Center, and other public and private organizations.

Cornelia B. Flora is professor and chair of sociology at Virginia Polytechnic Institute and State University. A past president of the Rural Sociological Society, she has published widely in the areas of international development, women's studies, community development, and popular culture.

Jan L. Flora is professor of agricultural economics and sociology at Virginia Polytechnic Institute and State University, specializing in the areas of community, agricultural, and rural change in the United States and in developing countries. He previously founded and directed the Kansas Center for Rural Institutes at Kansas State University.

Louise Fortmann is professor of natural resource sociology in the Department of Forestry and Resource Management at the University of California–Berkeley, where she studies environmental protest, property dimensions of natural resources, and poverty in resource-dependent communities. Together with John Bruce, she coedited *Whose Trees? Proprietary Dimensions of Forestry* (1988).

William H. Friedland is professor of community studies and sociology at the University of California–Santa Cruz. He is coauthor of *Manufacturing Green Gold: Capital, Labor, and Technology in the Lettuce Industry* (1981) among other books, and coeditor of the forthcoming volume, *The New Political Economy of Advanced Capitalist Agriculture.*

Lorraine E. Garkovich is professor of sociology at the University of Kentucky. Her research examines how social and economic changes in farm communities are linked to changes in the enterprise structure and family relationships on family farms. Her publications include *Population and Community in Rural America* (1990). She is currently coauthoring a book on contemporary farm families with Janet Bokemeier.

Jess Gilbert is associate professor of rural sociology at the University of Wisconsin–Madison. His research concerns land tenure issues and U.S. regional farming systems. He is currently examining New Deal agricultural policies in light of current theories of the state.

Nina L. Glasgow is senior research associate of rural sociology at Cornell University. Her research interests include communities' adaptations to changes in size; age composition of the population, especially relating to retirement migration; and socioeconomic characteristics of the rural elderly population.

Gary P. Green is associate professor in the Department of Sociology and the Institute of Community and Area Development at the University of Georgia. His research interests involve political economy and community. His current research projects assess local economic development incentives and examine self-development strategies among nonmetropolitan communities.

Rita R. Hamm is research associate of agricultural economics at North Dakota State University–Fargo. Her work focuses on the social and social psychological dimensions of high risk and controversial projects. She has published widely on the impacts of development and on waste storage and management in rural areas of the United States.

Daryl Hobbs is professor of rural sociology and director of the Office of Social and Economic Data Analysis at the University of Missouri. He is a past president of the Rural Sociological Society and a recipient of the society's Award for Excellence in Public Service. He has written more than 20 articles and papers on rural education and has served as a consultant to state and national education organizations.

Robert A. Hoppe is an economist at the Economic Research Service, U.S. Department of Agriculture. As a senior specialist in policy research, his work focuses on income levels, poverty, and income-support programs in rural areas.

Leif Jensen is assistant professor of rural sociology at The Pennsylvania State University. His research studies include economic coping strategies among low-income households in rural Pennsylvania, trends in underemployment among racial and ethnic minorities during periods of recession and expansion, and the socioeconomic status of immigrant children.

Thomas G. Johnson is associate professor of agricultural economics and an extension community resource development specialist at Virginia Polytechnic Institute and State University. His research, teaching, and extension activities concern rural economic development, development finance alternatives, entrepreneurship, impact analysis, local government service provision and decision making, transportation economics, and resource economics.

Marvin A. Kaiser is associate dean of the College of Arts and Sciences at Kansas State University–Manhattan and acting director of the Kansas Center for Rural Initiatives. He also serves as consultant for the Aging Unit of the United Nations Office in Vienna. He has published works related to aging issues.

F. Larry Leistritz is professor of agricultural economics at North Dakota State University–Fargo. His studies include analyzing the effects of nuclear and other waste products on rural areas and on the alternatives for mitigating such impacts. He has published numerous books, journal articles, and technical reports on the economic, fiscal, and other socioeconomic impacts of developments in rural areas of the United States and other developed countries.

Stephen B. Lovejoy is coordinator for the Center for Alternative Agricultural Systems, School of Agriculture, and associate professor of agricultural economics at Purdue University. His research and extension education programs concentrate on natural resource policy and how public policy alternatives influence agriculture, the environment, and rural communities. He has edited two books, *Conserving Soil* (with Ted L. Napier, 1986) and *Agriculture and Water Quality* (with John B. Braden, 1989).

Thomas A. Lyson is associate professor of rural sociology at Cornell University. His research focuses on agricultural biotechnologies, low-input sustainable agricultural systems, and uneven development in advanced industrial societies. His most recent book is *Two Sides to the Sunbelt: The Growing Divergence Between the Rural and Urban South* (1989).

Patrick H. Mooney is associate professor of sociology at the University of Kentucky. His current research concerns the history of agrarian social movements and class analysis in the United States. He is author of *My Own Boss?* (1988).

Charles Morris is senior economist and leader of the Financial Markets and Institutions Working Group in the economic research department of the Federal Reserve Bank of Kansas City. His areas of specialization are banking and financial economics.

Steve H. Murdock is professor and chair of rural sociology at Texas A&M University. He has examined the impacts of waste storage and management for low-level and high-level nuclear, chemical, and municipal wastes in rural areas throughout the United States. He is the author or editor of six books and many journal articles and technical reports on the social and demographic impacts of resource, technological, and industrial developments.

Ted L. Napier is professor of resources sociology in the Department of Agricultural Economics and Rural Sociology at The Ohio State University. He has received several awards from professional societies for his contributions to natural resources research. He has published extensively in sociological, development, and natural resources journals and is editor of four texts on natural resources issues.

Jerry R. Skees is associate professor of agricultural economics at the University of Kentucky. His current research program emphasizes crop insurance, Kentucky farm structural change and adjustments, and rural development. He has published numerous research articles for professional journals as well as publications for lay audiences.

Doris P. Slesinger is professor and chair of rural sociology at the University of Wisconsin–Madison. She chairs the North Central Regional Committee on Rural Health Services (NCR-127) and is a member of the editorial board of the *Journal of Rural Health*. She has published numerous articles on the demography and health of rural populations, including migrant agricultural workers, Hispanics, blacks, and American Indians. She is also author of the book, *Mothercraft and Infant Health: A Sociocultural and Demographic Approach* (1980).

C. Matthew Snipp is associate professor of rural sociology and sociology at the University of Wisconsin–Madison. His research and writing, in collaboration with Gene F. Summers, deal with poverty and unemployment on American Indian reservations. His most recent book is *American Indians: The First of This Land* (1989).

C. Shannon Stokes is professor of rural sociology, faculty associate of the Population Issues Research Center, and head of the Department of Agricultural Economics and Rural Sociology at The Pennsylvania State University. He has conducted research on agricultural development and population change in Asia and Africa. He is the author of numerous articles and is coeditor of *Rural Development and Human Fertility* (1984).

Gene F. Summers is professor and chair of rural sociology at the University of Wisconsin. He has written eight books and monographs and contributed articles to journals in several academic fields. His most recent book is *Community Economic Vitality: Major Trends and Selected Issues* (with Leonard E. Bloomquist, 1988).

Louis E. Swanson is associate professor of sociology at the University of Kentucky. His research and publications focus on the sociology of agriculture, community studies, and the political economy of rural and agricultural policy. He is editor of two books: *Agricultural and Community Change in the U.S.* (1988) and *American Rural Communities* (1990).

Ann R. Tickamyer is associate professor of sociology at the University of Kentucky. She has published extensively in the areas of gender, work, and poverty. With Cynthia Duncan, she has a review article on rural poverty in the 1990 *Annual Review of Sociology.*

Ronald C. Wimberley is professor of sociology at North Carolina State University. His research interests deal with rural sociology and sociology of agriculture issues. He recently served as editor and contributor for *Agriculture and Rural Viability* (National Association of State Universities and Land-Grant Colleges) and *New Dimensions in Rural Policy* (Joint Economic Committee of the Congress). He currently serves on the Census Bureau's advisory committee on agricultural statistics and on a Southern Rural Development Center task force on rural infrastructure.

Index